Organizing Crime
in Chinatown

Organizing Crime in Chinatown

Race and Racketeering in New York City, 1890–1910

Jeffrey Scott McIllwain

McFarland & Company, Inc., Publishers
Jefferson, North Carolina, and London

LIBRARY OF CONGRESS CATALOGUING-IN-PUBLICATION DATA

McIllwain, Jeffrey Scott, 1969–
    Organizing crime in Chinatown : race and racketeering in New York City, 1890–1910 / Jeffrey Scott McIllwain.
      p.   cm.
    Includes bibliographical references and index.

    ISBN 0-7864-1626-2 (softcover : 50# alkaline paper)

    1. Organized crime—New York (State)—New York—History. 2. Chinatown (New York, N.Y.)—History. 3. Chinatown (New York, N.Y.)—Social conditions. 4. Chinese American criminals—New York (State)—New York—History. 5. Chinese Americans—New York (State)—New York—Social conditions. 6. New York (N.Y.)—History—1865–1898. 7. New York (N.Y.)—History—1898–1951. 8. New York (N.Y.)—Race relations. I. Title.
HV6452.N7M37   2004
364.1'06'08995107471—dc22   2003021121

British Library cataloguing data are available

©2004 Jeffrey Scott McIllwain. All rights reserved

No part of this book may be reproduced or transmitted in any form or by any means, electronic or mechanical, including photocopying or recording, or by any information storage and retrieval system, without permission in writing from the publisher.

Manufactured in the United States of America

On the cover: Tiger hide ©2003 Photodisc.
Chinese man ©2003 Stockbyte

McFarland & Company, Inc., Publishers
  Box 611, Jefferson, North Carolina 28640
    www.mcfarlandpub.com

In memory of my parents, Dennis and Linda McIllwain,
with thanks for encouraging me to be curious and learn,
making my dreams a reality,
and teaching me the ropes of life in all of their splendor

Asian criminal groups have evolved from street gangs into sophisticated criminal syndicates that rival, and in some cases surpass, La Cosa Nostra, in terms of violence, economic impact, and the diversity of their illegal activities. Their criminal portfolios include narcotics trafficking, money laundering, contract murder, illegal gambling, loan-sharking, extortion, inter-state prostitution rings, and alien smuggling. And they are adopting the hallmark of traditional organized crime—corruption of our public officials—as their *modus operandi*.

William Weld
U.S. Attorney General
1988

In fact, for pay, the highbinder is ready to perpetrate any villainy, from perjury to murder, and his oath bound fellows, under pain of death, must protect him should he fall in the meshes of the law in the practice of his unholy vision. Talk of the Italian Mafia! There has never existed such another organization of desperadoes and villains as the Chinese highbinders, and these maintain their organization and ply their trade more or less openly in every city of the United States which maintains any considerable colony of Chinese.

Louis Beck
New York's Chinatown
1898

Acknowledgments

This study would not have been possible without the assistance of numerous teachers and mentors over the years. They include, but are not limited to, Meredith Reidy, Sandra Evans, Gary Smuts, Dennis Cox, Paul Knoll, Frank Mitchell, Terry Seip, Stanley Rosen, John Wills, jr., Michael Mochizuki, David Ellenson, Alex Hybel, Gerald Bender, Brendan Nagle, Chip Blacker, Joan Schaeffer, Harrison Kurtz, Alonzo Hamby, John Lewis Gaddis, Al Eckes, Donald Jordan, Alan Block, Philip Jenkins, Tom Bernard, Roy Austin, Richard Ritti, Dan Maier-Katkin, Bruce Bullington, John Sullivan, Ed Donovan, Michael Buerger, and Rosemary Gido.

Additionally, my professional colleagues provided major assistance, support, criticisms, and encouragement. Among them are Sean Griffin, Scott Johnson, Kim Menard, Howard Smith, Donald Lidick, Tim Carter, Susan Craig, Amy Patterson, Robin Ogle, Melody Lane, Tracy Melnick, Adrian Praetzellis, Margaret Purser, Robert Karlsrud, Pat Jackson, Homero Yearwood, Ken Marcus, Laurel Holstrom, Carol Cinquini, Jane Wright, Paul Sutton, Celleste Murphy-Greene, Lou Rea, Dawn Christiansen, Gayle August, John Dombrink, John Song, Sheldon Zhang, Ko-lin Chin, Joeseph Albini, Victor Kappeler, Willard Meyers, Ian Lewis Gordon, Ed Day, Dana Nurge, Timothy Gilfoyle, Eve Armentrout Ma, Stanley Rosen, Jay Albanese, and Michael Woodiwiss.

A number of representatives of the "real world" of the criminal justice system also provided valuable input, including William Plackenmeyer, W. Leighton Lord III, M. Cordell Hart, John Mattingly, Sam Theodora, John Browning, Dennis Conte, Sr., Thomas Budds, Debbie Crawford, Jim Horne, James Maurer, Mark Nye, Peter Ritchie, Mark Craig, Mark Warner, Mark Snyder, and Michael Dunbaugh.

Numerous archivists and librarians provided invaluable assistance in locating hard to find material. They include Kenneth Cobb of the New York Municipal Archives, Robert C. Morris of the New York Branch of the National Archives, Jane Thiele of the Lloyd Sealy Library at John Jay College, Bernard Crystal of the Rare Book and Manuscript Library at Colombia University, and the librarians of Sonoma State University's Reuben Salazar Library.

Additionally, the Pennsylvania State University Department of Sociology, Sonoma State University's Office of Sponsored Programs, San Diego State University's Office of Sponsored Programs, the Academy of Criminal Justice Sciences, and the National Endowment for the Humanities all provided funding that made the research and writing of this book possible. Thanks to the anonymous reviewers of my *Justice Quarterly* and *Crime, Law & Social Change* articles that serve as a basis for this book.

Over the years, a number of friends got me "over the hump" when it came to pursuing my career goals and the research for this book. Thank you to my Reva Circle "family," my friends at New Life Community Church, mis tios y tias en el Club Optimista Pan Americano de Los Angeles, the Cerritos "Mafia" (fellow Knabe-istas), my USC Trojan Family (especially John and Carole Peterson, Samantha Paynter, Todd and Stacey Sharp, Sam Sheldon, Pat Smith, and my consummate host, guide and theater guru in New York City, Sammy Buck), my Penn State Nittany Lion Family (especially Sean and Heidi Slater, Kevin Morgan, Scott and Jen Johnson, Eric Stromer and Stevie Rocco, John and Tracey Corte, and Susan Shields), the California Sigma Chapter of Phi Delta Theta International Fraternity (especially Brothers Doug Sorrel and Casey Caldwell), Laurielie Van den Bos, Heather Hulbert, Amy Johnson, Lessa Holzheizer, Sean Simmons, the Morse family, Don and Julie Knabe, Matt Knabe, and the entire Struiksma clan (the original Dutch Mafia).

My family deserves particular thanks for the sacrifices they made and endured that got me to where I am today. Thank you to my grandparents, Henry and Alice Estrada and Carlo and Helen Guarino and my aunts and uncles Craig and Dorothy Morrison, Rosie Chavez, Bob and Betty Conley, Don and Shirley Strommen, Cathy Guarino, and David and Tanya Guarino. Thanks also to my cousins, Valery and Michael Guarino, for providing me with hours of comic relief.

Every guy should have a sister to pick on and pester her entire life. I really lucked out with mine. Debbie McIllwain, thanks for letting me be your "big bro" in good times and bad. My step-mom, Fran Anderson, also deserves recognition for keeping me plump and happy over the years with her fine cooking and kind, giving heart. Thanks also to my wife, Donna Struiksma, for casting a warm ray of sunlight in an otherwise dark period in my life and for making me happy and complete.

Though they are no longer here to read these words, I would also like to thank my mother and father, Linda and Dennis McIllwain. As far back as I can remember, they shared with me the value of learning and instilled in me the desire to be the first in my family to earn a university education. They also taught me that an education alone does not make one a good person; character, integrity, and love of God and others do. In life and death, they provided for me in more ways than I can ever fully comprehend. As I completed writing this book, I was providing hospice care for my dad who was suffering from emphysema. I told him I was dedicating this book to him and mom. He said, "Oh, brother!" Thanks dad (and *semper fi!*).

Table of Contents

Acknowledgments   vii
Preface   1

PART I: RACE AND THE AMERICAN UNDERWORLD

1. Alien Conspiracy, Yellow Peril and the "Threat" Posed by "Non-Traditional" Organized Crime   5
2. Social Networks and the Organization of Crime   10
3. Social Networks and the Institutionalizing of *Guanxi*   25

PART II: ORGANIZING CRIME ON GOLD MOUNTAIN

4. The Four Vices and the Bachelor Society   41
5. Chinese Syndicates: Prostitution and Opium   50
6. Chinese Power Syndicates: Gambling and Muscle   67

PART III: NEW YORK, NEW YORK

7. New York After Chinatown   83
8. Chinatown Vice and "The Bowery! The Bowery!"   105
9. Setting the Stage for a Tong War   127
10. The Gloves Come Off   147
11. "The Dead Dove of Peace"   166

PART IV: ORGANIZED CRIME AND THE AMERICAN EXPERIENCE

12. Rethinking the Gangster Image — 183

Appendix: Comments on Literature, Sources, and Methodology — 189
Chapter Notes — 203
Bibliography — 231
Index — 245

Preface

Pick up any major text or article on the history of organized crime in the United States and you are bound to read a litany dedicated to professional criminals of Italian or Jewish descent. From David Cressey's *Theft of a Nation* to Francis Ianni's *A Family Business*, from Joseph Albini's *The American Mafia* to Daniel Bell's "Crime as an American Way of Life," the phenomenon commonly referred to as the Mafia—aka La Cosa Nostra, the Mob, the Outfit, the Syndicate or the Commission—dominates. This scholarship on organized crime has overwhelmingly focused on Italian and Jewish gangsters, much to the exclusion of all others.

Of course, there are some exceptions. The past two decades have produced a modest literature on new, emerging or nontraditional organized crime, which is another way of saying organized crime groups of non–Italian and non–Jewish descent. More recently, scholars of organized crime have concentrated on the phenomenon's transnational incarnations in crimes as diverse as money laundering, human smuggling and drug trafficking. In both cases, La Cosa Nostra is the standard by which all else is measured.

Scholars have generally ignored the possibility that such syndicates of non–Italian and non–Jewish origin may have existed before the waning days of the Cold War, let alone Prohibition, and that such syndicates could have been sophisticated, powerful and autonomous.[1] The justification for this oversight seems to be that Italian organized criminals and their Jewish "associates" *were* organized crime, while others were either subordinate to La Cosa Nostra or too inconsequential to matter. La Cosa Nostra became traditional organized crime; all others became nontraditional. Consequently, as the conventional wisdom holds, to understand the history of organized crime in the United States, one must immerse oneself in the details of such subjects as Lucky Luciano, Al Capone, Dutch Schultz Prohibition, Las Vegas, the Kefauver and McClellan Committee Hearings, Meyer Lanskey, Joe Valachi and Jimmy Hoffa.

This study counters the assumptions that the history of organized crime is the purview of Italian and Jewish gangsters; that organized crime became modernized with Prohibition; and that other ethnic groups failed to muster syndicates of any real substance, power or sophistication before the 1980s. This study focuses on the Chinese-American experience as a means to test these assumptions. It presents evidence that Chinese organized criminals across the United States were engaged in such classic organized criminal enterprises as gambling, prostitution and the importation, distribution and sale of narcotics between 1870 and 1910. Also discussed are the handmaidens to these enterprises, violent crime (extortion, protection rackets and murder) and corruption. To further illustrate these findings, an in-depth case study of organized crime in New York City's Chinatown from 1890 to 1910 is provided.

This study is not meant to be exhaustive. Rather, it serves as a first step to motivate organized crime scholars, criminologists and social historians to investigate the myriad of untapped historical resources that have the potential of forcing a fundamental revision of our understanding of the history and development of organized crime in the United States, as well as the relationship between race and crime in American society. This study does not rejuvenate or lend credence to a "yellow peril" approach to the Chinese-American experience. Neither does it advance old stereotypes that were used to justify discriminatory policies, laws, and practices, nor does it resurrect jingoistic sentiments that were used as a basis of pogroms against Chinese communities across the United States.

Indeed, this study attempts to assess organized criminal activity in the Chinese-American community on its own terms. By focusing on organized crime activities, like gambling, prostitution, and violent crime, it seeks to avoid what Jay Albanese terms the ethnicity trap-"when organized crime is defined in terms of the nature of the groups that engage in it, rather than the nature of the organized crime activity itself, and how and why various groups specialize—or fail to specialize—in certain activities."[2] By avoiding the ethnicity trap, organized crime in the Chinese-American community can be analyzed as both a criminological and historical phenomenon; the results of this analysis can be applied to the existing constructions of organized crime; and the significance of organized crime to the greater Chinese-American experience can be more accurately assessed.

Part I

Race and the American Underworld

1

Alien Conspiracy, Yellow Peril and the "Threat" Posed by "Non-Traditional" Organized Crime

In 1991 the United States Senate's Permanent Subcommittee on Investigations held hearings on Asian organized crime. Senator Sam Nunn (D-Georgia), the Chairman of the Subcommittee, set the stage for the hearings by noting that Asian organized crime "has proven to be no less interesting nor challenging than other, more traditional and more established, aspects of organized crime, such as La Cosa Nostra." The hearings, he continued, "respond to reports of a frightening increase in violent crime at the hands of Asian gangs and those organized criminals whom they emulate. These gangs have confirmed connections to the highest levels of Asian organized crime, both within our country and abroad."[1]

Senator Nunn's counterpart, Senator William Roth (R-Delaware), stated that since hearings on "emerging" criminal organizations had been held by the same Subcommittee in 1986, the challenges posed by these groups "have continued to grow as many of these groups have expanded their criminal activities." Roth expressed his fear that the clear progress made by the Federal Bureau of Investigation against La Cosa Nostra (LCN) would be undermined as new, emerging, organized crime groups, such as the Chinese criminals, simply stepped in and replaced LCN. As a result, one of the purposes of the 1991 hearings was "to identify and assess the nontraditional emerging crime groups that have the potential to develop into future LCNs, and to make certain that law enforcement has the necessary tools to prevent this from happening."[2]

Nunn and Roth were not alone in assuming that Chinese organized crime in the United States is both emerging and nontraditional. Almost without exception, according to the conventional wisdom of the government, academics, and the media, contemporary Chinese organized crime is a new phenomenon born of foreign culture and values, and is culturally insular in its manifestations. The following are a few examples of these assumptions:

- Scholars Ko-lin Chin, Robert Kelley and Jeffrey Fagan assert that Chinese organized crime has "neither infiltrated the larger American society nor victimized people who are not Chinese" because American society was "so alien to them."[3]
- Ko-lin Chin, perhaps the most recognized American scholar on Chinese organized crime, observed that since Chinese criminals in the United States "normally do not and could not relate to American society, they have little desire to expand their activities to a society that is so alien to them. Even if they were willing to do so, they would not be able to establish close relationships with public officials through corruption.[4]
- Journalist William Kleinknecht heralds the thesis that Chinese organized crime "remains largely an immigrant phenomenon with little influence outside the Chinese community." Even though he recognized that heroin trafficking by Chinese "affects a broad segment of society," Kleinknecht asserted that "Chinese gangsters otherwise limit their crimes to their own people." In this spirit, "Chinese crooks have not shown an ability to make the kinds of friendships in the political clubhouses that gave the Mafia unfettered access to the halls of power."[5]
- In an episode of the Arts & Entertainment Channel's *Investigative Reports* titled "The Dragons of Crime," host Bill Kurtis observes the following about Chinese organized crime: "A new threat is emerging on the streets of our cities. An organized violence that, according to the F.B.I., is quickly surpassing the age old threat of the Mafia."[6]
- In 1991 F.B.I. Director William Sessions testified before the Permanent Subcommittee on Investigations that the "newest and most significant challengers on the American organized crime scene are Asian criminal organizations." He stated that these organizations are attempting to gain "stronger footholds" in the United States. Of these Asian organizations, the Chinese "currently pose the most serious threat." Furthermore, "Only a few years ago, Chinese criminal groups operating in the United States were small and were disorganized. Now they are the most developed of the Asian groups and are rapidly expanding their operations outside the Asian community."[7]
- In a follow-up to the 1991 hearings, the Permanent Subcommittee on Investigations held hearings on "Asian Organized Crime: The New International Criminal" in 1992. These hearings portrayed crimes committed by Chinese organized crime groups— like immigrant smuggling and narcotics trafficking—as new threats to the United States and the international community.[8]

- In the wake of the June 6, 1993 grounding of the *Golden Venture* off of Rockaway Beach in Queens, New York and the subsequent detention of the roughly 300 smuggled Chinese migrants found aboard, President William Jefferson Clinton charged the National Security Council to coordinate the response to the newly designated national security threat posed by Chinese smuggling syndicates.[9]
- The Pennsylvania Crime Commission discusses the "future threat" of Asian organized crime in more understated terms: "While much of the organized criminal activity in the Asian community remains confined to ethnic enclaves, the introduction of video poker machines suggests an emergence of relationships with other non–Asian, organized crime groups. This development signals the beginning of what has been predicted: Asian organized crime groups will form criminal partnerships with other non–Asian crime groups."[10]

Throughout media, government, and academic analyses and descriptions, commonly used descriptors of what Chinese organized crime is and is not are routinely offered. These descriptors form the basis of the conventional wisdom about Chinese organized crime. Interestingly, when we consider what Chinese organized crime is *not*, we get common descriptors of traditional organized crime (Table 1):

Table 1

***What Chinese Organized Crime Is and Is Not: Establishing the Conventional Wisdom about Chinese Organized Crime*[11]**

What Chinese Organized Crime Is	What Chinese Organized Crime Is Not
new	old
recent	long-standing
emerging	established
developing	developed
evolving	evolved
organizing	organized
growing	grown
expanding	mature
strengthening	strong
nontraditional	traditional
marginal	central
international	national
foreign	domestic
infiltrating	impenetrable
threatening	defensive
challenging	status quo
insular	expansive

The result of this conventional wisdom is a *de facto* acceptance of the "ethnic succession" presupposition about organized crime. Originally conceived by Daniel Bell, the theory of ethnic succession holds that crime in the United States serves as a form of social mobility for various immigrant groups. Bell argued that as the Irish immigrants of the middle–1800s, the German-Jewish immigrants of the late 1800s, and the Italian and Sicilian immigrants of the early 1900s attempted to enter the mainstream of American life, some members of each immigrant group turned to illegal means to do so. Bell contended that as each wave of immigrants reached the United States, they received the bulk of attention from the criminal justice system. As the first group of immigrants joined the mainstream, public attention turned to the criminality of the dominant immigrant group following in its wake. This pattern repeated itself as one immigrant group succeeded another.[12]

In the absence of historically grounded research to challenge them, this conventional wisdom and notion of ethnic succession, and the ethnicity trap they implicitly entail, have manifested themselves in many government policies, scholarly works, police investigations, and reports by government investigative committees. This is despite the existence of almost a century's worth of rich primary and secondary sources addressing the existence of Chinese organized criminality and its active participation in the social system of organized crime in the United States.[13]

How do we extricate ourselves from the ethnicity trap and test the conventional wisdom? Alan Block provided a suitable approach when he tested the general thinking about traditional organized crime in New York City from 1930 to 1950. Block established that organized crime derives from its role as a historical phenomenon "whose changes mirror changes in civil society [and] the political economy."[14] The results of his study subsequently helped to revise the thinking about traditional organized crime. Similarly, this study turns to the past to gain an understanding of organized crime in the Chinese-American community that is not encumbered by myth.[15]

Historical evidence can lead to the development of a more historically grounded conventional wisdom, one in which Chinese organized criminals and the enterprises they operate can be appraised and addressed more accurately. An analysis of primary source documents and a variety of secondary works shows that the organized criminal enterprises existing in New York City's Chinatown from 1890 to 1910 and across the United States from 1870 to 1910 were similar to what we consider today to be modern organized crime. This evidence also shows that activities that were viewed previously as "tong wars" were often the manifestation of conflicts between highly organized Chinese criminal networks.

These networks coupled their criminal interests with legitimate functions in the Chinese-American community, took advantage of the criminal opportunities inherent in fundamental contradictions in American society and the American political economy, infiltrated and manipulated the political and social institutions around them, were influential in Chinese communities across the United States, and victimized both Chinese and non–Chinese Americans. Though they had their own unique, usually culturally based, differences from other groups, they were symbiotically connected to the underworld and upperworld criminal organizations of their day, regardless of ethnic origin. These connections manifested themselves as highly developed social networks that spanned across the United States and North America and reached across the Pacific to other Pacific Rim ethnic Chinese settlements and into China itself.

Far from being a contemporary phenomenon, organized crime in the Chinese-American community dates back to the earliest Chinese settlements on the West Coast. Since then it has been involved in the same illicit enterprises for which it is known today. For example, Chinese organized crime has engaged continuously in the illegal trafficking of immigrants and drugs, extortion, gambling, prostitution, slavery, labor racketeering, and political and police corruption. These illegal activities necessitated the development of extensive social networks composed of upperworld and underworld actors, both Chinese and non–Chinese. Turn-of-the-century Chinese organized crime was the equivalent of the modern organized crime described by today's experts. Consequently, one need not fear that Chinese organized criminals are a new international threat that will supplant "LCN" criminal enterprises. Just like professional criminals from other ethnic backgrounds, they are simply continuing to take advantage of criminal opportunities in the United States, a practice quite refined over the course of more than a hundred years and as American as apple pie. But before moving forward, it is necessary to develop a conceptual framework through which to view the process of organizing crime in the Chinese-American community. To do so necessitates a foray into the work of anthropologists and historians who researched traditional organized crime in the United States and Sicily.

2

Social Networks and the Organization of Crime

For over four decades scholars and government experts have debated how to best comprehend the actions of organized criminals and the symbiotic relationships they have with legitimate society. These debates have centered on three major paradigms used to define and comprehend organized crime. The first proposes that organized crime is best understood as a viable organization, a reflection of the institutional approaches that dominated sociology and business departments and major government hearings on organized crime during the 1960s.[1] The second rejects the formality of the institutional approach in favor of one based on exchange relationships between those with power and those who needed access to that power.[2] This paradigm, originating during the 1970s, is a reflection of scholarship in the fields of anthropology and, to a lesser extent, political science, which emphasizes the patron-client relationship. The third de-emphasizes the actors engaged in organized crime and focuses instead on the business of organized crime.[3] This "enterprise" paradigm began in the 1980s and reflects the influence of the field of economics on the study of illegal markets.

Proponents of these paradigms continue to argue their respective points at academic conferences, in scholarly articles and at government hearings. Still, no one has asked a simple question about these three paradigms: Is there a common underpinning to all three paradigms that can assist scholars in assessing the essence of organized crime? The answer is yes.

The lowest common denominator of organized crime is composed of human relationships; specifically human relationships engaged in the process of social networking for the provision of illicit goods and services as well as the protection, regulation and extortion of those engaged in the provision or consumption of these goods and services. This process of social networking occurs as a part of a social system of organized crime, a system that explains the remarkable consistency of the process of organizing crime across time and space. This process also has cultural variants, a phenomenon that explains the subtle and not-so-subtle differences between organized criminals of different ethnic heritages.

Social Networks

Beginning in the mid–1950s, anthropologists studying urbanization found that a sufficient understanding of the behavior of individuals in complex societies could not be achieved via the traditional sociological and anthropological approach of describing social organization in terms of institutions (economics, religion, politics, kinship, etc.).[4] As these anthropologists studied complex societies, they recognized a need for new concepts to describe the fluid social interactions of individuals and groups that they observed during ethnographic field research.[5]

They discovered that at its most basic level society organizes itself around relationships. Taking into account the social role, social status, and social position of individual actors, as well as the inevitability of the formation of relational ties among these actors, relationships form gateways to political and economic power for all involved. The essential element in achieving an actor's goals is the social network.

Anthropologists Stanley Wasserman and Katherine Faust defined social networks as "the relational structure of a group or larger social system consisting of the pattern of relationships among the collection of actors." The concept of a network, they note, "emphasizes the fact that each individual has ties to other individuals, each of whom in turn is tied to a few, some, or many others, and so on." Subsequently, the term "social network refers to the set of actors and the ties among them."[6]

A social network assumes the importance of relationships among interacting units. When using a social network perspective, linkages between units define relationships. Actors and their actions are not viewed as autonomous units, rather as interdependent. The linkages, or relational ties, between actors serve as channels for the transfer, or "flow," of material or nonmaterial resources. The network's structural environment provides opportunities for, and constraints on, individual action. Finally, a network perspective conceptualizes social, political, and economic structure as lasting patterns of relational ties between actors.[7]

Wasserman and Faust observed that there are several key concepts at the center of the discussion of social networks. The first of these is the *actor*, defined as a "discrete individual, corporate, or collective social units." Examples of actors are "people in a group, departments within a corporation, public service agencies within a city, or nation-states in the world system." Of course, the term actor "does not imply that these entities necessarily have volition or the ability to 'act.'"[8]

Next comes the *relational tie*. A tie "establishes a linkage between a pair of actors." There exist a wide-variety of ranges and types of ties. Most common are:

- Evaluation of one person by another (e.g., friendship, liking, or respect)
- Transfers of material resources (e.g., business transactions, lending or borrowing things)
- Association or affiliation (e.g., jointly attending a social event, or belonging to the same social club)
- Behavioral interaction (e.g., talking together, sending letters or e-mails)
- Movement between places or statuses (e.g., migration, social or physical mobility)
- Physical connection (e.g., a road, river, or bridge connecting two points)
- Formal relations (e.g., authority)
- Biological relationship (e.g., kinship or descent)[9]

At its most basic level, at least two actors are needed to create a tie. To understand ties among pairs, one must concentrate on the dyad as the unit of analysis. A dyad "consists of a pair of actors and the (possible) tie(s) between them." According to Wasserman and Faust, "dyadic analyses focus on the properties of pairwise relationships, such as whether ties are reciprocated or not, or whether specific types of multiple relationships tend to occur together." The *triad* unit of analysis allows us to examine relationships among larger subsets of actors. A triad is defined as "a subset of three actors and the (possible) tie(s) among them." Dyads and triads do not exist independently from other dyads and triads. Therefore, we can define a *subgroup* of actors as "any subset of actors, and all ties among them." Following the same logic, subgroups interact with other subgroups.[10]

One of the strengths of the network perspective is that it allows us to model "the relationships among systems of actors." A system "consists of ties among members of some (more or less bounded) group." A *group* is "the collection of all actors on which ties are to be measured." According to Wasserman and Faust,

> One must be able to argue by theoretical, empirical, or conceptual criteria that the actors in the group belong together in a more or less bounded set. Indeed, once one decides to gather data on a group, a more concrete meaning of the term is necessary. A group, then, consists of a finite set of actors who for conceptual, theoretical, or empirical reasons are treated as a finite set of individuals on which network measurements are made.[11]

A finite set (or sets) of actors is needed to prevent the data overload that would occur if boundaries were not set, as the network ties could go on indefinitely.

A *relation* is "the collection of ties of a specific kind among members of a group." Examples of ties that define relations are the set of friendships among pairs of children in a day care program, or the set of formal diplomatic ties maintained by pairs of nations in the world. Many different relations may be measured for any group of actors. For example, formal diplomatic ties among nations are one measure' and the dollar amount of trade is another. Likewise, one could examine the membership roster of a church group or a political party, track visitors to a newspapers' web site, or list the co-conspirators in a federal conspiracy indictment. Wasserman and Faust added, "It is important to note that a relation refers to the collection of ties of a given kind measured on pairs of actors from a specified actor set. The ties themselves only exist between specific pairs of actors." A *social network*, then, "consists of a finite set or sets of actors and the relations defined of them."[12]

Social Networks as Applied to Organized Crime: The Case of Mafiosi in Sicily

Social networks are certainly not exclusive to the realms of legitimate society.[13] Consequently, some anthropologists applied social network theory to the study of the underworld. Specifically, they attempted to discern the societal role and function of criminal subcultures in various cultures. Anton Blok was one such anthropologist. Like other anthropologists of his day, he set out to understand the role of social networks in a "complex society."[14]

The complex society Blok chose to analyze was the rural Sicilian community he calls "Genuardo."[15] To research his book, *The Mafia of a Sicilian Village, 1860–1960*, he spent two-and-a-half years living in "Genuardo," conversing with, and interviewing, the local people, as well as reviewing published material and archival documents. In his research, Blok sought "to account for the rural mafia in western Sicily in the 19th and 20th centuries through a detailed examination of the overall social networks *mafiosi* of a particular peasant community formed with other individuals." In this way, Blok was able to reveal "the conditions under which *mafiosi* became a powerful force in the West Sicilian hinterland."[16]

Blok's research deviated from the dominant sociological approach to organized crime existing at the time, an approach that viewed organized crime as a "corporation" run by a "board of directors" drawn from prominent organized crime "families."[17] As Charles Tilly stated in the foreword of *The Mafia of a Sicilian Village*, Blok "doesn't dazzle us with a Who's Who of 'chiefs' and 'families.' That way of dealing with the problem is often sensational, but its importance is fleeting...."[18] What Blok did instead is address the circumstances that created *mafia* by singling out the social, political and economic structures that keep it thriving. Blok examined "the rural setting in which the phenomenon originated and prospered, rather than with the cities in which it eventually multiplied." Blok used a combination of direct observation, historical reconstruction, and careful deduction "to display the destructive genius of the system."[19] He did not seek to discover who the *mafiosi* were, or even what their "character" was. Rather, he sought "to locate the connections between the prevalence of violence and the structure of economic and political life."[20]

To recognize these connections, Blok said, one had to "discover and understand the factual interdependencies between *mafiosi*, landlords, bandits, peasants, and many other individuals." When viewing these interdependencies, he did not assume that "groups, configurations, and societies are something abstracted from the individuals who form them." Therefore, by concentrating on the coalitions and larger networks of which *mafiosi* were part, Blok demonstrated "that these configurations are neither more nor less 'real' than the individuals who formed them." This enabled Blok to gain a better perspective on specific notions of society, social order, and social structure.[21]

Blok asserted that one way "to disencumber oneself from the reified abstractions which still loom large in conventional sociological and anthropological analysis is to shift one's focus from a short-term to a long-term perspective." Blok did not address the problems of Genuardo at a particular point in time. If he had done so, he would have had to focus on "what society *is* rather than form the question of how society *becomes* or *has become* in the past." According to Blok,

> To study a particular society in a given state and at a given point of time entails essentially static notions [of] order, social structure, and society which leave problems of change and development largely unexplored and hence unexplained. If changes in such "social systems" are perceived at all, they are seen as an unstructured flow, as incidental, "historical" changes.[22]

To clarify his point that the conventional anthropological and sociological views of social systems are static, Blok quoted Nobert Elias and J. L. Scotson, who emphasize,

> that sociological problems can hardly ever be adequately framed if they seem to be concerned with social phenomena exclusively at a given point and time—with structures which, to use the language of films, have the form of a "still." They approximate more closely ... what one can observe, and lead to comprehensive explanations only if they are conceived as problems and phenomena which have the form of processes, which participate in the movement of time.... The ruling concept of social structure has a strong tendency to make people perceive structures as "stills," as "steady state structures," while movements of structures in time, whether they have the form of developments or of other types of social changes, are treated as "historical"; and that often means in the sociologists' language as something apart from the structure, not as an indelible property of social structures themselves.[23]

"According to the present conventions of thinking," Elias and Scotson concluded, "history has no structure and structure no his-tory."[24]

Blok stated that it is inevitable that people form configurations with each other. Furthermore, he claimed that it is inevitable that these configurations "have their own structure through time." As examples, Blok pointed to sports teams or villages on one level, to nations on another. Regrettably, Blok observed, "sociological theories and concepts are inadequate to understand the problems of social development." Because of this situation, "we cannot visualize social change, or any change for that matter, save in terms of a series of static pictures." "A configurational approach to society," he added, "may help us break out of this impasse, because it focuses explicitly on the events of change, on structured, historical processes and the way they are interrelated."[25] In other words, "to consider local events in isolation from the long-term developments of the larger society would deprive us of the possibility of finding out and explaining how and why these events happened at all."[26]

Organized Crime: Structure and History in New York City

Historian Alan Block provided such a "configurational approach" when he produced a series of works addressing organized crime in the United States, focusing specifically on New York City. For the first time, a scholar used network analysis *and* history to analyze American organized crime. In an interview, Block divulged that as he was researching organized crime in New York City for his doctoral dissertation, he was baffled by the complete lack of evidence supporting the notion that a "national commission" or "national syndicate" known as the Mafia or La Cosa Nostra controlled American organized crime. What he had found instead was evidence of highly fluid relationships between groups of violent and nonviolent criminal entrepreneurs. Block recalled that for some time, he could not make sense of this glaring contradiction between the conventional wisdom of the institutional approach to the study of organized crime and the historical facts. Then he was introduced to the work of historically sensitive anthropologists like Anton Blok, Henner Hess Jeremy Boissevain, and Jane and Peter Schneider. By reading their work, Block became familiar with the social network perspective and the contradictory data before him suddenly made sense.[27]

Block realized that "the historical insensitivity and sociological primitivism of the popular account" of the history of American organized crime had been "carried forward and incorporated into the realm of academic scholarship," thereby fueling "flights of fantasy."[28] He maintained that previous works overlooked fundamental contradictions in the evidence that "were pushed aside by either ignoring history or transforming it into romance and demonology."[29] This particularly held true for New York City, long the primary focal point of studies on organized crime.

According to Block, it was "dismally clear that historical studies of organized crime outside the popular genre [were] virtually absent and sorely needed." The result was that much of the history of organized crime in New York City was in limbo. Block blamed this on "the handicaps of conservative ideology with its devotion to conspiracy theory,"[30] the idea that "organized crime is caused by a particular group of alien foreigners (most commonly, Italians and Sicilians) invading and infiltrating an otherwise law-abiding America and forming a highly structured, secret, nationwide criminal organization."[31] What Block meant was that the term organized crime was so linked to an alien conspiracy mythology in the literature that "employment of it increasingly implies acceptance of the conspiracy." Consequently, Block declared, "To write about organized crime [was] to saddle oneself with at least the outline of the ineluctable drive towards consolidation and confederation."[32]

What Block discovered during the course of his primary source research was something different. By conducting network analysis and treating organized crime as a historical phenomenon, Block found that "at the most fundamental level, the endless weaving of criminal conspiracies is the meaning of organized crime." If organized crime entailed belonging to a crime family or syndicate, or what the government styles La Cosa Nostra, there would have to exist "organizational restraint upon the activities of professional criminals." This, he stated, is unlikely given the historical record. He did not assert that "there are no recognizable hierarchies among organized criminals or that there are no boundaries to particular activities." According to Block, some do exist, "but they are challenged more often than not; territories and organizations are honored only in the breach." The key lies in the vast criminal opportunity existing in American society, the effect of which undermines the stability of hierarchies. This instability breeds ceaseless disputes over rackets and territories that, in turn, is frequently "characterized by immoderate instances of murderous treachery, which further frustrates organizational security and permanence."[33]

Alan Block echoed Anton Blok's conclusions about Genuardo when he observed that outside pressures, like population growth, industrialization, and rapid urbanization, present a constant need for change on the part of urban underworlds. As new technologies, laws, regulations, organizations, and public fads or fancies emerged, "quantitative and qualitative changes in urban structures and economies" occurred which "accounted for different patterns of organized crime in the nineteenth and twentieth centuries."[34] In other words,

> the history of the phenomena of organized crime is but a part of the social history of the U.S., in which the patterns of immigration, the rise and fall of the reform impulse, the organization of labor, the rise

of a middle class with a yen for travel and entertainment, the organization of policing and politics, and the expansion of financial institutions, are the mix and mingle within which criminal syndicates, criminal confraternities and cartels emerge and operate.[35]

Block underscored this point when he quoted economist and historian David Landes:

> Mass production and urbanization stimulated, indeed required, wider facilities for distribution, a larger credit structure, an expansion of the educational system, the assumption of new functions by government. At the same time, the increase in the standard of living due to higher productivity created new wants and made possible new satisfactions, which led to a spectacular flowering of those businesses that cater to human pleasure and leisure: entertainment, travel, hotels, restaurants, and so on.

Indeed, Block commented, "urban organized criminals who were specialists in vice, violence, and corruption penetrated segments of licit pleasure businesses while also controlling illicit ones." Since the state heavily regulates pleasurable commodities and leisure businesses that numerous people still desire, Block determined that an entrepreneurial climate for the avoidance of regulations exists. Consequently, this climate instigates the formation of criminal conspiracies that thrive on the systematic avoidance of regulation through corruption, stealth, duplicity, and violence.[36]

Social Systems and Social Worlds

Such findings did not sit well with the traditional, institutional view of organized crime in the United States. To counter the institutional perspective, Block conceived organized crime as both "a social system and social world." The *social system of organized crime*, he explained, "refers to the notion that organized crime is a phenomenon recognizable by reciprocal services performed by professional criminals, politicians, and clients." It is "thus understood to lie in the relationships binding members of the underworld to upperworld institutions and individuals." Additionally, the social system of organized crime recognizes that "organized crime is not a modern, urban, or lower-class phenomenon; it is a historical one whose changes mirror changes in civil society, the political economy. That is why, naturally, organized crime is increasingly taken to represent a series of relationships among professional criminals, upperworld clients and politicians...."[37]

Block conceded that there are numerous examples "when the fully-found system cannot be identified." For instance, corruption often makes it possible for one of the three elements—criminals, clients, or politicians—to be "absent from some criminal conspiracy from some variant of corruption." Block used the term "organized criminality" in such cases. This allows one to differentiate between the total system and what Block viewed as "the innumerable aspects possible within that system."[38] Nevertheless, both organized crime and organized criminality are

> manifestations of conspiracies that are slight variants of a common theme: the manner in which the city's political and economic power was dispersed and consumed. What the city had to offer was 'influence' which translated to money and power. The many ways in which influence was bought and sold, manipulated and multiplied is the thread of all the organized crime and criminality so far described. Those with influence had power and potential profit over those without. Webs of influence were spun out through kinship, friendship, relations of patronage, and straight cash purchase. These webs linked together diverse statuses, county and city government, and fairly entangled almost all aspects of criminal justice changing it to an engine of corruption. So pervasive were they that an official position in city government or its equivalent appears to have been a virtual license to engage in non-violent extortion.[39]

Block asserted that continuity is the mark of the overall system. Yet the system can be disrupted for a variety of reasons. For example, a politician or police captain can be caught taking bribes from a prostitute or gambling enterprise. When this occurs, the system, with its ever-fluid series of relationships binding upperworld and underworld actors together, adapts and survives.[40]

There also exists a *social world of organized crime*. According to Block, unlike the social system, the social world of organized crime "is often murderously chaotic because professional criminals are oriented by constant manifestations of personal power."[41] The social world encompasses the social life of professional criminals. The relational ties that form between professional criminals are often strained due to internal forces (rivalries, jealousies, ambition, etc.) or external forces (police crackdowns, indictments, market changes, etc.). With this strain comes the very real possibility of physical violence disrupting or terminating these relationships. For example, Alan Block's findings in New York City mirror those of Anton Blok's findings in rural Sicily: "Private violence and all it implies is the ground upon which the social world of professional criminals is constructed. And it is a world of some complexity in and of itself, difficult to grasp let alone to plot in some systematic fashion. An environment rent by private violence is deeply chaotic."[42]

Block recognized the contrast between the chaos of the social world and the stability and continuity of the social system. In his book *East Side-West Side*, Block clearly proved that the social system of organized crime "is virtually unbroken as a general system at the same time as the participants live in a whirl of change." By understanding both of these elements, he asserted, the reality of organized crime is determined.[43] According to Block, the reality is best understood by recognizing that there are two basic types of criminal syndicates operating in the United States.

The first is the *enterprise syndicate*. The enterprise syndicate "operates exclusively in the arena of illicit enterprises such as prostitution, gambling, bootlegging, and narcotics." Its purpose is to provide those non-violent goods and services prohibited or regulated by the state at prices set by market forces.[44]

Block named the second type the *power syndicate*. The forte of the power syndicate is extortion not enterprise. Block's research shows that "the power syndicate works in the arena of illicit enterprises and the industrial world, specifically in labor-management disputes and relations." Block noted that professional criminals in power syndicates are known for their ability to coerce. Coercion, Block said, "orients them in time and space; it is their job and identity." Furthermore, "approached from this angle, extortion is not simply a vastly under-researched crime, but a complex activity sorely needing its own 'sociology of occasions.' In addition, it is a compelling metaphor for a life-style of competitive individualism whose rigor ironically binds and rends so many segments of both upperworld and underworld life."[45]

Block acknowledged that neat categories such as enterprise and power syndicates cannot fully cover the "usually chaotic social world" criminals inhabit. Certainly, "syndicates of both stripes came and went, rose and fell with a great deal of rapidity making it very difficult to type them. Also, some syndicates displayed characteristics of both power and enterprise for periods of time. Others traveled the distance from one basic orientation to the other." Despite this complexity, Block asserted that "there seems little doubt that criminal syndicates can and should be seen as either enterprise or power depending on first the arena within which they functioned, and second on the issue of extortion." Accordingly, by using this approach, certain changes in the history of organized crime, which have passed for other sorts of developments, are understood more clearly.[46]

Power and the lack of power are of paramount importance in the complex world of illicit enterprises. According to Block, enterprise syndicates operate between two *zones of power*. The primary zone is the underworld itself. Looking at the historical record, Block realized the obvious:

> ...that enterprise syndicates are often preyed upon by highjackers, thieves, and extortionists. To achieve some security from this sea of potential enemies, an enterprise syndicate cannot appeal to criminal justice given that it is engaged in illegal activities itself. When the potential enemies become actual ones, it is forced to deal with underworld power brokers who may be the very ones preying upon the enterprise in the first place. In such cases the broker and his associates may be put on the payroll as protectors, or may actually take over the enterprise putting the original syndicate managers themselves upon an ever decreasing payroll.[47]

The criminal justice system forms the second zone of power. Its attitude toward illegal enterprises can be active, passive or criminal. These attitudes can fluctuate between and within different criminal justice agencies. Block stated that the enterprise syndicate must have a flexible structure in order to avoid a significant number of arrests of customers or operators and thus survive. Concurrently, the enterprise syndicate must attempt to purchase the passivity of law enforcement through bribes and payoffs.[48]

According to Block, both zones of power exert influence over enterprise syndicates, leaving the latter "weak and prone to exploitation in a variety of ways." For that reason, when assessing "evidence of centralization of an illicit enterprise through either consolidation or expansion one must be extremely wary of its significance." This is because

> More often than not the impetus for these developments comes not from the original managers but from outside or contingent forces. And when that happens the relationship between the new managers and the original syndicate(s) is at bottom extraordinary and therefore divisive as the rebellions, cheating and intra-syndicate violence reveals. The primary significance of the centralization episodes discussed lie in the conflicts generated rather than in centralization itself.[49]

In the end, Block resolved, the successful enterprise syndicate is the one which maintains a precarious balance between the two zones of power, a balance mandating the flexibility and decentralization found in a loosely structured environment.

As for power syndicates, they measure their success by their "ability to control others, which was the manifestation of their power." Block noted that to control others, they use methods ranging from persuasion to murder, in short "the politics of terror." By establishing dominance over a particular enterprise, they increase their personal power, thereby allowing them the ability to graft themselves on other enterprise syndicates, employers' associations, and trade unions.[50] Indeed, a casual observer may view power syndicates as an integral part of some highly structured organizations. Block cautioned that this may lead one to view them through an inappropriate organizational perspective:

> First and foremost because the organizational perspective tends to freeze time and hence change, thereby misrepresenting the nature of power syndicates. This nature is better captured by focusing on them as solid sets of mobile marauders in the urban landscape alert to institutional weakness in both legitimate and illegitimate spheres. They form, then, the loci of power in exceptionally competitive or unstable arenas.[51]

An organizational perspective is inadequate, he reasoned, because "the structure of power syndicates was simple and flexible allowing members to engage in a multiplicity of illegal activities and therefore to be involved in various complex networks in addition to their own."[52]

Block concluded that "the most precious commodity in this world is power," and that "individuals oriented themselves through a series of personal relationships which, if fortunate, added to their personal power and therefore their ability to successfully extort from those less fortunate." As is evident in the work of the network anthropologists, "the method to secure relationships was to do 'favors' for the already powerful." Yet the competitive and contingent nature of the social world of organized crime cannot ensure that one's patron "will remain powerful or indeed alive or that others will not be more successful in courting a patron, and so on." As a result, Block observed, this chaotic world dictates that individuals constantly tend their relational ties to other actors, as well as maintain a personal reputation of toughness, in order to prosper and survive. That is why "displays of power are constantly necessary for both personal and financial security in this most insecure world. Weakness undermines not only an individual's position but reverberates through the entire associational network which is always precarious."[53]

Because of the fluid nature of relationships in the social world of organized crime, Block found that in a variety of manifestations and in a variety of settings, "[power] is what it was all about." Throughout his work, Block provided examples showing that power is "taken as a sort of limitless commodity which carries with it the promise of almost endless profit" by gangsters like Waxey Gordon, Lepke Buchalter, Lucky Luciano, and Bengamin Siegel. According to Block, in all of the cases he explored,

> the formal expressions of power connoted by the term authority were never enough and were continually supplanted by the extra rush which the informal arrangements promised. Power not authority was paramount. And that because in the competitive areas discussed there was a demand for the edge. In real and fictive terms one needed the gun to eliminate competitors, to discipline workers, to secure the right vote. The gun and what it signified bridged the supposed gaps between under- and upperworld. The city was staked out with for sale signs, but only the really powerful need bother to register claims.[54]

In 1964 Charles Reich published his influential article "The New Property" in *The Yale Law Journal*. In this article, Reich discussed his theory about the *new property* that the administrative state dispenses. This property takes the form of permits, franchises, licenses, easements, and sinecures—the paperwork that allows the American economy to function. Just like a home, a car, and a business, he said, new property has real value. This is because one way or another, all of this new property falls under the purview of politicians and bureaucrats and is subject to patronage.[55] With Reich's theory in mind, Block found the following:

> Out of the maw of competitive capitalism and possessive individualism marched the extortionists—the entrepreneurs of violence whose function was to mediate this state of greed while they skimmed as much as they could for themselves. This issue of power then must be seen from two primary perspectives: the first is the political world itself and corresponds to the social system of organized crime; the second is

to view power as the leitmotif of the underworld, as a wedge into the social world of organized crime.[56]

Of course, access to patronage depended on an individual's or group's social network.[57]

Block concluded that when observing the social world of organized crime, it seems that "what professional criminals were all about was the process of organizing crime." Without an overriding authority, their domain was shaped by informal power, necessitating fluid associations that enabled them to respond efficiently to changing circumstances—the practice of actually organizing crime. Block added that by "looking exclusively through structural-functional lenses, the most important element of all is typically missed: the rigor of professional criminals in organizing crime because they exist within a world of rather tumultuous change." To be efficient and successful, an organized criminal needs to be very individualistic, "the least committed to particular structures; one of the major differences between the managers of illegal enterprises and the extortionists."[58]

What of the tension between the continuity of the social system and the turmoil of the social world? It is best understood, Block suggested, by recognizing that the stability of the system is "the ground of opportunity" for the residents of the social world of organized crime. Organized crime, then, is nothing more than an outgrowth of the political economy in which it operates.[59]

Block is not alone in this conclusion. Other scholars recognized that there exists a social system and social world of organized crime that reflects and exploits the inherent contradictions in American society. For example, Timothy Gilfoyle discovered the existence of the symbiotic relational ties between underworld and upperworld actors that led to the industrialization and commercialization of prostitution in New York City.[60] David Johnson provided glimpses of the social system and social world of organized crime as it pertains to gambling. He found that "gambling shifted, during the nineteenth century, from a profession populated by talented individuals to an activity run on business principles." He concluded that "gamblers created complex and subtle connections among themselves, their customers, politicians, and the police which redefined the context in which law enforcement occurred."[61]

In another article, Johnson conducts a systematic study of the history of America's intercity underworld, from which he offered a "generalized explanation for the process by which intercity associational networks evolved." He also traced the relationship between urbanization and these networks. As Johnson explained,

> important changes in the relationships between criminals and legitimate society did occur in the mid-nineteenth century. Those changes probably marked the beginning of a cohesive underworld based on extensive, stable institutions for the first time. Once devel-

oped, this underworld provided individual criminals with networks of relationships which could give them access to new ideas and help in testing their implications. Finally, innovations in transportation played a vital role in promoting intercity criminal activities.[62]

In a series of articles in which he discussed the history of organized crime in the United States, Mark Haller viewed various criminal enterprises as historical processes that necessitated fluid organizational structures and complicated social networks. For example, Haller explored the need for the creation and development of a social network by bootleggers during Prohibition, and how this network adapted to the repeal of Prohibition. This adaptation found those in the network using their relational ties to engage in cooperative ventures, legitimate and criminal, across the county.[63]

In another article, Haller viewed the structure of American gambling as a historical process. He identified some of the factors "that altered the economics and control of policy and numbers gambling, bookmaking, and casino gambling from 1900 to 1950." Shifting demographic patterns, technological advances, and the investment capital of former bootleggers shaped American gambling, not *La Cosa Nostra*.[64] Haller's research on organized crime in twentieth century Chicago led him to conclude that "organized crime, then, was an important part of the complex social structure of ethnic communities and the urban society." Organized crime, he stated, offered social mobility "out of the ghettos to the social world of crime, politics, ethnic business, sports, and entertainment." As he explained, "those who were successful at organized crime possessed the wealth and contacts to exercise broad influence within the ethnic communities of the city." Furthermore, "the economic activities of the underworld provided jobs or supplemental income for tens of thousands."[65]

In reviewing these and other works, it is quite clear that organized criminals and the enterprises they operate exist, succeed and fail solely at the whim of the networks with which they are involved. It is also quite clear that organized crime cannot be viewed as a static enterprise, somehow above the processes of time and space. To quote Block,

> Underworlds have an ebb and flow. Criminals are on top one moment, out of power a moment later, some return when conditions are again favorable, others spend their time in prison or penury. There were many factors capable of affecting criminal careers including seemingly endless reform movements seeking to eradicate vice, to eliminate gambling, to destroy political machines, to end alcohol consumption, to restore unions to democratic ways, and so forth. For criminals whose protection was dependent on a particular political patron, or committed to a vice activity under attack, fire storms of reform, some based on moral outrage' others the ambitions of political outsiders, could and did end careers. But the successful reform impulse also laid the foundations for new criminal careers as well. Pushing desired commodities deep underground, such as narcotics and alcohol, had a profoundly

uplifting effect for some organized criminals. The more illicit an activity became, the greater the profit margin for its vendors. Consumers had to pay more not only because of the sliding availability, but also as a kind of value-added tax based on risk.[66]

Organizing Crime

By focusing on the process of organizing criminal networks within the context of a social system of organized crime, one can transcend the current notions that organized crime should be solely viewed from either an organizational, patron-client or enterprise lens. Yes, some professional criminals formed formal and informal organizations. Yes, some gangsters possessed extensive patron-client relationships. Yes, an appreciation for the dynamics of criminal enterprises sheds light on the phenomenon otherwise known as organized crime. Nevertheless, it is quite clear that a social network approach provides a more efficient, effective and culturally sensitive means of identifying, analyzing and explaining the phenomenon. It allows us to focus on the process of organizing crime, which brings to our attention actors that otherwise may be excluded from traditional approaches. Consequently, organized crime can be viewed more clearly in terms of its role and function in a given society.

Human relationships form the least common denominator of organized crime. The actors composing these relationships engage in the process of social networking for the provision of illicit goods or services. They also protect, regulate and extort those engaged in the provision or consumption of these goods and services. These social networks can form syndicates that focus on the business of criminal enterprise or the business of projecting power. The social networks that create these syndicates also create an encompassing social system of organized crime, a system that explains the remarkable consistency of the process of organizing crime across time and space. The social networks that compose this social system of organized crime encompass the networks between underworld and upperworld actors, each of whom benefits from the actions or inaction of the other.

These social networks are never static. Rather, they are constantly changing, evolving, adapting, contracting and expanding due to internal or external forces and contingencies in the world around them. These social networks also transcend time and space, allowing professional criminals to engage in activities in small communities and on a global scale. These social networks manifest themselves in different ways for different reasons in different cultures, but they simultaneously transcend culture and allow for cross-cultural exchange.

3

Social Networks and the Institutionalization of *Gaunxi*

Of course social networks are not unique to Western societies. Willard Meyers III illustrates this point in his research on ethnic Chinese transnational crime. Concentrating on the post–Cold War world, he found that ethnic Chinese transnational crime "is an opportunistic entrepreneurial activity, conducted exclusively through individual and organizational *guanxi* networks." Systemically, ethnic Chinese transnational crime operates a global trade network in prohibited commodities and services. This system is composed of "bankers, suppliers, refiners, exporters, transporters, importers, and distributors, who are in, or have access to *guanxi* networks, which are able to be linked flexibly from point of origin to point of delivery."[1]

These points of origin and delivery are worldwide. Ethnic Chinese communities have developed globally for centuries from Asia to Latin America, from Europe to the Caribbean.[2] These fundamental international networks provide ethnic Chinese criminals with an inherent advantage over other ethnic groups by providing the logistical framework to engage in transnational organized crime. For example, one cousin in India supplies raw opium to another in Hong Kong where it is processed into smoking opium. His brother in Seattle imports it and sells it to his cousin in Portland who retails the commodity. As Block suggested, those immigrant groups "who shared a communal heritage with overseas criminals or otherwise were prepared to develop overseas contacts were far more successful than those without the heritage or contacts."[3]

These networks and their manifestations in the legitimate world are quite evident in the work of anthropologists, ethnographers, and archaeologists. For example, while excavating a nineteenth-century refuse pit that was firmly associated with Chinese merchants in a section of Sacramento, California's Chinatown, archaeologists discovered a variety of artifacts originating from overseas. These artifacts included art, porcelain, tableware, and food scraps. From these artifacts and corresponding ethnographic and historical research, the project's leaders inferred that these merchants were a part of a sophisticated international and domestic supply and distribution network that provided goods and services reflecting Chinese ethnic identity.[4] Another example is found in the work of ethnographer J. T. Omohundru. He researched the structure of Chinese merchant families and the trading patterns of Chinese residing in the Philippines.[5] Omohundru established that Chinese merchants relied on ethnic ties to "organize an entire commercial ethnic group," and that Chinese "middlemen" relied on specific individuals in China to provide goods and services when asked.[6]

Just like those operating within the law, Meyers found that transnational ethnic Chinese criminals are "symbiotically attached to the global economy and partially, or in some countries wholly, integrated into the domestic economy." According to Meyers, empirical data shows that these criminals are engaged in illegal activities like drug trafficking, immigrant and weapons smuggling, fraud and theft on a global scale, profiting hundreds of billions of dollars a year.[7] Meyers justifiably proclaimed that "the scale of global trade and depth of penetration of the global marketplace by ethnic Chinese transnational criminal organizations suggested by the above [crimes] is without parallel." The opportunistic nature of the activities of ethnic Chinese transnational criminals, as well as "their ability to rapidly assemble resources on a global scale to capitalize on any entrepreneurial opportunity presented," is also testament to the success of ethnic Chinese criminal networks.[8]

As opposed to Western society, which places emphasis on individual freedom for all, regardless of social station, Chinese are born into a hierarchically organized society. Within this hierarchy, individuals are "bound to others in an ever expanding web of social relations bearing mutually obligate bonds of varying strength." This term is called *guanxi* (or *quanxi*) in the Chinese language. As defined by Meyers, *guanxi* "embraces many concepts, some familiar to Westerners, such as connections, networks, and patron-client relations." The basis for *guanxi* is the dyadic relationship between two actors, a relationship that is naturally present for some, but for others must be acquired, cultivated, and maintained. It is best viewed as "a social strategy by which individuals in a hierarchical society seek to insure access to resources, which are controlled by powerful elites, who can arbitrarily allocate them."[9]

According to Meyers, "a *guanxi* bond has two interlocking components, which taken together serve as the basis for this social strategy." The first component is *renqing*. This is "the right of each party to request performance by the other of the undertakings implicit in the bond." The strength of the bond is measured by the degree to which a party feels obligated to carry out the request. *Bao* is the second component. This is the obligation to repay. This obligation is incurred when the request is performed. According to Meyers, "the repayment must be a *renqing* of at least equal, but preferably greater, value to the performer. Each party's ledger of *renqing* and *bao* must remain balanced."[10]

In forming the *guanxi* bond, the two actors do not view the dyadic bond as the ultimate goal. Each party also takes stock of the other's bonds to other actors as well. According to Meyers, "it is the expectation of each partner to receive not only the benefit of their agreement, but prospective benefits from the total of all agreements each has made in the past or may make in the future." Consequently, "by acquiring a storehouse of *guanxi* bonds to others who control, or have access to those in control of social resources, Chinese build a dynamic relational network that sustains them in time of need and advances their social status (*mianzi*)."[11]

Parental and filial bonds carry with them the strongest obligations of mutual reciprocity (*qinqing*). With these bonds serving as an individual's starting point, the individual can make bonds first with immediate kin, then distant kin. In the coastal provinces of Guangdong and Fujian, which provide most of the immigrants coming to the United States, villages are commonly centered around either single surnames or common lineage. This provides natural sources of affinal and agnatically derived *guanxi*. From family and kin come additional sources of *guanxi*, "sources that include neighbors (non-kinsmen), classmates, co-workers, persons sharing a natal place and other associative societal contacts."[12]

Though both Westerners and Chinese form relational ties that place them into social networks, there exists fundamental differences in how these ties are viewed by each party. Meyers defined these differences in the following manner:

> Western man forms bonds outside his immediate family circle. He does so to satisfy identifiable present needs unobtainable through individual endeavor. The terms are specific, formal, define performance and duration of obligation. The subject of an agreement and the content of an obligation are delimited by a state sponsored value system and a breach is enforced by reference to a state maintained mechanism extrinsic to the parties. Western man forms transactional bonds to obtain transactional benefits.

By contrast, Chinese actively acquire bonds to satisfy anticipated and contingent future needs. The terms are informal and the subject of agreement is constrained only by the parties' intrinsic value system. Performance is temporally and situationally defined; obligation is limited only by need and balance in accounts of repayment (*bao*) and could last for the life of the parties.[13]

Such a contrasting view on the role of social bonds has direct impact on the Western and Chinese concepts of social order, structure, and function. Meyers explained that there are two primary arenas in which this difference is manifested. The first are the roles of the legal system and the law. In Chinese society, "the particularistic social order of human relationships, face (*mianzi*) and the *guanxi* bond serve to define moral values, order behavior and resolve conflict." As a result, "the law is marginalized and the legal system relegated to a lowly position in a spectrum of mediative mechanisms, while at the same time available for manipulation by powerful sectors within the state and society at large." This stands in marked contrast to Western society, where the law "is seen as the fundamental expression of moral values and the legal system as the sole mechanism for enforcement of those values and as the ultimate arbiter of conflicting values."[14]

Such a fundamental difference in the view of social order, structure, and function presents fundamental contradictions when the two societies interact. In Chinese society,

> The marginal role played by law in favor of a relational system for defining values and the legal system for ordering behavior permits the existence and acceptance of a dynamic continuum of social behavior and activity along which, the lines between criminal, technically illegal and licit actions are blurred or non-existent. In this informal atmosphere, criminal groups can successfully compete with the legal system to enforce obligations and collect debts; the banking system to lend money; and the state in meeting the needs of individuals, business and industry. To the extent that criminal groups serve the demands of the society for goods and services that are unmet by the state, or provide them more efficiently, or at a lower cost, they are institutionalized in the society. In addition, criminal groups have in the past and do in the present serve the interests of the state by providing a mechanism to obscure the exercise of state power in domestic and even international spheres.[15]

For that reason, an American software company victimized by bootleggers operating in Fujian may attempt to compel the Chinese legal system to enforce its patent rights for years and still be unsuccessful. Similarly, a Chinese businessman defrauded by another in the United States may ignore the American legal system and instead go through an associational mediative processes within the Chinese community to seek justice.

The second difference inspired by different concepts of relational ties is the influence these ties have on social organization and social behavior. With regard to social organization, it is important to recall that a *guanxi* bond is not limited to the parties forming a dyadic relationship. It also encompasses each actor's social network. As Meyers stated,

> *Guanxi* restrains individual action and impels all endeavors to be undertaken in a consultative and associative manner. Little productive activity can be undertaken without the knowledge of those in your network and without employing or satisfying the mutual-obligate bonds of those with whom you have *guanxi*, who are or might be affected. Every sector of Chinese society, be it family, social, commercial, governmental, military, or criminal, is permeated with some form of association.

Thus, lineages, guilds, tongs, associations, partnerships, trusts and conspiracies are the rule in familial, social, commercial and criminal contexts.[16]

This sophisticated structure bears directly on social behavior. In the United States, one generally would not consider the impact on one's extended family, friends, neighborhood, town, union, church, clubs, and service organizations when asking for or granting a favor. However, this consideration, and the responsibility it entails, is a reality in Chinese society.

Meyers remarks that "in Chinese associations of any kind, webs of individual *guanxi* networks converge and diverge." It is up to the leaders of these associations to posses and maintain "many cross cutting strands that tie them to the members and to each other to form a larger and more stable web." Individual leaders also acquire "associational *guanxi*." Associational *guanxi* "links them and their organization to the leaders of other associations to form a still larger web." Associational *guanxi* "reduces competition, fosters cooperation, and permits efficient use of resources to attain organizational objectives. Associational *guanxi* is a central factor in explaining cooperation among ethnic Chinese criminal groups in transnational activities." This type of arrangement, Meyers explained, confounds Western authorities who, from their own societal perspective, view relationships between criminal groups as inherently competitive.[17]

This is reminiscent of culture conflict theory in criminology. As originated by Thorsten Sellin, this theory centers on the idea that "conduct norms," or rules that govern behavior, are relative and that they vary from culture to culture. This relativity instigates conflict between cultures. These conflicts come in two primary forms. The first he called "primary conflict." This happens when two different cultures govern the behavior of individuals and groups. For example, an immigrant is governed by the conduct norms of his or her native culture, as well as those of his or her host culture. Sellin called the second type of conflict "secondary conflict." Secondary conflict refers to smaller cultures that exist within larger cultures. Today, these smaller cultures are called subcultures. For example, wealthy merchants would have different subcultural conduct norms than a Chinese common laborer.[18]

Yet culture conflict does not preclude cultural integration, the process of uniting diverse groups in a society into a cohesive whole. Indeed, the two processes are not mutually exclusive. Because the two cultures have networking traditions, adaptive individuals in both cultures learned the cultural nuances of networking in both societies. Consequently, networks expanded in both directions, with these adaptive individuals often filling the classic role of middlemen in social, political and economic cross-cultural exchange. These middlemen, some of whom were professional criminals, eventually paved the way for broader acculturation, the process of becoming adapted to a new or different culture, to occur.

Institutionalizing Guanxi

As ethnic Chinese arrived in the United States during the mid–1800's, they brought with them their *guanxi* networks and their need to institutionalize these networks in the form of organizations and associations referred to as *hui*.[19] According to Dian Murray, *hui* had a long history in China:

> During the Qing dynasty (1644–1911), *hui* were organizations characterized by a ceremonial ritual, often in the form of a blood oath, that brought people together for a common goal. Some were organized for clandestine, criminal, or even seditious purposes by people who were alienated from or at the origins of society. Others were organized for mutual protection or the administration of local activities by members of law-abiding communities. *Hui* members originally organized for one purpose sometimes found themselves mobilized for different ends, and simultaneously involved in activities where the distinction between "legal" and "illegal," "protection" and "predation," or "orthodox" and "heterodox" blurred. However, all these groups, regardless of their special configurations, fell within the long organizational and cultural traditions of China.[20]

As manifested in the Chinese community in the United States, these organizations are divided into two primary types, distinguished primarily on the basis of requirements for membership.

According to Eve Armentrout Ma, who made a detailed study of the subject, one type of organization has restrictive membership requirements. The other does not. Membership for the former is determined by accident of birth. The most prominent of these are the *hui-kuan* (or regional associations), the Chinese Six Companies and related *hui-kuan* federations, and the surname associations (family associations). The most common types of organizations created with non-restrictive membership requirements are guilds, Christian groups, tongs and Triad secret societies. All of these organizations, regardless of membership requirements, represented "variations" on organizations existing in China.[21]

Ma explained that each of these organizations has legitimate functions in Chinese-American society. Generally, they provide a social net in times of crisis; represent, protect, and advance members' interests with Chinese and non–Chinese; provide credit; ship the bones of deceased members back to China for proper burial; provide information and assistance for finding jobs; maintain hostels in their various branches; and provide a sense of fellowship and community.[22] In short, they offer access to *guanxi* to all who qualified. Thanks to this *guanxi*, members were more likely to survive and succeed in the politically, economically, and socially hostile host society that was the nineteenth century United States.

For the purposes of this study, two types of non-restrictive organizations are of primary importance. These are Triad societies and tongs. Some observers equate all Chinese criminal groups, namely Triads, tongs, and street gangs, to a Chinese "Mafia," or they simply use the blanket term Triads.[23]

This type of generalization reflects a tendency on the part of some to want to impose a familiar, organizational paradigm of organized crime on Chinese organized criminality in order to make sense of it.[24] Whether the structures used are accurate or not is unimportant. As Ko-lin Chin accurately observed, "such a generalization would only blur our understanding of the distinctive character of [Triads and tongs]."[25]

According to Chin, Triad societies began as secret societies during the Ch'ing dynasty. Their purpose was political: to overthrow the Manchus and restore the Ming Dynasty. Members viewed themselves as patriots fighting against an occupying force.[26] Notwithstanding their noble incarnations, the Triads did not stay focused on patriotism. Chin explained how the Triad societies began to divert themselves to criminal pursuits in the new British colony of Hong Kong during the 1840s.[27]

Membership grew rapidly and spread overseas as political and economic turmoil ravaged China and members joined the diaspora. Consequently, Triad *guanxi* networks and Triad norms and values were spread to Chinese communities abroad. These norms and values establish obligations for the support and protection of the members of the Triad. They also condone and encourage criminal, deviant, and duplicitous behavior as long as it does not negatively impact fellow members of the Triad.[28]

In contrast to Triads, which spread through Chinese communities across the globe, tongs are unique to the experience of the Chinese in North America. The literal definition of tong means simply "hall" or "gathering place."[29] The role and function of the tong in the Chinese-American community has been subject to a long debate. Historian Richard Dillon offered one of the first explanations of the rise of the tongs. First, the Chinese placed a high value on their culture and way of life. Since many expected to return one day to China, they had no interest in becoming Westernized. So they formed tongs to reflect these values of culture and way of life.[30]

Second, Chinese could not make fair use of the American justice system due to discriminatory laws. For example, in California and several other states, Chinese were prevented from testifying in court. This prompted the creation of the tongs because they offered the threat of force to demand and extract justice. As a result, the tongs took on the social functions of arbitration, protection and exploitation in Chinatown.[31]

Third, the decline of the power of the Six Companies in Chinatowns across the country during the 1890s created a power vacuum that various tongs rushed to fill. As the tongs simultaneously gained and decentralized power, many Chinatowns experienced vicious power struggles and the proliferation of illegal activities. This conflict and criminal activity came to an end in the late 1910s only after harsh crackdowns by authorities in San Francisco and the efforts of the larger Chinese community itself.[32]

Stanford Morris Lyman criticized Dillon's explanations. Specifically, Lyman pointed to two errors on the part of Dillon. First, he criticized Dillon's pronouncement that the end of the tong wars marked the end of

Chinese criminality. Lyman maintained this was erroneous, for Dillon ignored evidence of criminality and conflict going on for decades afterward. Second, Lyman charged, Dillon made a "frame of reference error," omitting the tongs' role as "radical societies." Lyman argued that by simply viewing the tongs as "organized criminal gangs," Dillon overlooked the relationship between criminality and rebellions or revolutionary activity, a point that non–Chinese have failed to understand. Finally, Lyman added, "Dillon's error is no different from that of many criminologists who perceive Chinese tong depredations as a social problem caused by an unhealthy environment of prejudice and misunderstanding."[33]

Ko-lin Chin tempered Lyman's "radical societies" critique. Chin made it clear that the politically-inspired Triad involvement, be it by the Huang Pang or Green Pang, was focused on the control of the Chih Kung Tong, often referred to as the Chinese Freemasons, in the United States. Other tongs were of peripheral interest to the Triads.[34] Specifically, the Hip Sing Tong and On Leong Tong have not explicitly identified themselves as "overseas branches of the Huang Pang." Nevertheless, "some of these tong's leaders or members" have been closely connected to, or members of, the Huang Pang.[35]

In addition to this semantic critique, Chin also asserted that tongs other than the Chih Kung emerged as a protective response against the dominance of a few large family and district associations. They formed as smaller family groups and district associations banded together, gaining strength from the fact that they could recruit members without traditional restrictions. As the tongs gained strength, they began to conflict with each other and the elite associations. According to Chin, "the secretive nature of the tongs (unlike family or district associations, tong members were hard to identify) and the strong alliance among them when they fought with elite organizations enabled them to overpower the family and district associations." Consequently, "the tongs became the most powerful associations in the Chinese communities, prompting members of family and district associations to join at least one tong for additional protection." With their victory over the elites, the tongs usurped some of their obligations to the Chinese community, providing assistance to those in need and acting as arbitrators in group and individual conflicts in the community.[36]

Chin also joined Lyman's critique of Dillon's thesis that the power of the tongs subsided during the 1910s. Chin noted that "the power of the tongs did not decline nor did tong conflict subside after the 1910's." The historical record speaks for itself. In California, the tong wars lasted until 1946. In New York, they lasted until 1930. Since 1960, "disputes among the Chinese associations have been peacefully settled inside the meeting rooms of the Chinese Consolidated Benevolent Association."[37] However, Chin is careful to point out that a peaceful settlement does not erase the fact disputes still occurred.[38] In short, a lack of violent conflict does not equate a lack of conflict or criminal activity. For the researcher, the existence and nature of these disputes are nearly impossible to discover, for without a trail of bodies to arouse the attention of non–Chinese authorities, a public record is lacking.

Despite myths to the contrary, it must be understood that tongs are not inherently criminal organizations. Membership is drawn mostly from the legally employed or business owners. As Chin explained, "these members pay their fees regularly, visit the associations occasionally to meet people or gamble, and attend the associations' banquets and picnics a few times a year. They are not involved in the tongs' daily affairs or in decision-making. Only the officers and the employees are involved with the organizations on a daily basis."[39]

The leaders of the tong and its employees handle the external and internal affairs. Like any organization, tongs have factions that reflect themselves in this leadership as well as the general membership. According to Chin,

> Within each association, there are many factions. A senior member who does not identify with a particular faction is most likely to be elected president, a result of compromise among the factions. In other words, the person who occupies the highest position could be a puppet. He is selected because he is isolated and is acceptable to the many factions. Those who are more powerful and more ambitious are least likely to be elected as formal leaders. Nevertheless, they are the ones who pull the strings. Because of their anonymity, few people outside of the association know who they are and how they control the daily activities of the association.[40]

Of course, such arrangements allow factions of either virtue or guile to control that tong at any one time. Still, members of both dispositions fill the ranks and are capable of using their affiliation to increase and strengthen their *guanxi* with similarly minded brethren residing anywhere a branch of the tong is located. Consequently, a tong is not an organized crime organization *per se*, but a natural means of obtaining and using individual and associational *guanxi* for both criminal and non-criminal purposes.

Considering that each tong had, and continues to have, members associated with the Chih Kung Tong and other triads, it should come as no surprise that the tongs adopted the norms and values of the Triad subculture. According to Chin,

> Members are required to go through the Triad initiation ceremony when recruited, take the thirty-six Triad oaths of loyalty, and bow to the god of the Triad societies. They memorize Triad poems and slang and are urged by leaders to internalize the Triad norms of loyalty, righteousness, patriotism, and brotherhood. Although law-abiding members, who constitute the majority, may become familiar with Triad philosophy for a short while during the initiation ceremony, core members of the tongs are committed to Triad norms and values on a long-term basis.[41]

It is the association with "those who are unable or unwilling to become assimilated into either the dominant culture or the elite culture of over-

A romanticized image of a Tong War (Gong and Grant, *Tong War*).

seas Chinese societies find Triad subcultural norms and values attractive. In all societies where Triad norms and values are ascended, the dominant cultures were alien cultures from the Chinese point of view."[42]

As a result, found Chin, members of the Triad subculture have been designated Dark Society Elements by their fellow Chinese. Furthermore, "the shady world in which they dwell" is called the Dark Society, or *Jiang Hu*. *Jiang Hu* literally means "rivers and lakes" and it denotes the rootlessness of the members. Conventional Chinese norms and values are cast aside in the *Jiang Hu* world. Instead, Triad norms and values dominate. Despite its devious implications, a *Jiang Hu* person does not have to be a criminal, only possess a different set of values and live a different style of life. However, as Chin perceived, it is the *Jiang Hu* world that produces a favorable climate for criminals and Triad norms and values.[43]

Due to the institutionalized *guanxi* provided by various *hui*, professional criminals in the Chinese-American community had ready instruments available to assist them in capitalizing on the criminal opportunities inherent in the host society. One could reach out to a non-criminal "cousin" or "brother" to provide assistance or protection with full knowledge that mutually obligate bonds made it difficult to say no. Indeed, the *hui* could easily gain valued resources and expand its power in the Chinese-American community by assisting its criminal members. Without a strong faction to keep criminal members in check, an individual *hui* could find its reputation damaged or destroyed in both the Chinese and non–Chinese communities alike, thereby becoming the target of numerous attempts to cut or curb its criminal ties.

On the "Parochialism of Presentism"

Despite the basic recognition of *guanxi*, *hui* and Triad norms and values to Chinese criminality, there is only a scant discussion of their applic-

3. Social Networks and the Institutionalization of Gaunxi 35

ability to the genesis and development of Chinese organized crime in the United States. As a matter of fact, the treatment of Chinese organized crime in the United States is largely ahistorical. Even when it is addressed, the histories provided offer little or no primary source evidence about important historical issues. Additionally, the use of proper historical methods is practically non-existent.

Criminologist Ko-lin Chin, a highly respected researcher of Chinese organized crime, furnished a strong example of this practice in effect. Chin's collected works are very impressive, setting the standard for research on Chinese organized crime and street gangs, as well as the fields of Chinese criminality and criminal victimization. Chin also deserves recognition for being an instrumental part of the vanguard that has created opportunity for minority scholars and criminological research addressing minorities and the criminal justice system. He is highly regarded for a reason.

Still, although Chin recognized that "a historical analysis of the development of [Triads, tongs, and street gangs] is needed to understand the present stages and potential of these organizations,"[44] the histories he provides, particularly those of the tongs, rely almost exclusively on secondary sources. In other cases, it is not existent. For example, his recent work on Chinese immigrant smuggling fails to take into account the rich history of that crime that extends back in time to the first exclusionary laws passed by Congress. As a matter of fact, the Exclusion Era itself is not mentioned at all. Chinese immigrant smuggling is viewed as a purely contemporary phenomenon.[45]

In his book *Chinatown Gangs*, Chin rendered a thorough analysis of contemporary Chinese street gangs and their relationship to tongs and other Chinatown social and economic institutions. His theoretical frame of reference centered on theories of victimology and organized crime criminology, and he tested these theories against data compiled from surveys of local businessmen and interviews with male gang members, law enforcement authorities, and the leaders of community organizations.[46]

Nonetheless, except for a few minor exceptions, roughly a century of historical development of the Chinese street gang is basically unaccounted for in *Chinatown Gangs*. It merits less than two pages in a book over two hundred pages long.[47] For example, Chin asserts that Chinese street gangs began with immigration reform during the mid–1960s. But what about the well-known existence of *boo how doy*, the "hatchetmen" and "highbinders" of old? It is quite apparent from even a cursory review of the secondary—let alone the primary sources—that the *boo how doy* of the tong wars and contemporary Chinese street gangs serve identical criminal functions (e.g. extortion, protection of gambling establishments, violence, etc.) in Chinatown's underworld and that they are composed of the same demographics (young immigrant men). Yet Chin does not address this point, even though he recognizes the existence of *boo how doy*.[48]

In addition, Chin's analysis, though confined to New York City's Chinatown, does not consider the relationship of Chinatown to the pervasive social system of organized crime (with its multiethnic actors and upperworld and underworld professional criminals) that has historically dominated New York City, particularly the Lower East Side where Chinatown is located. The result is a reinforcement of the notion that Chinese organized crime only impacts and involves Chinese.

In another one of his books, *Chinese Sub-culture and Criminality*, Chin offers relatively more historical depth than *Chinatown Gangs*. Yet even this effort could be strengthened by a more in depth and critical historical analysis. For example, one of Chin's major themes is that the Chinese community in general, and the tongs in particular, "did not participate in American politics,"[49] and "even if they were willing to do so, they would not be able to establish close relationships with public officials through corruption."[50] But one cannot help but be overrun by evidence of corruption and numerous, substantive relationships with non–Chinese in the very works Chin cited as historical evidence in his own research.[51] At the very least, Chin's work would have benefited by providing more qualifying statements when historical fact contradicted his findings.

Another example is the scant four pages dedicated to the history of tongs in the United States in Chin's frequently cited dissertation, *Chinese Triad Societies, Tongs, Organized Crime, and Street Gangs in Asia and the United States*. The histories of the On Leong Tong and the Hip Sing Tong, tongs that play a large role in Chin's later analysis of street gangs are simply overlooked, as are numerous other tongs engaged in the tong wars he lists. He only focuses on the Chih Kung Tong.[52] Even in the section dedicated to tong wars, only two pages were dedicated to events before the 1960s, one of which is simply a listing of dates and corresponding tong wars. Additionally, the historical facts drawn from secondary sources that Chin presented were taken at face value. No primary source research was conducted.

To put this paucity of historical material into perspective, Chin ended his tong war section with roughly four pages dedicated to the circumstances surrounding the Golden Star Massacre that occurred in San Francisco in 1982.[53] Given the abundance of secondary and primary source material on Chinese organized crime, Chin's emphasis of one historical event that occurred less than a decade before he wrote his dissertation does not constitute a comprehensive history. Clearly, the history of Chinese organized crime in the United States is in need of additional scholarly attention if such standard works as Chin's overlook abundant source material and basic historical methodologies. Recognizing the historical limitations of Chin's work is particularly important for he is the most prominent author contemporary criminologists turn to for their treatment of Chinese organized crime.[54]

Most of the scholarly work completed on Chinese organized crime has provided unique and sorely needed insight into the world of Chinese organized crime. My only contention is that these studies would be strengthened if more attention were provided to history or basic historical methodologies. Granted, history is not and should not be the sole mark of quality for research and investigation. Nevertheless, when history is needed and used in research like Chin's, or in investigations like those of the United States Senate or the media, standard secondary sources are referenced and summarized without question. This leads to the wholesale acceptance of historical assumptions that may be unfounded. Instead of basing theory and policy on historical fact, scholars and policy makers create foundations composed of myth.

If these historical assumptions are not challenged and tested, their blanket acceptance by scholars, the media and policy-makers may undermine the theoretical frameworks, conclusions, and policy implications they helped create. Stephan Thernstrom called this same phenomenon "a parochialism of time rather than of space, as it were, the parochialism of presentism." Referring to the study of social mobility, Thernstrom offered a critique equally applicable to the study of Chinese organized crime:

> Let me begin with a simple, obvious, uncontroversial point—so obvious, indeed, that I would blush to make it but for the fact that so few students of social mobility seem to have taken it to heart. This is simply that some of the most interesting questions we might ask about the nature of a class structure today cannot be answered without reliable information about the nature of that class structure yesterday—and the day before yesterday, and even the century before yesterday! And that nowhere has the research necessary to supply such knowledge about class and mobility been carried out in sufficient historical depth.[55]

With regard to Chinese organized crime, we currently find ourselves in the position revisionist scholars like Dwight Smith, Joseph Albini, Alan Block, Mark Haller, and David Johnson found themselves when they studied "traditional" organized crime. As it stands, organized crime in the Chinese-American community is not viewed as a long-term historical process. Rather, it is viewed as a recent phenomenon that aims to become the new "Mafia" by replacing the old, a regurgitation of the old ethnic succession theory. With the exception of Meyers, social network analysis has not been used to discover how Chinese criminals organize crime in the United States. Chinese organizations and institutions are viewed statically, not as mechanisms of *guanxi* that can assist Chinese criminals in their endeavors.

To extricate ourselves from this position, one must do as the revisionists did: dig deep into the past and attempt to establish the *guanxi* networks that have made Chinese organized crime a crucial player in the social system of organized crime in the United States. Only then can we extricate ourselves from the ethnicity trap in which the study of Chinese organized crime is currently ensnared.

Part II

Organizing Crime on Gold Mountain

4

The Four Vices and the Bachelor Society

According to Marlon Hom, "the most unfortunate thing that could happen to an affluent Cantonese family was for its head or his son to become addicted to one of the so-called four vices—that is, womanizing among prostitutes (*piu*), compulsive gambling (*dou*), excessive indulgence in food and drink (*yam*), and smoking opium (*cheui*)."[1] It was said that each of these vices "would bring ruin to a man and his family—in the form of disease, failing health, loss of wealth and property, sale of wife and children, and so on—and, unless the addict quickly repented, he was doomed." After all, the ramifications did not end with the person who succumbed to the lure of vice, but extended to one's family who, along with their child, would lose considerable face. Therefore, "duty and responsibility to one's family" had to be "placed above one's individual interests."[2]

It was commonly held by Chinese that the only way one could avoid such destruction in one's life was to follow Confucian teachings of moral cultivation. Consequently, the immigrants who left China to seek their fortunes in the United States had already spent a life being "indoctrinated with Confucian family values." Upon their arrival to the United States, however, they were immediately thrust into a society where Chinese and non–Chinese vice entrepreneurs exerted strong influence. To quote Hom, "Chinatown's attitude toward these vices, which were so dramatized in Cantonese folklore, was quite ambivalent." A cavalcade of vice resorts would confront a Chinese immigrant upon his entry to San Francisco. Among them, "gambling and womanizing were accepted as necessary evils by a population of desperate men to whom escapist moments provided a remote hope of becoming rich or fulfilling their physical needs."[3] An unknown poet wrote insightfully of the consequences of this dilemma a century ago:

> My life's half gone, but I'm still unsettled;
> I've erred, I'm an expert at whoring and gambling.
> Syphilis almost ended my life.
> I turned to friends for a loan, but no one took pity on me.
> Ashamed, frightened—
> Now, I must wake up after this long nightmare;
> Leap out of this misery and find my paradise.
> But others laugh that old habits die hard and I'll never change.[4]

Of all the vices, sex probably had the strongest lure for the male Chinese immigrant. The reason was demographic. Immigration law curtailed the immigration of Chinese women in order to prevent Chinese men from creating families and establishing permanent residence in the United States. The result was an immigrant population commonly known as the Bachelor Society. Barred from pursuing married life and legitimate sexual relations, and emancipated from family pressures that would stress adherence to traditional values, these men eventually found sexual satisfaction with prostitutes.[5] After succumbing to this particular vice, the words of the Chinese sage Mencius, "food and sex are instincts," were often quoted as justification for such behavior.[6]

Despite such declarations, the four vices were still largely regarded "as wicked and serious threats to a person's well-being." However, the use of opium was singled out for particular moral sanction because of its imperialist overtones. British imports of opium had devastated the Cantonese immigrants' homeland. Subsequently, "numerous Chinatown vernacular rhymes ridiculed and cursed opium addicts; none showed any support for the drug, in contrast to their frequent toleration of gambling and womanizing."[7] The following poem reflects this sentiment well:

> The taxed gum is a tremendous burdened:
> Once addicted to it, it does you in:
> Pockets empty, clothes ragged,
> Furniture pawned, children sold...
> All for smoking opium.
> Indulgence shows no concern for the future:
> Talent and abilities all go down the gutter.
> No way to escape from it, even if you put on wings![8]

The four vices were not solely the domain of the Chinese. Other cultures have long had prohibitions against them, as well as their fair share of those who viewed the vices as popular recreational pursuits. Ivan Light stated that beginning about 1870, non–Chinese of the laboring class regularly frequented the whorehouses, gambling joints, and opium dens in American Chinatowns. Though Chinese patronage was high, Light concluded that "there seems no doubt that the dollars of the white visitors enabled American Chinatowns to support many more bordellos, opium dens, and gambling halls than would have been possible solely on the basis of Chinese patronage." Albeit whites made up a substantial portion of the clientele, the vice entrepreneurs who ran the establishments in Chinatown were overwhelmingly Chinese.[9]

What attracted non–Chinese to Chinatown vice establishments when there were plenty of others to patronize? Light suggested three reasons. First, there was a sense of "anonymity of patronage," a welcome quality for those living in shame of their actions. Second, Chinatown offered lower rates than their white competitors for similar illicit goods and services. Third, the Chinese paid particular attention to security that eased their clients' fears of apprehension. It was common knowledge that Chinatown's underworld purchased protection from the municipal police. In addition, Light stated, "many vice resorts boasted thick oaken doors studded with bolts, and sentries posted in warning. Coupled with the skylights and secret passages through cellars to the street, these precautions permitted fleeing customers to escape arrest in case of police raids...." Moreover, politicians who made careers of demagoguing against the "depraved" Chinese had no aversion to simultaneously taking kickbacks from Chinese vice entrepreneurs and guaranteeing their security.[10]

Given the profit generated by these vice enterprises, it did not take long for some men to extort them. Chinatown provided ample opportunities for those with physical power to regulate, protect, and disrupt the distribution of the four vices. Consequently, power syndicates rose to exploit, or work in conjunction with, vice syndicates. As authorities continued to regulate and criminalize these vices to ever-higher degrees, both types of syndicates were ready to take advantage of the increased criminal opportunities and potential for profit inherent within them. After all, they had a substantial non–Chinese client base and a formidable Bachelor Society of laborers to provide a steady clientele, a ready talent pool from which to draw recruits for their organizations, and a long history of organized crime in China to draw upon.[11] Just like non–Chinese bachelor laborer communities in the United States, the economic and social consequences of these developments were severe: "More debt, more disease, more death, and more disorder."[12]

To Gold Mountain

During the late 1840s and mid–1850s, difficulties in China—including severe economic hardship, the Taiping Rebellion of 1840–1864, the Red Turban revolt, and the Hakka-Punti wars in Kwangtung province—coincided with the exciting news that vast amounts of gold was there for the taking in a place called Gold Mountain, which existed far off to the east, over the Pacific horizon. News also came that there were plenty of jobs available, for there was a shortage of labor there as well.

Thousands of men, almost all from the areas around the port city of

Guangzhou (Canton), decided to take advantage of the opportunity presented to them and sailed to the United States. Others had no choice in the matter. Chinese merchants who had valuable "coolie" labor contracts to fill kidnapped them.[13] Dillon explained that the great preponderance of Cantonese immigrants during this time can be explained by two facts. First, the accessibility of their home region to first clipper, then steamship, lines between San Francisco and Hong Kong and, second, the existence of well-organized Cantonese companies which actively recruited immigrants from the surrounding province of Kwangtung.[14] The combination of these factors led to an ever-increasing number of Chinese immigrants in the United States from 1860 to 1890.[15]

The vast majority of these men (and it was almost entirely men) who came to the United States did not intend to permanently relocate. They simply came to the United States to earn their fortune, mostly as laborers, so that they could return to China as prosperous men, able to live comfortably and care for their families. Yet things did not go as planned for almost half of these immigrants. In the words of Eve Armentrout Ma, "continuing instability in their motherland, the difficulty and expense of the return trip, and the obstacles to possible future reentry into the American countries (of which the notorious United States Chinese Exclusion laws provide only one example) eventually led about half to settle permanently in the Americas."[16] Consequently, a permanent Chinese-American community joined the ranks of other overseas Chinese communities that had established themselves across the Pacific Rim over the previous six hundred years.[17]

In order to get to the United States, one needed to pay one's passage, an unrealistic prospect for a poor peasant laborer. To meet this need, Chinese companies began to offer "credit-fare" contracts. Under these contracts an immigrant would repay the loan that paid his passage by working for the creditor for a specified period of time, usually between five to seven years. The creditor would then sub-contract the immigrant's labor to various companies.[18]

Some equate such arrangements to slavery. Lisa See asserted that even though the international slave trade was barred in 1862, "foreign men tricked, coerced, or 'shanghaied' Chinese travelers into signing contracts for boat fare, which left them little better than slaves." From that point on, their fate merited that of Africans shipped across the Atlantic. According to See,

> Chinese, too, were loaded onto overcrowded ships where they lived below decks for the duration of their voyage across the Pacific. Conditions on shipboard were nightmarish. On some vessels, men found themselves stacked like cordwood in three-tiered bunks six feet long and thirteen and a half inches wide, with only seventeen to twenty-four inches of headroom. These holds reeked with the stench of humanity as hatches were battened down to prevent escape. The sojourners—men who promised to return to their home villages—were

given a bucket of water a day for washing and drinking. Food was also scarce. The foreigners knew from past experience that the fastest thing to break a man's spirit was hunger.[19]

Despite the veracity of See's comments regarding the transportation conditions of the Chinese laborer, she overlooked the complicity of Chinese labor brokers who had a vested interest in the trade on both ends of the supply and demand continuum. See also overlooks that many of these men voluntarily entered these arrangements. The result was that their situation is more accurately described as indentured servanthood, a status neither free nor enslaved. Nonetheless, she correctly states that this "willingness to assume such a burden was a sign of the immigrants' desperation and their optimism about prospects in the United States."[20]

Upon their arrival to the United States, the immigrants were separated into district groups and received at the docks by the representatives of the district associations.[21] From there they were sent to their various work assignments. Before the 1880s, Chinese immigrants found most of their assignments in mining and railroad construction camps, fishing villages, and agricultural jobs scattered throughout the hinterland. However, changes in employment opportunities and racial tension during the 1880s drove many to the cities where relative security was obtained in Chinatowns. "Not surprisingly," commented Eve Armentrout Ma, "by the turn of the century these Chinatowns supported a complex and dynamic social structure."[22]

By 1893, Ma continued, "Chinese immigrants had to a great extent managed to rise above the unenviable condition they found themselves in on their arrival. However, most were still plagued by a dearth of capital, and ignorance of the language of the country in which they lived, and, perhaps even more importantly, by the prejudice directed against them. Furthermore, they were subject to immigration restrictions and laws designed to limit their economic opportunities.[23] This prejudice was widespread in American society. According to Stewart Creighton Miller, "the arrival of Chinese in California provoked editorial fears across the nation, fears that can only be explained in terms of the unfavorable image of these people that preceded them to American shores."[24]

Despite a common perception, these views were not all the sole product of a violently nativist California and an influx of Chinese immigrants. Negative characterizations, fostered and promoted by the press, were quite common years before the arrival of substantial numbers of Chinese immigrants. As Miller discovered, a public that was exposed to negative stereotypes of Chinese for years readily responded to the cries of nativists. Long before 1840, "American traders, diplomats, and Protestant missionaries had developed and spread conceptions of Chinese deceit, cunning, idolatry, despotism, xenophobia, cruelty, infanticide, and intellectual and sexual perversity."[25] Mass marketed magazines and textbooks spread these stereotypes, coinciding with the development of the first recognizably modern mass media in the United States and the burgeoning public school system.

As Chinese immigrants arrived in California, these existing negative stereotypes were reinforced and thrown into the mix of a number of other social anxieties existing in American society. Consider the following editorial comment made in *The Missoula and Cedar Creek* in 1871: "Chinaman clings to his idolatry and heathenism with the tenacity of life; lives upon less than the refuse from the table of civilized man, and devotes his sister to the basest lusts of humanity, and makes her an unsexed prostitute to disseminate among devotees of base passions."[26] In one sentence, it hits on sexual purity, racial superiority, xenophobia, religion, and fear of disease, issues dominating the social politics of the day.

Additionally, as Miller pointed out, the Chinese had the misfortune of arriving "in the middle of the slavery controversy, when modern racist theory was being developed and when Americans were becoming more conscious of antisepsis and germs." Consequently, "editorial fears of 'coolieism,' of alien genes and germs" flourished. Miller concluded that these fears more adequately explain "the national decision to exclude the Chinese immigrants than does a California conspiracy."[27] As Susan Craddock established in her study of disease, poverty and deviance in San Francisco, "Disease may not discriminate, but it can help those that do."[28]

This twisted theory of race, health, and morality went a long way towards justifying the views of American nativists. As Miller explained, "the germ theory of culture hypothesized by racists helped to validate the cultural fears provoked by the arrival of the Chinese and placed the rejection of these immigrants on a seemingly more scientific basis." That is to say, "'Oriental blood' determined the 'Oriental thoughts' and 'Oriental habits' that precluded any possibility that the Chinese would be 'Americanized.'"[29] Such thoughts reached as high as the Supreme Court, where Justice Stephen Field determined that

Cartoon showing jingoism and the Chinese stereotype (*The Wasp*, 20 May 1881).

"our institutions have made no impression on [the Chinese] during the more than thirty years they have been in this country."[30]

Even the progressive Theodore Roosevelt looked down upon the Chinese. According to Roosevelt scholar Thomas Dyer, "Roosevelt did not respect the Chinese as he did the Japanese and placed them in a far lower position in the stages of civilization scheme." Roosevelt believed that "the Chinese had fallen into racial decadence, had lost the martial values, and were unable to assert themselves as a people. In fact, he so thoroughly deplored their racial character that he used the term 'Chinese' as an epithet of opprobrium." As Dyer related, as early as 1882, the future New York City Police Commissioner, New York Governor, and President of the United States agreed that Chinese immigration should be curtailed. It seemed "incredible" to him that anyone of even "moderate intelligence" could fail to see that "no greater calamity could now befall the United States than to have the Pacific slope fill up with a Mongolian population."[31]

Systematic Criminalization

In the face of the Judeo-Christian mores and the self-perceived social Darwinist supremacy of whites in the United States, the cultural weaknesses ascribed to the Chinese were many. They included idolatry, a penchant for gambling and opium smoking, and a fond desire to consume the flesh of rodents, cats and dogs.[32] Indeed, it was common practice during the nineteenth century to identify drug addicts with foreign groups and internal minorities who were actively feared and objects of massive social and legal restraints.[33] With regard to the Chinese, it was feared that smoking opium "facilitated sexual contact between Chinese and white Americans," a fear which lead to incremental efforts to legally prohibit its use in the United States.[34]

Of course the belief in perverted sexual practices by Chinese men, who were said to have a particular appetite for white women, was a main source of cultural antagonism. An 1876 article on Chinese servants in *Scribner's* warned its readers, "no matter how good a Chinaman may be, ladies never leave their children with them, especially little girls."[35] It was also believed that in order to lure young white women and girls into their evil clutches, the Chinese used opium to subjugate them. For instance, two seventeen-year-old prostitutes claimed in a Brooklyn court that they were lured into their "shameful life" at a young age by Chinese laundrymen who dulled their better judgment with opium.[36] As Miller commented, "the fear of perverted sexual proclivities on the part of the Chinese immigrants ... neither originated in California nor was it confined to that state."[37]

Nevertheless, there were those in American society who defended the Chinese. Most notably was Samuel Clemens, better known as Mark Twain. In *Roughing It*, the popular Twain spoke on behalf of the Chinese, pulling no punches when it came to those who demagogued against them:

> They are quiet, peaceable, tractable, free from drunkenness, and they are as industrious as the day is long. A disorderly Chinaman is rare and a lazy one does not exist.... He is a great convenience to everybody—even to the worst class of white men, for he bears the most of their sins, suffering fines for their petty thefts, imprisonment for their robberies, and death for their murders. Any white man can swear a Chinaman's life away in the courts, but no Chinaman can testify against a white man.... They are a kindly-disposed, well-meaning race and are respected and well treated by the upper classes all over the Pacific Coast. No California *gentleman* or *lady* ever abuses or oppresses a Chinaman under any circumstances, an explanation that seems to be much needed in the East. Only the scum of the population do it—they and their children; they, and naturally and consistently, the policemen and politicians likewise, for these are the dust-licking pimps and slaves of the scum there as well as elsewhere in America.[38]

Despite the noble and colorful efforts of Clemens, the Chinese found themselves with few friends and bearing the brunt of legislative onslaught on the federal, state and local levels.[39] After the 1868 signing of the Burlingame Treaty between the United States and China—which recognized the right of reciprocal immigration, privileges, immunities, and exemptions between the two nations—the Chinese community in the United States found itself subject to a number of discriminatory laws. For instance, in 1870, California passed an act denying female Chinese immigrants the right of entry unless they could prove to the Commissioner of Immigration that they were "of correct habits and good character." The year 1875 saw the passing of the federal Page Law, as well as the adoption of the new California Constitution, both of which added further restrictions to the immigration of Chinese laborers and women deemed to be prostitutes.[40]

The United States Congress then passed the Chinese Exclusion Act in 1882. The Exclusion Act suspended the immigration of skilled and unskilled Chinese laborers for ten years. Exempt from this law were Chinese teachers, students, merchants, and travelers, but no Chinese would be permitted naturalization from this date onward. The Exclusion Act was continued ten years later under the Geary Act, which also mandated that all Chinese in the United States must register with the U.S. government. In 1904, the Exclusion Act was extended indefinitely.[41]

The United States did not just seek to keep more Chinese out of the United States, but also sought to decrease the amount of Chinese already living there. With this in mind, Congress passed the Scott Act in 1888 that prohibited the return of Chinese laborers who had departed from the United States. In what would become a boom for immigrant smugglers, over 20,000 Chinese laborers had temporarily left the United States for China with re-entry certificates, permits declared void under this Act.[42]

A number of laws were also directed at harassing Chinese living in the United States—mostly, but not exclusively, in Western states. For example,

4. The Four Vices and the Bachelor Society 49

some states, like California, passed anti-miscegenation laws forbidding people of color, including Chinese, from marrying whites. Other laws did not allow Chinese to testify in court, forced Chinese students to attend segregated schools, and levied special taxes on Chinese miners and merchants. One such law, California's Foreign Miners Tax, accounted for half of the state's income by the time it was voided. Even municipalities got into the act. For example, in 1870 San Francisco passed the Sidewalk Ordinance that prohibited people using poles to carry goods from walking on the sidewalk, a measure obviously directed at the Chinese.[43] These laws were actively fought in the courts by the Chinese and, in many cases, found to be unconstitutional.[44]

The systematic criminalization of many areas of Chinese-American life did not solve the Chinese "problem." Instead the racist laws, tariffs, and ordinances created criminal opportunity as the supply of goods and services desired by Chinese and non–Chinese alike were forced to go underground. Once underground, the professional criminals who supplied these goods and services had to rely on either private violence or the corruption of public officials to protect their economic interests. Consequently, a segment of the Chinese-American community now found itself with the full-time occupation of organizing crime within the larger social system of organized crime already in existence in the United States. Enterprise and power syndicates began to form in earnest. Ironically, Chinese gangsterism in the United States was "the criminal epiphenomenon of an artificial bachelor society,"[45] created by the very immigration laws intended by jingoists to stamp out the "virus" of Chinese criminality in the first place.

5

Chinese Syndicates: Prostitution and Opium

Professional criminals in the Chinese-American community found themselves subject to the dynamics of the social system of organized crime in which they operated. Those forming enterprise syndicates were caught between the dual threats of power syndicates and the criminal justice system. In order to survive, the successful enterprise syndicate had to learn how to neutralize or mitigate both.[1] In Chinatown this meant that an enterprise syndicate would pay "tribute" to the *boo how doy*, otherwise known as highbinders and hatchetmen, of the tongs who extorted them. In other cases, they would rely on their *guanxi* networks to provide *boo how doy* to protect them from the extortion attempts of others. Operating in a society where corruption was already rampant, the enterprise syndicate would also pay bribes and kickbacks to corrupt officials in the political and criminal justice systems in order to neutralize the threat inherent in their authority.

In order to navigate this social system of organized crime, the Chinese enterprise syndicate had to successfully utilize the *guanxi* inherent in its varied associations; maintain a balance between *renqing* (right to request favors) and the *bao* (obligation to repay) in its *guanxi* network; and preserve and enhance its *mianzi* (social status) in the eyes of the Chinese community, particularly members who operated other criminal enterprises.[2] By implementing these strategies, Chinese enterprise syndicates avoided vertically integrated control and conducted their criminal activities with maximum flexibility and a minimum expenditure of resources. This flexibility, conservation of resources, and avoidance of vertically integrated control translated into successful endeavors for these syndicates. That is why the practice of *guanxi* by Chinese organized criminals is relied upon just as much today as it was over a century ago.[3]

Prostitution

The disproportionate gender ratio of the Chinese community in the United States during the second half of the 1800s is often pointed to as the key factor behind the proliferation of prostitution in Chinatowns across the United States.[4] This is due to the simple reason that, thanks to restrictive immigration laws, there were far more Chinese men than Chinese women in the United States (Table 2). This made marriage, and the implied sexual needs and desires it fulfilled, a rare possibility. As a result, members of the Bachelor Society turned to the prostitution industry en masse.[5]

Table 2
Sex Ratio of Chinese in the United States, 1860–1910[6]

Year	Male	Female	Percent Male	Percent Female	Ratio of Males to 100 Females
1860	33,149	1,784	94.9	4.1	1,858.0
1870	58,633	4,566	92.8	7.2	1,284.1
1880	100,686	4,779	95.5	4.5	2,106.8
1890	103,620	3,868	96.4	3.6	2,678.9
1900	89,341	4,522	95.0	5.0	1,887.2
1910	66,856	4,675	93.5	6.5	1,430.1

Source: United States Census of Population, 1960.

Lucie Cheng Hirata provided the most substantive evaluation of the Chinese prostitution industry in the nineteenth-century United States. According to Hirata, the trade began in China, where female children were often sold by their parents to the highest bidder during hard times. Other women were kidnapped or otherwise forced into a life of prostitution. Still, Hirata told how others entered the profession on their own volition, having been promised a substantial salary for providing their services under a contractual arrangement.[7] Benson Tong found that these prostitutes overwhelmingly came from the poorest groups of the peasantry class in Kwantung in Southern China.[8]

Lisa See described how the process occurred: "Just as the coolie laborers had signed their lives over to men of little honor for passage to the Gold Mountain, many of these girls—aged twelve to sixteen years—did the same, pressing their thumbprints into contracts they could not read. Although the purchase of any human being had been declared illegal in the United States, this trade flourished virtually unchecked."[9] The following is a translated example of such a prostitution contract:

> The contractee Xin Jin is indebted to her master/mistress for passage from China to San Francisco and will voluntarily work as a prostitute at Tan Fu's place for four and one-half years for an advance of 1,205 yuan (US $524) to pay this debt. There shall be no interest on

the money, and Xin Jin shall receive no wages. At the expiration of the contract, Xin Jin shall be free to do as she pleases. Until then, she shall first secure the master's mistress's permission if a customer asks to take her out. If she has the four loathsome diseases, she shall be returned within a hundred days; beyond that time the procurer has no responsibility. Menstruation disorder is limited to one month's rest only. If Xin Jin becomes sick at any time for more than fifteen days, she shall work one month extra; if she becomes pregnant, she shall work one year extra. Should Xin Jin run away before her term is out, she shall pay whatever expense is incurred in finding and returning her to her brothel. This is a contract to be retained by the master/mistress as evidence of the agreement.[10]

As this contract suggests, the life of the Chinese prostitute was an arduous one indeed. Consequently, a general sentiment held by non–Chinese Americans that Chinese women were frequent victims of violence took hold. This spurred many of strong Christian conscience to act. In 1876 the Reverend Otis Gibson, who provided shelter and salvation for runaway Chinese prostitutes, testified before a special Congressional committee charged with looking into the status of Chinese in the United States. Gibson noted that he had seen some of the contracts (like the one above) and concluded that they made false promises and committed outright fraud. Referring to prostitution as it existed in San Francisco's Chinatown, Gibson explained that the women lived in filthy, 10x10 ft. rooms, commonly referred to as cribs. Shih-Shan Tsai summarized the rest of Gibson's testimony:

> If the girls failed to attract customers, or refused to receive company because of illness or other reasons, they were beaten with sticks. When such punishment did not work, the house mistress tortured them in a variety of sadistic and cruel ways. A great many, terrified by such savage treatment, ran away before the expiration of their contracts. Some slipped back to China, others went to the country for temporary hiding; the most fortunate found shelter in the Gibson station-house. However, countless numbers of unfortunate girls were passed from owner to owner, never escaping their vicious captivity.[11]

Benson Tong found that prostitutes involved in brothel prostitution were actually afforded reasonable amounts of protection from direct forms of violence by clients, thanks to the organized crime syndicates who ran them. The violence that did occur was usually the result of the tenuous relationship between owners, customers and prostitutes, "all of whom sought to gain economic leverage," and usually precipitated by a customer who "thought he had purchased more than a woman was willing to give." As for the brothel owners, "the center of male authority and power in the establishment," they did use force on the women "to coerce compliance with their wishes, particularly to make reluctant new prostitutes accept their fates or to compel women to work harder and bring in more money." Tong also found that many Chinese prostitutes suffered rape and robbery at the hands of Chinese men.[12]

5. Chinese Syndicates: Prostitution and Opium

Because of the demand for prostitutes generated by the substantial Chinese Bachelor Society residing in the United States, a vibrant and profitable industry developed. Hirata asserted that there were two distinct periods of Chinese prostitution in California, each reflecting "the ever-increasing profitability associated with the industry." The first stage was "the initial period of free competition, during which the prostitute was also the owner of her body service." As the demand for prostitutes rose, however, so did the profits to be made from their labor. As a result, a second stage developed, "a period of organized trade, during which the prostitute was a semislave and other individuals shared the benefits of her exploitation."[13]

The first period did not last long because transportation expenses and business experience were in short supply for women seeking to take advantage of the situation. However, this situation did not prevent others who possessed access to both of these assets from recognizing that "the affluence of the male residents and the extreme (im)balance of the sexes suggested that a considerable sum of money could be made in the business." As the gender disparity continued to increase, professional criminals began to organize various aspects of the business. According to Hirata, "specialization occurred and a monopoly developed by 1854 under the control of the Chinese secret societies."[14] As early as that year, reported Lisa See, the Honorable Why Yea Tug Company had shipped to San Francisco six hundred girls to work as prostitutes.[15]

The second period of Chinese prostitution in California (ca. 1854–1925) established "a widespread organization of the trade with a network of specialized functions extending across the Pacific to Canton and Hong Kong." It took six specialized groups to keep the trade going: (1) the procurers who kidnapped, enticed, or purchased Chinese women; (2) the importers who brought them into America; (3) the brothel owners who profitted from their exploitation; (4) the Chinese highbinders who collected fees for protecting them from other highbinders; (5) the police who collected pay offs for keeping them from being arrested; and (6) the non–Chinese Chinatown property owners who leased their land and buildings for exorbitant rents.[16]

The procurers would secure the women by one of the three methods mentioned previously. The importers would then pay for the women and arrange for their passage to the United States. Upon arrival, the importers would auction the women to brothel owners. Hirata identified San Francisco's Hip Yee Tong as the dominant importer of Chinese women. According to Hirata, "it was estimated that between 1852 and 1873, the Hip Yee Tong alone imported 6,000 women, or about 87 percent of the total number of Chinese women who arrived during that period." The Hip Yee Tong levied a $40 fee on each buyer. Of this fee, $10 was paid to policemen for protection. Despite this fee, the importation of prostitutes was very profitable. Between 1852 and 1873, said Hirata, the Hip Yee netted an estimated $200,000 from the import business.[17] Marlon Hom concurred with Hirata's assessment of the Hip Yee Tong's dominance, and stated that the only reason they enjoyed their monopoly was due to the "law's protection and collaboration through bribery."[18]

Such activities prompted non–Chinese nativists, missionaries and their political allies to push for restrictive legislation aimed at destroying the Chinese prostitution industry. Consequently, California passed "An Act to Prevent the Kidnapping and Importation of Mongolian, Chinese and Japanese Females, for Criminal or Demoralizing Purposes in 1870." The federal government quickly followed suit in 1875, passing the Page Law that, among other immigration restrictions, disallowed entry of Chinese women into the United States for purposes of prostitution.

The combination of these two laws made it far more expensive to import women from China. The added expenses took the form of bribes that had to be paid to various U.S. consulate officials, customs officers, and immigration inspectors in China and the United States. For example, in 1879 it was discovered that one Counsel received from $10 to $15 for every woman shipped to the United Sates during his tenure in Hong Kong. These regulations also benefited attorneys. "Some lawyers," Hirata revealed, "colluded with the Chinese importers in obtaining habeas corpus decrees to allow the landing of Chinese women headed for the brothels."[19]

The 1882 Exclusion Act made it even more difficult to import women, for it prohibited the immigration of all women except those who were native born, married or born overseas to domiciled merchants. The importation did not end with the passage of this Act, however, because as the restrictions on the immigration of Chinese women became greater, Chinese entrepreneurs became that much more determined to meet the ever more lucrative demand of the market.[20] From the buyers' standpoint, the cost of delivery skyrocketed because of the increasing complexity and costs of importing prostitutes. According to Hirata, "after 1870, for example, young women who originally sold for $50 in Canton now brought $1,000 in San Francisco. And in the 1890s it was reported that as much as $3,000 in gold was paid for a single Chinese female in San Francisco."[21] Each successive law also "provided more opportunities for corruption. People soon found that U.S. immigration inspectors and interpreters could easily be persuaded to accept bribes for rendering favorable decisions and interpretations of the law."[22]

Nevertheless, these same market conditions made it more difficult for one organization to maintain a monopoly over the import portion of the prostitution industry.[23] The Hip Yee Tong gradually lost its monopolistic control over the traffic as other, more aggressive importers increased their market share. But overall, the import industry began to collapse under the weight of a "dwindling supply of females in China, the nearly prohibitive costs and difficulties of procurement and importation, and the loss of prostitutes from brothels in San Francisco to other cities and mining towns." As a result, brothel operators had to find non–Chinese women to meet the demand for services.[24]

5. Chinese Syndicates: Prostitution and Opium

With a large, ethnically mixed clientele creating demand and a small and ever-dwindling foreign supply, the value of the Chinese women to an enterprise syndicate increased. They became even more valuable as women of reputed questionable character were legally prevented from entering the United States. Originally, prostitutes came predominately from overseas before the passage of the Exclusion Act, but after 1882 local Chinese women became the major source of the new supply. Richard Dillon noted that by the time of the Spanish-American War, there were not enough imported Chinese women to meet the demand for their services. Therefore, those engaged in the prostitution trade found it profitable to kidnap the prostitutes of their competitors, as well as the respectable wives and daughters of those few Chinese men who had families. Once kidnapped, these women would be rushed inland to service the womanless mining and agricultural Chinatowns.[25] The kidnapping of Chinese prostitutes was common knowledge in the American West. For example, eight women were allegedly kidnapped for prostitution in San Francisco in just one week in February 1898.[26] However, this practice merely evoked a heartless comparison to horse stealing among non–Chinese.[27]

Kidnapping had its various forms. In many cases, *boo how doy* from a tong affiliated with a particular brothel would raid the operations of their competitors. In other cases, the wives of Chinese merchants and other elites were also kidnapped by *boo how doy*.[28] Of course, this practice led to violent conflicts between tongs seeking to either protect or expand the enterprises of their members or the enterprises of those with whom they were associated.[29]

As mentioned previously, in addition to kidnapping Chinese women, another course of action was for Chinese vice entrepreneurs to rely on non–Chinese prostitutes. This is particularly evident in New York City's Chinatown, where—due to migratory patterns, geography and competition from more established West Coast Chinese communities—most prostitutes controlled by Chinese enterprise syndicates were of European or African descent.[30] It is perhaps this shift in the ethnic composition ratio of Chinese controlled prostitution that accounted for the emerging "white slavery" concerns of non–Chinese during the late 1800s and early 1900s.

The profits for Chinese brothel owners were considerable. The literature on Chinese prostitution approximates that "an average full-time prostitute-worker receives four to ten customers per day, and the average career life of such a prostitute is estimated at four to five years." Therefore, concluded Hirata, "at an average of thirty-eight cents per customer and seven customers per day, a lower-grade prostitute would earn about $850 per year and $3,400 after four years." Even when one factors in the costs of maintaining a prostitute, the profits were still impressive. Hirata explained that "since women in lower-class brothels were generally kept at subsistence levels, the cost of maintaining them probably did not exceed $8 per month or $96 per person per year." This would leave a profit of approximately $754 per person per year. As a result, in what Hirata claimed are most likely conservative figures,

> if a lower-grade prostitute earned an average of $850 a year, and if we assume that the average brothel in 1870 contained nine prostitutes..., the owner's gross annual income would have been about $7,650.... If the rent and maintenance of the women are deducted from the gross income, the owner would still have received an annual profit of no less than $6,000. Even if we added other expenses such as protection fees paid to the police and taxes extorted by the tongs from brothels not owned by their members, the profit which the brothel owner received would still compare very favorably with the less than $500 average annual income of other occupations in which he or she might engage.[31]

In addition to the revenue generated by prostitution, many brothel owners forced their women to work as semiskilled workers when not entertaining clients. Hirata found that many sources refer to the fact that women provided services as seamstresses, the work farmed out by sweatshops contracted to manufacturers. The women would seldom get paid for this work, as all of the money would go to the brothel owner. Furthermore, brothel owners often owned or had a financial interest in gambling joints and opium dens as well. This provided yet another means of controlling the women, for the owners recognized that if they allowed the gambling debts and addictions of the women to take root and grow, the prostitutes would indenture themselves in perpetuity.[32]

The customer who sought the services of prostitutes was not confined to the Chinese bachelor. Chinese bordellos actively sought non–Chinese customers as well. Despite the stiff competition of non–Chinese bordellos operating elsewhere, Ivan Light explained that Chinatown bordellos relied upon special advantages in order to attract white customers. The first of these advantages was their lower price. According to Light, "in Chinatown a miner with a roustabout could obtain for four bits sexual gratification that would cost a dollar elsewhere." The second advantage was that "some white visitors apparently felt free to engage 'sing-song' girls in aberrant sexual practices which they would have blushed even to mention to the most jaded of white harlots." With this chance for unconventional erotic gratification, many non–Chinese men and boys frequented Chinatown bordellos instead of those of rival operations. Finally, Chinatown brothels benefited from "persistent rumors" that there existed a "difference in the 'slant' of the vagina of white and Chinese women." This final factor set up a cottage industry based upon the ten-cent "lookee." As Light explained, "this service was popular among white boys whose anatomical knowledge and budgets were both modest."[33]

Even Chinese women who were "rescued" by missionaries or ran away to the safety of the Protestant missions were not safe from the reach of their pimps and madams.[34] False charges of theft would be lodged against the prostitute and the police would be obliged to arrest her and take her away from her sanctuary. Once in jail, her "owner" would post her bail and take custody of her, forcing her back into the conditions she sought to

5. Chinese Syndicates: Prostitution and Opium 57

escape. If these measures did not work, *boo how doy* would carry out one of their responsibilities by either sneaking or crashing into the mission and forcibly kidnapping the prostitute.[35]

Sometimes a Chinese man would fall in love with, or take pity on, a prostitute and would help her escape. These men were then the target of a *boo how doy* dragnet. Chinatowns across the state could easily be notified by telegraph to be on the lookout for the pair and that a reward was posted. If the man had the resources, he could avoid the wrath of the *boo how doy* by offering compensation for the woman. However, most could never begin to pay such a sum and instead met violent ends.[36]

Missionary E. V. Robbens pointed to the complicity of non–Chinese attorneys in these exercises. Once a Chinese woman was fortunate enough to find shelter in a Missionary Home, she explained, tong-employed attorneys would challenge the missionaries with a writ of habeas corpus to appear in court so that a judge could decide the fate of the prostitute. "Graft is a tame word for such cruelty," commented Robbens.[37] In the end, this need for the protection and reclaiming of prostitutes reinforced the positions of various tongs or portions of tongs that provided a power syndicate function.

Such actions inspired legislation on the part of American politicians. Dillon recounts how San Francisco ordinances were passed that made it illegal "to sell any human being, such as a slave girl, or even to be in, enter into, remain in or dwell in any brothel." But according to reform members of the Chinese community, these ordinances were created not to clean Chinatown as its supporters stated. Instead, they viewed police crackdowns on prostitution as an effort to compel those involved in the business to pay for increased police protection.[38]

During the 1870s officials from the Six Companies (a powerful Chinese association which officially represented the concerns of Chinese living in the United States) wrote President Ulysses S. Grant to inform him that, yes, "unprincipled Chinese" were bringing in prostitutes from China. However, they asserted that the traffic was intent on meeting the gratifications of not just Chinese, but non–Chinese customers as well. Additionally, they informed the President, that it was non–Chinese attorneys who secured, and non–Chinese judges who approved, writs of *habeas corpus* on behalf of Chinese vice entrepreneurs that prevented prostitutes from being sent back to China. According to the Six Companies officials, "These women are still here and the only remedy for this evil and for the evil of Chinese gambling lies, so far as we can see, in an honest and impartial administration of municipal government in all its details, even including the police department. If officers would refuse bribes, the unprincipled Chinese would no longer purchase immunity from the punishment of their crimes...."[39] Regrettably, this appeal fell on the deaf ears of an administration that was too busy dealing its own self-generated corruption scandals.

Attorneys and corrupt judges were not the only obstacles faced by the Six Companies in its quest for reform. Ironically, their efforts to rid Chinatown of prostitutes by sending them and their sponsors back to China met resistance from a group that shared their goal of ending the trade, the American missionary organizations. The missionaries believed—with plausible justification—that the prostitutes would meet a horrible fate if they were returned to China as outlaws. As a result of this opposition, on three separate occasions, the Six Companies tried and failed to arrange for an extradition treaty that would allow Chinese prostitutes who were "rescued" in the U.S. to be deported to Canada.[40]

Non-Chinese property owners were also an integral part of the prostitution industry. E. V. Robbens attacked the "American capitalists" who helped "this traffic by building in our midst large buildings for the special purpose of brothel slavery...."[41] Hirata and Dillon also pointed to the practice of white landlords renting their structures to brothel owners.[42] This relationship between wealthy white landlords and vice entrepreneurs was not limited to Chinatown. In his thorough study of prostitution in New York City, Timothy Gilfoyle found that vice enterprises relied heavily on this fundamental link to the respectable upperworld for the existence of their operations.[43]

Needless to say, a vice entrepreneur venturing in prostitution without a larger support network would have found himself at the mercy of *boo how doy* extorters and kidnappers, the police, missionaries and the desire of his prostitutes to flee their oppression. As Ching Chao Wu observed, "in order to make their human property more secure and their financial loss less probable, the owners of prostitutes have to secure the tong's protection."[44] The quickest way of doing so would be for the owner to join the tong that governed the territory covering his operation and thereby increase and strengthen his *guanxi* network.

The tong therefore served as a mechanism of institutionalized *guanxi*. In assessing the tong's role in the organization of the prostitution enterprise, Wu concluded that, more often than not, the tong itself did not own prostitutes, though some of its members did. In his words,

> whether or not the tongs as an organization own any prostitute is a debatable question. It is generally believed that an owner of a prostitute must be a tong man. When he imports a prostitute into this country, he must pay his tong a certain sum of money for protection. A small weekly or monthly tax is also levied upon each prostitute as a regular income for the tong. In that case the earnings go to her owner. But, according to a Chinese report, there are cases where the prostitutes are bought by a tong and controlled by it. The administration of a tong is responsible for her. There are no special privileges granted to the tong members in connection with her. All the money that she makes goes to the whole organization.[45]

Opium

When discussing the recreational use of opium in the United States, it is impossible to separate it from the issue of race. The social equation "opium equals Chinese" is one most non–Chinese Americans had come to accept by the end of the nineteenth century. It was not always this way. The medical use of opiates had entrenched itself in American society by the early 1800s. Many non–Chinese addicts took daily doses of the narcotic in its various forms during the first seventy-five years of the nineteenth-century. Without a prescription, one could easily purchase a variety of opiates over the counter and there was little demand for opiate prohibition.

This attitude began to change in the wake of large-scale Chinese immigration. Dillon pointed to 1864 as the year San Francisco's non–Chinese first became concerned about smoking opium, for it was the year that opium became a very big business and the year authorities and the public began to take stock of the legal and illegal importation of the narcotic.[46] One of the first official anti-opium movements began in that city in 1875, after it passed an ordinance prohibiting the smoking of opium in smoking houses or dens, an ordinance directed at Chinese dealers and users.[47]

It is clear that the real motivation behind the 1875 San Francisco ordinance was not public health, but a desire for social control inspired by racial intolerance. Originally imposed upon the Chinese people by Great Britain as a means to achieve its imperialist objectives, opium smoking was brought to the United States by some of the thousands of working class Chinese men and boys imported during the 1850s and 1860s to build railroads and work in mines. When their jobs were completed, these Chinese laborers drifted to San Francisco and other cities, taking low-paying, labor-intensive jobs. Consequently, xenophobia and labor-driven economic concerns set the stage for anti-opium ordinances and laws.

The catalyst for these actions, however, was the rumor amongst non–Chinese that wealthy young men from respectable families and, more importantly, many young women and girls were being induced to visit the Chinese opium dens, where they were reputedly "ruined morally and otherwise." The San Francisco ordinance, like many similar laws passed in its wake, did not have the intended effect of bringing such ruination. Rather, it only pushed the practice underground while simultaneously giving it a forbidden fruit appeal to those non–Chinese who might not have otherwise tried it. Paying no heed to this lesson, Virginia City, Nevada, and then the State of Nevada passed similar ordinances and laws during the next three years.[48]

Even after these laws failed, the U.S. Congress joined the trend. Because opium can be smoked only after being specially prepared and because a weak brand of opium is used in this preparation process, Congress treated the opium "problem" under the revenue umbrella it would use against narcotics for most of the twentieth century. It consequently raised the tariff on opium prepared for smoking from $6 to $10 a pound in 1883. By 1887 the importation of the kind of weak opium used for preparing smoking opium was banned completely. The 1887 law also prohibited Chinese from importing opium and allowed only non–Chinese American citizens to manufacture smoking opium in the United States.[49]

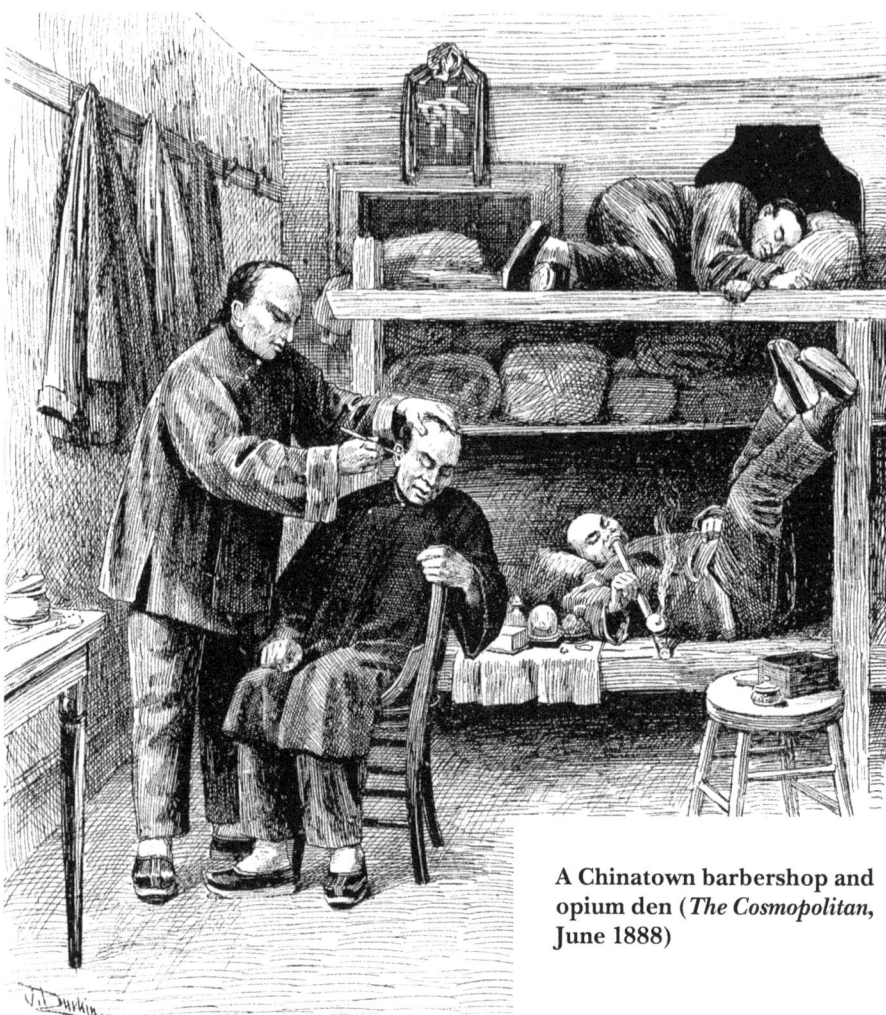

A Chinatown barbershop and opium den (*The Cosmopolitan*, June 1888)

These laws only served to decentralize the practice of opium smuggling by the Chinese and necessitated the use of more widespread and intricate *guanxi* networks to get opium shipments into the U.S. Fortunately for these criminal entrepreneurs, such *guanxi* already existed in the form of networks created for immigrant smuggling.[50] As a result, opium and immigrant smuggling were, in many cases, intertwined criminal enterprises. For example, while investigating the smuggling of Chinese immigrants across Puget Sound in 1895, an earnest U.S. Customs Collector discovered that opium was synonymous with the immigrant smuggling enterprise.[51] In a brilliant, cost-effective move still used to this day, illegal immigrants were sometimes offered credit-fare reductions for smuggling opium as they crossed the border. Smuggled immigrants made for an excellent, cost-efficient way to avoid the duties placed on opium. Similarly, they could make use of the same *guanxi* networks to assist in their importation, distribution and protection.

According to Richard Dillon, instead of harassing the Chinese, what the 1887 law actually meant was that the need for opium "would have to be met in the future by smuggling and by white firms fronting for Chinese customers." For instance, he noted that late in 1896, a $200,000 shipment arrived in San Francisco on a steamer for H.R. Davidson, an accountant of the Bank of British Columbia. Local Customs agents requested two new Customs agents, completely unknown to Bay area narcotics smugglers. They were Caleb West of Washington and Leslie Cullin of Oregon. The two agents not only discovered the supplier, Rosano & Company, but tailed the shipment and found its true destination to be the firm of Kwong Fong Tai. The Collector of the Port, John H. Wise, then stepped in and ordered all opium in port—from $300,000 to $400,000 worth of it—into bonded warehouses. Even with the ubiquitous smugglers working around the clock, the price of the poppy-seed paste doubled in San Francisco.[52]

An example of a similar practice is found in two *New York Times*

Searching Chinese immigrants for opium in San Francisco (*Harper's Weekly*, 7 January 1882).

articles from the following year.[53] On 27 February 1897, special agents of the Department of Treasury raided a warehouse and confiscated $400,000 in opium due to a violation of "the custody rules," which provided that Chinese could not import the narcotic.[54] The seized opium was owned by Kwong Fong Tai & Company, but it was consigned previously to P. Davidson, an accountant with the Bank of British Columbia, "who transferred it to the real importers as soon as it passed ... customs." Commenting on this case, government officials stated that "the system of acting as nominal importers to aid Chinese firms [had] been practiced for the last ten years." Due to the difficulties of showing that the letter of the law was actually violated, these same officials hinted that it was "improbable" that either Davidson or Fong Tai would be prosecuted.[55]

Three days later, a follow-up raid of the Kwong Fong Tai & Company store resulted in the confiscation of 1,000 lbs. of opium valued at $12,000. The *Times* reported that between the two raids, "practically all of the opium" in San Francisco was in the custody of government officials. As a result, the retail price of opium soared from $13 to $25 a pound.[56] The *Times'* statement that these two raids removed "practically all of the opium" from San Francisco may have been a bit hasty. This is due to evidence that other illicit opium importers existed at the same time and were quite extensive. For example, the year before the Kwong Fong Tai & Company raids, Customs authorities in that same city confiscated $750,000 worth of the narcotic from another smuggling ring.[57]

Nevertheless, as illustrated by these four examples and other cases, the Chinese opium smuggling syndicates of the late 1800s serve as fundamental examples of today's "modern" drug smuggling syndicates.[58] In order to successfully conduct their enterprises, Chinese opium smugglers made ample use of upperworld actors, organizations and business practices (like nominees, front companies and the corruption of government officials) to bring their product to a highly lucrative market.[59]

Anti-Chinese opium laws created this market and they allowed opium smuggling to become a large, complex and highly profitable business. Consequently, on 12 January 1888, the Secretary of the Treasury wrote to the Speaker of the House of Representatives to explain the unintended effect of these laws. The effect, he wrote, had been "to stimulate smuggling, extensively practiced by systemic organizations [presumably the Chinese 'tongs' or mutual benefit societies] on the Pacific coast. Recently completed facilities for transcontinental transportation have enabled the opium smugglers to extend their traffic to our Northern border. Although all possible efforts have been made by this Department to suppress the traffic, it is found practically impossible to do so."[60] The Secretary's advice was ignored, however, and Congress increased the duty from $10 to $12 per pound in 1890 and smugglers subsequently got $2 per pound richer.

It should be noted that during this time, the legal importation of opium was also a big business. According to Shih-Shan Tsai, a Chinese minister wrote of "the tariff revenues levied on Chinese imports by the United States Customs, 840,000 Chinese silver dollars were for rice, 150,000 for silk and cloth, and more than 750,000 for opium."[61] Nevertheless, the high duty on opium encouraged smuggling because by not paying the fee, moneys collected from the consumer for that purpose went straight to the coffers of the importer and retailer.

It was not until 1897 that the tariff was reduced to $6 per pound. According to one observer, the reason for this shift was "experience having at last taught that it could not bear a higher rate without begetting an extensive surreptitious manufacture or serious smuggling operations." After the tariff rate dropped, the amount of opium passing legally through customs progressively increased. Despite this successful reversal of federal policy, local and state governments continued to press for more anti-opium smoking laws and, there were twenty-seven such laws in effect by 1914.[62]

According to the findings of the U.S. Treasury Department, despite the suppression efforts of the federal, state, and local governments, there was a steady rise in the importation of opium from 1860 to 1909 (Table 3). In 1909 Congress finally banned all importation of smoking opium altogether. In the short term, this ban was effective only "in the sense that smoking opium imported through the customhouses fell to zero, but it did not solve the opium smoking-problem."[63] As Tsai observed, "when the United States Congress finally banned opium, the price per pound jumped from $12 to $70. The high price caused most of the opium dens to close their doors; nevertheless, illicit activities continued because desperate dealers knew how to operate around the law and squeeze profits from die-hard addicts."[64] Similarly, addicts turned to other drugs like morphine, cocaine and heroin to fill the void.

Table 3
The Rise in the Legal Importation of Smoking Opium, 1860–1909

Decade	Lbs. of Imported Smoking Opium	Number of Smokers Who Could Be Supplied
1860–1869	21,176	8,470
1870–1879	48,049	19,219
1880–1889	85,988	34,395
1890–1899	92,462	36,985
1900–1909	148,168	59,267

Source: Lawrence Kolb and A. G. Du Mez, *The Prevalence and Trend of Drug Addiction in the United States and Factors Influencing It*, Treasury Department, U.S. Public Health Service, Reprint No. 924 (Washington, D.C.: U.S. Government Printing Office, 1924): 14.[65]

Generally speaking, the legal importation of crude opium declined after 1900, except, that is, for smoking opium. According to David Musto, this was "in spite of its holding no special interest for prescribing physicians, patent medicine manufacturers, or wounded Civil War veterans." David Courtwright assessed the irony of this situation: "Smoking opium, solely a pastime, lacked any of the elaborate advertising campaigns which boosted morphine and cocaine preparations; it had a slow but steady rise in per capita consumption since import statistics began in 1860."[66] Even the repatriation of thousands of Chinese back to China in the wake of the 1890 Scott Act failed to push the rates downward. This was due to an ever-increasing use and abuse of the narcotic by non–Chinese.

In his meticulous study of the topic, Courtwright observed that opium smokers in the United States were generally Chinese and white, each with distinct reasons for indulging in the practice. Between the years 1850 and 1880, the typical Chinese opium smoker was usually a young man with a peasant background. He came to the United States as an indentured laborer. The money he earned was used to support his family, repay his creditors, create savings, and eventually pay for his return to his family as a modestly prosperous man. While in the United States, the laborer divided his time between his place of employment and the Chinese quarter of a city or town. It was in the latter that he would go on an "occasional spree." These sprees included the patronage of various vice establishments. Smoking opium was one of these vices, popular because it was "a social enterprise, carried on in a communal place."[67]

A few Chinese women were occasionally found in opium dens, but these women were overwhelmingly prostitutes. Courtwright cited one reference to this in a story found in *The San Francisco Chronicle* in 1886: "The Chinese women…, except those of the lower class, do not seem to be addicted to the habit as are the men." Nevertheless, he concluded, "contemporary portrayals of opium dens, verbal as well as graphic, generally depicted the Chinese occupants as men."[68]

As part of his research, Courtwright rhetorically asked, "Counting all types of users, what percentage of the Chinese immigrant community smoked opium?" His research found a number of diverse estimates. After all, "Those in the best position to know were the tong leaders, and they went to their graves—or back to China—without talking." Despite these differences, however, authorities "were virtually unanimous on one point: the addiction to smoking opium afflicted a significant portion of the Chinese immigrant community."[69] Due to their unavoidable and continuous contact with non–Chinese, this significant habit of the Chinese was bound to draw non–Chinese to the practice, a point commonly underscored in contemporary descriptions and illustrations of opium dens which found a multiethnic clientele partaking of the vice.

The best estimate on the emergence of smoking opium by non–Chinese is placed at sometime around 1870. Opium smoking was mostly, but not exclusively, an underworld experience; "prostitutes, gamblers, and petty criminals, their pimps, apprentices, and hangers-on" were those most frequently found "hitting the pipe." Courtwright clearly found that "evil men" predominated "ill-famed women" in this pastime. He also found that classism was prevalent in the public's attitude toward the issue, with media and social concern often expressing that "opium smoking had spread or was about to spread to the upper classes, particularly the 'idle rich' and other wealthy neurotics who had nothing better to do than dabble in dangerous vices." Nevertheless, Courtwright concluded that "while there were undoubtedly some upper-class opium smokers, it is unlikely that they ever comprised more than a small minority."[70]

Non-Chinese smokers tended to be young, an assessment applied to females as well as males. Contemporary studies, though drawn from a small sample, pointed to an ever-decreasing average age of use for males. Non-Chinese smokers paralleled Chinese in their geographic distribution:

> the earliest smokers were situated in western cities and towns; it was there that the white gamblers and prostitutes first learned to smoke opium. Later, as the Chinese fanned out into the South and East, the practice went with them. The presence of a few Chinese, in fact, was almost a prerequisite for opium smoking to take root in a given place. As a rule, the Chinese controlled the supply and ran the dens. Peripatetic white smokers helped spread opium smoking to places like New York City, Boston, and Chicago....

These findings in mind, Courtwright resolved that "it is doubtful that the practice would have flourished without the presence of Chinese communities in those cities."[71]

Ironically, Courtwright's conclusion provided a truthful, though exaggerated, basis behind the fear of Chinese-inspired "moral degradation" of white society peddled by jingoistic elements in U.S. society. The problem with many non–Chinese in the U.S. was that they could not and would not separate what could have been a relevant public health concern (drug addiction) from their yellow peril xenophobia.

In concluding his study on smoking opium use in the United States, Courtwright pointed to two forces—one demographic, the other legal—that brought about the decline and fall of opium smoking in the United States. The decrease in Chinese population from 1890 to 1920 was the demographic force. It "reduced by one-half the group with the highest proportion of addicts. This in turn reduced the overall rate of addiction to smoking opium, though it did not of itself end this practice."[72]

Yet it was the legal forces that were far more influential. As previously mentioned, a steady accumulation of anti-smoking opium laws and ordinances culminated with the 1909 Smoking Opium Exclusion Act. The increase of risk and price generated by the legislation between the years 1910 and 1915 compelled most non–Chinese smokers who had held out against a variety of state and local measures to stop or replace their habit with other drugs or narcotics. In short, the opium problem was not solved. Rather, addicts patronized alternative drug markets. The Chinese smokers who remained in the United States would follow in kind during the 1920s, 1930s and 1940s. Nonetheless, "capitulation did not take the form of the renunciation of opiates, as some reformers had hoped, but rather the adoption of new and more potent varieties."[73] Needless to say, it was the Chinese enterprise syndicates who continued to import and distribute these same narcotics around the world for years to come.[74]

Opium was but one more commodity that Chinese enterprise syndicates could smuggle for considerable profits. Just like the smuggling of prostitutes and immigrants, it was a practice made profitable and, to an extent, necessary by the imposition of prohibitive laws by the federal, state and local governments. These same laws made it necessary for these smugglers to employ non–Chinese for the actual smuggling of the merchandise, develop a sophisticated system of front companies (or "blinds") to hide their involvement, and ingratiate themselves into the rampant ethos of graft and corruption endemic to the politics and the criminal justice system of that day and age.[74]

6

Chinese Power Syndicates: Gambling and Muscle

In the words of Marlon Hom, "man's interest in games of chance is universal, and Chinese immigrants, like their European counterparts, brought their favorite games with them to America." Just like alcohol and prostitutes, he stated, gambling "was a fixture of the saloons of Western frontier towns. However, since the Chinese could not patronize the white man's saloons at the time, they had to create their own gambling operations in their own communities."[1] Vice or no vice, gambling offered one of the few acceptable and readily available options for recreational activity for Chinese in the United States.[2]

Stewart Culin was a highly recognized nineteenth century expert on Chinese culture in the United States. Based on his field research on Chinese games of chance, Culin explained the two forms of gambling that were the most popular with the Chinese-American community of his day.[3] The first, called *fan tan*,[4] was "usually played upon a mat-covered table, with a quantity of Chinese coins or other small objects which are covered in a cup." A *tan kun*, or "ruler of the spreading out," and a *ho kun*, or cashier, operated the game. The object was for "the players to guess what remainder will be left when the pile is divided by four, and bet upon the result."[5]

Culin observed that *fan tan* was "usually conducted by a company of several persons, and is almost invariable played in a room on the ground floor or basement," a practice which allowed passersby, directed by the doorman, easy access to the game. The doorman, often a *boo how doy*, was also charged with keeping out intruders and giving warning of danger when the game is in progress.[6] Based on his field research on the social pursuits of Chinese laundrymen, Paul C. P. Siu concluded that *fan tan* was one of the most popular gaming pursuits in Chinatown, and that it was organized and controlled on the local level by gambling syndicates.[7]

Culin stated that the second form of gambling popular with Chinese in the United States was *pak kop piu*, or "white pigeon ticket." *Pak kop piu* was a lottery run by a company. The company's store, usually located on the upper floors of a building, was where the drawings were conducted. The company would establish contracts with runners. Every day these runners would solicit bets from men working at Chinese laundries and other businesses in their assigned territory, as well as non–Chinese customers living and working in or near Chinatown. Local merchants also served as agents. The runners and local merchants charged a fifteen percent advance so that a dollar bet costs one dollar and fifteen cents.[8]

Culin explained that the lottery tickets were printed in and shipped from China in large quantities. Each five inch square piece of paper had printed on it the first eighty characters of the Chinese classic, *Ts'in-tsz' man*, or *Thousand Man Classic*. According to Culin, "this book, which contains precisely one thousand characters, no two of which are alike, is so well known in China that its characters are frequently used instead of the corresponding numerals from one to a thousand."[9]

Of the eighty characters provided on the ticket, twenty were drawn every night. The lottery company paid prizes to those who purchased a

A game of Fan Tan in a Chinatown gambling joint (*The Cosmopolitan*, June 1888).

certain number of characters drawn. Before the characters were drawn, the player prepared the ticket by marking the selected characters with black ink. Then this ticket was given to the manager along with the money wagered. The player's name, amount wagered, and characters selected were recorded in a ledger. The cost for selecting the ten numbers was one dollar. Eighty pieces of paper, each with one of the eighty characters on it, were then rolled into pellets and placed in a bowl marked one. Sixty of these pellets were then randomly removed and placed in three bowls marked two, three and four. One of the players was selected—and paid a small gratuity—to choose one of the bowls. The bowl selected provided

A Chinese lottery ticket, circa 1915 (author's private collection).

the winning characters. The numbers were then posted on a bulletin board in the store. Each step of this process was closely watched by the players to prevent fraud by the company, though Culin noted that this was not a fool-proof system.[10] Once the numbers were posted and the lottery agents notified their customers, the players checked their tickets and the game's operator checked the tickets against his ledger. Those who purchased ten numbers lost their stakes unless they chose at least five of the winning numbers. Winners were paid based on the odds correlated to the client's selecting a certain number of correct characters (Table 4).[11]

Table 4
Winnings for Each Dollar Bet in "Pak Kop Piu"

For 5 winning numbers:	$2.00
For 6 winning numbers:	$20.00
For 7 winning numbers:	$200.00
For 8 winning numbers:	$1,000.00
For 9 winning numbers:	$1,500.00
For 10 winning numbers:	$3,000.00

Source: Stewart Culin, "The Gambling Games of the Chinese in America," *Series in Philology, Literature and Archaeology* 1:4 (Philadelphia: University of Pennsylvania Press, 1891).

"Nevertheless," noted Culin, "the companies always deducted five percent from these amounts, and when the ticket has been sold through an agent, fifteen per cent, ten percent of which was paid to the agent."[12] According to Siu, in terms of its reach in the community, the "lotteries lead all other gambling in patrons. Many people, including women and children, who do not bet on fan-tan or play other games, are patrons of lottery tickets."[13]

In a society where gambling was largely illegal, gambling operations had to neutralize the police and politicians to stay in operation. To achieve this goal, Chinese criminal entrepreneurs relied heavily on bribery, just like their brethren in the prostitution industry. Undoubtedly, the influence of wealthy and respectable white landlords who profited from the exorbitant rents they charged the Chinese owners of both types of vice establishments came into play as well. One of the findings of San Francisco Chinatown investigator Willard Farwell was that white businessmen were "all too willing to allow their buildings to be turned into bastions for the gambling fraternity in Chinatown."[14] This echoes Timothy Gilfoyle's point made in his study of Victorian-era prostitution in New York City: underworld vice enterprises also lined the pockets of the city's wealthy landlords.[15]

A Chinese witness testified before the California Senate Committee in 1876 that there were an estimated 200 Chinese gambling houses in San Francisco and about a dozen in Sacramento. From small to large, each of these establishments paid "hush money" to the police. He testified that fan-tan gambling operators were required to pay $5 per week, whereas lottery owners paid $8 a month for the privilege of keeping their businesses open.[16] Reform-minded W. Maitland was more specific as he detailed the dark comedy that was police corruption in San Francisco's Chinatown:

> Gambling has, however, flourished in Chinatown, and has formed one of the most lucrative sources of income for the police force of San Francisco. Some months ago one of the three commissioners of police, having been informed of how things were being run, determined to make an investigation on his own account, and went to Chinatown, remaining on the outskirts. He sent some of the men to station themselves outside the gambling houses that were running full blast, and then sent word to the police captain in charge of the squad on duty in Chinatown to come and meet him, as he wished to see for himself about the Chinese gambling.
> A few minutes after the captain received this message, there was not a man nor light to be seen in any one of the houses, and the captain was able to conduct his commissioner through the streets where they were situated and prove to him how well the police were putting down gambling. Nevertheless, this too inquisitive commissioner was not satisfied, and the following evening he made a tour of inspection himself, without giving any warning, and the police, feeling no doubt, that after so recent and satisfactory a visit they had no reason to fear any further impertinent intrusion on their preserves, he found the gambling houses doing a roaring trade.
> The matter was taken up and investigated by the grand jury, and under their cross-examination this captain of police confessed, and indeed handed over a considerable sum of money that he had collected from the owners of the houses. According to his statement there was an arrangement between the police and the owners that, in consideration of the payment of a sum of, I think, $3,500 per month, their houses were not to be molested, and that they were to receive due notice of any danger, and furthermore that if either through neglect of the police, or through their having to make an occasional raid and haul up some offenders to show their strict attention to duty, the fines imposed were to be deducted from the next monthly payment. The money was collected regularly and distributed among the force according to rank.[17]

Chinese gamblers were not the sole benefactors of police corruption, but they were synonymously associated with it for decades. David Johnson established that the era in which Chinese gambling developed was quite favorable to this criminal enterprise, for "gambling shifted, during the nineteenth century, from a profession populated by talented individuals to an activity run on business principles."[18] Corresponding to this shift were other fundamental changes in American society. Most importantly were the changes in the structure and theory of policing in the years from 1840 to 1887. According to Johnson, it was during this time that "gamblers created complex and subtle connections among themselves, their customers, politicians, and the police which redefined the context in which law enforcement occurred. By creating conditions that severely restricted the ability of the police to suppress them, gamblers not only assured their own fortunes, but they also laid the foundations for modern organized crime."[19]

Ironically, these conditions came as a result of widespread efforts aimed at police reform. For the reformers, crime prevention was key to the new idea of police, "and many Americans hoped that law enforcement policies would now be more effectively implemented than ever before." As Johnson noted, "fortunately for the gamblers, the public's ingrained fear of centralized political authority resulted in the creation of police departments whose structure and activities reflected the democratic instincts of their local communities. Democratic decentralization provided gamblers with opportunities to protect themselves from the strictures of the law."[20]

This was due to their vast amounts of cash resources and a considerable influence on their voting employees and patrons. This fundamental organizational strength was readily parlayed into political power that was then used to keep the police in check. These ties were reinforced with social and economic ties to their communities that further insulated gamblers, Chinese and non–Chinese alike, from any significant interference in their affairs. In effect, Johnson concluded, "the shift to organized gambling made it possible for gamblers to neutralize the police because the law was subordinate to and dependent upon public agreement regarding its enforcement." Therefore, "the police had less independent ability to shape their own policies than the gamblers did."[21]

When the police could not or would not be bought, the gamblers needed a system to detect, thwart or avoid the raids. On one level, protection was often offered by Chinese *boo how doy* (though Ivan Light noted that "since no Chinese could safely exert bodily restraint against disorderly whites in Chinatown, the Chinese resort owners hired white guards to perform this service") when the police could not be bought.[22] On another level, physical barriers were used to protect patrons. Writing in 1910, Robert Wells Ritchie explained how the security system worked in New York City's Chinatown:

> A system of sentries was then instituted by the Chinese, and the gambling rooms were removed to the top stories of the house, or installed deep underground. Enormous doors of oak, studded with nails and equipped with peep-holes and ponderous iron bars, defended passage after passage in the subterranean corridors. A push upon an electric button by the watcher at the front door, and the massive slabs of wood glided instantly into place, confronting the baffled police with solid inches of stubborn oak and iron. By the time the axes and sledgehammers had beaten down the barriers, all signs of gambling would have disappeared, and the players would be safely in the streets. A few Ah Sins, bland and childlike as Bret Hart's immortal hero, and all resembling one another like so many pins, would be

found sitting innocently about their tables eating rice or chop suey, and looking with simulated surprise upon the thunderous intrusion of the police.[23]

Considering such inherent business risks from the criminal justice system and underworld extortion that operated within and outside of Chinatown, gambling operators needed a network to support them in carrying out their illicit service. This network was usually affiliated with a tong.[24] As Ching Chao Wu found, "gambling alone does not necessitate the organization of a tong." After all, he said, "the Cantonese have been gambling for ages in China without any idea of a tong." Wu asserted, "it is only when gambling is prohibited and the desire for gambling cannot be ordered to disappear by prohibition that a tong situation arises."[25]

In Chinatown, just like anywhere else, organizations arise to accommodate and protect gamblers when the law prohibits their livelihood. Though a tong may not necessarily own a gambling house, it can, in the words of Wu, "own the right to grant letters patent to all parties who wish to open a gambling house" in their territory. The tong "collects all protection money, takes out its percentage, and turns over the price of immunity" to the police. However, "if the policeman refuses to be bribed, then the money goes to the watchmen or spies who are in the employ of the tong" to protect the gambling establishment. If for any reason the tong fails in its duties, it puts up the bail and pays the fines of those caught gambling.[26]

WATCH DOG OF A GAMBLING DEN.

A *boo how doy* guards a gambling den (*Harper's Weekly*, 22 May 1875).

Power Syndicates

Understanding power syndicates is instrumental in understanding the workings of the underworld. However, we must be careful not to equate the sobriquet "tong" to the activities of power syndicates (e.g., conflict between Chinese organized criminals being labeled the "tong wars"). It is also not appropriate to assume that all members of a particular tong that had a reputation for violence engaged in the activities that would classify them as gangsters. That said, many branches of many tongs appear to have had a group of members or hired men who served this function. Yet family associations, district associations and political associations appear to have done the same. These men were known interchangeably as highbinders, hatchetmen, salaried soldiers or *boo how doy*.

The term highbinders was the most generally applied to all tong members regardless of their activities. The other three were applied only to those who provided power functions in the Chinese underworld.[27] Using rather fanciful language, Dillon illustrated this point when he described the relative place of violent Chinese organized criminals in the pantheon of violence in the American West:

> Perhaps no more desperate breed of fighting men were developed in the Old West than the 20 per cent or so of the tong membership who were "salaried soldiers" or *boo how doy*. These were the real highbinders—the professional hatchet men. Unlike the anarchical road agents, cattle thieves and brigands of the Hispano-American and Anglo-American frontier, the killers of this Sino-American frontier were fanatical and militarily disciplined. It was not mere bravado or vanity that led them to call themselves salaried soldiers; that is just the role they played.[28]

Some tongs, like New York City's Hip Sing Tong, had full-time members that were *boo how doy*. Whether or not a tong awarded membership to *boo how doy*, and whether this membership allowed *boo how doy* to assume leadership roles in the tong, appears to have been determined by the class orientation of the tong. It appears that a tong of respectable, elite merchants would not be inclined to share power with violent criminals. Tongs largely composed of members from a working class background, however, seemed more flexible on this issue.[29]

Whether possessing working class or elite backgrounds, the leadership of a tong would seldom willingly and directly engage in the actual fighting during a conflict. In the words of Carl Glick, it was not the "respectable" members who fought:

> Never, even in the early days in California, would a dignified Chinese "Rotarian" punch in the nose or fire a revolver in the direction of a rival Chinese "Kiwanian." He might have a pistol fired in his direction, too. And that wouldn't make sense. So, astutely, the peace-loving merchant hires an armed guard, or *boo how doy*, sometimes poetically called "hatchetman," although nobody knows just why. For the Chinese have discovered that a pistol shot is quicker, more effective, and also more merciful.... The merchants themselves did not descend to such crudities. And even while the war was on, two merchants of the war-

ring tongs would meet on the street, bow politely, smile, exchange flowery words of insult, then go their separate ways quite safe. It was the hired gunmen who took the risks.[30]

It was these "hatchetmen" who engaged in literal "warfare," not the tong leadership, although the latter simultaneously made for prime targets and lucrative clients.

If a tong did not have *boo how doy* of its own when a conflict broke out, it would either ally itself to another that did or, in some cases, draw lots among its own membership. Those who were selected in this process became the tong's gun men, earning a stipend for this service.[31] Another far more common solution was to recruit individual *boo how doy* to assist the tong in its cause. For example, a letter found on a Chih Kung Tong "hatchetman" in Victoria, British Columbia (dated 2 July 1887) became the first such contract to be discovered by Western authorities. Translated, it stated the following:

> To Lum Hip, Salaried Soldier.
>
> It is well-known that plans and schemes of government are the work of the learned holders of the seal, while to oppose foes, fight battles and to plant firm government is the work of the military. This agreement is made with the above-named salaried soldier on account of sedition from within and derision and contempt from without. You, Lum Hip, together with all other salaried soldiers shall act only when orders given; and without orders you shall not act. But in case of emergency when our members, for instance, are suddenly attacked, you shall act according to the expediency of the case and enter the arena, if necessary. When orders are given, you shall advance valiantly to your assigned duty, striving to be the first and only fearing to be found laggard. Never shrink or turn your back on the battlefield.
>
> You shall go under orders from our directors to all the vessels arriving in port with prostitutes on board and shall be on hand to receive them. Always be punctual; work for the good of the society and serve us with all your ability. If, in the discharge of your duties, you are slain, this tong undertakes to pay $500 sympathy money to your friends. If you are wounded, a surgeon will be engaged to heal your wounds, and if you are laid up for any length of time, you shall receive the additional sum of $250 and a subscription shall be opened to defray the expenses of your passage home.
>
> This document is given as proof, as an oral promise may not be credited. It is further stipulated that you, in common with your comrades, shall exert yourself to kill, or wound, anyone at the direction of this tong. If, in so doing, you are arrested and have to endure the miseries of imprisonment, this society undertakes to send $100 every year to your family during the term of you incarceration.[32]

Boo how doy had the freedom to affiliate with, or join, more than one tong. They also lent their services to their particular trade associations, unions and clan or district associations.[33] Just as an honest merchant sought to expand his *guanxi* by joining various associations and tongs, so did a *boo how doy*. If a *boo how doy* was involved with two particular organizations that became enemies, he would simply assert his neutrality and would be left alone by both.

During times of conflict, tongs would place rewards on the heads of key members of a rival organization. Depending on the importance of the target, the reward could reach four figures. With such an incentive, *boo how doy* were easily induced to violence. As Ching Chao Wu commented, "there is much to gain, and very little to lose. For, as the murder is usually accomplished in Chinatown, the chance to escape is very great. And even if they are caught, their tongs would do their utmost to save them."[34]

Sociologist Stanford Morris Lyman asserted that such conflict, commonly referred to as "tong wars," should not be viewed in the traditional Western ways. That is to say it should not be viewed as either the romantic mysteries of a strange, exotic people, something that just "erupted from time to time to upset the harmonious nature of peaceful, hardworking people," or as a social problem indicating social disorganization. Such perspectives are "too fanciful to be relevant for a sociological analysis of Chinatown's structure of conflict," "misunderstand the relation of conflict to Chinatown social organization," and do not comprehend "the socio-political aspects of Chinatown's patterns of antagonism."[35]

Rather, Lyman argues that conflict is systemic in Chinatown society, as it is in any other ethnic community. When conflict occurs, it usually concerns wealth, power, status, and women, and it is not without structure. Consequently, since every culture has conflict, every culture creates structures around engaging in and resolving conflict. Lyman found that customs dictate "whether and how these deadly quarrels would be initiated, fought, and resolved." These customs were slow to change during the initial phases of acculturation for an immigrant community. Consequently, these customs were "affected very little by the customs or the constraints of the larger society."[36]

Lyman concludes that rebellions, feuds and violence in Chinatown are a sign of order, not chaos. In Chinatown, he continued, "Disagreement, dispute, hostilities, and settlements are patterned. Traditional folkways govern the manner in which individual resentments should be channeled." Those who have complaints about an injustice have institutions to which they complain, and "their feelings may be assuaged (or hurt further)." No forms of hostilities are "chaotic and without organization. Indeed, the mode of hostility, the form of the targets of violence, and the way to cessation of a struggle are each institutionalized."[37]

Lyman does not address (for it was not his intent to do so) the differences between criminal and non-criminal use of such customs and traditions as a means of solving disputes. Yet these customs and traditions, these structures, are clearly used for both purposes; thus a benevolent association is as likely as a criminal organization to follow them when necessary. Therefore, power syndicates and *boo how doy* provided a necessary function in Chinese-American society. They were the instruments of waging and resolving conflict.

A tong's use of, and dependence on, *boo how doy* also correlated to the involvement of its members in criminal enterprise. As mentioned in the previous descriptions of enterprise syndicates specializing in gambling, prostitution and opium, there was a social function for power syndicates in these industries. For example, prostitution provided excellent opportunities for power syndicates, as the needs for protection and the lucrative draw for extorters were constant. Hirata found that in addition to "the tax levied on brothel owners who were not tong members, the tongs imposed a weekly tax of twenty-five cents on every Chinese prostitute. If any woman refused to pay, they promised to use 'harsh measures' to collect."[38] Hirata also found that

Highbinder, hatchetman, *boo how doy* (*The Call*, **January 7, 1900**).

> blackmailing Chinese prostitutes was another method employed by the tongs to extort money. Members of a tong, noted one report, "went around among Chinese prostitutes and told them a new chief of police had come in, and unless he received a handsome present, would shut up the houses. They collected from one and a half to five dollars from each one, and it was divided among the members of that society."[39]

Indeed, it was the *boo how doy* who manifested the terms "harsh measures" and "collection."

Tongs influenced or controlled by criminals were charged with the responsibility of preventing the escape of Chinese prostitutes, as well as their capture and return should they succeed in escaping. The lengths to which the tongs would go to ensure the return of a prostitute to her owner illustrates the value the women possessed. These tongs would offer rewards for a prostitute's return; they would kidnap her from her safe-haven; or they would file false charges of theft against her so that the police would arrest her and, once she was arrested, post her bail so that they could return her to her brothel, at which point the charges would be dropped. These tongs also targeted any male accomplice the prostitute might have had. The most common practice was to offer a reward for the man's capture. Local police and government officials were also given retainer fees to provide further insurance against the escape of a prostitute and any who chose to aid and abet. These tongs made ample use of the day's technology as well, using the telegraph to keep a network of informers spread across the country's rural and urban Chinese communities.[40] Of course, *boo how doy* would provide the leg work and muscle to ensure the return of the women or the payment in kind.

Power syndicates were also an instrumental part of the gambling business. They served as the muscle to ensure the safety of proprietors, patrons, and the cash box alike. They protected the proprietors from the extortive efforts of rival *boo how doy* as well as the encroachment of competition on their property rights. They also made sure patrons behaved themselves and that they paid their debts to the house. In exchange for their "services" (whether or not the proprietor asked for them in the first place was irrelevant) the power syndicates collected fixed prices or a percentage of the house's take.

Another area of criminal opportunity for power syndicates evolved from Chinese labor and industrial racketeering. The members of the various labor and trade associations found themselves under the influence of a number of rules and regulations stemming from their respective association or the governing body of many Chinese communities, often referred to as the Chinese Consolidated Benevolent Association (CCBA) or, most commonly to non–Chinese, the Chinese City Hall. These organizations needed their rules enforced. Power syndicates served this function.

For example, Special Agent Lee Meriwether of the United States Department of Labor, though originally perplexed about labor practices in San Francisco's Chinatown, eventually discovered hints of systemic racketeering taking place:

> A member of a Chinese union who disobeys orders is black-listed. If he makes himself especially obnoxious his name is handed down to the [Chih Kung]; then that Chinaman disappears. Nobody knows what has become of him. Perhaps he has returned to China or gone to the Eastern states, or perhaps he is dead. People do not know and do not care. Thus it is that the Chinese unions are enabled to enforce implicit obedience to their every mandate.[41]

Boo how doy, and the power syndicates they composed, were an instrumental force in the Chinese-American underworld. They extorted Chinese enterprise syndicates and legitimate Chinese businessmen. They provided "protection" from other *boo how doy* to the same, an underworld version of an insurance policy. *Boo how doy* also provided an enforcement mechanism for the various organizations Chinese immigrants established to oversee their collective affairs in the United States. Viewed as legitimate in the eyes of some, many others viewed this practice as a means for some of the elites in Chinatown who controlled these organizations to expand, consolidate and defend their own interests, not the interests of their community.

The social functions of power syndicates helped solidify upperworld-underworld ties in the Chinese social system of organized crime in the United States. Because of the association with enterprise syndicates and their function in the larger Chinese-American community, power syndicates and their individual *boo how doy* operatives often found themselves protected by politically powerful Chinese and non–Chinese upperworld actors who were paid to look after the interests of their clients, even if that meant their violent associates. Because of these connections many *boo how doy* often avoided arrest, prosecution or conviction at the hands of the criminal justice system.[42]

Part III

New York, New York

7

New York After Chinatown

The Greater New York area of 1880 was a mercantile city of two million people, mostly German-, Irish-, and American-born. The population engaged in the financial, commercial, and manufacturing activities tied to the area's role as the port handling the lion's share of trade with Europe. According to David Hammack, "by 1910 the metropolis was more extensively involved in the management of American industry than in the Atlantic trade, and while its own manufacturing sector remained healthy, it produced a considerably narrower range of goods." The population had grown to five million people who engaged in these activities. Besides those previously mentioned, it now included Russian-Jewish, Italian, Chinese, and Austro-Hungarian immigrants as well. Hammack observed that "in 1910 as in 1880, Greater New York contained about one out of every eight city- and town-dwellers in the United States."[1]

With these changes, Greater New York maintained its dominant position "as the largest urban region and the most important central business district in the nation's system of cities," a point reinforced by the 1898 consolidation of five counties (Richmond, Kings, Queens, New York, and The Bronx) into the City of New York. New York City and the surrounding metropolitan area was the most diverse manufacturing center in the United States. Employment in business management, legal, and other professional services, as well as services and trade for the nation's largest and wealthiest urban market, grew rapidly. The growth of these economic sectors more than made up for its relative decline to other cities in the areas of trade and financial services. As Hammack noted, "the key to Greater New York's continuing dominance in these years lay in its long-established advantages as the center of communication, trade, and finance both within the United States and between the United States and Europe."[2]

However, this economic power did not necessarily translate to widespread prosperity for its population. About half of the city's population lived in tenement houses. Those who could make it out of the tenements usually found new residences uptown, where lower middle- and middle-class neighborhoods began to spring up along ethnic lines. By the turn of the century, New York City "contained a disproportionate share of the nation's middle as well as its upper classes," the latter of which were defined by the opulence of Fifth Avenue.[3]

Politically, New York City was experiencing an intense battle between the forces of reform and those of corrupt Tammany Hall politicians. Beginning with the spirited investigations of the Reverend Charles Parkhurst, the city and the nation were simultaneously entertained and outraged by the disclosures made in the Lexow and Mazet Committee corruption hearings. These hearings established an intrinsic financial relationship between vice establishments, the police, and local politicians.[4]

For example, Timothy Gilfoyle identified three factors that allowed police protection of prostitution to exist in New York City during the half century after 1870. It is reasonable to assume that these same factors also extended themselves to other vices, such as gambling and the smoking of opium. First, the police system was decentralized, thereby giving ward politicians and police captains "a remarkable degree of independence" in choosing candidates for appointment and promotion. Despite efforts to control this phenomenon by the likes of Police Commissioners Theodore Roosevelt and Theodore Bingham, "high-level police authorities complained of their inability to control rank-and-file behavior." The second factor was that the New York Police Department "was based on informal authority with loose internal discipline." Police officers had a high degree of individualism and discretion, positive attributes when a blind eye to vice establishments could line an officer's pockets and assist with his chances for promotion due to the political influence of the established owners. The final factor was that most police officers took a fatalistic view of vice, "seeing it as necessary and inevitable."[5] In addition to Gilfoyle's points, it is clear that political patronage, a lack of civil service protection, and a dismal lack of training also had substantial influence.

Gilfoyle compared New York City's experience with prostitution to those of other cities. In contrast to San Francisco, New Orleans, St. Louis, or Cincinnati, New York City never formally legalized or regulated prostitution. The absence of legal prostitution further prevented the appearance of the kind of formal structures that controlled and organized prostitution in France and Great Britain during the second half of the nineteenth century. Yet the informal, *de facto* regulation adopted by Gotham's police and political machine served more or less the same function. Rarely extending beyond the ward or the precinct, this payoff system was secretive, always fluctuating and individually controlled. In the most commercialized sex districts, police knew madams, numerous prostitutes, their pimps and their addresses. The most successful regulated the street life and sexual commerce of the neighborhood. Eventually enterprise syndicates and extensive social networks were formed to achieve these goals.[6] Gilfoyle noted that this *de facto* regulation of prostitution in New York City reflected an inherent contradiction in its market economy:

> Private groups like the society for the Suppression of Vice, the Society for the Prevention of Crime, and the Society for the Prevention of Cruelty to Children adopted traditional public functions in their efforts to prosecute criminal offenders ignored by the police and others. In contrast, public officials—police and politicians—organized, regulated, and profited from the underground economy, ultimately resorting to private, sometimes illegal, methods of business. Significantly, these police activities frequently extended beyond prostitution. Police officers were also 'hired' to protect saloons and gambling dens, even to serve as strikebreakers on behalf of employers. Paradoxically, public officials resorted to entrepreneurial methods in their work, while private organizations assumed law enforcement responsibilities.[7]

The Reverend Charles Parkhurst, founder of the Society for the Prevention of Crime (Moss, *The American Metropolis*).

It is this informal, *de facto* regulation that Chinese criminal entrepreneurs encountered when they began to settle in New York City's Chinatown, located in the epicenter of that city's vice district, the Bowery.

The Chinese of New York City

By the mid–1870s a large number of Chinese had arrived on the East Coast to established communities, commonly called Chinatowns, in New York, Boston, and Philadelphia. These were not, however, the first Chinese in New York. Since the origin of American trade with China during the early–1800s, "a trickle" of Chinese had found their way to the eastern United States.[8] Louis Beck cited the Wo Kee Company, "the first purely Chinese mercantile established in the city," as being the nucleus around which that city's Chinatown formed. The small Chinese community in New York at the time followed the Wo Kee Company through two previous locations (the first on Oliver near Cherry Street, the second on Park Street) to its final resting place at 8 Mott Street.[9]

At first, the Chinese in New York City were viewed with patronizing curiosity. In 1856 *The New York Times* sent a reporter to investigate reports of Chinese idol worshipping on Cherry Street. Roughly 150 Chinese were reported to live near there at the time, mostly marooned sailors. Their leader was reported to be "Mr. Chimpo Appo," a racist play on the man's real name, Quimbo Appo.[10] The reporter was disappointed to find no idols, only "sundry Chinese ornaments which are undesirable." Even more disappointingly, it appeared that Mr. Appo was a Methodist who was a self-perceived missionary to the Chinese in New York. The reporter also revealed that the Chinese lived "fraternally" and "did not feast on rats and dogs, did not smoke opium, and occasionally married Irish ladies."[11] Miller assessed this article as reflecting the popular stereotype of the Chinese due to the questions asked by the reporter. However, "the report produced was more typical of the friendly curiosity that greeted the early stray arrivals from China on the East Coast."[12]

The famous *Harper's Weekly* artist Winslow Homer offered a benign view of the Chinese of New York City. In 1874 Homer ventured into the small Chinatown and located two "clubs." These clubs sought to "aid members in distress, and to extend a helping hand to young Chinese who might come as strangers to the City." One of the clubs was the "Poolon Kun Cee,"

Studying a New York "Chinaman" (*Harper's Weekly* 25 August 1888).

located at 34 Mott Street. It had 50 dues-paying members. For these dues, the members were allowed to make use of the eleven beds in "three dark and badly ventilated" rooms. The other club was located at 12 Baxter Street, but Homer provided no name for the club, though he did state it had a smaller membership.[13]

These attitudes began to change as Chinese migrated in large numbers to the East Coast, particularly New York City.[14] Chinese had been moving east since the early 1870s because they had increasingly become the targets of pogroms, lynchings and other forms of racial violence on the West Coast. One observer assessed this motivation bluntly: "Chinese men, terrified for their lives, began leaving the West for either China or the East Coast." The flight was so severe that by the turn of the century, "even San Francisco, to which most Chinese from the rural areas had fled, had had its Chinese population cut nearly in half because of the massive departures for China."[15]

Other factors also played roles in this exodus. The Six Companies, long charged with overseeing the affairs of the Chinese community in the United States, suffered from internal divisions and a challenge from the various tongs for leadership of the Chinese community. Additionally, the outbreak of a series of tong wars during the 1880s and 1890s undercut social stability amongst the Chinese and severe economic downturns shut down mines and railroad construction, leaving many Chinese out of work.[16]

Even professional criminals had reason to head east. Not only did an increase in police raids and missionary activities in San Francisco make for a hazardous working environment, but the dwindling of the Chinese population created a smaller core customer base for criminal enterprise. Many criminals recognized the bountiful opportunities found in the rapidly growing Chinese communities to the east, and, of course, all migrants now had the benefit of a transcontinental railroad system on which to travel eastward. Consequently, supply followed demand to New York and other cities on the eastern seaboard.

To the Chinese community, "New York" meant essentially everything east of and including Chicago.[17] The New York City metropolitan area, however, was the destination of an increasingly large number of Chinese immigrants. The net result was that the official Chinese population of New York City grew rapidly during the late 1800s.

Table 5
Chinese Population in the United States, 1870–1910

Year	New York City	United States
1870	120	63,199
1880	853	105,465
1890	2,259	107,488
1900	6,321	89,863
1910	4,614	77,531

Source: *United States Census of Population*, 1960.

Despite this official estimate of 6,321 in 1900, Louis Beck estimated the Chinese population immediately around New York City at between 12,000 and 13,000 in 1898. Beck stated that this number increases to 17,000 when one considers the entire metropolitan area. Chinatown itself, he said, held about 4,000 Chinese "traders, artisans, gamblers, amusement caterers and prostitutes." Thirteen thousand others, mostly laborers, were "scattered about the metropolitan area."[18]

Compared to the Census reports, this is a rather large discrepancy. However, Beck's estimate may be more reliable. Besides the fact that the census of this era possessed many methodological problems, in 1888 Wong Chin Foo[19] wrote a lengthy and detailed piece on New York City's Chinatown for *The Cosmopolitan*. He estimated the population at that time to be near 10,000. Further, he estimated that at that time there were a little over 2,000 Chinese laundries in the city of New York, between 880 and 900 in Brooklyn, and about 150 in Jersey City ("mosquito land, as Chinamen call it").[20] If there were only two people working in each laundry, this would have given us roughly 4,000 laundrymen alone in New York City at a time the census said there were 2,559 Chinese in total. Regardless of which figures are used, it is clear that the Chinese population in New York grew dramatically between 1870 and 1900, despite the passage and implementation of legislation barring the immigration and naturalization of Chinese immigrants.

The sudden increase in the Chinese population left other New Yorkers feeling uneasy. Press reports began to reflect the anti–Chinese sentiment spreading across the nation. As early as 1873, *The New York Times* took a less friendly take on the city's growing Chinatown, now composed of roughly 500 residents. This story was similar to many of those found on the West Coast. It portrayed the Chinese as gamblers who feasted on rodents, lived in filth, and worshipped hideous idols. Yet worst of all, to the reporter's inquiry about a "handsome but squalidly dressed young white girl" present in an opium den, the owner "replied with a horrible leer, 'Oh, hard time in New York. Young girl hungry. Plenty come here. Chinaman always have something to eat, and he like young white girl, He! He!'" The reader of the article was then informed by the reporter that this was a statement of fact, for many white girls were "lured" by the Chinese into Chinatown's opium dens.[21] Luc Sante explained this blatantly racist journalistic phenomenon:

> By the late 1870s it had become routine for cub reporters on newspapers everywhere to turn in their 'horrors of Chinatown' piece soon after being hired. These reports were largely fictitious, drawing on the sexual fantasies of the white middle classes, and using a certain propensity of the early Chinese settlers for marrying Irish women, as a loose basis for involved tales of white slavery and the forcibly induced drug addiction of white girls.[22]

In 1890 journalist and muckraker Jacob Riis published his highly influential book *How the Other Half Lives*. The book informed middle and

7. New York After Chinatown

upper class America about the horrible conditions found in tenement life in New York City. Tenements occupied by various ethnic groups were investigated by Riis, including the tenements of Chinatown. Riis bestowed unto Chinatown such less than generous descriptions as these:

CHINATOWN, NEW YORK.

On the streets of New York's Chinatown (*The Cosmopolitan*, June 1888).

> Whatever is on foot goes on behind closed doors. Stealth and secretiveness are as much part of Chinaman in New York as the cat-like tread of his felt shoes. His business, as his domestic life, shuns light, less because there is anything to conceal than because that is the way of the man. Perhaps the attitude of American civilization toward the stranger, whom it invited in, has taught him that way. At any rate, the very doorways of his offices and shops are fenced off by queer, forbidding partitions suggestive of a continual state of siege. The stranger who enters through the crooked approach is received with sudden silence, a sullen stare, and angry "Vat you vant?" that breathes annoyance and distrust.[23]
>
> Trust not him who trusts no one, is as safe a rule in Chinatown as out of it. Were not Mott Street overawed in its isolation, it would not be safe to descend this open cellar-way, through which come the pungent odor of burning opium and the clink of copper coins on the table. As it is, though safe, it is not profitable to intrude. At the first foot-fall of leather soles on the steps the hum of talk ceases, and the group of celestials, crouching over their game of fan tan, stop playing and watch the comer with ugly looks. Fan tan is their ruling passion. The average Chinaman, the police will tell you, would rather gamble than eat any day, and they have ample experience to back them. Only the fellow in the bunk smokes away, indifferent to all else but his pipe and his own enjoyment. It is a mistake to assume that Chinatown is

honeycombed with opium "joints." There are a good many more outside of it than in it. The celestials do not monopolize the pipe. In Mott Street there is no need of them. Not a Chinese home or burrow there but has its bunk and its lay-out, where they can be enjoyed safe from police interference. The Chinaman smokes tobacco, and apparently with little worse effect upon himself. But woe unto the white victim upon which his pitiless drug gets its grip![24]

With the organization of the Chinese Consolidated Benevolent Association (CCBA) around 1890, such stereotypical attacks appear to have given way to the idea that Chinatown was run by "respectable" Chinese merchants. Similarly, Chinatown became the object of favorable curiosity after the 1894 visit of Chinese Minister Li Hung Chang to New York City. Gong and Grant stated that Li Hung Chang's visit "opened up Doyers Street to the Chinese, as the merchants had to find stores to accommodate the American public, which manifested a chop suey and incense-burning hysteria" during and after his visit.[25]

Located on the former sites of the Moravian Burying Ground and the Henry Doyers Distillery,[26] the Chinese community in New York was centered in the Lower East-Side of the borough of Manhattan. Specifically, it anchored itself to the immediate vicinity surrounding Pell, Mott, and Doyers streets, right off the famous Bowery Street. Nearby was the commuter train stop at Chatham Square and the Manhattan, Brooklyn and Williamsburg bridges, which allowed Chinese from the metropolitan area to flood "Chinatown" on weekends and holidays. Within a few blocks was City Hall, the various federal, state and local courts, the Tombs prison, and the Elizabeth Street police station and police headquarters. Also nearby, and symbiotically attached to these government entities, was the headquarters of Tammany Hall, the powerful New York Democratic political club.

Because they composed roughly eighty-one percent of the Chinese population in New York City, Beck realized that such a large laundryman population constituted the main consumer market for Chinese businesses, licit and illicit, in Chinatown (Table 6).[27] Renqiu Yu relates a Chinatown description of this population as the "economic lifeline" of the Chinese community.[28] In 1888 Wong Fing Foo described this symbiotic relationship in the following manner: "There are now over thirty Chinese grocery stores in the city and most of these are in Mott Street, or in that vicinity of Mott Street called 'Chinatown.' ...These stores import all their good[s] from China direct[ly], and they depend entirely upon the laundrymen for support."[29] Ten years later missionary Helen Clark observed:

> For the population of Chinatown on Sundays is about four or five thousand, on week-days very much less. The difference may be accounted for by the fact that on Sunday the Chinese from all parts of New York and Brooklyn, and from Long Island, New Jersey, and Connecticut towns, flock to Chinatown to visit their friends and to do business. Since the American Sunday does not permit laundry work on that day, the laundrymen seize upon it as a general recreation day, and

7. New York After Chinatown

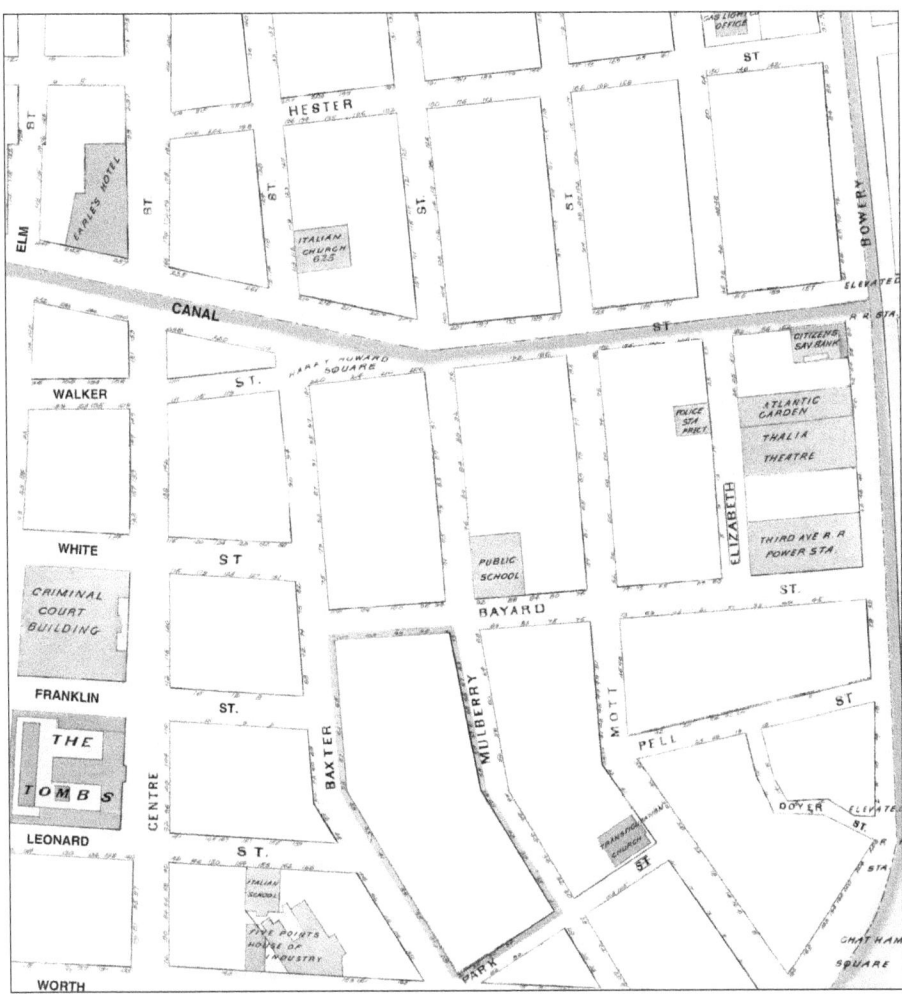

Chinatown and vicinity. Chinatown is centered on Mott, Pell and Doyers streets, adjacent to Chatham Square. Note the proximity of the fifth precinct police station on Elizabeth Street and the Tombs jail and criminal court building on Franklin Street (Robinson and Pidgeon, *Atlas of the City of New York*, 1893. Adapted by Melodie Tune, SDSU graphic designer).

go to Chinatown by hundreds. This, therefore, is the great business day of that region, and all the stores are open and every employee is constantly occupied."[30]

According to Beck, "most of the Chinamen within a radius of fifty miles visit the great center, if possible, at least once a week,"[31] where they would meet family and friends, pick up the latest news, buy products, eat at restaurants, and indulge in recreational activities, some legal, some not.

Table 6
Chinese Occupations in
New York City's Chinatown, 1898

Candy makers	3
Apothecaries (Chinese doctors)	50
Doctors (Chinese graduates of American Colleges)	2
Cigar makers	75
Laundrymen (within a thirty mile radius)	8,000
Operators on sewing machines	30
Manufacturers of clothes wringers and laundry supplies	4
Merchants, traders and clerks	175
Sign painters	4
Artists	7
Interpreters	15
Silver and gold smiths	2
Women of respectable families	40
Women—slaves and prostitutes[32]	3
Young female slaves	12
Vegetable peddlers	12
Transient residents, agents, officers of various associations loafers and outlaws	150
Highbinders	450
Bakers	2
Restaurant keepers and pastry makers	45
Farmers and vegetable growers	75
Total	9156[33]

Source: Louis Beck, *New York's Chinatown* (New York: Bohemia Publishing Company, 1898): 28–29.

Despite non–Chinese perceptions to the contrary, the "four vices" were not the only recreational activities in Chinatown. The famous Chinatown Theater, the centerpiece of Chinatown culture, hosted numerous entertainers from China. Located at 5 Doyers Street, "The Chinese Opera House" could accommodate about 500 people. The regular prices were twenty-five and fifty cents, with a seat in a private box costing one dollar. The doorman charged half-price for those entering an hour into the performance. The theater was highly profitable until the Parkhurst Society's pressure on the police to enforce the Sunday laws during the 1890s prevented performances on its most profitable business day.[34]

Chinatown Organizations

New York City's Chinatown was composed of a number of restrictive and non-restrictive organizations that provided various services and insti-

7. New York After Chinatown

IN A RESTAURANT.

A Chinese restaurant in New York's Chinatown (*The Cosmopolitan*, June 1888).

tutionalized *guanxi* to the Chinese community. Clan associations and district associations formed the core of the latter. Representing the six largest district associations, the powerful Six Companies maintained an office at Chinatown's "City Hall" at 16 Mott Street.[35] When the Six Companies encountered internal difficulties in 1896 and 1897, the majority of Chinatown's merchants settled their accounts with, and arranged for their independence from, the organization via the auspices of the Chinese counsel in New York City.[36] This important development essentially allowed for the formation of an independent governing association in New York City, the Chinese Consolidated Benevolent Association (CCBA).[37]

Leong Gor Yun states that the Chung Wah Kung Saw (as the CCBA was known as well) was registered with the Peking Imperial Government in 1884, and that it was registered in the State of New York as the Chinese Charitable and Benevolent Association of the City of New York in 1890.[38] The CCBA arose as anti–Chinese sentiments began to increase nationwide during the 1870s. It was realized by the various New York district and clan associations that each, on their own accord, could not protect their respective constituencies. Therefore, a single, unified voice was needed to represent the Chinese community. Just like the Six Companies on the West Coast, the CCBA took on the function as the community's representative to the Imperial government after a Chinese consulate was established in New York City in 1878.

In his analysis of Chinatown, Louis Beck described the CCBA as Chinatown's "government." The president of the Chung Wah Kung Saw[39] was known as Chinatown's "Mayor." Though not recognized by American law, the Mayor was the most powerful political figure at any one time in Chinatown. However, his position was not the result of a popular vote in the Chinese community, for although "an elective officer, the electorate is confined to the leading merchants of Mott, Pell and Doyers streets, who arrogate to themselves the right to make laws and regulations governing the entire Chinese community in all its ramifications, though, of course, subject to the general municipal laws, theoretically if not practically."[40] The Mayor of Chinatown was elected for a one-year term each March. For his service, he was provided with a salary of $1,000. His office was located at 16 Mott Street. Beck described the Mayor's duties as the following:

> He collects all dues and voluntary contributions, which amount to about $150 a month; the regular income from dues and other sources of the [Chung] Wah Gong Shaw, about $325 a month; the rentals of the [Chung] Wah Gong Shaw's property, $175 a month; and a tax on worshippers at the Joss House—50 cents for each devotional visit—which amounts to about $1,000 a year. Thus the total income of the mayor's office is between $8,000 and $9,000 a year.[41]

As Renqiu Yu observed, both the individual district associations and the CCBA were established "to meet the needs of the Chinese immigrants." However, both were also "authoritarian in nature." This is a reflection of the hierarchical nature of Chinese society as it adapted to a new host society. The merchant elite from the two largest district associations, for example, selected the officers of the New York CCBA. The largest was the Ning Yang Hui Guan that consisted of immigrants from Taishan. Merchants also dominated this association. The second was the Lian Cheng (Lun Sing) Gong Suo, which consisted of all of the non–Taishan immigrants in New York City. The general membership of each district association could not vote for their leaders or the leaders of the CCBA.[42]

Yu found that "according to the CCBA bylaws, its four officers—president, Chinese secretary, English secretary, and office boy—were to be elected alternately by the Ning Yang Hui Guan and the Lian Cheng Gong Suo." Eventually, the CCBA Standing Committee would be composed of seven permanent members, representatives from the Ning Yang Hui Guan, Lian Cheng Gong Suo, Chinese Chamber of Commerce, On Leong Association, Hip Sing Association, Mei Chi Party, and Eastern America Branch of the Kuomintang after its founding in China. These organizations had the right "to propose and vote for resolutions" and "to help the president handle all affairs."[43] It is not known which groups besides the Ning Yang Hui Guan and the Lian Cheng Gong Suo composed the Standing Committee during the time period encompassing our case study.

As opposed to San Francisco, New York City found the major tongs working in cooperation with the CCBA. According to Leong Gor Yun, "in all the important cities in the east and middle west, the Chinese Benevolent Association serves as a neutral meeting-ground for the Tongs. For this reason, and because in time of peace they use the Association to further the interests of their members at the expense of non–Tong members, the Tongs actively support the Association."[44] These New York City tongs apparently played both ends against the middle. On the one end, they served as the inherent threat behind the CCBA's political and economic power over the community. On the other end, they extorted membership from Chinese businessmen and laborers who needed a patron to protect them from arbitrary abuses of the CCBA's power.

As mentioned earlier, Renqiu Yu is one scholar who took a dim view of what he calls "the authoritarian nature" of the CCBA at the turn-of-the-century. His reasons were many and quite valid from an American point of view.

> While the rank-and-file Chinese immigrants had no right to vote, they were required by the CCBA bylaws to pay a variety of fees to support the association's existence. Every Chinese living in the greater New York area (including New Jersey and Connecticut) was automatically a member, whether he or she wanted to join or not. A member was required to pay a "foundation fee" of three dollars and an annual membership fee of one dollar, plus a so-called port duty of three dollars before leaving for China. In addition, each laundryman had to pay an extra annual laundry-shop fee of two dollars. Moreover, the CCBA bylaws required all Chinese business transactions to be conducted at the associations headquarters at 16 Mott Street for a fee of five dollars each. This was a unique practice only in New York. Through its regulation of business transactions, the official positions in the CCBA became profitable, since the Chinese hand laundries changed hands quite often. The account books of the CCBA were kept secret, thus giving rise to considerable suspicion of corruption and embezzlement.[45]

In other words, the rich and powerful created and imposed a culture of institutionalized extortion over the poor and powerless that went well above and beyond traditions of the mutual benefit society.

Beck was more charitable in his assessment. Continuing traditions started by the earliest mutual aid societies in Chinatown, he stated the responsibilities of the CCBA included "the maintenance of a Joss House and the proper use of it by the devotees of idolatry;" "seeing that the bones of dead Chinamen who had been buried six or more years are sent back to the nearest relatives in the town from whence they came;" "the settlement of disputes and accounts between Chinamen;" and "the regulation of fan-tan."[46] In his assessment, it was the CCBA's function as the handler of the remains of the deceased that composed the "secret" of its power in Chinatown. After all, "if one of their number should be convicted before the Chinatown mayor of an offense against any of the laws and regulations of the governing society, and the mayor should sentence him to a forfeiture of his right to have his remains sent home for burial, the culprit really believes that he is doomed to be an outcast devil in the world of the future."[47]

It seems, however, that there was another more monetarily based function that provided an even more important basis for the CCBA's power in Chinatown. The CCBA also controlled what was referred to as "the basic property right." Regardless of whether he owned the location outright or rented the location from another, the basic property right held that once a Chinese man was assigned a location for his business, he was to be paid an up-front fee by any other Chinese who took over the location from him. This fee corresponded to the value of the location. If the original business was being sold, this basic property right fee came in addition to the cost of the actual business.[48] The concept of basic property rights benefited those who arrived in Chinatown early enough to beat the population explosion during the 1890s, particularly those with capital, like merchants.[49]

It is clear that the concept of basic property rights affected non–Chinese, as well as Chinese, both inside and outside of Chinatown. Leong Gor Yun provided many examples like the following:

> One respectable American realtor and property-owner, whose office and buildings are in Chinatown, has been dealing with the Chinese for so long that he sometimes feels like a Chinaman. He thought he knew all there was to know about the Benevolent Association. As long as his buildings were leased, he did not worry; the Chinese pay their rent regularly. But when one of his tenants went into bankruptcy and closed shop, he encountered some difficulties that gave him a headache for years. His store remained vacant, though many Chinese tried to rent it; the bankrupt merchant claimed some $10,000 for his 'basic property right' in the store. Nobody could or would satisfy his demand. At length the owner grew tired of wasting his time negotiating with Chinese. He made a direct appeal to the proper authority, a personal friend of his, in the hope that at least his own government would do something for him. But the reply, though he presented his case to three different state officials in five years was always the same: "The government can do nothing in a case like this." He was helpless, but today he is a great deal wiser. He will not lease any of his stores to

7. New York After Chinatown

IN A JOSS TEMPLE.

Praying in the "Joss House," 16 Mott Street (*The Cosmopolitan*, June 1888).

Chinese unless an agreement is signed saying that the lessee waives all claims to "basic rights."[50]

Such cases were by no means rare. Yun concluded that these examples show that "under the pretext of protecting Chinese business, property rights are violated with no legal means of redress." Indeed, the Chinese community had no choice but to accept this "protection" thanks to its "widespread influence and support of the Tongs" that was "sufficient to bring any Chinese to terms."[51] In other words, the tongs, the local power syndicates, provided the "muscle" to enforce the CCBA's arbitrary decisions.

Even if basic property rights had a legitimate function within the sphere of Chinese customs, norms, and values, those who had strong, developed *guanxi* networks could easily corrupt this function to enhance their power and wealth. Those without these networks were at the mercy of the CCBA. Consider the following example offered by Yun:

> There was the case of an old man named Ching. He was well over sixty. He had labored in his dingy little laundry for twenty years, and hardly earned enough for two meals a day. Realizing that he had not much longer to live, he decided to go back to the old country. After many difficulties, he arranged to sell his laundry for $250. He and the buyer went together to the Association to report the transaction. Two weeks later he returned to the Association only to be handed a long statement by the president. He had "violated" everything. For more than twenty years he had neither registered his store nor paid his foundation fee, annual dues and store location fee. Added to these were various fines for non-compliance. Besides the $250 he was to receive from the sale of his laundry, he owed the Association $30 more. With difficulty he managed to say, "I rather not sell my laundry." "But the deal has gone through," said the president, "and you have to pay anyway." Ching's friends and distant relatives came to the rescue, and raised enough money to buy his homeward passage, and pay his debts to the Association, including his "port duty."[52]

It seems that with the backing of a power syndicate, the CCBA was able to provide patronage and extort those without it.

The port duty was yet another way the CCBA attempted to maintain control of the Chinese community. It charged roughly $3 for a Chinese individual to leave for China, mirroring the role of the Six Companies on the west coast. The CCBA even made charitable functions a business opportunity. For example, Yun takes a more skeptical view of Beck's assessment of the CCBA's burial responsibilities. To be buried in a CCBA-owned Chinese cemetery, one could purchase a grave for $25, but only if one had paid all of his dues when living. Defaulters or violators were charged $45 to be buried. To add yet another expense, if the living wanted the bones of the deceased removed from the grave and sent to China for proper burial, as was the custom, the CCBA would charge another $30.[53]

After listing such examples, Yun asked this question of the CCBA: If this is an organization dedicated to "maintain peace and undertake charity and public welfare," how does it define charity and public welfare in the light of such exploitive actions?[54] He concluded, "like chop-suey, this government is an American product. It uses racketeer methods and ingenuity, but it depends for its continued and prosperous existence on Chinese psychology, in this connection more precisely called passivity."[55]

Nevertheless, not everyone followed the edicts of the CCBA. Beck points to the existence of 25 to 40 Chinese peddlers who made "a business of catering to the wants of their countrymen scattered throughout the metropolitan area, or say a radius of thirty miles, taking Chinatown for a center." Their customer base was estimated by Beck to be about 13,000 laundrymen, laborers, and others, all having a fondness for peculiar items from their home country. These peddlers met the desires of these men by carrying "huge wicker baskets upon their shoulders containing their stock in trade." Each peddler had a well-defined territory to cover and permitted no intrusion. This territory was decided by a peddlers' union, which also set prices for its members.[56]

Because the peddlers charged an average of ten percent less than the Chinatown merchants, the latter was their "bitter enemy" who, in turn, denounced them as "stinging bees." As a result, these peddlers and their union operated without the license from the CCBA. Who won this rivalry is unknown, however it should be noted that these peddlers are not mentioned in later works dedicated to New York City's Chinatown.[57]

Notwithstanding the rebellious peddlers, it is clear that the authoritarian political, social, and economic structure of Chinatown at the turn of the century was consolidated at one address, 16 Mott Street (Table 7). The CCBA's headquarters at 16 Mott Street was commonly referred to as the Chinatown City Hall. According to Beck, besides serving as the headquarters of the CCBA, 16 Mott Street also housed the "Fan Tan Syndicate" in its basement; a leading mercantile company, the Quong Ying Lung Company, on the first floor; one of the largest Chinese restaurants in the second floor; the meeting room of the Mee Shing Gong Shaw,[58] a reported Confucian organization, towards the front of the third floor; the Chinese Laundryman's Union at the rear of the third floor; and the Joss House, center of Chinatown's spiritual life, which occupied the front of the fourth floor. The CCBA itself had its rooms in the rear of the fourth floor.[59] As mentioned earlier, the New York office of the Six Companies was also located here. Even Chinatown's official communication mechanism, a bulletin board called a "great institution" by Beck, was located in front of 16 Mott Street. It published the official bulletins of the CCBA and its member institutions, as well as the private announcements of members of the Chinese community.[60]

It comes as no surprise, then, that the merchant elites who ran the CCBA located their merchant's association, the On Leong Tong, right next door at 14 Mott Street.[61] Beck offered a rather lofty assessment of the On Leong Tong.[62] He viewed it "as a social organization which confines its membership to the higher class of Chinese residents." In his assessment, the On Leong sought "to encourage and promote good order and becoming respect to the laws of the land and city which gives the Chinamen hospitality and protection." According to Beck, "most of the merchants of Chinatown are members of this meritorious organization."[63]

Table 7
The Locus of Power in Chinatown:
Chinatown's "City Hall," 16 Mott Street, Circa 1898

16 MOTT STREET

Fourth Floor

Joss House, Office of the President
of the CCBA, and Six Companies Office

Third Floor

Mee Shing Gong Shaw ("Confucian Organization," aka
Mei Chi Party) and Chinese Laundryman's Association

Second Floor

King Heong Lau (top-tier restaurant in Chinatown)

First Floor

Quong Ying Lun Company (mercantile)

Basement

Fan Tan Gambling Syndicate

Source: Information from Louis Beck, *New York's Chinatown* (New York: Bohemia Publishing Company, 1898): 16. Illustration created by Jeffrey McIllwain (9 April 1997).

Since the On Leong Tong was a wealthy merchant tong and some of its most prominent members controlled Chinatown's gambling syndicates, access to New York City's power structure was possible. This access resulted in an alliance between the On Leong Tong, Tammany politicians and supporters, and the New York City Police Department. Although this alliance was largely fueled by money and graft, individual personalities also made this relationship possible.

The President of the On Leong Tong and Chinatown's Mayor, Tom Lee (Wang A. Ling[64]), knew that in order to increase his *guanxi* and his power, he needed to reach out to the local non–Chinese powers of New York City. He became a stalwart Tammany political ally who reportedly turned-out all four of Chinatown's votes early and often in every election.[65] He attended the Chuck Connors Association benefits for Tammany Hall and he invited Tammany leaders to On Leong Tong banquets. For example, on 12 February 1900, the On Leong Tong gave a dinner for its American business, political, and other friends at 14 Mott Street to mark closing of New Year's festivities. Tom Lee hosted sixty guests, including judges, aldermen, assemblymen, representatives of the police and D.A.'s office, and prominent businessmen, lawyers and doctors.[66] In 1894 Lee was appointed Deputy Sheriff, his commission signed by Tammany Under Sheriff John B. Sexton.[67] Besides his money, this *guanxi* was a source of Lee's—and by extension the On Leong Tong's—power.

Lee was not the only On Leong Tong member with ties to New York City's political and social establishment. Beck points to the close relationship between Chu Fong, a successful merchant of 21 Mott Street and prominent member of the On Leong Tong, and his "many friends in social and political life, numbering among them several ex-mayors, and others now and formerly high in official circles, among them ex–Mayors Strong and Van Wyck."[68] Another powerful member was Lee Shew, a cousin of Tom Lee's. Beck stated that it is Lee Shew, not Tom Lee, who held the real power in Chinatown. The sixty-year-old Lee Shew was the leader of the Lee Family Association in the Eastern States, with membership approximating 8,000. He was known as "an enterprising merchant, the proprietor of two large stores in New York and one in Boston." He was "a member of the firms of Sang Chung, 24 Mott Street, and Sun Chung Lung, 3 Oxford Street, Boston."[69]

Tom Leem, the "mayor" of Chinatown (Asbury, *The Gangs of New York*).

There is no question that the On Leong Tong represented the legitimate and illegitimate interests of the wealthy elite in Chinatown. It served as an associational *guanxi* mechanism that allowed its members access to the rich and powerful within and outside of Chinatown. It existed to protect the interests of the merchant class, as well as to counter the power of the rival Hip Sing Tong. Gong and Grant cite this as the primary inspiration for the formation of the tong. They state that gambling house keepers were afraid that the extortive actions of the Hip Sing Tong would ruin them. They subsequently had to resort to a defensive measure. Louie Yong Hock and Moy Dong Yue had gained the backing of Tom Lee, whom Gong and Grant assert was head of a powerful gambling trust, to organize a tong. Subsequently, the On Leong Tong was formed to protect these interests.[70]

Calvin Lee asserted that the Hip Sing Tong, along with the Kwang Duck Tong, formed in California in 1854. According to Lee, "initially they were organized for the purpose of mutual aid and protection, but soon they became involved in vice, mainly prostitution and gambling."[71] Gong and Grant reported that the New York branch of the Hip Sing Tong originated as a grouping of mostly smaller families looking for protection against larger organizations. They discussed forming a tong and, as luck would have it, a Hip Sing named Laing Yue from Portland was in New York and attended a meeting at their clubhouse on 10 Pell Street. He told them that the Hip Sing Tong was the only major tong that would allow independence for each of its branches. The families liked this idea and Laing Yue helped them incorporate into the Hip Sing Tong.[72]

For a time, the Hip Sing Tong struggled against other tongs and guilds, primarily the Four Brothers clan association and the Chih Kung Tong (the Chinese Freemasons).[73] At one point, members of the more powerful Four Brothers stole the Hip Sing sign from its headquarters, a great insult to the Hip Sing. Undeterred by the strength of their opponents, the Hip Sing Tong declared war on the Four Brothers. After a short time of skirmishing, the sign was returned and allegedly carried triumphantly through the streets by a young Hip Sing named Mock Duck, thereby restoring Hip Sing prestige.[74]

Beck was far less charitable in his assessment of the Hip Sing Tong. As far as he and his merchant sources were concerned, the Hip Sing were the root of all evil in Chinatown:

> In fact, for pay, the highbinder is ready to perpetrate any villainy, from perjury to murder, and his oath bound fellows, under pain of death, must protect him should he fall in the meshes of the law in the practice of his unholy vocation. Talk of the Italian Mafia! There has never existed such another organization of desperadoes and villains as the Chinese highbinders, and these maintain their organization and ply their trade more or less openly in every city of the United States which maintains any considerable colony of Chinese.[75]

Beck viewed the Hip Sing Tong as a fraternity of "professional" criminals with about 450 members in New York. According to Beck,

> These men are not criminals because of mere love of crime, any more than a man is a surgeon because of a fondness of inflicting pain. It is their chosen profession, and they practice it for the money they make from it. They are shrewd enough to understand that many of the pursuits of their countrymen, esteemed innocent by them, are unlawful in this country, and may only be carried on surreptitiously. This affords these cold blooded professional scoundrels their opportunity. Every gambling game of any kind is compelled to pay them tribute under pain of exposure to the police. Every inmate in a house of shame must in like manner pay, lest the evidence be produced to send her to Blackwell's Island. Every opium joint must contribute a liberal share of its receipts, lest its doors be forced open by the guardians of the law, who are as carefully kept away from the submissive places. For the rest, if a quarrel occurs between two men, one of whom is able and willing to pay to have the other put out of the way, the highbinder is ready to undertake the job. Or if anybody has fallen under the disfavor of the law this enterprising free bootleg will for a suitable "fee," provide the evidence to secure his acquittal. Again, when a neighbor has made himself personally obnoxious, the ever ready highbinder will secure his conviction of any crime that may be trumped up against him in order to secure his removal from the place.[76]

They did not directly operate gambling dens, opium joints and brothels. Indeed, Beck's description clearly illustrates that the Hip Sing Tong operated as a power syndicate. They extorted criminal enterprises and contracted their violent power to the highest bidder and the CCBA.

Beck asserted, however, that the Hip Sing were not viewed as criminals by the Chinese, "whose moral ethics differ so widely from Western civilization." That is why they were recognized by the CCBA. He explained that the Hip Sing Tong had chapters in every major city in the United States and that a "bond of union exists between them, and members transfer from one to the other as, for any cause, they have occasion to change their residence from one city to another."[77]

According to Leong Gor Yun, in "the On Leong as well as the Hip Sing, the president, vice-president, secretary, treasurer and a 'diplomat' are elected by the members, while some forty councilors are appointed by the president." The Hip Sing, however, reflected their proletarian roots by allowing its rank-and-file, even its gunmen, to have some voice in Tong affairs. Conversely, the On Leong reflected the egalitarian structure of the CCBA, of which many of its members were closely tied due to membership in other organizations. The On Leong viewed their contracted, mercenary "hatchet-men" as "typical underlings of [its] aristocratic 'gentlemen' leaders."[78]

It can be said that this fundamental difference in the power structures accounts for why the Hip Sing Tong "always had more daring fighters," but the On Leong Tong had "always been richer, first because its sphere of interest is greater, and second because its members [were] mostly wealthy merchants and restaurant-owners."[79] Nevertheless,

> neither tong maintain[ed] its sphere for legitimate business, and neither [drew] its income from stores. Their financial strength, consequently their power, [was] derived from illicit enterprises such as gambling, white-slaving, and opium. It [did] not necessarily mean that the Tongs operate[d] or finance[d] these establishments, but it [was] well-known among the Chinese that they receive[d] tribute from all of them. How they lev[ied] and collect[ed] this tribute [was] a matter of conjecture, except for the gambling houses, which [paid] a daily percentage of their take.[80]

Despite their legitimate social, political and economic functions in Chinatown, a chronicler of New York City's underworld described the tongs of turn-of-the-century New York City as "a form of organized criminal society dealing in rackets and protection." Scanning the historical record, he concluded, "in New York the tongs controlled gambling, especially fan-tan and lotteries, settled local disputes, handled relations with cops and politicians, and promoted and directed opium sales and consumption." "The diversity of operations," he concluded, "is strikingly reminiscent of later consortiums, such as the Mafia."[81]

The increasing control of the CCBA, the On Leong Tong, and other social institutions dominated by the wealthy elite on the growing population of single Chinese men moving to or near New York City's Chinatown created deep senses of inequity and injustice. Men seeking their fortunes found their efforts continuously thwarted by the Byzantine rules and regulations imposed on the community by those with wealth and power. Consequently, the late 1890s to the 1900s would find conflict over labor issues and property rights boiling over to the point of rebellion against the authoritarian elites. Given its strong ties to, and responsibility for, Chinatown's disenfranchised laborers, the Hip Sing Tong became the vehicle by which this conflict would reach the elites. The resulting conflicts, called "tong wars" by non–Chinese, would illustrate the importance and social function of both power syndicates and enterprise syndicates to the community. Regrettably, this violence would also reinforce negative stereotypes of Chinese-Americans that were already well-established in the non–Chinese mind.[82]

8

Chinatown Vice and "The Bowery! The Bowery!"

Chinatown was not just a center for Chinese business and recreation. Chinatown's proximity to the Bowery found more than a few native-born and immigrant non–Chinese at work there as well. John Kenny ran the Chatham Club on Doyers Street that counted amongst its clientele a number of pickpockets and thieves. Paddy Mullins had a higher class joint around the corner on Mott Street—next to Chinatown "Mayor" Tom Lee's headquarters—where the aristocrats of the underworld congregated. "Nigger" Mike Salter (a Jew) had his two-floor opium den at 12 Pell Street, and his beer saloon and dance hall, "The Pelham," on the first floor, which catered more to slumming tourists than lords of the underworld. It is at "The Pelham" that Irving Berlin, "the singing waiter," had his first success.[1] Other prominent entertainers like Eddie Cantor and Harry and Al Jolson got their starts in these neighborhood saloons as well.[2]

In the wake of Minister Li Hung Chang's visit to Chinatown, it became a popular place for the middle class and wealthy to go "slumming" and enjoy a bowl of chop suey. The fascination with Chinatown was summed up by former New York police officer Cornelius Willemse in his memoirs:

> It's an old story to the police. Visitors are more or less of a nuisance in Chinatown and a good many times they're disappointed. For they've built up such fantastic ideas of what goes on down there that if they don't see a few Chinamen disappearing down traps in the pavement pursued by somebody with a hatchet or a long curved knife, they haven't had any fun and they go home disappointed.[3]

Some of the Bowery's entrepreneurs made a tidy profit exploiting these racial stereotypes. The famous Tammany hack Chuck Connors, who could easily be found at the Chatham Club, ran tours of Chinatown for those non–Chinese who wanted to gloat in their moral "superiority" over Chinese "degradation."[4] Connors, recognizing a fine business opportunity when he saw one, translated his fame into a profitable career as a "lobby-gow," a term used to describe a Chinatown tour guide. Never one to disappoint a paying customer, Connors established fake opium dens where "wild-eyed," "stoned" Chinese actors played their parts for stunned Americans.[5]

Immortalized by press reports, Connors was a national celebrity. He is perhaps best known for immortalizing the "dese, dem and dose" manner of speaking.[6] Connors translated his fame into a service for Tammany Hall by hosting the annual Chuck Connors Association banquet for Tammany Hall. Every year, the political and business elite of New York would attend this fund-raiser.[7] However, Chinatown was not Connors' own political fiefdom. That honor went to Big Tim Sullivan, as of 1893.

In May 1902 Tammany Boss Richard Croker gave up his position and left New York for Ireland in virtual exile thanks to the miasma of corruption and graft surrounding him. By September of that year, Charles Francis Murphy succeeded him. Murphy was a man of few words who was prescient enough to never put his instructions on paper. He was close friends with Big Tim Sullivan, who had helped him oust the notoriously corrupt former Police Chief Bill Devery from Tammany's Executive Committee. Devery coveted Murphy's position, but his expulsion ended his political aspirations. As far as Murphy was concerned, Devery's expulsion had the added benefit of publicly "cleaning up" Tammany Hall's direct links to commercialized vice. Indeed, these links had cost Tammany Hall a number of recent elections. With Croker and Devery gone and his power consolidated, Murphy ordered an end to such blatant graft by his District leaders.[8]

However, Murphy made one exception to this order out of political necessity: Big Tim Sullivan could maintain his lucrative kickbacks from underworld establishments in Chinatown and the rest of the Lower East Side. This exception arose less from friendship and gratitude than from the practical reality that, left to his own devices, Big Tim would become a rival. Indeed, Big Tim had flexed his muscle before, when he prevented his political enemy, Richard Croker, from allowing Tammany's own token reform committee, the Committee of Five, from even entering the Bowery two years before. Murphy recognized this power and had no intention of following in Croker's footsteps.[9]

In exchange for this concession, Sullivan used the Jewish Monk Eastman Gang and the Italian Five Points Gang to turn out votes in and around Chinatown come election day, as well as to collect tribute from local vice enterprises.[10] Despite the fact that Chinatown was the dividing line between Five Point Gang and Monk Eastman Gang turf, Luc Sante reported that neither of these gangs would touch Chinese interests. After all, the tongs independently controlled opium distribution, gambling, and political patronage in their territories, "much more directly than the Caucasian gangs ran anything, since the latter were usually only enforcers for more powerful and unassailable forces." Indeed, noted Sante, "the tongs merged the functions, resources, and techniques of politicians, police, financiers, and gangsters, and enforced their levy with no opposition."[11]

Implicitly tied to political corruption, yet maintaining its own separate identity, was police corruption. Going beyond the realm of a mere "fringe benefit," graft was for the chief and patrolman alike "a cardinal value by which they measured their livelihood."[12] This was the era in which the Lexow Committee exposed the "lavish extent of graft extorted from thousands of businesses, from pushcart to steamship company" by the police.[13] In this spirit, officers of the Elizabeth Street police station collected a reported $15–$25 a table each week for "protection" of the Chinese gambling dens.[14]

The notoriety of Chinatown brothels and opium dens spread far and wide. Chinatown shared its clientele with the adjacent Bowery district and together they became synonymous with urban vice and licentiousness. The moral despair and squalid conditions that was the fusion of the Bowery and Chinatown gained national attention when Charles M. Hoyt's musical comedy, 'A Trip to Chinatown,' became a hit in 1892. "The Bowery," the lead song in Hoyt's musical, swept the country: "The Bowery, the Bowery!/They say such things and they do strange things/On the Bowery, the Bowery!/I'll never go there any more!"[15] Despite the song's warning to stay away from the area, many did flock to Chinatown, and a profitable Chinese vice industry developed alongside the others already established on the Bowery.

Chinatown Vice: Gambling

Gambling was the backbone of vice enterprises in New York City's Chinatown. Ivan Light asserted that the first Chinese-operated gambling den opened in New York City in the early 1860s in the shop of the aforementioned Wo Kee. From the outset, noted Light, Wo Kee's shop drew more than just Chinese customers to his upstairs gambling hall and opium den, which, "with an increasing white trade, prospered mightily." Then, as the number of single Chinese men with disposable income increasingly migrated to New York, Chinatown's "gambling resorts multiplied until by 1890 Chinese-operated pai-gow and fan-tan parlors had become standing attractions for rowdy whites visiting the Bowery district."[16] As one contemporary reform-minded observer stated, "flaming posters in Chinese characters, are sufficient to inform all, except certain thick-witted, blue clad personages, that the Chinamen are engaged in their national vices, regardless of the law of the land."[17]

Of course, successful gambling operations immediately attracted the attention of the police, ever on the prowl for more ways to line their pockets. As a result, they immediately began to raid the gambling houses, often smashing up the various types of gambling paraphernalia they found. The message was sent: Pay up or the raids will continue. The gambling proprietors acted accordingly. Payoffs commenced and the gambling houses found themselves notified in ample time before a raid, so that they could prepare to thwart the efforts to shut them down.[18] It is difficult to determine whether or not the gambling establishments were tipped off by bribe-induced police or by their own lookouts. What is clear is that police raids were very sporadic, usually coming in brief crackdowns motivated out of either a need to satisfy reformers inside or outside of the department, or by a newly assigned Captain looking for an increase in his weekly tribute. After one such series of raids, the following announcement was posted in Chinese gambling dens. It explained the impact of the raids on customers.

> The gambling houses are reopened again. As extra expenses must be paid as a new rule has gone into effect. Instead of the old percentage of 7 percent deducted from the winnings of over 50 cents, a new percentage has been established. Henceforth, a percentage of 7 percent will be deducted from all the winnings and a percentage of 14 percent from all winnings over $25. Every gambling place must post this notice on the wall where it can be easily seen. Inspectors of the Gamblers' Union shall visit all gambling houses to see that this law is enforced, and any failure to comply with said law shall be punished by a fine of $10, half of which shall go to the informer. Given under hand and seal in the 17th year of Quong Soi, King, and the 9th month (October). New York Bin Ching Union.[19]

Battles between rival gambling and police factions over Chinatown also provided a motivation for police crackdowns. For several weeks during the fall of 1898, former Police Commissioner Andrew D. Parker attempted to get the Police Department to raid Chinatown, which was "largely a big gambling house, divided by partitions." Tammany Police Chief William Devery, a bastion of police corruption, had been saying for weeks that there was "no public gambling in New York, but said he would see what could be done." A few days later, the Captain in charge of the Elizabeth Street Station was transferred and Captain Titus replaced him.[20]

The Oriental Benevolent Association and the "Ming Duck Tong" retained Commissioner Parker as counsel in their efforts to root out the gambling.[21] The concern of these two parties seemed to be that the gambling enterprises were so successful that they were forced to pay higher rents to the local landlords. This, in turn, drove up the rent for legitimate businesses in Chinatown, forcing some to go out of business, others to relocate, and still others to turn to vice enterprises for added revenue streams. Parker's informers told him "a certain Chinaman who lives in a house uptown[22] made the rounds every Monday and collected from every gambler $13 for each gaming table in his place." Police said they had heard of this collector, but that the sum, between $500 to $1,000 per week, "goes into a fund to employ lawyers when any of the gamblers gets into trouble." Since the police did not seem eager to assist Parker, he took a reporter and artist from *The New York Herald* on a tour of Chinatown, where they found gambling to be "wide-open."[23]

This exposure politically damaged Chief Devery. Soon after, Captain Titus began to make raids on alleged gambling dens. These raids, however, were unsuccessful, leaving one paper to conclude, "John Chinaman continued to laugh yesterday at the discomfiture of those who would have raided the realms of the fan tan, broken up the bamboo tables and thrown the scores of players into police station cells." Apparently responding to a "hot tip," Titus and his men raided the alleged dens on Mott, Doyers, and Pell Streets, only to find that their intended prey had just vacated the establishments. "I'm sorry," said Titus, "they did not keep at it until I could get a whack at them." Titus blamed the fact that he had only been in Chinatown for ten days, "and a man can't accomplish all he would like to do in that time."[24] Soon after, Titus conducted another raid, but "when the detectives reached the upper room the Chinamen there looked as innocent as lambs and there was no evidence found."[25] Whether this was bad luck on the part of Titus or a smoke screen to protect the interests of the gamblers and their police protectors is unknown, though the reputations of Devery and Titus lend credence to the latter interpretation.

New York Police Chief William Devery (*The Commercial Advertiser Sunday Pictorial Review*, 5 January 1901).

Who owned and operated the gambling establishments of Chinatown? Louis Beck argued that gambling establishments were independently owned and operated. However, they had to cooperate with other organizations to ensure their success. Beck established that a fan tan operation formed when about ten men came together, each contributing $30. Out of this $300, a location was rented, a table was purchased, and other basic expenses were covered, for a total expense of about $30. Protection money also had to be paid, which ran about $15. The remaining $240 to $250 was reserved for the bank, or capital, for the game.[26]

The owners and operators of the game also had to join the Fan Tan Syndicate. In 1891 Police Inspector Nicholas Brooks began a series of gambling raids in Chinatown. Brooks said that it was after one of these raids, in which 40 men and women were arrested, that the Fan Tan Syndicate was formed.[27] According to Beck, the Syndicate—with its power backed by its close ties to the CCBA—was a "voluntary" organization run by "Chinamen of prominence and influence" who undertook "the regulation of the game in general;" adjusted disputes among the warring "joints;" fixed the number of games allowed; and exercised general supervision over that particular form of gambling.[28]

It seems that the Fan Tan Syndicate also may have been behind a clever scheme to protect its customers during a raid. Beck found that substitutes for arrest were often hired for two dollars apiece. These hangers-on welcomed every raid because they could pick up some easy money. Using this substitute scheme, regular customers were seldom held. About fifteen minutes after the raid, the gambling would resume just as if nothing had happened. The police officers would take the substitutes to court on a charge of disorderly conduct. The magistrate would ask the police for proof and proper identification of those arrested. By design or default, the police seldom had the answers the magistrate desired. Consequently, those arrested would soon be discharged after enjoying "hearing the court give the police a piece of its mind."[29]

Beck also pointed to another organization that had to be ameliorated. This organization was the Hip Sing Tong. Beck's sources informed him that all of the gambling establishments paid tribute money to the Hip Sing Tong "for the privilege of carrying on the game without molestation or disturbance." The tribute was paid on a fixed-scale: "Games located in basements or on the ground or main floor are assessed $15 a week per table. Sixty of these tables are in existence, besides ten policy shops."[30]

Beck found that an unnamed but well-known man within the Chinese community would collect the protection money every week. It was commonly believed by the residents of Chinatown that some of this money was turned over in turn to the police, "though on that point there [was] no direct evidence beyond the inference gathered from the fact that the patrolmen do not discover the games which are so well known to everybody else." This is underscored by a story Beck heard of one proprietor, whose place was at 28 Pell Street, who so distrusted the collector that he insisted that a former Mayor of Chinatown tied to the Hip Sing Tong should collect the money. Soon after, an officer from the Elizabeth Street Station called on the proprietor and told him to pay the regular collector.

Captain Titus of the New York Police Department (*The Commercial Advertiser Saturday Pictorial Review*, 5 January 1901).

The proprietor refused, saying he would only make payment directly to the police or the ex-Mayor.[31] Frank Moss, a well-known reformer and former New York Police Commissioner, summed up the state of affairs between Chinatown gamblers and the New York Police Department. He found that the Chinese community "had no concern in our government or in the affairs of our City, except as far as they may be protected from the operations of our laws upon their customs and habits. They have learned that money buys peace, and they have purchased peace at a liberal price."[32]

It is very telling that Beck's sources encouraged a perception to his non–Chinese audience that the Hip Sing were those responsible for the gambling-related payoffs in Chinatown. Indeed, this story is not as clear-cut as it may seem at first glance. First, Beck relied heavily on the elite merchant class of Chinatown as his sources. As Beck himself noted, these merchants helped form the On Leong Merchant's Association, who were "bitter enemies" of the Hip Sing Tong. Second, in all of the primary and secondary sources used in this study, none, other than Beck, concluded that the Hip Sing Tong controlled gambling in Chinatown or the police of the Elizabeth Street Station. Actually, it is overwhelmingly held that it was the head of the On Leong Tong, Tom Lee, and his cronies who controlled both. Third, the Fan Tan Syndicate, which tightly regulated the trade, was closely tied to the CCBA and its leadership, many of whom were members of the On Leong Tong. Fourth, Beck's reference to the "former Mayor of Chinatown" pointed toward Tom Lee. Nowhere was evidence found of a Hip Sing Tong member holding the presidency of the CCBA during this period of time. Yet, Tom Lee was commonly referred to as "the former mayor of Chinatown." He was also widely viewed as the man who "controlled" the gambling operations in Chinatown.

Clearly, Beck's sources misled him to some degree. The gambling activities mentioned above surely occurred under the auspices of the Fan Tan Syndicate and, by extension, the On Leong Tong. For his part, Frank Moss confirmed this connection. Conducting his own study of Chinatown in 1897, he concluded, "Of late years the gambling fraternity has protected itself through an organization called the On Leong Tong."[33] Moss cited the results of an 1891 investigation that found twenty Fan Tan games at fourteen Chinatown addresses and eleven Chinese Lottery Companies at eight Chinatown addresses. Each of these businesses paid a weekly sum of $16 to Tom Lee and the On Leong Tong. Consequently, these businesses paid $544 each week, for a combined total of $28,288 in protection payments for the year.[34]

The origins of this connection are underscored by facts overlooked by all observers but Tyler Anbinder in his history of the greater Five Points neighborhood in which Chinatown was located. Anbinder found that none other than Tom Lee was actively engaged in organizing gambling and opium concerns as early 1879. Lee, then approximately 40 years old, actively used his Tammany Hall connections and his high-profile attorney, Edmond E. Price, to arrange for protection for Chinatown's then small number of vice establishments. By the early 1880s, Lee used his Tammany Hall provided Sheriff's badge and demanded payment from all of Chinatown's estimated two-dozen gambling houses. If they did not comply, his police allies would sweep in and arrest the proprietor and his patrons.[35]

Eventually, the victims of Lee's extortion attempted to fight back. They documented his actions and turned over evidence against him to the District Attorney. On May 1, 1883, Lee was indicted for "keeping a gambling establishment" at 17 Mott Street and taking payments from other gambling establishments. In what would become a hallmark of Lee's style, he responded aggressively against his accusers in the press and in the courtroom. He relied on allies in the Chinese and non–Chinese communities to attack the motivation of his accusers and bolster his own reputation as a legitimate merchant. Additionally, Lee had *boo how doy* threaten witnesses to the point that their attorney complained they were "in a state of abject terror."[36]

Simultaneously, a young pastor named John Barry, of the nearby Transfiguration Church, began agitating against Chinese opium dens, which he and like-minded reformers viewed as "girl traps." Although other pastors and social reformers believed Barry's crusade was exaggerating the truth, Barry succeed in securing one indictment against an opium den proprietor named Ah Chung. Ah Chung freely admitted to selling the narcotic, but said that he paid Tom Lee for the right to do so and therefore it was legal. Apparently, nobody told Ah Chung that Chinese property rights did not supersede American law in cases like this.[37]

Facing these new allegations, Lee readied for trial on the gambling charges. However, prosecutors refused to file charges for his involvement with opium protection rackets. This victory may have enhanced the already effective efforts to dissuade witnesses from testifying against Lee. By the time the preliminary hearing was held on May 16, "the prosecution could muster but a single witness, and with Lee's men ominously filling the courtroom, even he changed his testimony." The charges were then dropped and Lee was reinstated as a Deputy Sheriff. Through the auspices of the Fan Tan Syndicate, Lee would continue to monopolize the industry until challenged by the Hip Sing almost twenty years later.[38] As Moss wrote in 1897, "Of all the men in Chinatown, who knew the location of gambling houses, policy-shops and opium joints, and who enjoyed the acquaintance of their keepers, there never was one who equaled Tom Lee."[39]

This does not mean, however, that the Hip Sing were not involved with the gambling industry to some degree. After all, the Hip Sing, commonly referred to as "highbinders" in New York's Chinatown, were the local power syndicate. Indeed, there was most likely an uneasy arrangement reached by the Hip Sing Tong and the Fan Tan Syndicate via the auspices of the CCBA with regard to gambling. In exchange for a portion of the gambling revenue, the Hip Sing provided gambling establishments physical "protection" from unruly Chinese and other extorters, while the Fan Tan

Syndicate, with its ties to Tom Lee and Chinatown's merchant elite, provided protection from outside authorities like the police and maintained a regulatory role over the enterprise. The Fan Tan Syndicate also benefited from the fact that Hip Sing muscle provided ample incentive for a gambling establishment proprietor to pay his scheduled dues.

From the standpoint of the Fan Tan Syndicate, this arrangement made sense for two reasons. First, by keeping the gambling establishments under one protection scheme, it prevented conflict between the owners of these establishments. Conflict, and the violence that often resulted, drove away customers and damaged not just the gambling industry, but Chinatown's other businesses as well.

Second, the Hip Sing Tong was composed of "lower class" thugs who were better off pacified than incited.[40] Moss reported that the Hip Sing were considered "Chinamen of less social standing" than those of the On Leong, which lead to a history of the former antagonizing the latter.[41] In the words of Beck, the Fan Tan Syndicate, and by extension its On Leong backers, probably "would be forced to pay even heavier tribute should the Hip Sing Tong swing around and assume an attitude of hostility to it."[42] They also saved the syndicate from having to hire their own *boo how doy* to guard the establishments. Ameliorating the Hip Sing was a sounder financial alternative than constant conflict. From the Hip Sing perspective, such a role translated to a legitimate function in Chinatown's power structure, especially when coupled with similar activities in the opium and prostitution markets.

Missionary Helen Clark alluded to the Hip Sing involvement with these enterprises two years before Beck's work was published. In 1896, she wrote in *The Century Magazine* that the "terrible" and "evil" Hip Sing Tong operated in New York City. Conscious of the impact of her revelation on anti–Chinese sentiment, the sinophile missionary placed the Hip Sing in the context of other dubious, ethnically-associated organizations to prevent its being singled-out in public opinion:

> Yes, even in New York this evil society exists; but against that let me place the imported Mafia of Italy, the nihilism of Russia, the anarchism of Germany and Italy; and while we weigh one against the other, let us remember that while the Hip [Sing] Tong may sometimes become the instrument of private vengeance for personal wrongs, the anarchist club and nihilist society hurl their death-dealing blows at great social and political institutions, and attack and destroy the pure and innocent without reason or cause.[43]

Despite countrary claims made by her critics, Clark was convinced of the cross-cultural roots of violence.[44]

Beck commented that the Hip Sing "tactfully" sought to avoid too much trouble with "the respectable members of the Chinese colony, [its] victims being those usually engaged in pursuits generally known to be unlawful under the laws of the land."[45] Yet it appears that many of the "respectable members of the Chinatown colony" had a vested interest in these operations, particularly gambling and opium. After all, it was the merchant elite who controlled the capital in Chinatown. Some invested in gambling, some funded the importation, distribution and sale of opium, and some controlled the power emanating from Chinatown City Hall at 16 Mott Street. This may be why the On Leong Merchants' Association held the Hip Sing Tong in such low regard.

Such organizational dynamics were also evident in the lottery business, which was even more popular and profitable than fan-tan. According to Beck, the roughly nine lotteries operating in Chinatown formed a union that placed all of them under centralized supervision. It dictated one uniform price for lottery tickets and established the commission rate for the lottery agents. Each lottery was required to maintain a bank of $3,000. The union established that lotteries held two drawings a day, one at 3:30 P.M. and the other at 9:30 P.M. Of course, the odds of winning the lottery were extremely high, "careful calculation" giving the managers sixty-five percent of the chances, with the players receiving but thirty-five percent.[46]

The lotteries employed about 150 agents who went around and sold the tickets and collected money from Chinese players throughout the metropolitan area. They also found a steady market in the many white denizens of Chinatown, especially the prostitutes. Agents received a commission of about ten percent of what they collected. However, an agent could not be employed unless he was a member of the Lottery Agent's Union, which cost $5 to join, or $25 for a life membership. The Union, in turn, protected the agents if they got into trouble with the police or the lottery managers.[47] Given that Tom Lee was in control of the lottery industry by the early 1890s, it is almost certain the he controlled the Lottery Agent's Union alongside the Fan Tan Syndicate.[48]

Beck also provided evidence that Chinese moneylenders were related to gambling operations in Chinatown. He pointed to Lo Ping, "the loan man," who was "a merchant of high standing in Chinatown, a member of the Lee Wah Lung Company, at 10 Pell Street." His rate was five percent a month and his loans were approved and enforced by the CCBA. Lo Ping was associated with Jo "The Plug" Sung. He was a prosperous lottery agent operating out of 18 Mott Street. Beck stated that The Plug's business totaled $200 a day, of which he received a seven percent commission (about $14 a day).[49]

Chinatown Vice: Opium

The picture of opium use during nineteenth-century New York City is as diverse as those contemporaries who commented on it. Despite these differences, some common themes emerge, including its multi-ethnic client base, a relationship to corrupt police, ties to the Chinese community, and a strong relationship to prostitution and gambling.

8. Chinatown Vice and "The Bowery! The Bowery!" 115

Scene from a Chinese lottery shop (*Harper's Weekly*, 22 May 1875).

On 17 May 1896, journalist and author Stephen Crane reported on opium use in New York City. He began his report by shattering the illusion that opium smoking in the United States was a particular pastime of the Chinese. Rather, he reported, "the greater number of smokers are white men and white women." In Crane's words, "Chinatown furnishes the pipe, lamp and yen-hock, but let a man once possess a 'layout' and a common American drug store furnishes him with the opium, and afterward China is discernible only in the traditions that cling to the habit."[50] Ninety years later, Luc Sante would use the phrase "the democratization of opium" to describe the emergence of its widespread popularity in New York City during the late 1800s.[51]

Crane very liberally estimated that there were roughly "25,000 opium-smokers in the city of New York alone." For many years, one could indulge in the practice in one of two neighborhoods in New York City, either in the Tenderloin or in Chinatown. He reported that after reformers targeted the vice, both the Tenderloin and Chinatown were affected adversely. Though these reform efforts disrupted the opium trade for a while, the opium smoking culture continued to exist. Crane explained that the prevalence of opium in the Tenderloin District was due to the fact that "that part of the population which is known as the sporting class adopted the habit quickly. Cheap actors, racetrack touts, gamblers and the different kinds of confidence men generally took to the habit. Consequently, opium raised its 'yellow banner' over the Tenderloin, attaining the dignity of a common vice."[52] As a result, Chinatown was not to be singled out as the sole harbinger of the evil that was opium use in New York City.

In his classic work on urban slums, *How the Other Half Lives,* Jacob Riis elaborated on the popularity of opium with Chinese and non–Chinese:

> From the teeming tenements to the right and left of it come the white slaves of its dens of vice and their infernal drug, that have infused into the "Bloody Sixth" Ward a subtler poison than ever the stale-beer dives knew, or the "sudden death" of the Old Brewery. There are houses, dozens of them, in Mott and Pell Streets, that are literally jammed, from the "joint" in the cellar to the attic, with these hapless victims of a passion which, once acquired, demands the sacrifice of every instinct of decency to its insatiable desire.[53]

The practice was so rampant and devastating that Riis concluded bluntly, "Mott Street gives up its victims only to the Charity Hospital or the Potter's Field."[54]

Augustine Costello painted a similarly bleak picture of the "opium habit" in New York City, circa 1885. In his memorial and testimony to the virtue of the New York Police Department, *Our Police Protectors,* Costello viewed the opium habit from the perspective of the (honest) police. He explained, "A comparatively new criminal agency has been at work in certain sections of the city, spreading the fruitful seeds of contamination, and throwing additional responsibilities on the already overburdened shoulders of the police. The agency in question is the 'opium habit.'" Despite the law's "repressive hand," Costello asserted that the habit "counts its victims by the thousands in this city alone." Yet his concern for the victims had definite race and class limitations: "Unfortunately this pernicious habit is not confined to the children of the flowery kingdom; a legion of opium smokers to the manner born, and many of them people of respectability and refinement, are slaves of the habit."[55]

The opium habit was not just a moral outrage to the likes of Costello. It was also illegal in New York City as of 15 May 1882.[56] Costello asserted that smoking opium entered New York City about 1873 as the Chinese population began to increase.[57] Another estimate placed the date five years earlier, stating that it began above the aforementioned Wah (Wo) Kee's grocery store at 13 Pell Street.[58]

Less racially even-handed than his contemporaries Riis and Crane, Costello assigned the blame for the opium habit squarely on the Chinese. As he explained, "the habit has been rife among the Celestials for generations," and that "those who know the New York Mongolians best say that there is not one of them but 'hits the pipe' regularly every day."[59] The fact that the British East India Company forced the habit on China in the first place seems to have eluded him.

For years, Costello continued, "the Celestials carried on their opium smoking with the utmost secrecy [in Chinatown], and very few outsiders knew of the existence of their haunts, or what went on in them." The press eventually discovered the custom and printed, "highly colored stories about scenes in the 'joints,' descriptions of the fashionable ladies who were alleged to be slaves of the habit, and all sorts of the improbable details of gorgeously fitted-up dens and wealthy patrons." Costello recognized that these stories were "without foundation in fact," but also explained "the general public took kindly to them." He cited a veteran police Captain who told him that "he had yet to hear of a wealthy or refined person who was in the habit of smoking opium in the joints: 'And I ought to know something about the joints,' he added, 'for I have made a study of them for years.'"[60]

Regardless of the veracity of the press accounts, the fact is that they drummed up curiosity in "that large class of people who are ever on the lookout for a new sensation." According to Costello, "men, and in many cases, women, who had tried all other forms of dissipation and found them palling to their tastes, began to visit the resorts and to smoke the poppy juice." Those who were of "weak constitution" soon found the habit "fastened firmly upon them." Costello found the primary users to be "the lower order of theatrical people" who found opium "a new and agreeable substitute for whiskey," and they formed "the greater part of the white devotees of the pipe in New York."[61]

To his credit, Costello pointed out that the many stories that were published "about Chinamen dragging young girls into their dens and stupefying them with drugs ... are untrue and without foundation." To his discredit, however, Costello quoted Captain McCullagh of the Elizabeth Street police station in response to that benign assertion: "Surely they are bad enough without adding imaginary evils to the list of offenses laid at their door." "The Chinamen," McCullagh patronizingly continued,

> are one of the most harmless classes of dwellers in New York. They interfere with no one, they never fight or hurt one another, and you never find them drunk or disorderly on the streets. But the opium makes sad work of them. Smokers who look reasonably stout and strong become ghastly pale, and shake like sufferers from the palsy when kept without the drug for a few days.[62]

Costello ended his exposition by noting that since 1882 the police raids upon opium joints resulted in 100 arrests. The number of arrests increased from 12 in 1882, to 19 in 1883, to 69 in 1884. In Costello's opinion, the increase in these statistics called for "no comments showing the spread of the vice."[63] Despite this proclamation, it may have been the case that the number of arrests escalated as police decided to send a message of a more entrepreneurial motivation: pay for protection or the raids will continue. If such a move did occur, it implied that there was an increase in opium use that needed to be exploited. Even if the raids were legitimate, their effectiveness was questionable. Costello quoted one "well-known" police Captain who predicted "raiding the joints won't stop the smoking," because "it only drives the Chinamen from one house to another, that's all. As long as Chinamen are Chinamen they will continue to smoke it."[64]

Two decades later, Costello's concern over the apparent increase in the opium habit was confirmed by Dr. Hamilton Wright, one of three American members to the International Opium Commission. Wright stated that there were over 6,000 people in New York who were "slaves to the opium habit" by 1908. He asserted, without proof, that "nearly all of the Chinese in the great cities are addicted more or less to the habit of smoking opium, but no more than one-third of them take it to a harmful extent." Wright also revealed that there had been a steady increase in the importation of opium into New York City since 1878. In 1878, imports of smoking opium amounted to 54,000 lbs., but by 1907, imports had increased to 151,00 lbs. This was despite the fact that "there was a larger Chinese population in 1878 than 1908, and laws against importation were less severe."[65] This increase lends credence to previous assessments that demand generated by non–Chinese was instrumental to the growth of the market.

A latter day observer, Ivan Light, found that "stupefied white smokers" were often found in police raids of Chinatown opium dens. Light established that opium addiction forced many white women to become prostitutes in Chinatown as a means to pay for their daily "hits" from the opium pipe. Light also noted the existence of white-owned opium dens in New York City which competed with the Chinese-owned dens for white customers. He did not reveal, however, how the white dens received their opium.[66]

Light also placed the use of opium by non–Chinese "whites" into perspective. "As a proportion of all whites," he stated, "those who patronized Chinatown opium dens were minuscule." Still, "the whites were many; the Chinese few." Consequently, non–Chinese patronage formed a significant part of Chinatown's total opium business.[67]

Needless to say, New Yorkers perceived smoking opium as a moral and public health problem necessitating criminal sanction. Yet one person's problem is another's opportunity for profit, hence the organization of crime around this enterprise. Even otherwise respectable businessmen took advantage of the opportunity; some storekeepers, laundry shops, and even barbers would offer a rudimentary opium den—usually consisting of a cot or two and the necessary paraphernalia—for their patrons. The smuggling of opium proved to be a lucrative enterprise as well. By avoiding the prohibitive tariffs imposed by the United States government, smugglers could pocket the tariff money that they recovered from retailers.

How was opium smuggled into New York City at this time? The historical record is not definite, but there still exists enough evidence to make some generalizations. Evidence suggests opium was imported from India or China, refined in Hong Kong, British Columbia or Mexico, and smuggled across the border from Canada and Mexico or directly through the ports of major U.S. cities. The evidence also illustrates that the practice was a multi-ethnic one controlled by Chinese enterprise syndicates.[68]

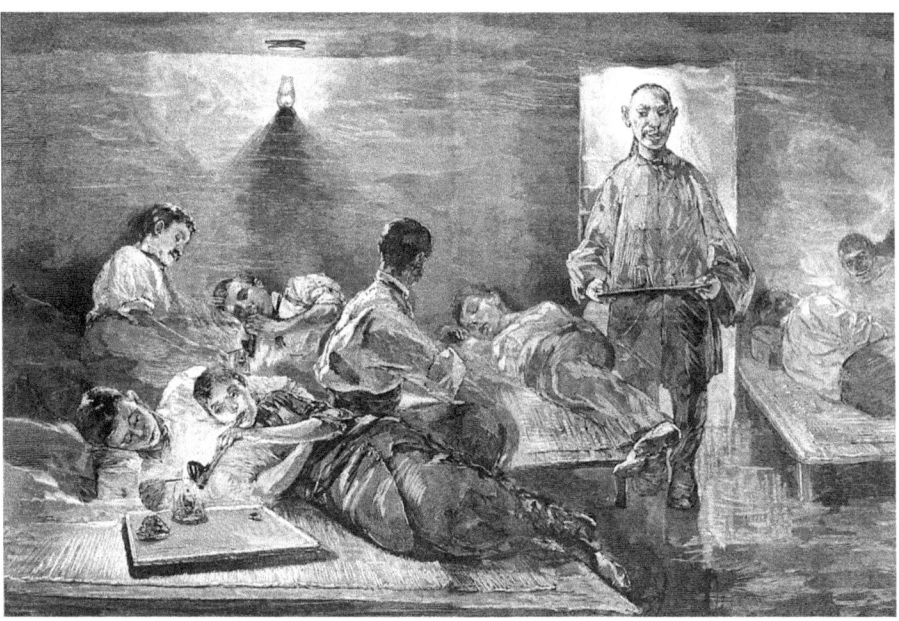

A New York opium den with a multi-ethnic clientele (*Harper's Weekly*, 8 October 1891).

Beck found that there were about 20 or more places in Chinatown that sold opium in twenty-five and fifty-cent portions. He says that the raw opium was purchased wholesale from local druggists.[69] The best brands of opium, Fook Yuen and Li Yuen, came from Hong Kong and were sold in cans on which the government imposed a duty of $5 to $6 a pound. The retail price was about $8 for one half pound. Four brands of opium, Ti Yuen, Ti Sin, Wing Chong, and Quan Kai, were refined in British Columbia. These brands were targeted with the duty, but it was far more lucrative to smuggle them across the border. Beck described a segment of the smuggling process as follows:

> [Opium is] smuggled into the United States by French women, who are employed for the purpose by the Chinese. The manufacturer in Victoria, B.C., makes a shipment to Montreal and then the women take the stuff and carry it over the border to some city or town, such as Burlington, where they leave it until they have [a] sufficient [quantity] to ship to New York City. The woman who smuggles the drug gets a commission.[70]

In another case, two Chinese men, Yung Sen and Ah Lip, were charged with the unlawful possession of raw opium worth $3,000. As a result of an investigation by U.S. Customs Inspector Galby, Yung Sen was arrested with a bundle of opium worth $500. An address found in the bundle led the police to a laundry at 26 Jefferson Street, Manhattan. Ah Lep was arrested there with $2,500 worth of packaged opium. Papers found with the packages led the authorities to the residence of John Schneider, a photographer, at 168 East 168th Street in the Bronx. He was arrested for being Yung Sen's and Ah Lep's confederate. The investigation also led authorities to a laundry at 16 Moore Street, Manhattan. The laundrymen employed there, Lee Fung, Lee Fung Chang, and Ching Lung Lin, were arrested after forty pounds of opium was found there. The opium was marked with a label from a Jefferson Street laundry. The investigation revealed that an R. H. Taylor sent opium from Albany to John Schneider. The package was marked "engineer's supplies." Schneider, who accepted the packages on consignment, apparently served as a front by which the opium was funneled to its Chinese importers.[71] Once again, it is evident that criminal inclination, ability, and opportunity, not race, were the determining factors for the ethnic composition of criminal enterprises created by Chinese organized criminals.

Another reported case not only reinforced the multi-ethnic nature of this trade, but also directly implicated the On Leong Tong. In February, 1905, police raided an On Leong pai gow game at 20 Mott Street. As the prisoners were being led away by police, a reporter from *The New York Sun* took down the following, incidental quote from "Chinatown Bill," a local, apparently knowledgeable of events in the community. Pointing to a group of slovenly white men congregating near the arrested Chinese, Chinatown Bill commented, "'Them white men under the pile is the white slaves of the On Leong Tong that does their dirty work. They have acquired the opium habit, them white men, and they will do anything for a little dope."[72] This would reinforce the idea that Tom Lee, now head of the On Leong Tong, was still behind the opium trade, almost 22 years after he reportedly organized it through his use of extortion and police and political pressure.[73]

Granted, this may have just been speculation on the part of Chinatown Bill, or even fabrication on the part of the reporter. However, given the incidental manner in which it was reported, as well as the age-old linkage of addiction to criminal activity, this prompts one to ask whether or not Chinese opium smugglers used non–Chinese opium addicts to smuggle and transport opium so that they could avoid the repercussions of the Exclusion Act. Regrettably, no direct evidence could be found to clarify this possibility. However, the abundance of non–Chinese working for Chinese opium smugglers implies that addiction may have been a motivation for at least some of the former.[74]

It must also be noted that authorities were not always on the right side of the law when it came to the opium trade. Though this case makes no mention of Chinese, it is indicative of the troubles faced by those who sought to enforce the law. In 1895, *The New York Times* reported that an Assistant U.S. Deputy Marshall was being suspended by his superior for hampering the investigation of an opium smuggling gang near Buffalo.

8. Chinatown Vice and "The Bowery! The Bowery!"

Joseph Weil and "Jerry" O'Leary were the suspected leaders of the gang in question. The opium was smuggled over the border by two black porters employed by the Grand Trunk Railroad. The porters would turn the opium over to Weil and O'Leary, who would then divide it into small packages. A young woman would then take the packages to the express office for shipment out of town. Before Weil and O'Leary could be served with search warrants, the Assistant Marshall tipped them off.[75]

In another case, Customs House agents raided an alleged opium den at 15½ Mott Street, seizing $150 worth of smuggled opium and cigars. Two men, Lee King and Woh Fong, were arrested. A third man at the door of the establishment was allowed to escape after giving the agents a $150 bribe (in real and counterfeit money). According to *The New York Daily Tribune*, the agents said they accepted the money "because they knew they could get the man again, and could pounce on the others and make the raid without hindrance."[76]

Leong Gor Yun discussed another route to the East Coast. He observed that "for some time there has been a smuggling ring organized by Chinese in America with the help of Chinese and white seamen. The opium is smuggled in from India, England, the Dutch East Indies and the Philippines, and thence to a depot in Cuba." Yun explained, "none is smuggled from China, because a can in Macao costs $100, whereas a can from one of the other sources costs $50." From Cuba, he said, the opium was smuggled into the United States by way of New York, Philadelphia, Norfolk, or New Orleans. The West Coast found seamen smuggling it from Japan to San Francisco, Los Angeles and Seattle.[77]

Yun explained that the opium came in "cans about the diameter of a silver dollar, two inches deep, and containing two ounces of opium." This provided an average smoker enough opium to last for some time, for "a lump the size of a house-fly makes two smokes." Because the cans were so small, "the actual smuggling [was] sometimes done by means of belts worn by the seamen; others successfully [walked] ashore with the cans loose in their pockets." For such a risk, "a seaman working for the ring gets twenty percent of the retail price; working alone he makes as high as 250% profit on a can that costs him $10."[78]

Most opium smuggling cases reflected the need for a multi-ethnic operation on the part of the Chinese enterprise syndicates engaged in opium smuggling. This stemmed in part from the desire of the Chinese opium smuggler to avoid deportation under federal law for engaging in the practice. However, some Chinese ignored the risk, a point evident in the 1903 indictment of 20 Chinese in Philadelphia for smuggling opium.[79]

One of those arrested in this case, Sam Jin, turned informer and provided damaging information against the other 19 defendants. On 25 October 1903, Sam Jin collapsed and died in a Chinese tea store at 19 Bowery in New York City. The cause of death was reported as a cerebral hemorrhage. Hearing of his death, a Philadelphia-based U.S. Government Inspector,

A. F. McLaughlin, came to New York to look for Sam Jin. He immediately contacted Captain Flood of the Elizabeth Street Station. McLaughlin told Flood that Sam Jin was "lured" to New York by those desiring retribution for his testimony in Philadelphia. Furthermore, McLaughlin stated that he had reason to believe that Sam Jin had been murdered by highbinders, a name commonly used to describe members of the Hip Sing Tong in Philadelphia and New York. Flood then had his detectives arrest Tuck C. Lee and Quong Jon of 19 Pell Street (also the residence of the Hip Sing leader, Mock Duck),[80] as well as the brother of the deceased, Sam Kee, of 35 Pell Street, under suspicion of homicide. Also arrested was Dr. Giovanni Corsiglia of 12 Franklin Street. Corsiglia was the attending physician, but he failed to report the death (which he stated was caused by apoplexy) to the Health Department and the Bureau of Vital Statistics, a crime punishable by fine or imprisonment.

Though foul play could not be proved by the coroner, it is interesting to note that in 1906, Dr. Corsiglia served as bail-bondsman for Yeh Wah and Louie Young, two men suspected of running a Hip Sing-affiliated policy shop and gambling den at 128 Park Row.[81] Before bail was secured, Hip Sing leader Mock Duck was arrested by police for attempting to secure the release of the two men with a bribe.[82] Considering that the attending physician, who did not report the death to the proper authorities, is associated with the Hip Sing Tong at a later date, and that two of those arrested were associated with the residence of the tong's leader, it seems safe to speculate that perhaps the death was not due to natural causes, but rather it resulted from criminal *guanxi* binding the Philadelphia and New York branches of the Hip Sing Tong.

The impact of opium on New York City's underworld was diffuse, but widespread. It did not solely involve the Chinese community, but a broad spectrum of New York City's ethnic landscape. This is true for the importation, distribution, wholesale, retail, and consumption levels of the trade. However, in almost all cases found here, Chinese ran the enterprises. Non-Chinese only assisted in the logistics of smuggling or purchased opium from Chinese smugglers for sale in their own vice establishments.[83] They also provided an increasing customer base as the numbers of Chinese residing in New York City began to decrease after 1900. This point was lost on the non–Chinese press and the public, who erroneously continued to view the problem as stemming from an intrinsic, race-based moral defect in the character of Chinese. Finally, opium encouraged the corruption of public officials and (though it was the exception, not the rule) it necessitated the use of violence when the smuggling networks needed to resolve internal and external disputes.

Chinatown Vice: Prostitution

According to historian Neil Shumsky, Americans of the late 1800s considered prostitution to be "evil, animal, and unhealthy—but also inevitable." It was tolerated as long as they also believed that it could be segregated and restricted to a certain segment of the social order. At the same time, they saw social benefits to be derived from the existence of a separate red light district. It served, in their eyes, as a means of controlling the lower and working classes and of protecting respectable women from the supposedly rampant sexuality of immigrant men. Such a district helped establish the boundaries of proper behavior; those who accepted the sexual norms of proper society avoided the district, while those who rejected propriety frequented it.[84]

Such was the case of prostitution in New York City's Chinatown.

According to Leong Gor Yun, unlike Chinatown bordellos on the West Coast, bordellos in New York City's Chinatown were well stocked with non–Chinese prostitutes who far outnumbered Chinese prostitutes. Furthermore, there existed a fundamental difference between these bordellos and those owned and operated by non–Chinese in New York City: "Chinese-owned bordellos on Mott and Pell Streets attracted white as well as Chinese clients, whereas white-owned competitors on these streets attracted only white customers."[85] This was due to the extreme disparity in the ratio of Chinese men to Chinese women in the State of New York (Table Eight) dwarfing the already immense gender disparity existing on the nation-wide level.[86]

Table 8
Chinese in the State of New York by Sex and Sex Ratio, 1880–1920

Year	Male	Female	Total	Males/100 Females
1880	837	12	849	6,808.3
1890	2,902	33	2,935	8,793.9
1900	7,028	142	7,170	4,949.3
1910	5,065	210	5,275	2,519.9
1920	5,240	553	5,793	947.6

Source: *United States Census of Population* (1970).

Jacob Riis also noted the curious absence of Chinese women in New York's Chinatown. As he reported in *How the Other Half Lives*, no women were met when one ventured to Chinatown, "none at least with almond eyes." The reason he gave was simple; there were none. According to Riis, "a few, a very few, Chinese merchants have wives of their own color, but they are seldom or never seen in the street. The 'wives' of Chinatown are of a different stock that comes closer to home."[87] Indeed, the absence of the blatant racial hostility found on the West Coast combined with the lack of Chinese women on the East Coast made miscegenation a common occurrence in New York's Chinatown, with most brides being Irish immigrants and African-American women.

Louis Beck supports the assertions of Riis, as he found only three Chinese prostitutes in New York City when he conducted his Chinatown survey in 1898. However, Beck was quick to point out that a number of "white women of the most degraded class" served as prostitutes in the apartments of Chinatown, ministering "exclusively to the passions of the Chinese."[88] Beck linked these prostitutes to opium smoking, since female addicts turned to prostitution to support their habit. He also noted that "highbinders" (the Hip Sing Tong) levied a heavy tribute on them, "in default of a license to buy and sell them outright, as they [did] the Chinese women."[89] This point was affirmed by Yun, who stated that even if they were independent, the white prostitutes had to be "on good terms" with the tong in order to ply their trade.[90]

Nevertheless, Beck noted that the Hip Sing were not satisfied with simply extorting non–Chinese prostitutes. Rather they were "eager for the development of the traffic" of Chinese women and that they had "made some promising beginnings in it."[91] After all, he continued, the traffic of Chinese women was regarded as "one of the most profitable investments" a professional criminal could make.[92] Beck's allegation that the Hip Sing were heavily involved with the prostitution trade may have some validity, particularly with regard to a developing traffic in Chinese prostitutes. The Hip Sing Tong had a nationwide network of branches, particularly on the West Coast, that could have provided the Chinese women for such an emerging market as New York City. Chinatown missionary Helen Clark, who observed in her work that Chinese merchants "bought" their wives, as well as young "slave girls," from Vancouver, San Francisco, or Boston, alludes to this networking system. The importance of the network to the Hip Sing is manifested in the fact that they seriously "protested" Clark's "daring rescues" of a number of slave girls by issuing "murderous threats." Considering the capital invested in the women, Hip Sing anger comes as no surprise.[93]

Beck also observed that because the prostitutes usually confined themselves indoors, a cottage industry of white, African-American and Chinese "hand messengers" developed to do their bidding. They were known in the Chinatown vocabulary as *low gui gow*, translated as "a common woman's dog." Beck estimated that there were about fifty *low gui gow* serving the prostitutes of Chinatown. Thirty-five whites, fifteen blacks, and five Chinese were employed regularly in this capacity. For general errands, they received tips running from five to twenty-five cents. However, they stood to earn up to a dollar for directing Chinese men to where the "'pretty Mellican girls'" lived.[94]

Multi-ethnic in composition and customer base, the bordellos found in New York's Chinatown complimented the larger prostitution industry located throughout New York City. The business of prostitution found in New York City's Chinatown differed from similar enterprises found in Chinese communities on the West Coast in that it was not centered on Chinese women. This is because New York City's Chinatown boomed after the U.S. government passed restrictive immigration policies, thereby precluding the importation of women from China to meet the demand generated by a thriving East Coast Chinese bachelor society. Those Chinese prostitutes who did make their way to New York City did so as part of *guanxi* networks that reached to the West Coast and Canada. Many of these networks appear to have been controlled by the Hip Sing Tong, which also extorted numerous non–Chinese prostitutes who operated in Chinatown.[95]

Summary

New York City's Chinatown was the epicenter of Chinese life on the East Coast during the nineteenth and early twentieth centuries. It was located in New York's Lower East Side, an area where thousands of immigrants from a host of nations lived in squalid conditions. New York's Chinatown was one of many ethnic enclaves in the mosaic that was New York City. Unlike Chinatowns on the West Coast, it did not have to suffer the undiluted ire of xenophobic whites. Technological developments in the area of transportation made it possible for single Chinese men living throughout the Northeast to travel to New York City's Chinatown on weekends and holidays so that they could meet with family and friends, purchase goods and services, and exchange news and information.

Chinatown was located immediately off the Bowery, a decades-old red light district. The social system of organized crime was already well entrenched in this district when Chinese immigrants began to arrive during the 1870s. To say the area was wide-open to criminals may be an overstatement, but not by much. Consequently, professional Chinese criminals found a hospitable environment in which to set up shop. This environment was made even more hospitable by two factors. First, the virulent, all-pervading racism directed towards Chinese in the Western United States was largely muted by New York City's longstanding experience with immigrant communities.[96] Second, corrupt politicians, police officers, and other criminal justice officials loved the green of money far more than they feared any yellow peril. They were more than willing to enter arrangements with Chinese criminals as long as the price was right.

With the emergence of a substantial Chinese community composed overwhelmingly of single men with disposable income, Chinese merchants met a demand for the number of goods and services that these men desired. Since some of these goods and services were deemed illegal by authorities—namely smoking opium, prostitution, and gambling—it should come as no surprise that professional criminals within the Chinese community capitalized on this demand. It should also come as no surprise that these criminal entrepreneurs recognized the sizable profit potential in the numerous non–Chinese denizens of the Bowery who desired the same proscribed goods and services. Consequently, professional criminals within the Chinese community formed enterprise syndicates to organize the gambling, prostitution and opium businesses in their own community.

Because they were forced to operate outside of the law, these syndicates had to neutralize three possible threats. First, utilizing *guanxi* relationships, they had to provide tribute to Chinatown's powerful ruling elite for the "property right" to conduct business without interference. These elites then assisted with the elimination of the second and third threats. They arranged for pay offs to the police, courts, and public officials of New York City, and arranged for *boo how doy* to protect proprietors and patrons alike from extortion, thieves, rowdy customers, and outbreaks of violence.

The Chinese criminal entrepreneurs learned early on that in order to establish and successfully operate a criminal enterprise in New York's Chinatown, it needed to be plugged into the larger social system of organized crime and the networks that composed it. After all, a Chinese immigrant who did not speak English, was new to the city, and desired to open a gambling establishment, brothel or opium den, would have to determine which cops, politicians, and judges to pay off. He also needed to ensure that his basic property rights, and any of a host of other fees and sinecures, went through the proper associations and individuals in Chinatown's ruling hierarchy. He also had to ensure that thugs and gangsters did not disrupt his business and chase away his customers.

The best avenue to success was to become part of established *guanxi* networks. For a criminal enterprise operating in New York City's Chinatown, this meant one of two options. The first option was the On Leong Tong, which represented the interests of the elite in Chinatown, as well as most of its traditional institutions. Its power lay in the social, economic, and political status of its leaders. These men dominated Chinatown's government and were closely tied to the larger social system of organized crime encompassing Mott, Pell, and Doyers Streets and the rest of the Bowery. The result was that the On Leong Tong President, Tom Lee, and other key members of the tong dominated the lucrative "property rights" system associated with opium and gambling in Chinatown.

The second option was the Hip Sing Tong, which was the power syndicate in Chinatown. Its power lay in the sizable number of professional criminals within its ranks, as well as its highbinder reputation. This reputation was solidified by the number of *boo how doy* associated with the organization who served as the power syndicate behind the CCBA's edicts. The Hip Sing Tong also had established networks with enterprise syndicates in other cities located throughout North America.

Despite readily evident class tensions between the elite On Leong Tong and the working class Hip Sing Tong, these two "options" coexisted for roughly a decade. The On Leong did not have, nor desired to have, the muscle necessary to control the troublesome Hip Sing. The Hip Sing did not have the connections or capital to rival the On Leong as Chinatown's primary *guanxi* network. Each tolerated the other, but the relationship was precarious and it seemed only a matter of time before one of the two organizations decided the other needed to be kept in check. Time ran out when Mock Duck came to town.

9

Setting the Stage for a Tong War

During the spring of 1899, Mock Sai Wing, more commonly known as Mock Duck, arrived in New York City from California.[1] Reportedly born in San Francisco in 1879, he was approximately 20 years old when he arrived.[2] He was part of the small but influential Mock clan in San Francisco. The Mocks reportedly suffered and endured much at the hands of the larger, more powerful clans that formed the Six Companies, an institution that dominated Chinese life in the U.S. during the second half of the nineteenth century. Because of this domination, a merchant named Mock Wah became instrumental to the burgeoning tong movement during the Gold Rush days.[3]

The tongs were initially organized for the purpose of mutual aid and protection of the small clan associations from the larger clan associations. The first two tongs created were the Kwang Dock Tong[4] and the Hip Sing Tong, both founded in 1854. Eventually, some members of these tongs became involved in vice enterprises, mainly prostitution and gambling.[5] This was a natural progression for individuals who found legitimate pathways to success blocked by not just both the anti–Chinese economic and social policies implemented by jingoistic politicians and the collapse of railroad and mining labor opportunities, but also by fellow Chinese affiliated with the dominant clans and voluntary associations.

Upon Mock Duck's arrival in New York City, the Hip Sing Tong, as well as the rest of Chinatown, immediately regarded him as a significant player. Perhaps this was due to his clan affiliation. In addition to Mock Wah being involved in the early tong movement, another Mock, Mock Wing, served as the President of the San Francisco branch of the Hip Sing Tong during the early 1870s. Whether Mock Duck was directly related to Mock Wah or Mock Wing is unknown, although Mock Duck's real name, Mock Sai Wing, closely resembles that of Mock Wing's and suggests a possible relationship. What is known is that upon Mock Duck's arrival in New York City, the Hip Sing Tong and the rest of Chinatown immediately regarded him as a significant force. Luc Sante, a chronicler of New York City's underworld, called Mock Duck "a lone wolf, a character straight out of *Yojimbo* or *A Fistful of Dollars*."[6] For one so young, such significance was rare. After all, Chinese culture emphasizes respect and reverence of elders, not brash young men like Mock Duck.

Like many American organized criminals, Mock Duck is shrouded in myth, exaggeration and half-truths. Mock Duck was clearly a gambler of some renown, famous in Chinese communities across the United States as a gambler's gambler. It was rumored that he would bet his substantial fortune on whether the numbers of seeds in an orange was odd or even. As a mark of success, he allegedly wowed Chinatown by changing his American suits three times a day.[7]

Other descriptions of Mock Duck were far less benign. For example, contemporary scholars often cite the following demonization of Mock Duck written by Carl Glick:

> In the spring of 1899, Mock Duck, a Hip Sing hatchet man, breezed into town from San Francisco. He was a fat, moonfaced man with a big queue, who wore expensive silk clothes that needed washing and ironing. But he was an extremely reckless man, carrying two guns, a hatchet, and a snickersnee. When fighting he often squatted down on his haunches and blazed away with his eyes closed. He seldom hit anything but his fire was so terrific that he became a danger to everybody around, friend or foe. The sight of him always made people nervous.[8]

This description is typical of the sensationalism or mystery used by authors to describe Mock Duck. Yet such descriptions are apparently exaggerated.

A photograph of Mock Duck at this time shows him to be young, slender and a sharp dresser in the "Western" style of the day. He was never found in possession of a gun, nor any other type of weapon for that matter. He was not a violent hatchet man or a *boo how doy* in the traditional sense. When asked under oath in a 1902 if he was ever convicted of a crime, Mock Duck stated that he had never been convicted, but that he was fined $10 for fighting with a man. He hastened to add that there was no trial in this case and that the Police Court magistrate levied the fine despite his ardent protests that he never hit the other man.[9] Although a miasma of violence circled Mock Duck, he was never convicted of a violent crime. Even contemporary sources described Mock Duck as a man who pulled the strings, the brains behind Hip Sing brawn. Indeed, a reputation for violence is often as effective as violence itself for a man of Mock Duck's stature and position.[10]

It could be argued that the sight of Mock Duck could reasonably make others in Chinatown nervous. The reason for this nervousness stemmed less from the potential of Mock Duck "to blaze away with his eyes closed," than the simple realization that he was a target of On Leong assassins, whose bullets could have easily and mistakenly found other targets, and the fact that the Hip Sing Tong that he represented provided the predominant "muscle" in New York City's underworld. The fact that he was viewed as the leader of the Hip Sing *boo how doy* certainly did not soften his reputation either. Indeed, Mock Duck's very presence in Chinatown often correlated to increased violence between the Hip Sing Tong and the On Leong Tong. This violence would then dissipate when he left town on either tong-related business or to protect his own hide.

Would You Like Your Prices Fixed or Starched?

Violence first broke out in the fall of 1899, a few months after Mock Duck arrived in Chinatown. On 22 August 1899, Chin Gin[11] allegedly committed suicide in his 19 Doyers Street restaurant, using the creative method of swallowing ammonia.[12] Eight days later, Chin Gin's friend, Loo Choo,[13] was found dead at the 253 West 53rd Street

The "Terror of Chinatown," Mock Duck.

laundry he managed. He was slumped over his counter, stabbed through the heart. After finding Loo Choo's cash drawer full, the coroner's physician, Dr. Weston, discounted robbery and determined that the deceased had committed suicide, probably due to grief over the reported suicide of his friend the week before.[14]

Such a speculative announcement raised questions in the press. For example, neither blood nor a knife was found at the crime scene. Weston and the police maintained that one of the many people who made their way into the shop after the body was discovered probably spirited away the knife. Ten feet away from the body, however, a pair of scissors hung from a partition and the blades appeared to be covered in dried blood. After a cursory glance, Weston concluded that the discoloration "appeared to be rust."[15]

The press was not the only face of cynicism in the wake of these official pronouncements. Some of the police on the scene also discounted the suicide theory. Their doubts began when four detectives investigating the case found the deceased's family far from cooperative. Loo Choo's brothers, Loo Lin and Loo Tom, were well-to-do restaurateurs who owned a popular restaurant at 14 Mott Street.[16] The restaurant shared its building with the headquarters of the On Leong Tong. Consequently, it was the location of numerous On Leong banquets, including many attended by non–Chinese, Tammany Hall-associated businessmen, attorneys, judges, cops, politicians and political operatives.[17]

When these two men first arrived on the scene of their brother's murder, they reportedly threw themselves over the body and cried that he was murdered. According to *The New York Times*, "when the detectives asked them whom they suspected, the Chinamen merely pointed southward" toward Chinatown. Before turning "secretive" a few moments later, Loo Lin insisted that his brother did not commit suicide. He pointed to the fact that his brother was in good health and had no troubles. Loo Choo was managing a successful business and Loo Lin produced the receipt for a $200 money order that the former sent to his wife and two children in China several days before his death.[18] The owner of the laundry, Wah Kee[19] of 808 Seventh Avenue, told police that Loo Choo had told him previously that he had a few enemies.[20]

Despite the many unresolved questions stemming from both of these "suicides," the police and coroner's office did not investigate further. Were they suicides? Not likely when viewed in the context of the events of the following week. On Sunday, 3 September 1899, "highbinders" instigated a riot that occurred in front of 19 Pell Street, the residence of Mock Duck.[21] *The New York Herald* reported that "warring factions" engaged the highbinders.[22] *The New York Journal* stated that the riot was between the Oriental Benevolent Society, another name for the CCBA, and the Chu Chung Society of Brooklyn. The latter was a "combination" formed to reduce laundry prices, a move challenging the policies of the CCBA.[23]

Fighting broke out at seven o'clock that evening when Chin Sam of 16 Pell Street allegedly pulled out a revolver and shot the man with whom he was arguing, Charlie Lee, in the abdomen.[24] After Lee was shot, many revolvers were drawn and over a dozen shots were fired. Fighting then moved to the front of 10 Pell Street. A spectator, Quong Lo, was shot in the ankle. As police from the nearby Elizabeth Street station rushed to the scene, Detective McClusky confronted Ching On[25] of 11 Pell Street. Ching On reportedly raised his revolver to McClusky's face, only to have it knocked down by the detective. The revolver discharged and a bullet lodged in the detective's thigh. McClusky clung to Ching On long enough for another detective to subdue and arrest him. Police Captain Titus called out the reserves and the rioters were run down or chased away.[26] Though twenty Chinese were arrested and arraigned, only five were held for trial.[27]

A review of newspaper coverage suggests that this riot was the culmination of at least a year's worth of tension between the Chinese Laundryman's Association and dissident laundrymen.[28] The Chinese Laundryman's Association was attempting to fix-prices at a level that was unacceptable to the dissidents. The tension derived from an inability of the two interests to agree on what prices customers should be charged for their services. When an agreement could not be reached and the prices were simply imposed by the owners, violence broke out.

Before going further, it is important to understand the reasons behind the Chinese Laundryman's Association's power. The choice of New York City as a destination for eastward-bound Chinese is attributed to a group of laundrymen once employed by James B. Harvey, owner of the Passaic Steam Laundry, which had been established in 1856 on the east bank of the Passaic River in Belleville, New Jersey. During the 1870s, Harvey shipped one hundred fifty Chinese from San Francisco to replace his plant's strike-prone Irish female workers who often disrupted businesses. Other plant workers on the East Coast took note of Harvey's solution to the labor problem and talked of shipping out their own Chinese workers. However, their enthusiasm waned when Harvey's Chinese workers reportedly turned out to be just as independent as the Irish women.[29]

By 1885 all of the Chinese at the Belleville laundry plant had either left on their own, or on their supervisor's, accord. These Chinese laundrymen then took the logical step: they opened their own shops in Newark and New York City. In his study on the subject, Renqiu Yu recognized these men as the pioneers of the Chinese laundrymen's community in the Greater New York area. These men wrote to their "cousins" and friends back West and encouraged them to take advantage of the favorable businesses climate and open their own shops. According to Yu, "by 1879 the number of Chinese hand laundries in New York City was large enough to alarm the white power laundry owners. The first issue of their trade journal discussed the 'menace' of this Chinese competition in the industry in a long editorial."[30] By 1898 the number of Chinese-owned laundries in the New York City metropolitan area had grown even larger, to 8,000 laundrymen (which constituted more than eighty percent of the Chinese work force in the area).[31]

In 1900 these Chinese laundrymen charged their customers the following rates: shirts were ten cents apiece; handkerchiefs, two cents each; cuffs and collars, also two cents each; and so on. These rates were roughly comparable to rates charged at non–Chinese laundries.[32] According to Yu, a Chinese laundryman earned between $8–$15 dollars a week. The employer provided his room and board.[33] This estimate reflects Louis Beck's contemporary claim that a two man laundry earned, as an average, about $1,000 a year in 1898.[34]

Beck's study of Chinatown also revealed the existence of two organizations meant to protect the interests of the Chinese laundrymen. The Chop Sing Tong,[35] or New York Union, represented those laundrymen employed in Manhattan, The Bronx and Jersey City, New Jersey. It was located at 24 Mott Street. The Sing Me Tong represented laundrymen working in Hoboken, New Jersey and Brooklyn. It was located at 16 Mott Street, headquarters of the CCBA.[36] It comes as no surprise that the power of these organizations came from their close connection to the CCBA. As Yu observed in his study of New York's Chinese hand laundries, Beck provided the only known account of these organizations.[37] Hence, "we do not know when and why they ceased to exist." What we do know is that by the early 1930s, these two tongs were gone and Chinese laundrymen in New York City had no organization of their own.[38]

Still, the unions Beck described do not correspond to those described in the contemporary press. All of the press accounts point to a Chinese Laundryman's Association being located at 16 Mott Street. The press clearly stated that the Brooklyn-based Chu Chung Society challenged the Chinese Laundryman's Association. The Chu Chung Society wanted to reduce laundry prices, a move contrary to the Chinese Benevolent Society (the CCBA).[39] Beck asserted that the Sing Me Tong represented Brooklyn and that it was based at 16 Mott. Yet it seems unlikely that a dissident group would locate their headquarters downstairs from its nemesis, the CCBA. Also, not a single reference to either Beck's Chop Sing Tong or Sing Me Tong by the press could be found. Weighing the available evidence, it seems like Beck mistakenly inverted the names of the two organizations.

Nevertheless, it appears that every Chinese laundryman in the metropolitan area at the turn-of-the-century had to be a member of one of the two associations. Beck explained that to become a member, one paid a $5 admission fee and subsequent monthly dues. Dues were set at twenty-five cents per month per person working in any one laundry.[40] In return, the laundry associations protected the business territory of its members from encroachment by Chinese competitors. It accomplished this by sending its "agents" to the encroacher in order to convince him to pick up and leave. Often times, the associations would offer the encroacher another territory, but only after his fines and dues had been paid.[41]

According to Beck, the associations also fixed the prices that were to be charged by their members for work. These rates are similar to those given by Yu above. It was understood by all laundrymen that they could not charge less than these prices. If a laundryman charged less, the association or its agents would use their "power and influence" to convince him to follow the rules. The associations would also use the criminal and civil courts to prosecute the laundryman on trumped-up offenses.[42]

On 22 November 1898, twenty-year-old Jim Sang[43] of 9 Pell Street was arrested for burglarizing the laundries of Lou Yen and Yee Sing.[44] The press reported that Jim Sang was suspected as well in the burglaries of many other laundries during the previous three months.[45] An interpreter hired by *The New York Journal* "expressed the belief that [Jim Sang] was one of the 'scab' laundrymen who have been warring against the 'Tap San Kan Shaw Tong,' or Chinese Laundrymen's Union."[46]

That same day, Ah Hop Sing[47] reportedly became a "fugitive from the mysterious vengeance of the many organizations of his countrymen." Ah

Hop Sing owned a laundry at 1877 Third Avenue. According to *The New York Herald*, he

> decided that his laundry should be run on the American plan. First, he abolished the Chinese checks, and instead introduced good, plain English print. This caused his countrymen to frown. When he introduced an American pen and ink instead of the pot and paintbrush and then hung his windows with attractive, snow-white lace, frowns gave way to scowls. When he cut his prices in true American style, every Chinaman, from 104th to 116th Street, and there is a laundry in almost every intervening block, began to mutter, and many mysterious warnings came through the mail.

These warnings disturbed Ah Hop Sing so much that he began to neglect his business. After he failed to pay his rent, his landlord threw his tubs and his patrons' laundry into the street. All lost, Ah Hop Sing reportedly fled town.[48]

Ah Hop Sing was not alone in his defiance. Other members of the Chinese Laundryman's Association disagreed with the price-fixing standards the Association established. Many wanted to undercut their competition to attract more customers, thereby increasing their business and profits. Increased profits were especially attractive to those laundrymen who desired to more expediently pay off either their credit-fare passage or the loans they needed to start their business.

By September 1899, it appears that members of the Brooklyn-based association were in agreement with the price-cutting strategy. A rebellion against the Chinese Laundryman's Association ensued and violence broke out. The press reported that "highbinders" were employed by one of the two sides. The term highbinders may have been used with no specific group in mind, but when compared to its common usage in the press and other accounts of that era, it equated to the Hip Sing Tong. Nevertheless, it seems that the Hip Sing Tong may have absconded from its traditional role as the muscle for the CCBA and its members, such as the Chinese Laundryman's Union, and was working for the dissidents.

There are two major reasons for this interpretation.[49] First, the Hip Sing Tong represented the disenfranchised of greater New York's Chinese community. Price-fixing favored the wealthy men who owned many laundries in and around New York City. With their direct access to, and influence with, the CCBA and the leaders of the Chinese Laundryman's Association, these men were able to force their self-enriching policies on all laundrymen. These policies also helped eliminate competition from smaller outfits. Ironically, the muscle of the CCBA, the Hip Sing Tong, most likely enforced these prices for a number of years. As dissent began to take the form of open rebellion in 1898, however, the Hip Sing Tong faced a quandary. By continuing to support the CCBA, it risked alienating itself from its core constituency, the working class men who formed the backbone of the Chinese laundry industry.

The second reason is that the Hip Sing Tong apparently needed new members and a new sense of mission. Gong and Grant explained that at about this time, the New York branch of the Hip Sing Tong was a complacent, directionless organization and that many men were leaving its ranks.[50] This may explain the appearance of Mock Duck in New York. If Mock Duck (Mock Sai Wing) was directly related to Mock Wing, former President of the San Francisco Hip Sing, he may have been dispatched to revitalize the organization and expand its interests in New York's Chinatown. After all, the trend of eastward migration by many Chinese ensured that it was New York, not San Francisco, that promised increased membership, revenue and organizational influence on Chinese-American life in the future.

This also explained the reception Mock Duck received in New York upon his arrival. For a young man, he possessed a tremendous amount of authority that translated to power within the Hip Sing Tong and fear in the rest of Chinatown. Although he was not physically intimidating, he had a reputation for violence. Yet many young men have such reputations, but they do not translate that reputation into authority and power. Likewise, Mock Duck's wealth alone could only get him so far in Chinatown society. After all, he had to overcome the traditional impediments faced by youth seeking leadership positions in Chinese culture. Nevertheless, Mock Duck's wealth, reputation, authority, power and ambition provided the Hip Sing Tong with a degree of political, organizational and financial independence from the CCBA that it previously did not enjoy.[51] This independence prompted the Hip Sing Tong to attempt to stake a more significant place in Chinatown's social system of organized crime, a move that would upset the social world of a number of Chinese organized criminals in the years to come.

Eventually, the powerful *guanxi* of the leaders of the CCBA and the Chinese Laundryman's Association proved more powerful then the protests of the dissidents. Prices remained fixed. On 14 March 1901 the press announced that the Chinese Laundryman's Association[52] joined a "community of interests" with non–Chinese rivals. The other members of this community included the Steam Laundryman's Club and the Laundryman's Protective Association.[53] Prices were fixed at ten cents for a shirt, two cents for a cuff, and two cents for a collar.[54]

On the surface, the formation of this cross-cultural "community of interests" seems implausible considering the prevalent racial ideologies of the day. However, money and political patronage appear to have obliterated any overt racial conflict. The Chinese Laundryman's Association was formed under the auspices of the Chinese Merchants' Association, a pseudonym of the On Leong Tong.[55] This comes as no surprise given that the president of the On Leong Tong was Tom Lee (the CCBA president and the "mayor" of Chinatown), who owned a large number of Chinese laundries in New York City. He owned so many, in fact, that he purchased a substantial amount of property in Williamsburg, Brooklyn to house his employees.⁵⁶ Given the strong connections of the On Leong Tong and Tom Lee to Tammany Hall, as well as Tammany Hall's connections to organized labor and the European immigrants of New York City who filled the ranks of the working class, it is reasonable to infer that the "community of interests" was made possible through political patronage. By forming a new, cross-cultural combination, the Chinese and two American organizations each benefited from the lack of competition.

Skirmishes and Mobilization

Life was tense for the Chinese-American community during the summer of 1900. The Boxer Rebellion was in full swing in China, and American and Allied forces were experiencing a number of military setbacks. For the first time in their collective experience, New York City's Chinese population feared anti–Chinese riots and pogroms like those on the West Coast. As it stood, the violence only manifested itself in isolated confrontations between individual Chinese and their non–Chinese attackers.⁵⁷ However, a rumor was floating around New York City that Boxers were organizing in Chinatown.⁵⁸ Though this rumor was baseless, it raised tensions dramatically. Chinatown's leadership was quick to make a public statement that the Boxers were not from the same part of China as Chinatown's Cantonese and they issued a statement denouncing the Boxers.⁵⁹

The statement did not ease tensions. For a community that experienced years of discrimination and violence at the hands of non–Chinese back on the West Coast, a prudent course of action was to leave town. Many did just that. The press reported a mini-exodus of New York Chinese leaving for China. Chinatown leaders posted warnings for those who remained to stay off the streets at night and to avoid non–Chinese. Some Chinese began to wear American clothing to draw less attention to themselves.

Others decided to take their safety into their own hands. As a result, many Chinese flocked to Bowery pawnshops and purchased pistols for self-defense. Considering the collective experience of Chinese in the Western U.S. with riots, pogroms and lynchings, these actions appear prudent and reasonable.⁶⁰ The unintended consequence of this proliferation of firearms in New York City's Chinatown was the ready availability of hand guns that could and would be used in the course of future organizational and individual conflicts.

Responding to the request of community leaders, Captain Titus of the nearby Elizabeth street station kept more of his men in the station house as a precautionary measure to protect the Chinese community.⁶¹ Chinatown's businesses suffered as non–Chinese tourists and Chinese visitors stayed away from the district. A serious shortage on foods imported from China—things they could not find domestically like bird's nests, shark fins, bamboo shoots, etc.—also occurred.⁶² The need for protection, goods, and services in this time of crisis forced Chinatown's residents to rely on their respective associations for assistance. Consequently, the already dominant presence of Chinatown's social institutions, especially the CCBA and the On Leong Tong, increased within in the Chinese community.

It was during this time of unrest and uncertainty that violence reemerged on the streets of Chinatown. On Sunday, 12 August 1900, a fight broke out in the first floor hallway of a tenement at 9 Pell Street. Witnesses say that Charlie Lee, Sin Que, Mock Wing Ching, Goo Wing Chung, and Lung Kin[63] were talking in the hallway, but as the afternoon wore on, the conversation became heated. The initial cause of the fight is unknown, but shortly after 6:00 P.M., Lung Kin allegedly either attacked or insulted Goo Wing Chung. Goo Wing Chung pulled out a .41 caliber "bulldog-type" revolver and shot Lung Kin in the abdomen. He would later die from this wound. Lung Kin was a Chinese Freemason, a member of the Chih Kung Tong, and Goo Wing Chung was a Hip Sing.[64]

A young man named Thomas Herlihy heard the shot and went to investigate. As Herlihy approached the door of 9 Pell Street, Goo Wing Chung, with the smoking revolver in hand, ran past him and entered 8 Pell Street. Goo Wing Chung knocked down John Phillips as he fled up the stairs. Seeing the pistol, Phillips followed Goo Wing Chung to a room on the second floor. Phillips then notified the police of the assailant's location and Goo Wing Chung was arrested. Police also arrested Sin Que, Charlie Lee, and Mock Wing Ching. When searched, they found one .41 caliber and one .38 caliber revolver on Sing Que; a razor sharp dirk, brass knuckles, and a five pound, eighteen inch iron bar on Charlie Lee; and a .38 caliber revolver and a two pound blackjack on Mock Wing Ching. Only the affiliation of Sing Que was reported. He was a Chinese Freemason, a member of the Chih Kung Tong.[65]

As the police arrested these men, a large and disorderly Bowery crowd began to gather on Pell Street. Reflecting the Boxer Rebellion-inspired tension of the day, they began to shout "Boxers!," "Anarchists!" and "Lynch the Chinks!" as police arrested the suspects. As a precautionary measure, Police Inspector Brooks had his men disperse the crowd.[66]

Goo Wing Ching was later convicted of the murder of Lung Kin. The conviction was secured in part by the testimony of a Newark tailor named Ah Fe.[67] Ah Fe was a member of the Chinese Freemasons. Though not listed in the original news reports, Ah Fe reportedly witnessed the murder of Lung Kin. He testified to this fact in court.[68]

On Friday, 21 September 1900, Ah Fe was allegedly in Chinatown to visit his cousin. As he walked on Pell Street, he encountered Sue Sing of 19 Pell Street.[69] Ah Fe and Sue Sing immediately exchanged words and both drew revolvers. Several shots were fired. Bullets struck two innocent bystanders sitting on the stoop in front of 23 Pell Street. Mary Mazzaki was shot in the right thigh and nine-year old Mary Paginelli was shot in the ankle. One of the bullets, however, found its intended target. As Ah Fe retreated up Pell Street, one of Sue Sing's bullets ripped through his back and passed through his extended right arm. Ah Fe stumbled to 28 Pell Street, where he collapsed as he attempted to climb the steps of the building located there. Before he died, Ah Fe identified Sue Sing as his assailant to the police.[70]

The trial of Sue Sing involved the use of evidence by Assistant District Attorney Francis W. Garvan that enabled him to show the murder was committed by "members of the [Hip] Sing Tong, or the highbinders, and was the result of [Ah Fe's] being a witness against one of the members of the organization." Garvan planned to show that Sue Sing did not act alone, but was joined by two other Hip Sing, Dong Sue and Mock Duck. *The New York Press* reported that the "cousin" Ah Fe was visiting was Sing Que, his friend and fellow Lung Kin homicide witness. As the two met, said Garvan, they were confronted by the Hip Sing men. The Hip Sing threw hot pepper into the eyes of Sing Que. Blinded by the pepper, Sing Que somehow managed to stumble into the basement of 19 Pell Street where friends protected him. His friend Ah Fe was not so fortunate.[71]

Garvan received his evidence from Tom Lee, whom he called "the good Chinaman." According to *The New York Daily Tribune*, Lee belonged to "the better element of Chinese in this city, known as the Lung Gag Gong, or Chinese Freemasons." Because of his assistance, Tom Lee stated that the Hip Sing Tong had placed a $2,000 reward on his head.[72] On April 20, District Attorney Philbin requested that the police provide protection for Tom Lee after an unknown Chinese man followed Lee to his home at 161st Street and Morris Avenue on the previous Friday night. Once Lee entered his house, the man waited outside for a time, and then rang the doorbell. Ever the gentleman, Lee had his wife answer the door and she told the man that her husband "was not receiving right now." The man then "lurked in the shadows" a bit longer before he went away.[73] In spite of his self-imposed brush with danger, Lee's evidence helped secure the conviction of Sue Sing, who pled guilty to the charge and was sentenced to a life term in the infamous Sing Sing prison.[74]

The conviction of Sue Sing, however, did not end the investigation into Ah Fe's murder. On 10 July 1901, Dong Sue, an alleged accomplice of Sue Sing, was extradited from Boston to New York to face the charge of murder. Dong Sue was reportedly arrested several months before in Boston, but his lawyer, the distinguished attorney Harvey J. Pratt, provided a time consuming—but eventually unsuccessful—extradition fight that delayed his trial date.[75] The adjudication of Dong Sue's murder charge is unknown.

As for Mock Duck, he was tried twice for the murder of Ah Fe. Indicted by the same Grand Jury that indicted Dong Sue and Sue Sing, Mock Duck posted bail and reportedly fled to Buffalo to ponder his options. According to *The New York Times*, "Tom Lee, "the good Chinaman," learned that Mock Duck had fled to Buffalo. He had him shadowed and gave information that led to his arrest. For this Tom Lee has had paper thrown in his face, and believes that there have been two attempts made to assassinate him. Those were frustrated by the timely appearance of policemen."[76]

To counter Tom Lee's active efforts to see him sent to prison, Mock Duck assembled a high-powered defense team. Chief counsel was Abraham Levy, a powerful, well-known attorney whose law partner was Henry Unger, a former Assistant District Attorney who had worked in the Indictment Bureau. Also serving as counsel were George Glaze, Stephen Brague, and the well-known reformer Frank Moss, former president of the New York Police Board, associate counsel to the Lexow Committee, senior counsel to the Mazet Committee, and counsel to the Reverend Charles Parkhurst's Society for the Prevention of Crime.[77]

Moss had previous contact with the Hip Sing during his 1897 study of New York, *The American Metropolis*. He viewed the Hip Sing Tong as "a benevolent corporation chartered under the laws of New York, approved by the Supreme Court, and expressly designed to aid the Chinese to learn American ways, and to advance them in religion and mutual helpfulness."[78] Coming from Moss, this was a generous assessment, for "as a body," he viewed the Chinese "as a dangerous, useless and disgusting lot of people."[79]

In his mind, however, Moss distinguished between "good Chinese" and "bad Chinese." Thanks to his history of fighting Tammany Hall and police corruption, he viewed the On Leong as the latter due to their gambling operations and their contributions to the system of bribery and graft that stood in the way of true reform in New York City. Effective deception and manipulation of Moss by the Hip Sing led him to view the Hip Sing as the maligned enemy of the On Leong. The Hip Sing portrayed themselves as reformers to Moss and explained On Leong animosity towards them as similar to what Moss and his reform colleagues received from Tammany Hall and corrupt cops. Empathizing with these claims, Moss was convinced and the Hip Sing and Mock Duck had their marquee, reform attorney.

During the trial, Wong Get, the Hip Sing Tong's interpreter, advised Mock Duck's attorneys that in order to ensure that the testimony of Chinese witnesses was true, it would be necessary to have them swear an oath over a slaughtered chicken. The oath stated, "If I do not tell the truth I hope God will punish me as this chicken has been punished." Levy brought this to the judge's attention and it was decided to order a number of live chickens from a poultry dealer. *The New York Times* commented that the court would probably become "a scene of slaughter, fuss, and feathers."[80] The effectiveness of the chicken oaths is unknown. However, the ritualistic killing of chickens when taking an oath is practiced by some Chinese secret societies and such oaths were and are taken quite seriously.[81] Indeed, it is safe to say that this practice was more effective than having a non–Christian Chinese man swear an oath on a Bible, which in his eyes would be nothing but a meaningless book.

The perceived lack of reliability of oaths made by Chinese in U.S.

courts led to laws in Western states that banned Chinese from testifying in court. Jingoists claimed that Chinese could not be trusted to abide by oaths because of a defective moral character intrinsic to their race. Federal courts and the courts of non–Western states did not agree with such transparent efforts to marginalize and disempower the Chinese community. The issue of credibility of Chinese oaths remained, however, with some courts practically recognizing that there was an inherent culture conflict surrounding oaths and morality.

In Chinese culture, one's *mianzi* (face) was of supreme importance. *Mianzi* was earned and maintained by respecting and adhering to the mutually obligate bonds inherent to one's *guanxi* network. Moral decisions were those that preserved *mianzi* and protected those in one's *guanxi* network.

Frank Moss, reform warrior (Moss, *The American Metropolis*).

Consequently, at the turn-of-the-century, if an American Court asked a Chinese man to testify against his patron or cousin, he would not because to do so would be immoral. Swearing on a Bible (once again, just another book in the eyes of a non–Christian) would not remove this culturally mandated obligation. Consider the following exchange between a Chinese witness and a defense attorney:

> Q: Now do you know what the book was that you swore on?
> A: Jesus Christ's book.
> Q: Jesus Christ's book?
> A: Yes, sir.
> Q: Are you a Christian?
> A: I am not a Christian.
> Q: How?
> A: I am not a Christian.
> Q: Do you believe in that book?
> A: I come here in the court, and they direct me to swear on that book, and I swear on that book.
> Q: You swear on that book simply because you have been directed to swear on it?
> A: How do you mean.
> Q: How do I mean?
> A: Yes.... Yes, sir, everybody that comes here swears on that book.
> Q: Does that book bind your conscience?
> A: Yes, sir, it binds it because, if not, Jesus Christ will condemn me.[82]

Which held more sway in this case, Jesus Christ or loss of *mianzi*? This fundamental question faced all U.S. courts when their Judeo-Christian foundation of oath taking encountered non–Judeo-Christian witnesses. Some courts banned the testimony of those who did not ascribe to the Judeo-Christian oath. Others, like our example in the Mock Duck trial, recognized that this obligation may be relinquished if a culturally specific oath tied to Chinese moral constructs (in this case sworn over a slaughtered chicken) was provided. Other courts, like the one in which the testimony above occurred, simply let juries decide whether or not the witness was credible.

Slaughtered chickens aside, there is no further record of the first trial in *The New York Times* and *The New York Daily Tribune*, nor is a transcript of the first case available. We do know, however, that the trial ended in a hung jury, prompting a retrial of Mock Duck on the same charges. The second trial, for which a transcript does exist, began on March 20, 1902, before the Honorable Rufus B. Cowing in the Court of General Sessions of the Peace for the City and County of New York. Mock Duck reassembled his legal team of Moss, Glaze and Brague. Assistant District Attorney Arthur Train was the prosecutor.[83]

The prosecution's case alleged that Mock Duck was not only at the scene of the crime, but that he organized it and took part in the shooting. They provided a parade of Chinese and non–Chinese witnesses to testify to that effect. Yet the defense provided effective cross-examinations, illustrating that the witnesses called had ties to the Chih Kung Tong (the Chinese Freemasons), the On Leong Tong, or Tom Lee. Indeed, Tom Lee provided most of the witnesses to the prosecution himself. The defense also hammered away at the numerous discrepancies in prosecution witness testimony.

Mock Duck's attorneys offered a two-tiered and, on the surface, contradictory defense strategy. The defense began by producing a string of witnesses who testified that at the time of the shooting Mock Duck was at the Fulton Market buying a terrapin and vegetables with an acquaintance. The defense also called witnesses who testified under oath in the Coroner's investigation but were not called by the prosecution to testify at trial. In a major blow to the prosecution, these witnesses did not place Mock Duck at the scene. Collectively, these witnesses provided a strong alibi and underscored the defense's assertion that Tom Lee and his Chih Kung and On Leong brethren were using the District Attorney's office as a surrogate to prevent the reform-minded Mock Duck and the Hip Sing from meddling in their affairs.

Switching gears, the defense recognized that the prosecution's entire case rested on the assumption that a principal crime was committed. The defense believed otherwise and it attempted to establish that no principal crime occurred because the murder of Ah Fe was a case of self-defense. The defense called none other than the accused triggerman, Sue Sing, to testify as to why he pled guilty to murdering Ah Fe. Sue Sing told the jury that Ah Fe and Sing Que had threatened him a few days before the attack because he was a Hip Sing and an associate of Mock Duck's. As a matter of fact, he stated, the two men chased him, pistols in hand, three day's before the attack.

Sue Sing then testified that when confronted by the men on the day of the murder, he originally fired in self-defense. He then came to the heat-of-the-moment conclusion that since his life was threatened and he was the victim of two attacks already, he had to be proactive. He subsequently pursued Ah Fe and shot him in the back. Facing the death penalty if convicted, Sue Sing recognized that if he had not pursued and shot Ah Fe, he would have had a better position to claim self-defense. Therefore, he pled guilty to second-degree murder to avoid conviction of first-degree murder and the electric chair. By introducing this justification of self-defense for Sue Sing's killing of Ah Fe, a remarkable legal maneuver given Sue Sing did not have occasion to use it himself, the defense argued that Mock Duck could not be guilty of the killing.

The two people who could have refuted Sue Sin's testimony, as well as the testimony of the defense's parade of witnesses, were Ah Fe and Sing Que. Since the former was killed in the fight, that left Sing Que. Yet Sing Que was killed in a Pell Street fire before Mock Duck's first trial. Although details are scarce, it appears that foul play was involved. However, the Court prevented a "claim of incendiarism or persecution" in the case of Sing Que's death. Therefore, there is no record of the details surrounding his death. With Ah Fe and Sing Que dead, the jury had to rely on a cavalcade of witnesses with disparate versions of the events in question.

In his closing, Frank Moss relied on this tableau of confusion to press his case for reasonable doubt. Yet he recognized that race may enter the equation, so he attempted to head it off in his closing arguments by reminding the jury of its higher calling:

> The greatest of the inalienable rights of man is life. It is the direct gift of God. It is sacred. It should not be taken by man, except in obedience to God's command, and in a way that God would sanction. The sweetest of man's rights is liberty. Life is worth very little without liberty, and surely, in the country of liberty, even with those who do not know its full value, perhaps, it becomes an American citizen not to infringe upon the liberty of others, not to shut them off from liberty, except in obedience to a conscience, clear itself and clear of any offense against God, when it renders a decision. The life and liberty of this man, Mock Duck, since the time of his indictment down to the present hour, have been in the keeping of his counsel. We have been charged with the life of this man, who is under accusation, as we believe, by a conspiracy of his enemy. We have been charged with his liberty, with his sacred life; and gentlemen, we have tried to acquit ourselves of that responsibility just as earnestly, just as ardently, just as religiously as though Mock Duck were Cornelius Vanderbilt. That responsibility that has weighed upon us, we are about to pass off of our

shoulders onto yours, and I pray God that responsibility may go upon your shoulders as you are prepared for it.[84]

Moss also reminded the jury of what could result if this higher calling was sublimated to human frailty:

> Look well to yourselves, gentlemen. Look well to your own hearts and consciences, to your own standing before the great Tribunal, the great Power from which life comes, the great Power which sanctifies liberty, the great Tribunal which will sit infallibly upon Mock Duck. If he be guilty, it will never let him go, that Power which, while it sits upon Mock Duck, sits upon you, while you sit in the place of God, as he writes it in the hearts of men. If it be so, that, within a few months from now, in the grounds of Sing Sing, the electric current be turned on, and the blood of Mock Duck be made to seethe in his veins, and his tissues melt with heat, and his tortured nerves to be wrung in anguish, and his spirit to be sent, unbidden, to the presence of his Maker, will it be, think you, the hand of the jailer that turns on the current, that really does that act...?
>
> I tell you gentlemen, if that thing happens to this living man, it will be you that will do it, it will be the Foreman, Mr. Wolf, and the Second Juror, Mr. Bixby, and the third, Mr. Paspary, and the fourth, Mr. Pine, and every one of you. You may wake, some night, if that thing be done, and recall the circumstances of this trial, and recall some bias that you have allowed to exist in your minds, some prejudice against counsel, some individual judgment about a witness, and you will think about those things, and you will say, "I wish I had the case in my hands once more." But it will be too late. Aye, gentlemen, when, after having rendered your verdict, you go out of this Courtroom, it will be too late. You cannot take it back.[85]

On 3 April 1902, *The Sun* reported that for a second time, a jury could not reach a verdict in the case. With two mistrials under his belt, Mock Duck walked away a free man.[86] He came very close to an acquittal, however, as the jury was hung eleven to one in his favor.[87] His lack of an acquittal, however, would haunt him for years to come since it gave prosecutors cause to have him rearrested on the outstanding indictment at any time.

Thoughts on Motivation

So what caused the feud between the Chinese Freemasons and the Hip Sing Tong? Gong and Grant maintained that the "Gee Kung Tong" (Chih Kung Tong) did not approve of the fact that Chinatown gambling houses were beginning to take notice of, and send tribute to, the Hip Sing Tong. Gong and Grant asserted that a war between the two began over this issue and that while this war was going on, a new tong, the On Leong Tong, was formed. As mentioned earlier, Louie Yong Hock and "The Silver Tongued Orator" Moy Dong Yue gained the backing of Chinatown

9. Setting the Stage for a Tong War

Mayor Tom Lee and his "gambling trust" to form the tong in 1899. According to Gong and Grant,

> The On Leong Tong was inspired by the unruly element that had crept into the Hip Sing Tong. Gambling housekeepers were afraid that the Hip Sings would ruin them, and so had to resort to a defensive measure. The On Leong Tong was organized for the sole purpose of opposing the Hip Sings, and keeping the latter's members away from gaming places. Of course the Hip Sing resented this, so a bitter feud started.[88]

Their version of events, however, does not hold up when tested against the available historical record. First, the On Leong Tong existed before 1899, a point illustrated in 1898, when Columbia University student Louis Beck surveyed New York City's Chinatown for his thesis, and in 1897, when Frank Moss surveyed Chinatown as part of his book on New York City.[89] Second, Beck also revealed the fact that the Hip Sing Tong already received tribute from gamblers, while Beck found that the On Leong Tong controlled gambling in Chinatown.[90] Finally, Beck, Moss and press reports make no reference to a New York branch of the Chinese Freemasons (Chih Kung Tong) during the 1890's. Given that Beck and Moss covered every major organization, association and business in Chinatown, and that the Chinese Freemasons were well known in other cities, it seems odd that they were not included in his work. The most likely scenario is that a chapter did exist there, but was overshadowed by other organizations that were more powerful and relevant to the New York Chinese community at that time.[91]

Perhaps the answer is found in the role of the Chih Kung Tong as the American arm of the Hung Mun Triad Society.[92] Calvin Lee explained that the Chinese Freemasons, as the Chih Kung Tong was known, began its activities in San Francisco in 1863. The Freemasons were "dedicated to the overthrow of the Manchu Dynasty, but in the United States it also became involved in various illegal activities" as a means of generating revenue for the organization and some of its members.[93] Nevertheless, the conflict between the Hip Sing Tong and Chih Kung Tong did not appear to be over Chinese politics.

Eve Armentrout Ma offers us an interesting framework for interpretation. She explained that in the United States, there was a centralization of sorts with regard to the various lodges (tongs). She said that "many 'lodges' actually consisted of a head lodge ... and sublodges scattered over a wide geographic area." At the turn of the century, she found, the Chih Kung t'ang (tong) "exercised a loose hegemony over all the others in North America":

> The larger, inclusive organization can best be called the Chih-kung t'ang federation, to distinguish it from the Chih-kung t'ang lodge which headed it.... The headquarters of the Chih-kung t'ang lodge and federation were located in San Francisco.... Lodges owed

only limited obedience to the Chih-kung t'ang federation, although the federation was the only one with the right to conduct the official Triad ritual.... In addition, the federation could collect certain fees from the members of the various lodges and was supposedly the arbitrator of conflicts between lodges.[94]

Ma's analysis lends credence to criminologist Ko-lin Chin's argument that tongs and Triads shared Triad norms and values.[95]

Consequently, the Chih Kung Tong may have been in partnership with the On Leong Tong at this time, a bond formed by shared Triad norms and values. Four pieces of evidence suggest that this may be the case. First, Tom Lee was recognized as being the president of the New York branch of the On Leong Tong and the Chih Kung Tong, not to mention the Fan Tan Syndicate. According to *The Sun*, Tom Lee was also head of the "Lee Company" which reportedly controlled Chinatown's gaming interest. *The Sun* reported that the Lee Company engaged the services of the On Leong Tong for protection, a move that makes sense because Tom Lee was in charge of both organizations.[96]

Second, some viewed the Chih Kung Tong as controlling gambling at this time. Gong and Grant[97] asserted this and so did *The New York Times* in a 9 September 1900 investigative report on gambling in Chinatown. The Chinese informant *The New York Times* cited in the piece asserted the following:

> Everything in the gambling line is controlled by the Gee Kung Tong (sic.). Occasionally most men who were not members of the society have set up gaming places, but they did not last long. The methods by which the society puts these independents out of business are various. If all kinds of petty torments fail to make them close up, knives or pistols are made to appear. The society will not be interfered with.[98]

Third, by September 1904, overwhelming evidence points to the On Leong Tong as the tong behind gambling in Chinatown. This backs up the fourth piece of evidence: after the Chih Kung Tong and Hip Sing Tong conflict, Gong and Grant stated that the On Leong Tong itself began to protect the interests of the gambling industry. This effectively removed the Hip Sing Tong from its longstanding power syndicate function in New York's Chinese community.[99]

How could two different entities, the On Leong Tong and the Chih Kung Tong, control all of Chinatown's gambling at the same time? How can the Chih Kung Tong be viewed as using extortion when it was widely recognized that the Hip Sing Tong was the local power syndicate? Why would the Chih Kung Tong and the Hip Sing Tong fight such a short war? These are questions for which there are no clear answers. The judge in Mock Duck's second trial specifically precluded testimony and evidence that addressed the large conflict that resulted in Ah Fe's murder.[100] The available evidence, however, suggests that the following scenario was likely.

As mentioned previously, it seemed that the laundry dispute may have signaled the first step in a Hip Sing quest for increased power in New York City's Chinatown. The formation and success of the aforementioned "community of interests" on the part of the Chinese Laundryman's Association suggests that the Hip Sing Tong supported the losing side of the struggle. The winning side, which included merchants like Tom Lee, had strong pull in a variety of Chinatown institutions like the CCBA and the Fan Tan Syndicate. As a consequence of its actions, the Hip Sing Tong may have had to give way to a new, more controllable and reliable power syndicate, the Chih Kung Tong, with regard to its function in Chinatown's gambling industry. If this was the case, to protect its interests and preserve its *mianzi* (face) in the Chinese community, the Hip Sing Tong had to take action. As a result, Chih Kung Tong members Lung Kin, Ah Fe and (possibly) Sing Que were murdered.

The murder trials of the men accused of killing Ah Fe were especially significant to Tom Lee, the apparent unifying factor in the anti–Hip Sing Tong movement. If the Hip Sing Tong's aggressive new leader, Mock Duck, could be sent to prison, the Hip Sing Tong would be kept in check and the Chih Kung Tong could retain its position as Chinatown's new, more easily controlled power syndicate. When the juries in the two Mock Duck trials could not reach a verdict, the membership or leaders of the Chih Kung Tong, after losing two of its members to Hip Sing *boo how doy*, reasonably had second thoughts about continuing its new role.

Admittedly, this is inferential reasoning, but it does explain why the New York branch of the Chih Kung Tong—known more for its concern over political issues in China then criminal opportunity in New York's Chinatown—was mentioned as a power syndicate for only a brief moment in time between a period of Hip Sing Tong protection and a period of attempted self-protection by the gambling industry itself. It also explains why the press and Gong and Grant reported the "formation" of the On Leong Tong at this time, despite the fact that the On Leong Tong had already existed for years.[101]

Alas, what Gong and Grant viewed as a formation was more likely an evolution of the On Leong Tong's organizational role in Chinatown. Instead of purely representing merchant concerns as it had before, the On Leong Tong now took on the dual functions of power and enterprise syndicates. By forming a partnership between the Fan Tan Syndicate and its chief partner, the Lee Company, the On Leong Tong became the official patron and protector of the interests of all three. Of course, being the most prominent member of all three organizations, Tom Lee served as the broker and linchpin of this arrangement. These roles ensured that he was responsible for the positive and negative consequences resulting from this partnership and the organizational evolution it inspired.

Evidence of the partnership between the On Leong Tong, the Fan Tan Syndicate, and the Lee Company, as well as the On Leong Tong's subsequent venture into organized criminal activity, is found in two *Sun* articles which appeared roughly four years after these developments would have occurred. These articles asserted that the On Leong Tong provided protection services for the Lee Company and, by extension, the Fan Tan Syndicate.[102] At first Tom Lee and the On Leong Tong may have contracted with the Chih Kung Tong to provide needed protection services. Then, after the Chih Kung Tong lost their skirmishes with the Hip Sing Tong, the On Leong Tong probably began to recruit and train its own *boo how doy*.

The Hip Sing-Chih Kung conflict serves as an important pretext to the coming tong war between the On Leong Tong and the Hip Sing Tong. First, it signaled a willingness on the part of the Hip Sing to use deadly force as a means of defending and advancing its positions in Chinatown politics. No longer was its strength implied via threats, reputation and mere presence. Second, it solidified the existing class and clan divisions between the Hip Sing Tong and Chinatown's ruling elite. From this point on the Hip Sing Tong desired equal, not subservient, footing with the On Leong Tong in the power structure of New York's Chinatown.

Whatever his motivation, the powerful Tom Lee personally chose to challenge the Hip Sing Tong by making use of his extensive *guanxi* networks. Specifically, Lee and his cronies actively targeted the influential and disruptive up-start Mock Duck for removal from the Chinatown via their allies in the criminal justice system. Regrettably for the former, they failed in their efforts, thus opening the door for reprisals from Mock Duck and his fellow Hip Sing. Two years later, Tom Lee, and the newly strengthened On Leong Tong faced just such a reprisal. This reprisal instigated New York City's first major Tong war.

10

The Gloves Come Off

From 2 April 1902, the day the second trial of Mock Duck ended in a hung jury, to 21 July 1904, when the Hip Sing-aided Society for the Prevention of Crime conducted its first gambling raid on On Leong establishments in Chinatown, there is no evidence in the New York press of tension between the Hip Sing Tong and the On Leong Tong. A few gambling raids in Chinatown were reported between December 1902 and February 1903, reflecting the fact that the new reform District Attorney William Travers Jerome was providing tips to, and corresponding political pressure on, an otherwise apathetic Elizabeth Street precinct. This police apathy, and the corruption that inspired it, is inferred from the fact that most Chinese-operated vice establishments were almost always empty when the police arrived on the scene, and when alleged gamblers were arrested they were discharged for lack of evidence rather quickly.[1]

During this time there were only three reported cases of Chinese-on-Chinese violence, but there is no reason to believe any of these cases were more than isolated incidents.[2] The only organized violence that occurred on the streets of Chinatown during this time was between perpetual rivals the Monk Eastman Gang and the Five Points Gang, the widely recognized evolutionary predecessors of "modern" organized crime syndicates. This feud began when a member of one gang assaulted a member of the other in a saloon. Tammany Assemblyman Thomas Foley mediated a quick end to the conflict after only three days of fighting.[3]

Only Gong and Grant offer a description of events concerning the activities of the Hip Sing Tong and the On Leong Tong during this period. Their cryptic and brief discussion, however, does not mention the dates of these activities. In addition, their claims cannot be corroborated from the available historical record. Nevertheless, their description is the only one we have and it merits consideration.

According to Gong and Grant, the formation of the On Leong Tong in 1899 caused a "war cloud" to hover over Chinatown. During this time, the Hip Sing organization went through some fundamental changes that would determine major aspects of the first On Leong-Hip Sing war. Foremost of these was a change in leadership. Their President, Ton Bok Woo, returned to China at about the time of Ah Fe's murder. Ton Bok Woo, a former Chinese military student, was made Hip Sing "chief" when he came to New York. Gong and Grant state that he was a powerful and fearless man. Reportedly, he was so strong that he was barred from all of the penny arcades along the Bowery because he was likely to ruin the punching bags and other machines for testing one's strength. Legend had it that once, during a Hip Sing feud with another party, two rival hatchetmen came up behind him at his third floor apartment at 22 Pell Street and drove knives deep into each of his shoulders. Instead of collapsing, the giant Ton Bock Woo, with the knives buried in his body, grabbed each of the men and knocked them both out. Then, with one man under each arm, he dragged them into the street below where he called his fellow tong men who summoned the police. It was only then that he collapsed.[4]

After Ton Bok Woo left for China, Huey Gow succeeded him as the Hip Sing leader and he ruled the tong with an iron hand, working closely with Mock Duck and the tong's interpreter, Wong Get.[5] With this new leadership in place, the Hip Sing Tong became more aggressive. First, the Hip Sing Tong recruited more *boo how doy* from San Francisco, including Sing Dock, known as "The Scientific Killer" for his precise and well-planned acts of violence.[6]

Upon arriving in New York, Sing Dock allegedly spent three months quietly learning the political and strategic situations in Chinatown. He then began to organize a fighting contingent in New Jersey. After he trained them in small unit military tactics and the art of firing pistols, he and his men were ready for battle. Sing Dock sent out decoys into On Leong territory, trying to lure them into battle. Eventually, the On Leong challenged the Hip Sing to a fight. The fight was to occur in a Brooklyn cemetery. Sing Duck strategically planned for the upcoming battle, mapping out the cemetery, positioning his men and training them on specific small unit tactics. On the appointed night, however, Sing Dock was disappointed because the On Leong did not show. Furious, he cut off branches of trees in the cemetery before his return to Chinatown so that he could prove the cowardly On Leong stood up the brave Hip Sing. Though he had failed to get his battle, Sing Dock did force the On Leong leadership into hiding, for at this point in the feud, only the leaders of the two tongs were marked for death. Feeling frustrated, Sing Dock left for San Francisco. No sooner did he get there than the fighting began in earnest back in New York.[7]

The loss of face on the part of the On Leong Tong was exacerbated by the courage of none other than Mock Duck. For example, before Sing Dock and his extra "muscle" made their way to New York, tensions had increased between the On Leong Tong and Hip Sing Tong. A skirmish occurred when a Hip Sing member went to visit a cousin on Mott Street, which was On Leong territory. Immediately, On Leong *boo how doy* were sent to the tenement where the luckless Hip Sing's cousin lived. The *boo how doy* waited outside for the Hip Sing to leave. When word reached Hip Sing headquarters, the tong's council met and decided not to help him due to his own foolishness. In spite of this decision, Gong and Grant alleged that upon hearing of his compatriot's trouble, Mock Duck walked calmly onto Mott Street and went boldly through the lines of the On Leong. He called to his trapped colleague to come out, which he did. Out of shock or respect, the *boo how doy* did not do anything as the two returned to Doyers Street. But after the shock wore off, the On Leong leadership was incensed at their loss of face. Consequently, they placed a $1,000 price on Mock Duck's head.[8]

This incident, coupled with his survival of assassination attempts and his emergence unscathed from two murder trials, created a reputation of invulnerability for Mock Duck. Neither Chinese nor Western foes could stop him. Likewise, this incident fed his existing reputation of being a fierce warrior and the organizer of almost every planned Hip Sing attack against its enemies.

Besides the recruitment of more *boo how doy*, the most important change Huey Gow made was to increase the Hip Sing Tong's contacts with the world outside of the Chinese community. The centerpiece of his plan was the formation of an alliance with the nemesis of Tammany Hall and crooked cops, the Reverend Charles Parkhurst and his reform juggernaut, the Society for the Prevention of Crime. Since the Hip Sing Tong had no institutional power base due to entrenched On Leong corruption of public officials, they decided to manipulate the reformers' zeal to cripple On Leong gaming operations and their Tammany Hall and police protectors. From the perspective of the Hip Sing, it was a classic case of "my enemy's enemy is my friend." Consequently, the Hip Sing Tong provided evidence to the Parkhurst Society's counsel, Frank Moss, so that he could bring indictments and prosecute cases against On Leong members. Mock Duck and Wong Get, both English speakers, were chosen to solicit and maintain the friendship of the Parkhurst Society, as well as the Society's allies in the press.[9] Wong Get and the Hip Sing President, Huey Gow, had a longstanding relationship with Moss that went back to his days on the Lexow Committee.[10]

With their new allies in place, the Hip Sing Tong was ready to make their power play by the summer of 1904. Legend has it that one day Mock Duck approached a dejected-looking Wong Get and asked what his trouble was. Wong Get responded that he was contemplating Tom Lee and his "delicious gambling pie." Wong Get believed that the Hip Sing Tong should "share some of the crumbs." "'Crumbs! Who wants crumbs?' Mock Duck cried. 'We'll have half of it!'"[11]

Mock Duck then went to the On Leong headquarters and demanded that they grant the Hip Sing Tong jurisdiction over half of Chinatown's gambling dens. The Hip Sing Tong, he explained, was no longer content with its delegated role of enforcers and its subservient status to the On Leong Tong. It wanted to become, and believed it deserved to become, a wealthy enterprise syndicate and a recognized Chinatown power. The On Leong leadership reportedly laughed at Mock Duck's request.[12] But according to Luc Sante, "it wasn't a laughing matter when two weeks later the On Leong boarding house on Pell Street caught fire and two On Leong died in the flames."[13] Both tongs held council meetings soon after and war was declared.

On 21 July 1904, Superintendent Thomas McClintock of the Parkhurst Society led officers from police headquarters on a raid of six policy operations located on Pell, Mott and Doyers Streets. The raid was conducted over the heads of the Elizabeth Street police because of what McClintock politely perceived as a "dereliction of duty" on the part of Inspector Titus and his men. One of the Elizabeth Street detectives criticized the raid because of the fact that McClintock relied on the advice of "Wong," a man known to represent another faction of gamblers in Chinatown. He was most likely referring to Wong Get.[14]

Two weeks later, on 16 August 1904, Tom Lee and two of his associates, William A. Hang, a cigar manufacturer, and Charles Foon Foos, a Mott Street merchant, were arrested and arraigned before U.S. Commissioner Shields in the Federal building. They were charged with having voted in elections, despite the fact they were not legally entitled to vote according to the naturalization laws that barred immigrant Chinese from citizenship privileges. Assistant U.S. Attorneys Marx and Houghton, who had charge of naturalization frauds, said they knew of others who possessed allegedly false citizenship papers and that these persons would be arrested soon. Lee obtained his citizenship papers, it was alleged, in the Criminal Courts of St. Louis in 1876.

Ever since Tom Lee established residence in New York City, he had taken quite an interest in politics, voting in every election, usually supporting the Democrats. The specific charge was that Lee registered to vote for a Second District Assemblyman on 10 October 1903. William A. Hang also possessed a full certificate of naturalization, granted by the County Court of Richmond, Indiana, on 6 October 1892. Charles Foon Foos received his papers from the Court of Common Pleas in Passaic, N.J. on 24 March 1890. The timing of the arrests suggests that the U.S. attorney's office received information and a gentle nudge from the Hip Sing Tong or its Parkhurst Society allies. The Hip Sing Tong would have made such a move to undermine the value of the political influence the On Leong Tong had with Tammany Hall.[15]

Despite their arrests, the three men did not seem worried, perhaps believing that their political patrons would protect them. Yet this protection, if it existed at all in this case, had mixed results. On the one hand, William Hang pled guilty to the charge.[16] On the other hand, it appears that Tom Lee offered a successful defense against the charges because he remained in New York City for years to come. The fate of Charles Foon Foos remains a mystery.[17]

As mentioned previously, the tong war heated up when Sing Dock returned to San Francisco in late 1904. The On Leong were bristling for a fight due to Hip Sing cooperation with the Parkhurst Society, as well as direct assaults on On Leong honor by Hip Sing members. For example, on 18 September 1904, police swarmed in on the On Leong headquarters at 14 Mott Street after some Hip Sing entered an On Leong meeting and "proceeded to batter the faces" of the On Leong men. Several shots were fired, but no one was killed. Acting Captain Eggers's men of the Elizabeth Street station arrested six Hip Sing.[18]

One month latter, on 17 October 1904, an influx of visiting Chinese and "rubberneck" tourist wagons were "entertained" by a tong fight in which the On Leong "scored" against the Hip Sing. Hip Sing member Tam Wah Toy was shot in the stomach and killed by On Leong member Luie Fong. The skirmish began earlier that evening at On Leong headquarters at 14 Mott Street. Five Hip Sing dashed upstairs and tore up the room where Tom Lee and his "minions" were smoking. Soon after, just after the "rubberneck" wagons dropped off passengers at about 9 P.M., a shot was fired across the street at 17 Mott Street. Tam Wah Toy fell, fatally wounded. Witnesses saw an "undersized" Chinese man throw down a revolver and run from 17 Mott Street to On Leong headquarters. The man who ran, Luie Fong, was arrested later that night after a Hip Sing witness, Huie Fong, told police where their suspect was hiding.[19]

Huie Fong was a member of the powerful Huie family, which wielded considerable influence with the Hip Sing Tong.[20] The family's head, the Reverend Huie Kin, was an ordained Presbyterian minister and, according to *The World*, the reputed leader of the Hip Sing Tong.[21] Whether *The World* meant *the* leader or *a* leader is unclear, but either capacity is possible due to the murky nature of internal tong politics.

Information on the Reverend Huie Kin is sketchy, relegated to a few newspaper reports during a brief span of time. Attempts to find

Mott Street from Chatham Square (Moss, *The American Metropolis*).

other sources to illuminate his life were unsuccessful. However, there is a chance that Huie Kin may be the same person as, or at least a close relative to, the man Gong and Grant credit with being the President of the Hip Sing Tong at this time, Huey Gow.[22] This possibility is based on the phonetic similarities of "Huie" and "Huey," the possibility of one of these name's being a "paper name," and the amount of importance attributed to both Huie Kin and Huey Gow.

Regardless of his official role in the tong, Huie Kin must have had considerable influence, for he and his family came under repeated physical attack by On Leong *boo how doy* during this period. The week before the murder of Tam Wah Tay, the *Tribune* reported that On Leong members attempted to "wipe out" the Huie family at 12 Pell Street.[23] Unfortunately, the *Tribune* or other newspapers provided no further details of this incident. Attacks against the Huies would force the family to take center stage in this conflict again come January 1905.

The On Leong Tong retaliated against the Hip Sing Tong on 3 November 1904. At 1:30 A.M., Mock Duck was shot and almost killed as he ascended the steps from the basement at 18 Pell Street.[24] On Leong member Lee Sing[25] fired the two shots, one of which went through Mock Duck's stomach. Lee Sing fled, but was caught by Chinese bystanders who turned him over to Detectives Power and Corr at the Elizabeth Street station. Interestingly, the local newspapers were sympathetic to Mock Duck, who had earned a positive reputation as a "twenty-seven year old Parkhurst Society worker." The papers reported that he was hunting fan tan gamblers, it is said, when he was fired on.[26] References to his previous trials on murder charges were conveniently absent.

Superintendent McClintock of the Parkhurst Society spoke of the assailant's motivation in the Tombs Police Court the day after the arraignment. McClintock explained the following to the Court:

> The case is very simple. There is a society of gamblers and merchants who want gambling in Chinatown and who pay for police protection to some one. There is a society of Chinese reformers also. The gamblers say that many of these men are only reformers until they are paid to keep their mouths and eyes closed as to gambling. Mock Duck was a reformer and was shot because it was believed he gave information to the Parkhurst agents. No one in Chinatown believes that [Lee Sing), who was arraigned today, tried to shoot anybody on Sunday night. It was a put-up job against the reformers and the detective seems to have arrived at just the right moment. What appears to be a feud between two secret societies is really a war between the police and the Parkhurst Society.[27]

The following January, the preliminary hearing for Lee Sing, represented by On Leong Tong attorneys D. Frank Lloyd and Edmund H. Price, was held. City Magistrate Charles Flammer stated that he "would be doing this man a gross injustice by putting him on trial," but that it was Mock Duck's word (the word of a "professional gambler") against an apparently honest man who, Hip Sing witnesses aside, appeared to be in the wrong place at the wrong time. With three other men who took part in the attack remaining unidentified, another key witness in China, and an apparent lack of motive for the Boston laundryman to attack Mock Duck, the Magistrate discharged Lee Sing. Attorneys Samuel Marcus and Frank Moss, representing the People and Mock Duck, argued that the prima facie case was made, but the Magistrate was unmoved. He did, however, state that he prolonged the hearing for the People and Mock Duck because he did not want to feel as if he was "discouraging" the good work of the Parkhurst Society.[28]

The attempted murder of Mock Duck marked the beginning of a change in the press coverage of the Hip Sing-On Leong war. Before this incident, the image of the Hip Sing Tong was that of the "Highbinders," widely viewed on the West Coast—and by extension New York—as a very violent, mysterious group. As for the On Leong Tong, it was commonly referred to in the positive, Americanized terms of "Freemasons" or "Merchant's Association." Its president, Tom Lee, was viewed as "the good Chinaman" and the venerable, wise and meek "Mayor of Chinatown." After this incident, the public perception of these organizations, and its leaders, was reversed. The Hip Sing Tong alliance with the Parkhurst Society cemented its perceived role as a reform faction bent on driving out vice and police corruption from Chinatown. The On Leong Tong was viewed as purveyors of vice and the friend of crooked cops and Tammany hacks.

By this time, Sing Dock had returned from San Francisco. Ironically, a close friend of his, Gin Gum, was recruited by the On Leong Tong to serve as their interpreter and he arrived at roughly the same time. Gin Gum was a capable leader and helped turn a discouraged and reeling On Leong Tong around after its early setbacks at the hands of the Hip Sing Tong and the Parkhurst Society. According to Gong and Grant, before leaving California for New York, Gin Gum and Sing Dock promised to never advocate the harm of the other during the conflict. Openly enemies, they were secretly friends throughout the entire conflict.[29]

On Friday, 25 November 1904, a skirmish occurred outside of 10½ Bowery that typified the On Leong's collusion with the local police. The previous Wednesday morning, some On Leong stole the Hip Sing crest from Hip Sing Tong headquarters. This act was a direct challenge and a message of warning to the Hip Sing Tong. As a result, the Hip Sing members readied themselves for a more violent On Leong assault. They quickly realized that a recuperating Mock Duck would make a prime target.

The assassination of Mock Duck remained a primary objective of the On Leong. After recuperating from his wounds at the hospital, Mock Duck was released. Soon Mock Duck was convalescing at Hip Sing headquarters, where he enjoyed the luxury of a twenty-four hour bodyguard of *boo how doy*. Mock Duck was scheduled to give testimony the next week against his assailant, Lee Sing, in the Court of General Sessions. When the On Leong *boo how doy* attacked Hip Sing headquarters, it was logical to assume that

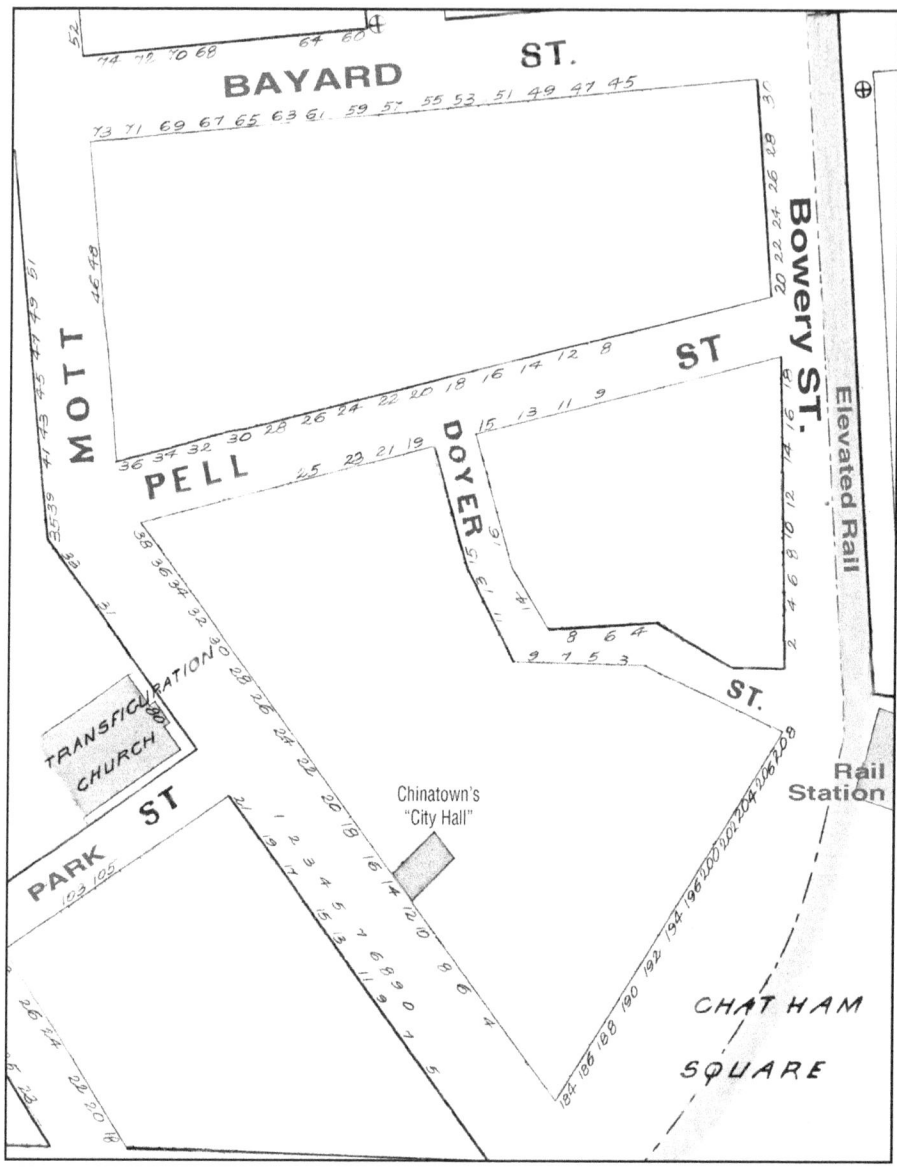

The streets and addresses of New York's Chinatown (Robinson and Pidgeon, *Atlas of the City of New York*, 1893. Adapted by Melodie Tune, SDSU graphic designer).

they would come after Mock Duck. After all, a dead man could not testify against their tong brother.

Knowing that there would be shooting in the streets after Mock Duck was taken from the hospital to the Hip Sing headquarters on Tuesday, November 22, all of the local merchants closed up their stores. The hit on Mock Duck was originally scheduled for Thanksgiving night, November 24, but Inspector Brooks was notified and a number of extra police were stationed in Chinatown to prevent trouble. When the On Leong *boo how doy* eventually reached Hip Sing headquarters a couple of days later, gunfire erupted between them and the Hip Sing guards. Though no tong members were hit, two non–Chinese were shot in the crossfire, one of whom died later that evening.[30]

Gong and Grant provided another motive for this assault. In their version, it was Hip Sing President Huey Gow (or Huie Kin[31]) that was the intended victim. Warned beforehand that an attempt would be made on his life when he returned from the theater to Chinatown via the Chatham Square rail station, Huey Gow ordered his men to watch out for him. He also ordered that Sing Dock, who was very ill, not be told of the situation, for undoubtedly he would rush to the fight, probably even taking it to the enemy. When Huey Gow did return, On Leong *boo how doy* followed him to Hip Sing headquarters. Reinforcements were called for as the alarm was carried throughout Hip Sing headquarters. Wong Lock, Sing Dock's lieutenant, went downstairs to investigate and was immediately fired upon by the On Leong massed outside the building.[32] He and three other Hip Sing gunmen ducked for cover behind the steel posts of the elevated railway and began to return fire. Sing Dock, hearing the shots, ran down the stairs, two pistols in hand. He immediately took charge of the Hip Sing men and soon the On Leong *boo how doy* were on the run. At this point, Huey Gow grabbed the ill Sing Dock and dragged him upstairs. When the police arrived, the four Hip Sing men were arrested.[33]

Whether Mock Duck, Huey Gow, or both were the targeted victims of the assault, the incident still reveals the nefarious relationship between the On Leong Tong and the police of the Elizabeth Street station. Despite the fact that the On Leong were the clear aggressors in this incident, when the Elizabeth street station police arrived on the scene, they arrested the four Hip Sing guards. Only two of the On Leong aggressors were arrested, but only to serve as material witnesses. Such shenanigans would not go unnoticed by the reform community or the press.

Superintendent McClintock of the Parkhurst Society defended the accused Hip Sing and was furious at the actions of the police. He stated that "two weeks ago last Sunday, precinct detectives accompanied by a member of the On Leong, walked through the streets of Chinatown and searched members of the Hip Sing, pointing out by the latter for firearms. They searched not less than seventeen men, but found only one revolver." McClintock then took dead-aim at the corrupt Elizabeth Street police and their cozy relationship with the On Leong Tong:

> I have no hesitation in saying that the police are siding with the On Leong in this matter. They arrested only members of the Hip Sing last night. The On Leong started the fight, and the only ones from their membership taken into custody were two men who came along willingly as witnesses. We raided a score of the sixty gambling places in Chinatown last July, and members of the Hip Sing Tong have been our chief witnesses or have given us the first information leading to the raids. From an investigation we have since made we are led to believe that each one of the gambling places there was paying a weekly tribute of $15 and that a prominent member of the On Leong was handling the money.[34]

In terms of the On Leong "ownership" of public officials, a new twist occurred in the wake of this incident. In December 1904, Frank Moss, counsel for Parkhurst's Society for the Prevention of Crime, prophesied wholesale slaughter in Chinatown unless the police took steps to eradicate gambling in Chinatown. This was done before Magistrate Ommen in the Tombs Court. Assistant D.A. Garvan, the prosecutor of Mock Duck during his murder trials, replied to Moss' statement, "That is a most remarkable statement, it seems to me, to come from a former Police Commissioner." Moss responded by going straight to the key issue:

> Unless the gambling is stopped at once, I tell you there will be more murders, and I want the District Attorney's office to realize it. The control of the gambling privilege is the bone of contention between the two great Chinese secret societies—the Hip Sing Tong and the On Leong Tong. The only way to stop this contention, which will result in serious trouble, is to eliminate the gambling houses in the whole Chinese quarter. I am amazed to see the police and the District Attorney's office apparently protecting the gambling syndicate in this section.

Garvan told Moss that if he had solid evidence, the D.A. would act on it. "Yes," Moss replied sarcastically, "and you appear here on behalf of the On Leong Tong as though you were a paid attorney of that infamous organization."[35]

Continuing a corrupt police tradition, Captain Kear of the Elizabeth Street station responded to Moss's allegations in the most innocent manner: "As to gambling in Chinatown, I know of none. If there was any I would suppress it. I think that I know about as much about Chinatown as Mr. Moss does. As soon as I find any evidence of gambling I will arrest those interested."[36]

Not wanting to pass up the opportunity presented by a corrupt rival, Captain Flood of the adjacent Eldridge Street station led a raid the next night and arrested 56 Chinamen who were engaged in gambling on the top floor of a five story building on Bayard Street, which is adjacent to Chinatown. All arrested were said to be members of the On Leong Tong. Before this raid, most of the raids made on Chinese gambling joints occurred on the other side of the Bowery in the Elizabeth Street station's territory. This raid was widely viewed as a way for the reformers to embarrass Captain Kear, the Elizabeth Street station police and the district attorney's office, as well as to send a message to the On Leong that they were not fully protected, despite what their Elizabeth Street lackeys led them to believe while taking their protection money.[37] As *The Sun* concluded of this raid,

> The Hip Sings seem to have the On Leong on the run. They have made gambling in Chinatown almost impossible, and this last stroke shows that they are going to keep after it, with the help of the Parkhurst people, until they run out of the city. According to Chinese procedure, there are two courses open to the Lee Company, owners of the gambling interest and employers of the On Leong. One is to let the Hip Sing in on the graft—a thing for which that company has worked for two years. The other is to have the On Leong resume their shooting, with a view to scaring the Hip Sings out of the game.[38]

As a result of this raid, evidence of police frame-ups and corruption, and the public sympathy gained from the shooting of the "reformer" Mock Duck, the Hip Sing Tong possessed all of the momentum. It appeared that they were well on their way to realizing their goals of defeating the On Leong Tong and controlling their own enterprise syndicates. They did not know, however, that their momentum would soon be taking them in the opposite direction.

The Tide Turns

A week after the Hip Sing Tong instigated their successful raid against the On Leong on Bayard Street, the On Leong Tong began to flex its considerable muscle. It began when the Elizabeth Street police raided a gambling room in the basement of 5 Mott Street and 18 Hip Sing were arrested for gambling. On the promise to provide investigators further evidence, Sing Moh, an alleged proprietor of the establishment, was held, while the other seventeen were released for lack of evidence. Attorney E. F. Price, on behalf of the accused Hip Sing members, said that the arrests "showed spite on the part of police, who have been accused before of favoring the On Leong Tong.[39]" As for the accused, they said that they "were in the act of raising a fund for a big dinner when the police broke in."[40]

Aware of these incidents, the Parkhurst Society chose to view them as set-ups or rumors. For example, Thomas McClintock stated that the Parkhurst Society had not been duped to take part in a "blackmailing scheme" against the On Leong Tong. As a matter of fact, the reputation of the Hip Sing Tong did not detour their alliance against Chinatown graft and vice. In the sarcastic assessment of *The Sun*, "Although the Hip Sings elsewhere are thugs, murderers, dealers in slaves, and blackmailers, Mr. McClintock believes that the New York Hip Sings are rather worthy persons. Something in the Atlantic breeze may soften the nature of the sternest Hip Sing and make his heart pure."[41]

Despite their professed innocence, Hip Sing apologies and platitudes rang hollow. The Hip Sing Tong was expertly manipulating the Parkhurst Society. The whole time the Hip Sing were playing the part of the reformer for the Parkhurst Society and the New York City press and public, they were implementing a duplicitous agenda. By eradicating On Leong gambling establishments, not only did they financially hurt On Leong members, they created opportunity for their own. It appears that after the raids, Hip Sing members would take the gaming operation over, thereby increasing the power and presence of their tong in Chinatown. A power syndicate thereby took on the added functions of an enterprise syndicate. Their reform-minded American counterparts took the Hip Sing Tong's reform agenda at face value, but over time Hip Sing manipulation could not be ignored and the relationship would eventually be terminated.

In addition to their powerful Parkhurst Society allies, the Hip Sing countered On Leong efforts to shut down their operations and to blunt police harassment by using American law. They reportedly sought court injunctions against police raids at Hip Sing related establishments unless probable cause was shown. *The New York Times* provided an example of such a case:

> Alleging that the police are oppressing the members of two Chinese literary organizations in Chinatown, Daniel O'Reilly and Maurice Meyer, counsel for the Chinamen, obtained from Justice Blanchard an order directing Police Captain Kear to show cause Monday in the Supreme Court why an injunction should not issue restraining the Captain and his men from interfering with the Chinamen's club rooms.

Chong Bock, President of the Wing Fut Club, signed one petition to the court and Chu Wing Kin, President of the Clan of Chu, signed another. Not only did they ask the court for an injunction, the plaintiffs also asked for damages from the Police Captain for picketing the Wing Fut premises at 20 and 22 Pell Street and the Chu Clubhouse at 10 and 12 Doyers Street.[42]

This legal and political sparring eventually escalated to the violence Frank Moss prophesied in December. It broke out at 1:00 A.M. Tuesday morning, 31 January 1905. According to two police detectives, a "well-dressed Chinaman, Americanized in every respect—queue cut off, derby hat, lace shoes, and looking like a Chinese Sunday-school teacher—" "entered the building located at 17 Mott Street, a known On Leong hang out located across the street from On Leong Headquarters. A minute later, two shots rang out from the building.[43]

Upon hearing the shots, the detectives hurried into the building. When they reached the second floor landing, they found the "well-dressed Chinaman," later identified as none other than Huie Fong, "gasping and flopping like a landed trout, with blood pulsing from two holes in his breast." He died soon after their arrival. Standing over the dying man, the detectives sensed movement nearby and turned towards its direction. With the detectives' attention inadvertently drawn, Yee Lee, an On Leong Tong-associated laundryman, bolted from his hiding place. The detectives quickly chased Yee Lee down and arrested him.[44]

Huie Fong reportedly lived at 8 Bowery, a Hip Sing lodging house next door to the Hip Sing headquarters that was the sight of the On Leong attempted assassination of Mock Duck or Huey Gow the previous November.[45] The Sunday night before Huie Fong was murdered, there was a Hip Sing-inspired police raid of On Leong gambling establishments at 28 Mott Street, 24 Pell Street and 18 Doyers Street. This crackdown occurred soon after other raids aimed at preventing the On Leong from establishing new gambling dens in the neighboring Eldridge Street precinct.[46] After the first set of raids, the On Leong Tong reportedly issued the following decree: "For every raid [of their establishments], there would be a dead Hip Sing." Huie Fong, *The Sun* reported, was murdered in retaliation for these raids, as well as for the fact that "he was hated in Chinatown for other reasons than his prejudice against gambling...."[47]

On 24 February 1905, prosecutors charged that the On Leong assassin mistook Huie Fong for the Reverend Huie Kin. Huie Kin himself testified that he was the intended target of the assassin. The assassin mistakenly shot and killed Huie Fong, Huie Kin's cousin.[48] This would have made Huie Kin, not Huie Fong, the man who was so "hated in Chinatown."[49]

Despite Huie Kin's statement, there was still a very strong reason why the On Leong Tong would want Huie Fong dead. After all, Huie Fong provided valuable testimony against Luie Foung, the man who shot and killed Tam Wah Toy roughly four months earlier.[50] Needless to say, both Huie Kin and Huie Fong made valuable targets for the On Leong Tong.

Speaking on behalf of the On Leong Tong three days after the shooting, Gin Gum had a different spin on the incident: "Huie Fong was killed by his own Hip Sings. They were laying [in wait] for an On Leong and got the wrong man. It was their plan to shoot Tom Lee just when all the firecrackers were going loudest, so that the police wouldn't notice."[51] Considering the harsh Hip Sing response to Huie Fong's murder, however, Gin Gum's words lack credibility. Undoubtedly, one of the two Hip Sing versions (or even a mixture of the two) is what transpired.

The day after the murder of Huie Fong, Chinatown was covered with placards offering a $3,000 reward for the death of Tom Lee. The reward was offered by the Hip Sing Tong as retribution for the attempted murder of one of its leaders and the actual murder of one of its members. In addition to Tom Lee, three other On Leong leaders[52] were held directly responsible in this manner. According to On Leong member Lee Moy, rumor had it that the Hip Sing Tong sent for *boo how doy* from its sister branch in Boston to murder these men during the upcoming Chinese New Year festivities, which were to begin the next day. In response to the actions of the Hip Sing Tong, Tom Lee requested and received a personal bodyguard of Elizabeth Street police officers and detectives, who guarded his person and his 16 Mott Street office.[53]

At first there was no violent retaliation by the Hip Sing Tong. However, an undisclosed "stool pigeon" informed the police about a pai gow establishment at 33 Mott Street, which the police then raided early in the morning on 13 February 1905. Which tong suffered as a result is unknown, though considering the address, it was most likely the On Leong Tong.[54]

The same day as this raid, *The Sun* reported a rumor that was floating around Chinatown. The rumor held that war between the two tongs "may soon be called off and that Chinatown gambling may be resumed as merrily as ever." In one of the few examples of excellent reporting about this conflict, *The Sun* explained the dynamics at work:

> Street rumor, which takes the place of newspapers in Chinatown, now has it that the Hip Sings have formally offered to quit informing for an even $10,000 to be paid by the Lee family through the On Leongs to the head of the Hip Sings. The privilege would be worth the price, for when gambling flourishes all Chinatown is prosperous, but the On Leongs have no faith in a Hip Sing promise to quit. They argue that, if they pay up, the Hip Sings will be back again in a few months for another payment. Therefore the offer is not likely to be accepted.[55]

The Hip Sing Tong apparently made its offer and the On Leong Tong apparently refused it, because soon after the anticipated Hip Sing retribution came to fruition.

On 25 February 1905, Hip Sing member Ong Fong[56] shot Tom Lee's "lieutenant," Lee Yu, in front of 36 Mott Street. As *The New York Times* reported it, Ong Fong was in Chinatown with Superintendent McClintock of the Society for the Prevention of Crime when the crime occurred. The police said Ong Fong pursued the 58-year-old Lee Yu through Pell and Mott Streets and, in the presence of McClintock, fired three shots at his victim, one striking him in the head.[57]

Before he died, Lee Yu reportedly identified Ong Fong to police as his assailant, saying his motivations came from the recent feud between their two tongs. Policeman Lang of the Elizabeth Street station said he witnessed what happened as well. According to Lang, Ong Fong admitted he shot Lee Yu, and said he did so because Lee Yu slapped him in the face. However, McClintlock directly countered Lang's statement. McClintock insisted that Ong Fong did not do the shooting and was completely innocent, that the police were making a terrible mistake. McClintlock maintained that the shooter was the very person he and Ong Fong were searching for that day. McClintock was to serve a warrant on this man, but never got the chance. Despite McClintock's voucher, Elizabeth Street police arrested Ong Fong.[58]

The manner in which these events were carried out do not make sense when one considers both the moral station and public reputation of the reformer McClintock and the well-known corrupt practices of the Elizabeth Street police. It was very likely that the identifications given by the victim and the officer, as well as Ong Fong's alleged confession, were bogus. If this was the case, it would have been just one more staged attempt by Elizabeth Street police and the On Leong Tong to sully the reputation and credibility of both the reformers and the Hip Sing Tong.[59]

Additionally, there is a reasonable possibility that Ong Fong is Dong Fong, a leader of the Hip Sing Tong that Frank Moss befriended during his work on the Lexow Committee during the mid–1890s. Moss stated that Dong Fong had a reputation as an "old villain" in Chinatown, but he trusted the man to identify gambling joints in Chinatown.[60] What Dong Fong's or, by extension, the Hip Sing's motivation was in providing this service is unknown. If Ong Fong is Dong Fong, this would explain an additional grudge the On Leong Tong would have against the man. Furthermore, it suggests the On Leong Tong/Hip Sing Tong feud may have originated during the days of the Lexow Committee.

The Return of Mock Duck

"Chinatown in Terror; Mock Duck Is Back" was the headline of *The World* on 18 March 1905. Earlier that day, Tom Lee and his lieutenants stated that Mock Duck had been in San Francisco to recruit more *boo how doy* and that he had just returned to Chinatown with his recruits in tow. Allegedly, Mock Duck wasted no time putting these men to use, for an On Leong member named Ju Hong[61] stated that he saw Mock Duck direct two *boo how doy* towards him as he was leaving his store at 24 Mott Street. One of the *boo how doy* placed a revolver in Ju Hong's belly, only to be prevented from firing by a detective who happened to witness the scene. The two *boo how doy* were arrested.

Commenting on Mock Duck's alleged involvement, Captain Kear of the Elizabeth Street station proclaimed, "He is a dangerous character. While he was away, quiet reigned in Chinatown. We have had weeks of rest."[62] The police subsequently arrested Mock Duck for allegedly threatening the lives of On Leong members. Rumor had it that Mock Duck was seen passing out papers on the streets of Chinatown earlier that day, papers which advertised substantial prices for the heads of Tom Lee and half-a-dozen other "Chinese notables."[63]

In addition to the Elizabeth Street police and the On Leong Tong, reform District Attorney William Travers Jerome wanted Mock Duck off the street as well. Consequently, he charged Mock Duck, once again, with the five-year-old murder of Ah Fe. At Mock Duck's arraignment, his counsel, Frank Moss, appealed to the Court:

> The District Attorney acted properly, undoubtedly. In having Duck arrested on the information that came to him, that he had come back from California to commit murder. As a matter of fact, this is untrue. Duck is the most inoffensive person in Chinatown. The persecution of him is due to the fact that at certain times he aided a certain

society in getting evidence about gambling in Chinatown, and has been invaluable to that society.

Moss then pointed out that Jerome had dismissed a murder indictment on the same charge some months ago. Jerome, handling the case himself, rose, smiled broadly at Moss, then fired back at his former partner-in-reform:

> This simple, angelic creature, as counsel would have it appear, has been twice tried for murder. The first time the jury voted ten to two for conviction. There are at least ten men who believe he is guilty of murder. It is true that I consented to the dismissal of the indictment charging murder because I had doubts if it would ever be possible to get a conviction. I still have those doubts. But when valuable information is laid before me to the effect that he intended to come back to New York bent on murder, I don't think we should pick and choose the methods.

Not wanting to miss an opportunity to slam his rivals Parkhurst and Moss, Jerome continued: "I might add that until a certain society in this city began to "monkey" and "butt in" around with Oriental affairs, we heard of nothing but gambling in Chinatown among the classes there. Since that certain society interfered plenty of shooting scrapes have been there."[64] Ever the pragmatist, Jerome was less concerned with gambling than he was with disruptions in the social world of organized crime that led to bloodshed on the streets of New York City.

Interestingly, there was more at stake for the opposing counsel in this legal contest than the fate of Mock Duck. As mentioned, Moss and Jerome were once former allies during the heyday of the reform movement. Moss and Jerome served on the Lexow Committee together and, along with John Goff,[65] defended officer Charles Gardner, a well-known ally of the Parkhurst Society. Police Chief William Devery, long the principal target of reform investigations into New York Police Department corruption, sought to discredit Parkhurst by framing Gardner for bribery.[66] Through these and other

District Attorney William Travers Jerome (O'Connor, *Courtroom Warrior*).

contacts, Moss and Jerome earned their substantial reform credentials side-by-side.

Eventually, Moss and Jerome split over the treatment of a Parkhurst Society-backed police captain, Max Schmittberger, who provided valuable testimony during the Lexow Committee hearings on police corruption. Once a "bag man" for his Captain, Schmittberger collected money from gambling houses and horse rooms for himself after he was promoted to the same rank. He would then turn over a percentage to his superior officers. Schmittberger broke the police "code of silence" when he testified before the Lexow Committee, explaining how the police collected graft from illegal activities, as well as what happened to the money once collected.[67]

Despite his valuable testimony, Jerome objected to Schmittberger's corrupt past and therefore he attempted to block Schmittberger's advancement within the New York Police Department. Moss and the Parkhurst Society, on the other hand, believed in forgiveness and asserted that the man had redeemed himself because of his valuable testimony and subsequent service to the reform cause. The split between Jerome and Moss became quite acrimonious and personal. It also became even more aggravated when Moss backed Mock Duck and the Hip Sing Tong, a man and an organization Jerome viewed as responsible for the new glut of violence in Chinatown. Add to this their battle over the symbolic leadership of New York City's reform movement and one can better appreciate the larger issues at stake in this trial.[68]

Nonetheless, the arrest of Mock Duck did not dissipate tensions in Chinatown. Instead the Hip Sing Tong and the Parkhurst Society "sent a message" to Jerome, the On Leong Tong and the Elizabeth Street police that they were not going to back down. On 24 April 1905, the Hip Sing Tong again took the offensive against On Leong gambling establishments. A "spectacular" raid resulted in roughly 200 Chinese being arrested. Police Commissioner McAdoo gave the order after he received tips from the Hip Sing Tong about gambling establishments. His main motivation, it seems, was responding to public pressure to act on the police inactivity resulting from the corruption of the Elizabeth Street precinct.[69]

The sheer numbers of gamblers arrested reportedly caused the Magistrate to lose his patience a dozen times. When it was all over, he remarked that it was "the worst farce he ever saw." With so many men in custody, chaos reigned at the station and the courtroom. Present at the court was Superintendent McCormick, Assistant D.A. Lord, Deputy Assistant D.A.s Kernochan and Corrigan, and lawyers Daniel O'Reilly[70] and Stephen J. O'Hare, who represented a number of the defendants. Standing with McCormick were two Chinese men who attempted to identify the defendants. One of these two was Jim Wing, a Methodist missionary and a trusted informant for the Parkhurst Society. The other was Chow Young, an employee of the Parkhurst Society. The chief ally of the Parkhurst Society and the Hip Sing Tong in this operation was a reform police Captain named Eggers. Eggers was reportedly so successful with his raids that he had a price placed on his head by unidentified parties. For their part, Tom Lee and others said the places Captain Eggers raided were merely boarding houses.[71]

Despite public displays of solidarity, the Parkhurst Society was catching on to their manipulation at the hands of the Hip Sing Tong. Referring to the arrests of both Hip Sing and On Leong in the raid, an increasingly skeptical Inspector McClintock observed the following:

> This is a fair sample of the cunning of the Chinese. Back of all this is nothing but the fight between two rival factions of On Leong Tongs and the Hip Sing Tongs. That kind of bickering, with an occasional instance of bloodshed, goes on wherever Chinamen congregate in numbers. The moment the white men try to meddle, the Chinese turn and make the white men take part in their fights. You see it right here. These fellows have already got almost every executive officer of this county and city mixed up in this squabble. The On Leong Tongs began by gaining the support of the precinct police. Then the Hip Sing Tongs made up to the Parkhurst Society and posed as reformers and informers. The next countermove by the On Leong Tongs was to get the assistance of the District Attorney. Then the Hip Sing Tongs went straight to Commissioner McAdoo.[72]

Police Commissioner McAdoo had his own explanation for his actions. After citing gambling and blackmail as the two biggest evils of Chinatown, he publicly stated,

> This action was taken to convince Chinatown of two things: That the law against gambling and kindred vices is the same in Chinatown as in the rest of the city; and above all, second, that paying blackmail or giving money to anyone for protection is wasting it; that there is only one "man higher up" in New York, and he is at 300 Mulberry Street, and I am that man: that the more money they pay the less protection they will get.[73]

A couple of days later, Tom Lee was arrested on the charge of extorting money from gamblers. This was yet another episode in what the press now labeled the "queer war" between the rival tongs which pitted District Attorney Jerome, various factions of the NYPD and the Parkhurst Society against each other. Superintendent McClintock of the Society instigated Lee's arrest by directly or indirectly giving him marked money that was soon found in the possession of police officers.[74] According to *The New York Times*, Commissioner McAdoo or Captain Eggers were not forewarned as to the identity of the man to be arrested. Rather a resourceful Superintendent McClintlock reportedly called the Commissioner and said he had a warrant for the arrest of a Chinese gambler based on his own sting operation. Commissioner McAdoo assigned Detectives Hickey and Standish, who met McClintock and Agent Robert S. McLellan of the Parkhurst Society. They proceeded to arrest Lee during his lunch at 14 Mott Street.[75]

According to McClintlock, "Lee had been for some time exacting $15 a week or fraction of a week for each gambling table in Chinatown," a number estimated at roughly 95. McClintlock said that he had evidence to show that all of this money did not stay with Lee either, that some of it went to those "higher up." Jim Wing, a former preacher and a Hip Sing, provided the evidence against Lee. Needless to say, McClintlock's unilateral and underhanded actions severely damaged relations between the Police Commissioner and the Parkhurst Society.[76]

Meanwhile, the On Leong Tong retaliated against the Hip Sing Tong for its role in Tom Lee's arrest. As mentioned earlier, the On Leong Tong nudged the District Attorney's Office into the fray on their behalf. Subsequently, Mock Duck was charged once again with the 1900 murder of Ah Fe and arrested, only to be released soon after on the condition he leave town. Mock Duck and Tom Lee were both brought in to "discuss" the situation with Commissioner McAdoo. After the meeting, McAdoo said he told both men that gambling must stop and they and their tongs must stop carrying pistols.[77]

Words aside, McAdoo wanted to teach both of the tongs a lesson. He ordered that no sightseeing autos were to be allowed in Chinatown. From now on, he declared, they must park on the Bowery and walk in on foot. Officially, McAdoo said he ordered this because firefighting apparatuses could not pass the large sightseeing busses on the narrow streets. Unofficially, McAdoo's real intent was to instigate strong economic repercussions on the entire Chinatown community and, hence, force the two tongs to settle due to merchant and community pressure from Chinese and non–Chinese alike. As an added incentive, McAdoo ordered Acting Captain Eggers and his officers to actively look for violators of the excise law. For the first time in many years, Chinatown's drinking establishments were forced to shut down at 1 A.M.[78] Since the saloon was the gateway to the larger engines of commerce and vice in the area, this action had strong potential for success. After all, customers could easily find other neighborhoods where the police were less interested in policing and regulating their recreational pursuits.

Nonetheless, McAdoo underestimated the animosity between the two tongs. Undaunted by the Commissioner's moves, on 30 May 1905 the On Leong Tong reciprocated for the raids inspired by the Hip Sing Tong during the previous four weeks. About 75 Elizabeth Street police raided Hip Sing gambling establishments in "the biggest and most spectacular daylight raid Chinatown ever witnessed." The police took 28 prisoners and several wagonloads of gambling paraphernalia. Tom Lee was at his home on Riverside Drive when the raid occurred. When asked if he instigated the blow to the Hip Sing "solar plexus," he responded, "Fine day for Declaration Day; fine day to plant flowers on grave." Sixteen "Chinamen" served as spies for police and appeared as witnesses. In a commentary on the newly dashed hopes for peace, *The New York Times* predicted, "the dead dove of peace will probably be served to Mock Duck in Chinatown's leading restaurant."[79]

11

"The Dead Dove of Peace"

The Hip Sing Tong waited until August for their next, and most extraordinary, move. According to Gong and Grant, it was a move planned and carried out by Sing Dock and a new Hip Sing mercenary named Yee Toy. It occurred when some Hip Sing entered the packed Chinese Theater on Doyers Street from front and back. Then a string of firecrackers were lit. The firecrackers signaled a volley of gunshots and a flurry of knife attacks on targeted On Leong. Some of the Hip Sing blocked the exits so that the numerous patrons in the packed theater were trapped.[1]

Three On Leong were killed instantly and at least 20 were seriously injured. Police arrested twenty, but some escaped, including Sing Dock and Yee Toy. Roughly twelve of these men were eventually incarcerated. Sing Dock's friend Gin Gum of the On Leong Tong cited jealousy and revenge for On Leong testimony against Mock Duck in a recent gambling trial as reasons for the attack.[2]

Later that evening Mock Duck was arrested for planning the ambush, despite having an excellent alibi. Earlier that evening, near Chatham Square, one lone patrolman arrested twenty-four Chinese gamblers affiliated with the Hip Sing Tong. Upon hearing of this, Mock Duck rushed to pay their bail. He was at the police station when the shootings took place.[3]

The day after the attack, Mock Duck was out on $1,000 bail. Within minutes, he was reportedly on the streets, almost near tears but still consoling others. One press account sarcastically called him "the smiling ally of virtue," reminding its readers of his connection to the Parkhurst Society. Mock Duck and fifty other Chinese were arraigned in Centre Street Court that morning. Half, including Mock Duck, were turned over to Coroner Scholer by Magistrate Breen to determine if charges could be substantiated. The other half of the Chinese arraigned were arrested in the previously mentioned gambling house raid in Chatham Square.[4]

The Chinese Theater Massacre proved a critical blow to the Hip Sing image in the American media. Specifically, the media that had fostered

Outside the old Chinese Theatre on Doyers Street (Asbury, *The Gangs of New York*).

Mock Duck's reformist reputation now vilified him. For example, *The New York Times* turned decisively against Mock Duck in an 8 August 1905 editorial entitled "Alibi of Mock Duck." This blatantly racist piece began by stating that the "wisdom of the East must be met with the brute force of Western unbelief." It compared the "reformer Duck" to his legal adversary, D.A. William Travers Jerome. It noted Mock Duck's use of "large caliber pistols and Black Art" in his evil endeavors. Mock Duck was viewed as a "canny oriental," which inspired "a number of rather disjointed reflections and a new admiration for the wisdom of the East." By looking at Mock Duck, the report maintained, it was no wonder that the West preaches exclusion of Chinese.[5]

Another harsh *New York Times* editorial published on the same day differentiated between "respectable" Chinese and others. It explained that gambling, associations, personal quarrels and assassinations were "somewhat tolerable," but riots that were "carefully planned" and "ruthlessly carried out" created a new level of social concern. It noted that the "prime condition" for residence in this country for "natives and immigrants is decent orderliness and respect for the rights of others as defined by law and by the consensus of public opinion." Organizations of violence and murder could not be tolerated, for they could "set up a rule of their own in defiance of the law for members of such organizations." It concluded that if they attempted to continue with this behavior, "the Chinamen who are already here will be treated with the utmost severity according to their deserts."[6]

The New York Daily Tribune also threw its two cents in with a prominent anti–Mock Duck article. This article served as the first contemporary history of the conflict. This history, however, is fundamentally flawed, relying of hearsay and perpetuating myth. Nonetheless, it is the historiographical foundation of subsequent journalistic and scholarly treatments of the conflict. Long time non–Chinese residents of Chinatown told the paper that the Chinese Theater ambush was not the climax of a war, as the police had said, but just the beginning. They noted that a circular for an explosives company was found on one of the suspects, indicative of future violence. Gambling, the paper reported, was the root of all the violence. To underscore this opinion, it pointed (with no justification of fact) to the "over 50 Chinamen slaughtered in the quarter over gambling rows."[7] Turning to authorities like D.A. Jerome and Commissioner McAdoo did no good, it argued, because they were respectively incompetent and corrupt.

The New York Daily Tribune reported that it was the success of the On Leong Tong and Tom Lee with gambling enterprises that reached San Francisco and brought Mock Duck to town. The On Leong members laughed at the young Mock Duck when he demanded a share of the gambling revenue, for why should they share their spoils with him? Mock Duck then tried to undercut the protection given to gambling establishments by the On Leong Tong. Nonetheless, the gamblers refused and reported him to the On Leong Tong. At this point, Mock Duck allied himself with the Hip Sing Tong and took what Chuck Connors said was a reform role as the "Jerome of Chinatown" by allying himself with the Parkhurst Society.[8]

New York's Chinatown, unlike San Francisco's, did not have a tradition of "Highbinders." Hence, reported *The New York Daily Tribune*, the first Hip Sing efforts were sloppy and ineffective, resulting in innocents getting shot, and Mock Duck employing professionals from San Francisco. Red posters went up in Chinatown putting a $3,000 price on Tom Lee's head and a smaller sum on the head of the On Leong Tong's Secretary, Gin Gum. The On Leong began to feel the heat and Tom Lee got scared and asked for police protection. After several murders and charges and countercharges of police corruption, Commissioner McAdoo pulled Elizabeth Street detectives off the case and charged Acting Captain Eggers' squad to keep the quarter clean. Mock Duck was told to leave the city, which he did (to San Francisco), but returned soon after with new "schemes."

The New York Daily Tribune's assault on Mock Duck's character then commenced in bigoted earnest. Using the typical language of "yellow-peril" journalism, it proclaimed, "Probably New York has never known a more successful 'boogie' man than he has become." He was worse than gangster Monk Eastman, members of the Five Points Gang, and even Jack the Ripper. His address was "wherever you hear the bark of a .44." Little Chinese children were warned, "Watch out, Mock Duck will get you!" As for the grown up children, they "almost turn pale under their yellow skins." According to Chinatown's residents, Mock Duck possessed supernatural abilities: bullets could not kill him, his eyes could see around corners, and his ears could hear a pin drop. Nevertheless, despite his reputation as a cold blooded killer, the police, who hated Mock Duck for the troubles he caused them, admitted that he never pulled the trigger. However, they quickly added, he did make the plans which resulted in the deaths of many.[9]

Reading this article, one must wonder if the reporter was paid by the On Leong Tong or its allies to write it. If one were to take it at face value, the tong war is better viewed as the evil Mock Duck versus the long-suffering On Leong Tong. Ignore the Hip Sing Tong, it implied, for they were just a means to an end for this dastardly villain, the physical incarnation of the yellow peril. Any hint of social, political, economic or criminological context is absent. Regardless of the report's veracity, this article, coupled with those of *The New York Times*, utterly demolished the reform reputations of Mock Duck and the Hip Sing Tong.

The repercussions of the Chinese Theater ambush were not limited to public perception for the Hip Sing Tong. On the morning of 12 November 1905, at a laundry on 11th Street and Avenue B, Hip Sing member Hup Lee was forcibly tied down onto his ironing board by five On Leong and slowly flayed him alive and hacked him to death while his feet were being tickled with a feather. Policeman Drescher of Union Market Station was warned by "fire house crank" Charley "the Hog" Smith that something was up at the laundry. Drescher burst into the room and arrested three of the assassins after a lively rooftop chase. Hup Lee identified two of the men before he died at Bellevue Hospital.[10]

On 14 November 1905, Deputy Assistant D.A. Kernochan summoned Tom Lee for questioning. Lee was to meet his lawyer, Frank Lloyd, at the corner of Franklin and Centre Streets beforehand. But before leaving, Lee was warned by his two lieutenants Gin Gum and Charlie Jong that four Hip Sing planned to kill him on his way to the office. Among them, they reportedly said, was Mock Duck. Lee then ran to the Criminal Courts building and alerted nearby police officers. The two cops noticed two men hiding on Leonard Street, but they escaped. Tom Lee claimed that Mock Duck was one of them. Tom Lee then informed the officers that the Hip Sing Tong had placed a $3,000 price on his head.[11]

Six days later, on 20 August 1905, shots were fired on the roof of either 13 or 15 Doyers Street, right above the infamous "Bloody Angle" formed by a sharp turn in the narrow, alley-like street. Acting Captain Tracy and his men responded, but once they got there, they heard shots on Pell

The "Bloody Angle" of Doyers Street as viewed from Pell Street (Asbury, *The Gangs of New York*).

Street. All but two of the cops responded to Hip Sing Tong headquarters on Pell Street. The victims were in a back room on the third floor. They included three members of the prominent Huie clan: Huie John Yok and Wee Wong, both severely wounded, and Huie Yee and Huie See. All gave their occupations as laundrymen. According to *The New York Daily Tribune*, four On Leong entered the Hip Sing headquarters and, "with less ceremony than the Japanese at Port Arthur," opened fire on the Hip Sing, wounding four. Later, an On Leong named Tom Su was arrested after being identified by witnesses.[12]

Two days later, the first public indications of the customary intervention by neutral parties to end the war began. In this case, F. F. Shah and Lock Wing, the Chinese Consul and Vice-Consul to New York City, reportedly called on Assistant District Attorney C. J. Nott to ask what his office could do to end the slaughter. According to *The New York Daily Tribune*, Shah was worried about the effect a few bad Chinese would have on the rest of the Chinese community. Several years ago, a similar outbreak was quelled in San Francisco when the Chinese Counsel warned the belligerents that their relatives in China might be harmed or killed if the fighting did not stop. *The Daily Tribune* speculated that the same threat was repeated this time as well.[13] This appeal was followed a few days later by an appeal by local merchants to China's Minister in Washington, Chentung Liang Chiang, to intervene in the conflict.[14]

Meanwhile, on 29 August 1905, Coroner Scholer's investigation into the Chinese Theater shootings led to the verdict that Ung Quong, Don Kim, Lee Dock and Loy Fook were the shooters, and that Mock Duck instigated and planned the attack. Mock Duck denied the accusation that he went to a gun shop the night before to purchase bullets for Colt revolvers. Wah Ju, janitor at the theater, said that he saw Mock Duck at the theater before the incident, then he disappeared for a while, only to come back

11. "The Dead Dove of Peace"

with seven or eight of his followers. Wah Ju also said he saw Mock Duck distributing fireworks to these men. The shooting followed soon after. Coroner Scholer stated that there was evidence establishing that Mock Duck was in the theater before the shooting and that, despite his denial and alibi, he had purchased ammunition. Assistant D.A. Kernochan wanted Mock Duck held without bail, but Scholer decided to set it at $5,000.

Two Central Office detectives testified that Li Gin, who died in the hospital, identified Ung Quong as the man who shot him and Don Kim as the man who shot and killed Li Yook. Dong Wah, a Westchester laundryman, swore that he saw Don Kim shoot Li Yook. Lee Chung said he saw Don Kim shoot, but did not see his victim. Li Ho identified Lee Dock as the man who shot and killed Ung Taing. Sam Sing testified he saw Ung Quong shoot Wah Kim. He also identified Lee Dock and Loy Fook as men who fired shots, but didn't know who their targets were. Finally, Tom Lee was said to have given information assisting the Coroner's inquest.[15]

While the criminal justice system was addressing crimes committed in the past, the violence continued in the present. On 17 November 1905, a "Wang Company man" named Moy Gung mistakenly murdered Loie Sung. Earlier that day, a Hip Sing named Woo Toy attempted to kill a Wang Company member named Moy Gung, but was unsuccessful after Moy Gung wrestled away the revolver. Both were arrested.[16]

Later that day, after being released into the custody of his (and Tom Lee's) counsel, Frank Lloyd, Moy Gung mistook Loie Sung for Woo Toy and killed him. Reportedly, a truce had been in effect after Mock Duck was taken to jail in The Tombs for the Chinese Theater shooting. The motive for the initial attempted hit on Moy Gung was not known, though *The New York Daily Tribune* speculated that it may have been precipitated by the alleged defection of Tom Lee's "Americanized," Yale graduate, nephew and secretary, Lee Toy, from the On Leong Tong to the Hip Sing Tong earlier that week.[17]

More police pressure on the Hip Sing Tong began on 15 January 1906. Captain Tracy ordered raids on gambling parlors and opium dens. Two successful raids occurred as a result. Detectives Miller, Cunniff, and Duffy arrested John Yohe of 11 Pell Street for selling policy numbers in one raid. In the other, detectives of Inspector Hogan's staff raided another Pell Street address and arrested nine men and confiscated ornamental opium paraphernalia. Captain Tracy promised he would "stamp out all Chinese gambling, even if he had to arrest every Chinaman in the district."[18]

On 24 January 1906, the Hip Sing Tong launched another ambush. The result left two On Leong dead and two seriously wounded. The On Leong were taken by surprise on Pell Street during Chinese New Year celebrations, traditionally a day of peace. As a result, the On Leong were off-guard. Before the incident occurred, the police had quelled a dispute between unknown men in front of a Pell Street shop. Fifteen minutes later, one dozen On Leong came off Mott Street onto Pell Street and entered a lodging house at 32 Pell Street. They were reportedly visiting relatives.[19]

The Hip Sing set up ambush positions in a nearby alley. Once the On Leong exited the building, the Hip Sing opened fire. The On Leong rushed across the street, returning fire. Tom Lee's cousin, Lee Soon, and a Mott Street laundryman, Chin Ying, were killed instantly. Fellow On Leong members Gong Yeong and Lee Toy, most likely Tom Lee's aforementioned nephew, were wounded. Captain Tracy and his officers quickly responded to the scene of the crime and six arrests were made, including four Hip Sing and the two wounded On Leong. Mock Duck was immediately sought by the police, who found him in his underwear at his residence on 4 Mott Street. Mock Duck said he knew nothing and the detectives did not arrest him. Despite this alibi, non-tong members said Mock Duck was on Pell Street not long before the shooting, talking to his fellows in vehement tones.[20]

Giving Peace a Chance

The week before the ambush murders of Lee Soon and Chin Ying, *The New York Times* reported that a peace agreement had been worked out between the two rival factions. Local merchants had mediated the agreement and NYPD Captain Tracy was informed that all grievances were to be put aside. He was also told that a big peace dinner was to be hosted by the Hip Sing Tong at the headquarters of the Chinese Freemasons on Pell Street. However, the On Leong leadership supposedly feared treachery and its members did not show up for the dinner.[21]

This development may explain the ambush on January 24. Perhaps the Hip Sing were responding to the breech of the agreement or, perhaps, it was the fact that Lee Toy was one of those targeted by the ambush. Earlier it was mentioned that he had defected to the Hip Sing Tong. There may have been some sort of treachery on his part that precipitated the ambush. *The World*, however, had a more practical explanation: the men who were killed were witnesses ready to provide alibis for the men accused of carving up Hup Lee on his ironing board on 12 November 1905.[22]

The police leadership finally had enough. On 26 January 1906, First Deputy Police Commissioner Waldo went on a "fact finding mission" to Chinatown with Captain Tracy and Detective McDonald. They interviewed Tom Lee and Gin Gum of the On Leong Tong and Mock Duck and Wong Get of the Hip Sing Tong. In Hip Sing headquarters, they noticed an unusual, though indicative, shrine of sorts; a painting of Frank Moss with the words "In God We Trust" engraved below it sitting opposite a joss. When asked for their assessment of the situation, Mock Duck and Wong Get blamed Tom Lee and the On Leong Tong. "Tom Lee told truth as a very young boy," they allegedly said, "but now he's a very old man." After the interview, all of the men walked outside. Waldo, it was reported, noticed that when Mock Duck walked by On Leong owned shops, the merchants closed them up. This was after Mock Duck pointed out his and his fellow Hip Sing's "persecution" for their righteous acts benefiting the

Parkhurst Society. For his part, Tom Lee diplomatically appealed for Waldo's intervention to end the bloodshed.[23]

Progress must have been made during these interviews, for the formal peace process began on 31 January 1906. Judge Warren W. Foster was chosen to mediate the peace talks. Also in attendance were the Chinese Emperor's Representative and a member of the Chinese Department of Treaty Revision, Dr. F. F. Tong; Chinese Consul to New York, Kit Fu Shah; and Guy Maine of the Chinese Reform Association. Representing the On Leong Tong were Moy Tow, Gin Gum, and Tom Lee. The latter stayed out of the negotiating room, communicating through his lieutenants. Thomas Dinnean was their counsel. Huey Gow, William Lee York and Louis Quong represented the Hip Sing Tong. Frederick A. Ware and Ely Rosenberg served as their counsel. Unnamed others also attended.

The press gave Judge Foster most of the credit for the truce that developed from this sit-down. One report revealed that the Hip Sing wanted "to smoke the peace pipe then and there," but the On Leong said the whole affair should be settled between the tongs themselves. This bickering, and the finger pointing which went along with it, was headed off by Foster with the following words:

> This business has gone on too far already, and it must be stopped at once. The rivalry between the tongs has reached such a stage that it reflects on the good name of this city, and threatens the business of that particular section. Now, if you wish your business to go on successfully, if you want to encourage sightseers down there, you must stop this bloodshed. If you can't agree among yourselves, then the law will bring a settlement.

A member of one faction observed that the two tongs would get along amicably if only "the bums and loafers" were driven out. These words were apparently heeded, because during the course of the meeting, the Hip Sing Tong effectively disowned Mock Duck, publicly blaming him for committing rash acts.[24]

This action illustrated a few points about both Mock Duck and his fellow Hip Sing. First, it showed that Mock Duck was expendable to the New York branch of the Hip Sing Tong. They could exist, and would continue to exist, without him. It also showed that he was not the omnipotent demon the non–Chinese press made him out to be. This was partially reflective of the internal politics of Hip Sing Tong at the time.

According to a later *New York Times* report, when Ton Bok Woo left Chinatown roughly five years before, it allowed for Mock Duck's power to grow proportionately within the tong. But in 1905, Ton Bok Woo returned from China. A split in the ranks of the Hip Sing Tong ensued. When Mock Duck was jailed for the Chinese Theater ambush, Ton Bok Woo successfully gained control of the Hip Sing Tong. Ton Bok Woo's ally, Wong Quon Sing,[25] was chosen as a replacement for Mock Duck's ally Huey Gow as President. This is most likely the reason why neither Mock Duck nor Wong Get attended the peace conference.[26]

Due in part to these leadership changes, the final result of the negotiations was an armistice that was declared until a treaty could be signed two days later. On 2 February 1906, details of the peace treaty were given:

- Guns and other weapons were banned in public.
- Tribute or taxes could not be levied, directly or indirectly, on any business or Chinaman under any pretext besides dues to a society.
- No member could be forced to pay a sum for a concession, privilege, favor or business opportunity.
- Members could not purchase or accept weapons as a gift.
- Tong members could not interfere with their rival's property.
- One representative of each society, in conjunction with the Chinese Counsel, had to investigate any treaty infractions, recommend "such sales as will tend to improve" Chinatown, and punish by fine any member guilty of misconduct.
- This committee should meet once a month.
- Gambling had to be discouraged and avoided.
- Both of the societies and members of the Chinese government had to promote peace and prosperity.
- Each society had to file "peace bonds" of $1,000 that, apparently, would be forfeited to the government if the peace was not maintained.[27]

What should have been greeted with aplomb from the press was treated skeptically, and rightfully so. For example, the very notion of a peace process itself was questioned in a *New York Times* editorial. It asserted that the peace process equated Chinese tongs to sovereign states. Instead, declared the *Times*, they must be held under, not above, American law, just like everybody else. The editorial granted that the situation was complex, but as criminals they did not differ from any other group. The editorial concluded by stating that *The Times* would breathe a sigh of relief like everybody else over recent developments, but other solutions should have been pursued.[28]

On 11 February 1906, the Hip Sing Tong hosted a peace dinner at 14 Pell Street, the Wang Ying Low Company restaurant. The On Leong did not attend because the peace treaty had not yet been ratified yet. Perhaps fearing an ambush, the On Leong were skeptical of the intent of the Hip Sing. To save face and stall for time, however, Tom Lee and the On Leong Tong sent their formal regrets. Periodically during the dinner, the Hip Sing in attendance would jubilantly yell "victory." The Americans who attended the dinner included Judge Foster's representative, Jacob Newman; Alderman and Hip Sing Tong counsel Frederick A. Ware and his wife; Hip Sing Tong counsel Ely Rosenberg; Lee York of the Philadelphia Chinese YMCA; and Agents McLelland and Hamilton of the Parkhurst Society. The President of the Hip Sing Tong, Wong Quon Sing,[29] and its Secretary, Yep Shung[30] hosted the dinner.[31]

The On Leong Tong hosted their own "far less pretentious" dinner in a Chinatown restaurant and a special performance at the Chinese Theater the next evening. Gin Gum, the master of ceremonies for the dinner, told the press that the Hip Sing Tong had been invited, but that they did not respond. Also invited to the dinner, but not attending, were various Supreme Court and General Sessions justices, District Attorney Jerome and Judge Foster. Although "principal police officials" were also invited, the only police presence in Chinatown that night were the roughly 45 officers that had been assigned to Mott, Pell and Doyers Streets as a safety measure ever since the Hip Sing festivities of the previous night. In addition, six plain-clothed officers were stationed at entrance points to On Leong headquarters. This mass presence surely reflected the little confidence police officials had in the peace treaty.[32]

This lack of confidence may have been well placed. While the two tongs celebrated, a rumor floated around Chinatown that suggested that Mock Duck and Wong Get were in the process of creating a new tong. This rumor, noted *The New York Times*, was the principal topic of conversation at the On Leong dinner.[33] It was also given credence during the Hip Sing dinner when the press, noting Mock Duck's absence, reported that he was "in the cellar" with the Tong.[34]

This rumor may be the by-product of Mock Duck's and Wong Get's loss of face and it would certainly be reasonable to assume that the two men would have taken this type of action. However, the lack of corroborating evidence about the actual formation of a new tong, coupled with Mock Duck's continued affiliation with the Hip Sing Tong in later accounts, may imply that the rumor was only a ruse on the part the Hip Sing Tong or On Leong Tong.[35] By identifying Mock Duck and Wong Get as the "troublemakers" behind the violence, and distancing themselves from them, both tongs gained credibility and enhanced their sullied reputations within the Chinese and non–Chinese community.[36]

Nevertheless, the rumor was enough to inspire some action against Mock Duck. On February 21, a week after the rumor was printed in the press, Mock Duck was arrested for the attempted bribery of two policemen. During the raid of a non–Chinese saloon at 12 Park Row, police fortuitously stumbled upon some Chinese men who were allegedly selling policy slips. The men were taken to the Elizabeth Street station, and, upon being notified, Mock Duck went there to post their bail. According to the police officers, Mock Duck offered fifty dollars for the release of his "cousins." He was subsequently arrested.[37]

Many parties had a vested interest in having Mock Duck behind bars, among them the police, the On Leong Tong, and the Hip Sing Tong. However, Mock Duck's counsel, Abraham Levy, did not blame them during his client's first appearance before Magistrate McAvoy. Rather, Levy accused Superintendent McClintock of the Parkhurst Society of framing his former client. Evidently, it was Mock Duck's perspective that the motivation for such an action was clearly drawn from his previous manipulation of the Parkhurst Society throughout the Hip Sing-On Leong conflict. This conspiracy theory, however, did not sway McAvoy. Taking note of the prosecutions reference to Mock Duck's danger to the community, bail was set at an exorbitant $5,000.[38]

Not able to raise bail, Mock Duck languished in The Tombs jail for almost two months before Levy won a reduction in the bail from Recorder John Goff, the old reform ally of Moss and Jerome. "For many moons," Levy informed Goff, "the authorities have charged this defendant with various crimes, and he is credited with being the head instigator of much of the past trouble of Chinatown; but he has never been convicted in any instance." He then told the court that the District Attorney's Office had not brought Mock Duck to trial for almost two months. When asked by Goff to explain this delay, Assistant District Attorney Garvan cited the ongoing investigation of the defendant's possible role in several murders. Undoubtedly knowing that the high-profile Garvan was the unsuccessful prosecutor of Mock Duck for the Ah Fe murder, Goff surely detected a hint of a personal vendetta toward the defendant. As a result, Goff did not accept the excuse and reduced Mock Duck's bail to $2,000, explaining that he believed the allegations of the District Attorney's Office and police were "exaggerated."[39]

The arrest of Mock Duck undoubtedly paved the way for the formal peace dinner between the On Leong Tong and Hip Sing Tong that took place on 29 March 1906. The CCBA hosted the dinner at Chu Gow's Port Arthur Chow House. The guest list reflected a small but impressive glimpse of the *guanxi* networks of the two tongs. In attendance were Judge Foster; Dr. F. Froman Tong, High Commissioner from the "Sun of Heaven;" President Joseph H. Singleton and Secretary Jue Chu of the Empire Reform Association; D. Caddy Herrick[40]; the former head of the Committee of Five (a Tammany-affiliated reform committee), Lewis Nixon; the Chinese Counsel General and the Chinese Vice-Counsel to New York City, General Shan Lock Wing; Sheriff "Tom" Foley; City Court Judges McCarthy and Colan; magistrates Moss, Steinert, Steen, Zeller, and Barlow; Congressman Henry Goldfogle[41]; and Fung Y. Mow of the Star Rescue Mission. Also in attendance were the officers of the two tongs. For the Hip Sing Tong, President Wong Quon Sing, Treasurer Huey Gow, and Secretary Yep Shung attended. Representing the On Leong Tong were its President Hoe Poch,[42] Vice-President Cheng Hun Sing, and Treasurer Lee Gong Yee.[43]

Despite the signing of the treaty and the subsequent feast, skeptics of the truce remained. Asked about the treaty, Chinatown saloon owner Scotty Lavelle—who reportedly knew "more about Chinatown than Chuck Connors ever forgot"—stated that the peace was a sham, noting particularly that the $1,000 "peace bond" was a joke.[44] Two days after the feast, *The New York Times* reported, "it now appears that while the peace is genuine enough, it has a strictly commercial basis." All the treaty did was divide the gambling profits between the On Leong Tong and the Hip Sing Tong. The five-year war had seriously decreased gambling profits due to street violence and police raids. As a result, the local economy was hurt as well. The On Leong leaders realized it was more lucrative to compromise with the Hip Sing Tong than to continue the war, so they went to the negotiating table. The resulting agreement established a holding company to divide gambling profits.[45]

The Art of Peace

The establishment of an equitable gambling trust sounds like a proper motive for peace, but was there another, more clandestine, motive as well? Indeed there was. The following March, it was announced that City Hall was taking steps to demolish Chinatown. Manhattan Borough President Ahearn had set March 20 as the date for a public hearing before the local improvement board to discuss wiping out Chinatown and establishing a small park within the boundaries of Bayard Street, the Bowery, Chatham Square and Park Row, Worth Street and Mulberry Street. Mayor McClellan was on the record favoring the plan and many of the interested property owners had signed the petition for the park that would cost $2,000,000.

Chinatown's land was assessed at $588,200, therefore its property owners, like Tom Lee and his On Leong brethren, would make out pretty well if they sold out. Possible relocation sites for its many Chinese residents included sites in Brooklyn, The Bronx and some land on the other side of the Williamsburg Bridge. Not surprisingly, Tom Lee and some of his associates owned a large part of the Williamsburg land and may have had interests in the other areas as well.[46] Considering the financial stake of Tom Lee and his associates and their strong political connections, it seems possible that they only agreed to peace with the realization that they were fighting for geographically-tied gambling rights that would not exist two years after the truce was signed.

By May, the American press made sporadic references to "stirrings" in Chinatown. In one case, three men, Lee Doong, Lee Foy Man and Chin Fin, signed a statement accusing Captain O'Connor of the Elizabeth Street station "with having Chinese collectors of tribute and with 'lifting the lid' on the fan-tan and the lottery houses on Mott, Pell, and Doyers Street." Only in the precinct for three weeks, Captain O'Connor adroitly dressed these accusations head on:

> It may be true that the Chinamen are collecting tribute and saying that they are getting money for the police ... and if they are I would like to have the chance to locate some of them at it. But the Captain is getting none of it, you may rest assured. I have been raiding the gambling houses in the Chinese quarter and doing the best I can to break up the gambling, but I always remember that this is the result: If the Captain raids them he is charged with making the raids to get the Chi-

namen in line for collecting money from them, and if he doesn't raid them, he has the charge made that they are all in line and paying.

Besides adversely affecting O'Connor, the allegation also put Tom Lee in the spotlight. With his recently recaptured credibility on the line, Lee was forced to respond to the possibility that the treaty, with its no gambling provision, was a sham, and that, in fact, a gambling trust was the result. Lee and Chin Sam (perhaps the same Chin "Four Flusher" Sam acquitted for the murder of Charlie Lee during the laundry riot of 3 September 1899[47]) denied the allegations and said that they were "hunting" for the men who made the allegations, men they accused of using fictitious names.[48]

What did this incident mean? The very fact that the allegation was made in the first place—coupled with the possible anonymity of the accusers and that there was apparently no follow-up by all sides involved—implies that a warning was being sent to Tom Lee and the On Leong Tong. Considering the broader political and criminal context of the allegation, namely the impending park proposal, perhaps the Hip Sing believed a light retort was called for. Perhaps this drove the public allegation of impropriety.

This retort, however, did not appear to work as intended, because another "stirring" occurred on May 22. *The New York Daily Tribune* reported that "some strange power [was] working below the quiet surface of apparent harmony between the tongs." The disruption of this harmony was evident in the fact that leaders of the Hip Sing Tong and On Leong Tong met at the office of the Chinese Consul to discuss "the gambling situation." The specific conflict that inspired the meeting was unknown to the reporter, but he implied that it was a refusal to go along with the Consul's mediative suggestions that prompted the On Leong representative to depart the meeting before a resolution was achieved.[49] The reporter, and a representative of the Hip Sing Tong, both predicted that conflict would begin if the matter was not rectified soon.[50]

How, why and when this particular conflict ended is unknown. What is known is what any visitor to contemporary New York City can see with their own eyes: The park proposal did not go through because a park was never built on the site of Chinatown. To this day, it is still centered on, and has grown subsequently around, Mott, Pell and Doyers Streets. Perhaps the failure of the proposal to go through was a sign of On Leong capitulation to pressure from the Chinese government, the police or other parties to honor the spirit of their agreement with the Hip Sing Tong. Conversely, perhaps the proposal died a natural political death. It should be noted, however, that the peace created by this truce did not last long after the park proposal died, for a second On Leong-Hip Sing tong war erupted a year later.[51]

Who won the first tong war? It is best viewed as a draw between the Hip Sing Tong and the On Leong Tong. The Hip Sing Tong gained the gambling "property rights" they sought from the start. It also increased its power relative to that of the On Leong Tong in the Chinese community, as well as in the larger, non–Chinese social system of organized crime of New York City. It did, however, lose the positive reform reputation it established with the American press and public during the early stages of the conflict. Yet this was a minor point, for the Hip Sing Tong did not have this reputation when the conflict began, therefore there was no real loss.

As for the On Leong Tong, it maintained its dominant position in Chinatown, even though it had to make room for another powerful voice in the affairs of the Chinese community. The conflict allowed the On Leong Tong to test the strength of their upperworld connections and they found them to be quite useful and effective. Although powerful On Leong members lost some of their share of existing gambling interests, they were compensated for these losses when gambling and other enterprises expanded into newly formed Chinese communities within the Greater New York City area.

The On Leong Tong-Hip Sing Tong conflict described here is improperly called a tong war. War implies a sense of permanency in victory, a permanency that is obviously absent in the rivalry and conflict between these two tongs that has lasted for roughly one hundred years. Instead of being viewed as a tong war, the conflict should be viewed as just the first of many battles between opposing organized crime syndicates, a reflection of the chaotic social world of organized crime and the larger social system of organized crime that is part and parcel to the American urban experience that was turn-of-the-century New York City.

Part IV

Organized Crime and the American Experience

12

Rethinking the Gangster Image

This historical study counters the conventional wisdom of academics, the media, and the government which collectively insist or imply that Chinese organized crime is either emerging, nontraditional, or both, or that it personifies a new international criminal threat to the United States. A century ago, Chinese organized criminals were involved symbiotically with the politics, economics, and social life of the Chinese-American community; infiltrated these aspects of life in the larger American society; and victimized Chinese and non–Chinese alike. Remarkably, they did this in the face of difficult language and cultural barriers, not to mention rampant institutional racism that was, at its best, discriminatory and, at its worst, violently hostile.

This study also indicates an interstate and international structure for these criminal networks. This counters the general belief that Chinese organized crime is only local in origin and influence. On the domestic level, illegal goods and services were demanded and supplied across neighborhood, city, county, and state lines. Concurrently, criminal enterprises such as opium smuggling and the trafficking of women necessitated organizational structures or connections overseas to ensure supply.[1]

This study also establishes that organized crime in the Chinese-American community is a long-term historical phenomenon. Its manifestations can be attributed to fundamental contradictions in the American society, politics, and economics that created numerous opportunities for professional criminals of all backgrounds and, in some cases, specifically for professional criminals of Chinese descent. For example, the illegal traffic of women, laborers, and opium were unintended consequences of anti–Chinese laws. Another example is that despite a hostile, racist climate, Chinese criminals were, for all intents and purposes, able to purchase protection and, to a fair extent, some semblances of equality and economic and political opportunity from corrupt politicians, police officers and government bureaucrats.

Nevertheless, placing organized crime in the Chinese-American community in the context of only the American experience should not be considered an exclusive approach. It should also be viewed as a product of Chinese culture and society as well, a point underscored by the research of scholars like Chin, Lyman, and Meyers. A strong, developed tradition of organized criminality existed in China long-before Chinese immigrants came to Gold Mountain. Consequently, professional Chinese criminals were familiar with crime and corruption as a way of life in China, and found it easy to adapt to the American manifestations of the same.[2] Additionally, Chinese criminals were able to adapt their tradition of *guanxi* to an American social system of organized crime already predicated on extensive upperworld/underworld networks. As a result, there certainly were more than enough non–Chinese willing to work in partnership with and, in some cases, as subordinates to Chinese enterprise and power syndicates, a mirror-image of conditions in the legitimate world. Organized crime was (and is) an equal opportunity employer in which multiethnic and multiracial networks focused on making money and gaining power, despite larger societal pressures to drive a wedge between groups on the basis of ethnicity and race.

Indeed, on a variety of levels the Chinese-American experience is one of broad engagement with the non–Chinese institutions and people of the United States. The idea of Chinese-Americans being passive in the face of widespread, race-inspired discrimination, violence and social control is a myth, a point underscored by research on the courts, the law, social integration, politics and economics. Indeed, the Chinese-American struggle for equal opportunity is a very active and long-standing one.[3] It should come as no surprise, then, that this broad engagement also occurred in the context of the social system of organized crime in the United States. Interestingly, engagement here resulted in one of the few areas in which Chinese-Americans could expect, and actually receive, a level playing field with non–Chinese in the United States, a playing field in which *guanxi* and the *Jiang Hu* subculture were not only adaptable, but critical instruments of success. In the end, the race-conscious social designations of "yellow" and "white" did not matter as long as they created the green of dollars when blended together.

While other Chinese-Americans worked diligently and bravely to remove racist laws and regulations, Chinatown gangsters instead saw opportunity for profit and power in these same laws and regulations. When Chinese organized criminals acted upon these opportunities, a small yet powerful segment of a historically victimized community became victimizers, not just of their own community, but of the larger society as well. They victimized their community not only in the direct costs of peddling traditional vices and engaging in extortion and acts of violence, but also by perpetuating a seedy criminal stereotype that was easily embraced by non–Chinese constantly looking for alien conspiracies. The result was a more poisoned racial climate; even harsher anti–Chinese rhetoric, laws, and policies; and the creation of ever more economic, social and political barriers for the entire Chinese-American community. Of course, ultimate blame remains with those who let xenophobia, racism and jingoism define the Chinese-American experience. However, Chinese gangsters certainly disrupted and intensified an already precarious situation.

These points are collectively embodied in the story of the social system of organized crime in New York City's Chinatown. This system was a fusion of two criminal sub-cultures, one Chinese and one non–Chinese. Both were composed of underworld and upperworld actors, as well as those who straddled the fine line between these two worlds. A Chinese social system of organized crime operated separately and independently from the larger "American" social system of organized crime.[4] However, it was simultaneously a key component of the American social system. At first glance, this duality may appear contradictory. Yet it is easy to comprehend when one considers the types of criminal activity in which Chinese gangsters engaged.

For example, some Chinese power syndicates specialized in enforcing the "property rights" of Chinese businesses and thereby worked entirely in a Chinese social system of organized crime. Conversely, some Chinese criminals formed enterprise syndicates that ran pai-gow games, opium dens, and brothels that served a multiethnic clientele, while also participating in the long-standing tradition of payoffs, bribery and graft routinized by non–Chinese upperworld actors.

In addition to systemic and organizational concerns, let us not forget the role of the individual in this phenomenon. When all is said and done, the men involved with organized criminal activity made conscious decisions to use their *guanxi*, power, or any other applicable attribute they possessed to break laws and victimize others in pursuit of illegitimate means to achieve the larger societal goals of social and economic mobility. In addition, it is this very emphasis on *guanxi* that allowed people like Tom Lee and Mock Duck, people who operated freely in the underworld of vice and violence, to form alliances with members of the upperworld. To view Chinese organized crime and criminals as the sole product of Chinese culture and American imperfections is to make a mockery of the countless Chinese who did not become organized criminals and who stayed clear of the "four vices." If this distinction is not made absolutely clear to the public by researchers, the media, and policymakers, the next wave of alien conspiracy, along with its implicit racism, will exacerbate racial tensions already underlying American society.[5]

The lessons to be learned here are not quirks of history. Rather, they point to the foundations of present-day Chinese organized criminal activities in the United States, and to their historical role in, and contributions to, the American social system of organized crime. By analyzing past and present tong wars, power syndicates and enterprise syndicates, in the light of the findings of this study, we can understand more clearly the true nature of Chinese organized crime and how to counter it. Avenues for exploration might include the activities of Chinese professional criminals during the Prohibition era when the attention of the criminal justice system was directed towards non–Chinese bootleggers, kidnappers and bank robbers; the relationship of the Cold War China Lobby to Chinese organized criminals; of the flight of capital and criminals to the United States following the "fall" of mainland China to Chinese Communists; and the relationship of San Francisco-based Chinese organized crime to the broader social systems of organized crime, including police and political corruption, existing in California.

This study can also help dispel a key assumption underlying the general study of organized crime in the United States: the assumption that "modern" organized crime evolved from Prohibition.[6] Despite strong historical evidence to the contrary produced by scholars like Block, Gilfoyle, Haller, Hirata, Jenkins and Potter, Johnson, Light, and Paulsen, there persists a notion that "modern" organized crime sprang miraculously from a pre-speakeasy vacuum.[7] In attempting to trace the origins of present-day organized crime, for example, experts have looked to the predecessors of the organized crime syndicates that emerged with Prohibition, such as the Monk Eastman Gang and the Five Points Gang. Yet when we compare the turn-of-the-century Hip Sing Tong and On Leong Tong with their Five Point Gang and Monk Eastman Gang neighbors, we arguably see that the tongs were far ahead of the gangs in organizational development, criminal sophistication and breadth and depth of criminal networks. With allowances for the technological, political, and socioeconomic changes of the last century, today's "modern" organized crime reflects the Hip Sing and On Leong far more than their fledgling contemporaries, the Five Pointers and Monk Eastmans.

It seems that some scholars focus on the Prohibition era as the source of modern organized crime for two reasons: a failure to come to terms with historical fact as it applies to the "Mafia mystique," and a general lack of historical research on "nontraditional" organized crime groups. Both reflect Albanese's "ethnicity trap" and the general failure of historians to fully address the many nuances of urban history and the history of crime and minority groups in the United States.[8] As Block observed more than a decade ago, "It is dismally clear that historical studies of organized crime outside the popular genre are virtually absent and sorely needed," a result of "the handicaps of conservative ideology with its devotion to conspiracy theory," which have "left much of the history of organized crime ... in limbo."[9]

Chinese organized crime is not "emerging." It has existed in the United States for more than a century. It is "nontraditional" only in that it operates largely in Chinese communities and reflects Chinese values and culture. Yet it also operates with similar effectiveness and vigor in the context of Western society, values, and culture.[10] With few exceptions, Chinese organized crime uses the same methods and displays the same behavior as do other ethnic organized crime groups. In addition, Chinese organized criminals are mischaracterized when they are called "new international criminals," because they have operated internationally since they first had the opportunity to do so in the United States.[11] Finally, although recent influxes of Chinese capital and immigrants to the United States suggest that the criminal activities of Chinese organized crime poses an *increased* future threat to this country due to demographic shifts, the threat itself has existed for years. However, it was overlooked, and unrecognized, or minimized in the presence of other concerns like Prohibition, World War II and the Cold War.

For more than a century, Chinese organized criminals have relied on Westerners' ethnic stereotypes, racist assumptions, and historical ignorance to minimize and distort its activities in American society and activities the social system of organized crime. Chinese organized criminals surely have followed the advice of the great Chinese military strategist Sun Tzu: "Be so subtle that you are invisible. Be so mysterious that you are intangible. Then you will control your rivals' fate." Perhaps a new generation of scholars will lead us to fresh, potentially vital avenues of inquiry and policy formulation that encompass the entire social system of organized crime, not just some of its select, stereotyped components. Then a new, more truly American gangster image, one focused on criminal activities and the social, political and economic structures that create them instead of the race and ethnicity of the criminal, will emerge.

Appendix: Comments on Literature, Sources, and Methodology

This study tests the conventional wisdom about Chinese organized crime against the historical record. The use of history in a social scientific framework is not a new phenomenon.[1] Many scholars have implemented historical methods within the fields of criminal justice and criminology and have produced works testing certain assumptions and theories. This is particularly evident in the sub-field of urban history, where many fine works have illustrated the usefulness of history in understanding crime and the criminal justice system. Among them are Timothy Gilfoyle's study of prostitution and the commercialization of sex in New York City; Mark Haller's study of the changing structure of American gambling; David Johnson's study of intercity criminal activity from 1840 to 1920; Alan Block's studies of cocaine use and female organized criminals in progressive-era New York City, as well as his analysis of the organization of crime in New York City from 1930 to 1950; and George Chauncey's study of the interaction of New York City's "gay male world" with the criminal justice system.[2]

Historian Roger Lane summarized the usefulness of history for social scientists when he wrote, "For nonhistorians, all of this interdisciplinary activity may be useful in at least two ways. It is one of the oldest and most valued functions of history simply to provide perspective, to separate deeply rooted phenomena from new ones, or to demonstrate, for example, that what is was not always so, and thus need not always be." In addition, he concluded:

> Whether as raw material or as filtered through a professional's analysis, history may serve also as a body of data which criminologists ... may employ for a kind of retrospective testing of current hypotheses. This function, in particular, has considerable unrealized potential, if only because it has been so rarely recognized. Traditional historians may take an almost malicious delight in its negative application,

demonstrating that much modern theory does not work when applied to the past.[3]

Yet Lane also realized that "the bridge between history and the other social sciences has been traveled, so far, largely in one direction only, and that the traffic has been limited in nature." For example, "public policy makers will find that we historians have rarely addressed their concerns directly, while social scientists may note that we have often used their concepts and methods awkwardly, without generating any useful ones in return."[4]

Using guideposts established by Gary King, Robert Keohane, and Stanley Verba, this study uses history as a means of making contributions to the study of Chinese organized crime and the theory of organized crime that can be appreciated from historical, social scientific, and professional perspectives. The first contribution is to provide "a systemic study addressing an area seen as important by scholars in the literature but heretofore underdeveloped."[5] Second, this study tests accepted hypotheses in the literature suspected to be false or inadequately confirmed, and it investigates whether they are indeed false or whether some other theory is correct as well.[6] These hypotheses include Chinese organized crime's emerging nature and its culturally insular manifestations.

Third, this study evaluates unquestioned assumptions in the literature.[7] The assumptions that Chinese criminals lack the desire and ability to be involved with the American political process, either directly or indirectly via corruption, and that the end of the tong wars and the tongs' involvement with Chinese politics somehow dictated an end to Chinese organized crime are two examples.

Finally, this study places organized crime in the Chinese-American community into historical perspective.[8] To date, the literature does not view Chinese organized crime as a historical process, and it views it as separate from the larger context of the social system of organized crime in the United States. This is despite the fact that Chinatowns were often located in the most crime-plagued sections of cities. Placing Chinese organized crime within this context will afford a new look at an important topic and previously underexamined in the organized crime literature.

Collecting Facts, Recognizing Fiction

Generally speaking, there is a conspicuous lack of sensitivity to historical methods and primary sources when it comes to the study of crime. As a result, many unqualified historical assumptions figure into theories on the subject. For the theories to remain valid requires proof of these assumptions. Yet how do we discover proof in the past?

Richard Myren and Carol Henderson Garcia noted the similarities between historians, who call their work research, and reporters and detectives, who call their work investigation. "Despite that difference," they stated, "all would probably agree that their result is rarely absolute proof, absolute certainty. The best that they can hope for in most circumstances is a very high degree of probability."[9] They quoted Robert Jones Shafer, who summarized the issue for historians:

> No facts speak for themselves to lighten the historian's task, not even facts as objects..., to say nothing of facts as events or ideas. So, facts must be made to speak, in the light of the historian's various purposes, erudition, sense of the fitness of things, and abilities to deal with problems of proof and probability. And there is the rub: the proof is rare and probability comes in many sizes, only to be judged with art and a sense of responsibility.[10]

Historians, said Myren and Garcia, "must support their assertions with proof that will convince their peers that they have exercised a professional 'sense of responsibility.'"[11] For this study, that responsibility begins with the collection of facts, which brings us to the sources from which they are derived.

Criminologists have tended to avoid checking primary sources when it comes to the study of organized crime. They often accept "uncritically the community's legends about itself—surely the most ethnocentric of all possible views."[12] Thanks to revisionist scholarship, the historical naiveté of these criminologists has waned with regard to "traditional" organized crime. This historical naiveté, however, does continue to exist for those groups labeled "nontraditional" like Chinese organized crime.

The sociological literature also lacks a rigorous treatment of Chinese organized crime within a historical context. The literature addresses the social construct of Chinatowns and presents many analyses of the tongs' political, economic, and social roles in the community, conflict and conflict resolution, and general Chinese criminality. However, this literature does not address the historical relationship of some tongs with organized criminality *per se*.[13] Because of this obvious gap in the criminological and sociological literature, I decided to examine primary source data and present my findings as an historical case study of Chinese organized crime in New York City.[14]

I consulted four types of primary source data for this study. The first is composed of contemporary histories and sociological treatments of New York City's Chinatown and tong warfare. These were valuable, for they presented data gathered first-hand by the authors. The best example of a New York City Chinatown study is Louis Beck's *New York's Chinatown;* however, Frank Moss's *The American Metropolis*, Carl Glick's *Shake Hands with the Dragon* and Leong Gor Yun's *Chinatown Inside Out* provide informative treatments as well.[15] Though not directly addressing New York City's Chinatown, Ching Chao Wu's *Chinatowns: A Study of Symbiosis and Assimilation* incorporates an excellent collection of primary source documents relevant to this study.[16] Other treatments, however, like John Stewart Burgess' *A Study of the Characteristics of the Cantonese Merchants in Chinatown, New York, as Shown by Their Use of Leisure Time*, proved disappointing in that they did not address issues relevant to this study.[17]

For my purposes, Louis Beck's research proved the most valuable. His was the first in-depth study of New York's Chinese community. Recognizing in 1898 that "the presence of the Chinese in the United States has been a fruitful topic of angry political discussion, of legislative investigation, of congressional legislation, and of judicial inquiry for twenty years," he was also keenly aware that the American public knew very little about the Chinese in the United States. That is to say, they knew very little outside of the "yellow peril" writings and orations of anti–Chinese jingoists. To help rectify this situation, Beck wrote *New York's Chinatown* in order

> to portray the everyday life of those Chinamen who have made the heart of New York City their home—their business occupations, social habits, amusements, religious observances and whatever else is peculiar to them as a race; drawing the pictures from actual life, uninfluenced by favor or prejudice; exaggerating in no particular; concealing no faults; omitting no feature of profitable study; to the end that the reader will be enabled to reach a fair and just conclusion on the questions involved.[18]

Even almost a century after it was completed, Beck's work is still exceptional for the data and insights it provides on New York City's Chinatown. Making use of historical evidence, interviews, surveys, and participant observation, he wrote the first comprehensive treatment of the subject. For example, Beck gave the first detailed description of the Chong Wah Gong Shaw, also known as the Chinese Consolidated Benevolent Association (CCBA), as the supreme authority in New York's Chinatown. He discussed the functions of family, district, and labor associations operating under the CCBA's authority. He also identified the Hip Sing Tong as representative of the criminal element in Chinatown, calling them by their Chinatown reputation of "highbinders."

Still, Beck's analysis suffers from two major weaknesses. The first is temporal. Being the first to address New York City's Chinatown and presenting one of the first social scientific studies examining a Chinatown in the United States, Beck did not have a developed scholarly literature to consult. Second, despite his desire to be "uninfluenced by favor or prejudice," both factors crept into the work. As for the former, Beck relied heavily on Chinatown's merchant class for his information. Hence, the On Leong Tong[19] gets quite favorable treatment at the expense of its "bitter" foe, the Hip Sing Tong, or "Highbinders' Society." He described the On Leong Tong as "a social organization which confines its membership to the higher class of Chinese residents ... which seeks to encourage and promote good order and becoming respect to the laws of the land and city which gives the Chinamen hospitality and protection." According to Beck, "most of the merchants of Chinatown are members of this meritorious organization."[20]

Meanwhile, Beck dedicated an entire chapter to the Hip Sing Tong and its criminal behavior, and he vilified one of its leaders in a profile found in another chapter. Beck's sources skillfully manipulated him into presenting the Hip Sing Tong as the sole organization responsible for—and profiting from—the operation and protection of gambling dens and houses of prostitution. These sources also called the Hip Sing members blackmailers and violent, unstable gunmen.[21] As we see in this study, the On Leong Tong represented the status quo of organized crime in Chinatown until the Hip Sing Tong challenged their hegemony. Clearly the On Leong Tong perspective influenced Beck's work.

Betsy Huang offers a third criticism. She notes that Beck's study, as well as other sociological studies of Chinatowns, sought "to identify the distinctive traits that constitute an authentic Chinese identity." However, she states, such studies are superficial and prone to stereotype. Specifically, she criticizes Beck and others for regarding Chinese as a collective, examining and judging them "by their operations as a community and not as individuals," and heightening "the sense of an alien collective to the white population at large." Her criticism is right on the mark, especially as it applies to Beck. Indeed, Beck does portray the New York Chinese community "as utterly incomprehensible aliens, a reaction that is symptomatic of the early stages of an encounter with a foreign culture [and] is disguised by his supposed objective ethnographic voice." The result is that Beck's treatment is quite prejudiced.[22]

Despite these faults, Beck made a distinct contribution to the Chinatown literature in three areas. He was the first to implement the ethnographic methods that will be used by many Chinatown scholars for the next hundred years. He provided the first "objective" glance at Chinatown and its institutions, subjects explored by future scholars who would implement his methods. Finally, Beck's work serves as an excellent primary source, providing us with both quantitative and qualitative information on turn-of-the-century New York City's Chinatown that is found nowhere else.

I found only three books written before 1964 that were dedicated solely to the history of Chinese criminal organizations. All three, however, are inadequate or incomplete treatments of the subject. The first, *Tong War!*, was published in 1930 and romantically recounts the early tong wars fought in American cities like San Francisco, New York, Philadelphia and Boston.[23] The authors are Eng Ying "Eddie" Gong, a reputed leader in New York City's Hip Sing Tong, and Bruce Grant, a New York City reporter. *Tong War!* is of primary importance to the history of conflict in New York City's Chinatown, for it is the cornerstone on which almost all other direct or indirect treatments of the subject are based.[24] However, *Tong War!* is to the study of tong warfare what the testimony of Joe Valachi is to the study of Italian and Sicilian organized crime: a purported gospel, riddled with errors of fact and omission among the truths.[25] It is not a scholarly treatment by any means.

The second, Richard Dillon's *The Hatchet Men*, published in 1962, offers a fine historical treatment of the various tong wars that occurred up to the 1900s, but it has two fundamental flaws. Not only is it outdated in terms of developments in the fields of Chinese-American studies and criminology, it also fails to provide footnotes by which to check the evidence presented. In addition, it concentrates only on conflict in California, ignoring the unique and rich history of Chinese organized crime in other Western states and the East Coast.[26]

The third, C.Y. Lee's *Days of the Tong Wars*, serves only as a regurgitation of the work found in *The Hatchet Men*, *Tong War!*, and a few other sources. It suffers from the same criticisms found in *The Hatchet Men*, though it does provide one chapter on New York that is drawn liberally from *Tong War!*[27]

Of the three books, Gong and Grant's *Tong War!* provides the only detailed treatment of events in New York City. *Tong War!* also provides the only known first-person account of the events in question. Still, *Tong War!* reflects the limitations of Eng Ying Gong's individual perspective. For example, he overlooked—by either ignorance or design—key events, personalities, and motivations involved in the historical process to which he was a reported witness or participant. Similarly, his co-author, Bruce Grant, brought a bit of journalistic sensationalism to the treatment reflective of the "yellow peril" genre of pulp fiction that was popular during the 1930s.[28] One must use a skeptical eye when reading *Tong War!*, for it forms the foundation of folk traditions and myths about tong wars in the United States.

In a related example, Martin Booth urged caution when studying the history of Triads because, "as with any folk tradition, the links between the story and the real past are—at best—tenuous, and are likely to have been so at the start. But there are a few identifiable links that can be teased out of the mythological and symbolic narrative."[29] Such is the case with *Tong War!* Still, the "links between the story and the real past" are much less tenuous here than those in Booth's case. Accordingly, the links are more plentiful when teased out of the narrative.

With these cautions in mind, *Tong War!* does provide a unique first-person perspective of someone apparently in the know about the events in this case study. Because of Eng Ying Gong's perspective, the book provides some behind-the-scenes glimpses of the running feud between the Hip Sing Tong and On Leong Tong, thus making *Tong War!* a solid and valuable primary source when viewed in the context of other material.

For the purposes of this study, *Tong War!* is also important in that it establishes a definite link between vice enterprises and conflict between rival organizations in New York City's Chinatown. This link is also evident in a non-related 1930s report sent to the Chinese government by its ambassador to the United States. As translated by Ko-lin Chin, it reads as follows:

> Narcotics and gambling are the causes of the tong wars. The tongs are generating unlimited amounts of income from operating opium and gambling dens. The tongs are so rich that a tong would spend tens of thousands of dollars for a building, and a tong's annual expenditures could be more than a million dollars. The tongs are well organized, their leaders very dignified. Each has about twenty to thirty branches, with ten to twenty thousand members. The tongs recruit a bunch of thugs (hatchetmen) to run opium and gambling dens, and to revenge and kill when the situations call for action. If a thug kills a person, the tongs will reward him with several thousand dollars; if he is killed, his family will receive a subsidy of ten thousand dollars. A hatchetman's subsidy is higher than a senior government official's. A group of hatchetmen is similar to a regular army, and the tongs resemble the warlords.[30]

Since this linkage of vice and violence is common to what is considered modern organized crime, the first tong war between New York City's On Leong Tong and Hip Sing Tong was chosen as the subject for this case study.

The treatments of California's tong wars by Gong and Grant, Dillon, and Lee also provide strong evidence of the same connections on the West Coast.[31] When viewed along with other secondary and primary source material, these three works provide us with a national picture of Chinese organized criminal enterprise and violence from approximately 1850 to 1920. Information on this subject was so plentiful and of such quality that I was also able to provide an assessment of the general development and state of Chinese organized crime in the United States during this time frame.

For a sense of the social, political, and economic contexts of the first tong war in New York City, my sources related to the case study. These sources included relevant accounts of New York City, its institutions, neighborhoods, and personalities. They also included reform pamphlets, travel guides, reform commission and municipal reports, local histories, and sociological studies.

I discovered some statistical data in these sources. Once evaluated, however, it quickly became apparent that these data were unreliable. This is often the case with statistics collected long ago. Michael Maltz explained that the use of all types of quantitative data in historical projects can be problematic. For example, what kind of statistics were collected? Who collected them? How accurate are they? These are questions that have been posed by researchers and statisticians ever since the International Association of Chiefs of Police and the Wickersham Commission began urging the collection of such data during the late 1920s and early 1930s.[32]

The reliability of statistics kept before the establishment of the Uniform Crime Reports is beset by even more problems. Historian Eric Monkkonen made this point when he evaluated municipal reports as indicator sources. As he noted, most crime records can be found in annual reports published by the mayor's office of a particular city. Generally, the police department would submit its report to the mayor, who would then publish them as part of an "Annual Report" or "Annual Message." Yet these reports often suffered from various forms of measurement bias. For example, the numbers used in reports were drawn from the likes of arrest blotters and then summarized in the annual report. Without proper oversight, the police or the mayor's office could easily manipulate these numbers for political gain and defense.[33] Similarly, some data were overlooked and not recorded because of the lack of sophistication and automation in the records keeping process.

These patterns were evident in some of the documents I consulted for this study. A case in point is the number of accounted-for suicides, homicides, and violent or accidental deaths found in official New York City vital records compared to those reported in the press. The press reported two suspicious suicides by Chinese in 1899,[34] yet neither is listed in the city's vital records.[35] For the period of this study (1899–1907), only four homicides with Chinese victims are recorded in official records, two in 1906 and two in 1907. However, newspaper sources report sixteen homicides for the same time period (Table 1). Without a doubt there is a significant discrepancy when it comes to the use of official statistical data for our case study, with reliability leaning heavily toward the press. Consequently, quantitative data as found in municipal indicator sources are not used in this study.

The third form of primary source data is contemporary newspaper accounts of related events. The use of newspapers in this capacity is nothing new. Scholars from C. N. Reynolds (1935) to Richard Dillon (1962) to Ko-lin Chin (1986) have used them as a major source of their data on tong activity.[36] For this case study, I consulted newspapers from 1890 to 1910, including all issues of the *New York Times* (1890 to 1910) and the *New York Daily Tribune* (1894 to 1906). The New York County District Attorney's scrapbooks (1898 to 1908)[37] provided me with numerous clippings compiled from the New York City newspapers of the day.[38] Within these scrapbooks, I

Table 9
Number of Chinese Homicides in New York According to Various Records, 1899–1907

Year	reported in press, tong-related	reprinted in press, unknown motivation	reported in official records[35]
1899	0	0	0
1900	2	1	0
1901	0	0	0
1902	0	1	0
1903	1	0	0
1904	0	2	0
1905	7	0	0
1906	2	0	2
1907	0	0	2
Total	12	4	4

(Total reported in press: 16)

Source: Haven Emerson and Harriet E. Hughes, *Population, Births, Notifiable Diseases, and Deaths Assembled for New York City, New York, 1866–1938: From Official Records* (New York: The DeLamar Institute of Public Health, College of Physicians and Surgeons, Columbia University, 1941): Nos. 172–175 inclusive; and numerous press reports.

found comprehensive coverage of criminal events, personalities, cases, and related matters in 19 New York City newspapers.[39] Because of the competition between these newspapers, they provided "checks and balances" for each other when it came to facts and perspective on a given story. Consequently, the accounts found in these newspapers compose the bulk of primary sources used to generate data for this study.

I found the fourth form of primary data in various documents located in New York City area archives and libraries. The New York Municipal Archives housed the most material, including the district attorney's closed-case files and papers of the Magistrates' Court, Court of General Sessions, and Supreme Court. These records proved quite valuable by confirming and elaborating on the facts presented in the newspapers, as well as by rectifying the factual gaps or inconsistencies occurring in the same. Unfortunately, many of the records needed for this study have been misplaced, destroyed, or otherwise lost to time. For example, the paperwork surrounding the murder trials of the prominent Hip Sing gangster Mock Duck was either filed incorrectly or misplaced.

These problems were not unique to the New York Municipal Archives. Indeed, my search for relevant primary sources at other locations was beset with far more failures than successes. The Trial Transcript Preservation Project at John Jay College, City University of New York, provided transcripts for many trials of Chinese gangsters, but, regrettably, it did not have any for the period covered in this study. It did, however, provide the transcript of a later trial of Mock Duck on gambling charges that provided valuable background information about the defendant. A transcript for a Mock Duck trial, this one for murder, was located at the New York Public Library.

The New York branch of the United States National Archives houses federal court and immigration records. Yet what seemed to be a promising archive proved disappointing for the purposes of this study. First, my search for documents related to a well-publicized federal court case against three leaders of the On Leong Tong for voting fraud resulted in the discovery of just one scant record of a guilty plea by one of the defendants. I could not locate the records on the other two men. Likewise, I could not locate information on several of the federal opium smuggling cases reported in the press.

Second, the database created to serve as a guide to the thousands of Chinese immigration files located in the archive was oriented toward genealogical work. Hence, it did not state which cases involved smuggling or provide information about the adjudication of the individual cases. This created a situation that would have necessitated my sorting through approximately 10,000 individual files to discover evidence elaborating on the structure and operation of Chinese smuggling operations in New York City. Therefore, this impressive data source could not be used for this study.

The Society for the Prevention of Crime and the Edwin Patrick Kilroe collections located at Columbia University's Rare Book and Manuscript Collection also proved dead ends. First, a thorough search of the records of the Society for the Prevention of Crime[40] found no reference to its highly publicized involvement in Chinatown during the early– to mid–1900s. For example, the files on gambling began in 1906, at the tail end of the first tong war, and dealt with non–Chinese gambling concerns in New York's Tenderloin district; correspondence between the Reverend Charles Parkhurst and his society's counsel, Frank Moss, stops in 1902, long before Moss' involvement in the Chinatown conflict as counsel for the Hip Sing Tong; and there is only one unrelated letter between the bickering, though politically tied, reformers Parkhurst and District Attorney William Travers Jerome. Second, the records of Tammany Hall, as found in Edwin Patrick Kilro's "Collection of Tammaniana," provided no information on the relationship of Tammany Hall and its members to the leaders of the On Leong Tong, even though this relationship is clearly evident in press accounts.

The lack of materials in both of these collections does not preclude the fact that these records may have existed at one time. According to one of the curators, the material in these collections was incomplete when they were donated to the Columbia University Libraries. As a result, for both collections, records are complete in some areas, but sporadic or nonexistent in others.

Working with a student fluent in Chinese, I looked for Chinese language sources that could be used in this study. We made, inquiries to the New York Public Library and New York's Museum of Chinese in the Americas. We quickly found that what little was available did not address the events in question in this study. For example, Chinese language newspapers focused largely on events in China, obituaries, advertisements for shipping schedules, and other items of general interest to the Chinese-American community. Crime coverage was nonexistent. As much as it would have benefited this study to have crime reports written by Chinese journalists, diaries of

Chinatown residents, or journals of Chinese criminals, the perspectives of numerous Chinese men were found in English language newspaper coverage and criminal justice records.

In sum, the process of discovering and retrieving relevant government, organizational, and personal records and documents was a process marked by failure and success. The failures prove a lesson learned by Eric Monkkonen: "Most historians who work with nineteenth-century criminal justice data are continually thwarted in their search for systematically preserved sources."[41] The successes, however, were abundant. The quantity and quality of the data collected for this study are comparable to, or exceed, that used in other historical studies of organized crime in New York.

Methods

As mentioned previously, the available quantitative data I found during the course of my research proved unreliable. This prohibited the implementation of quantitative methods in this study. Similarly, the failure of traditional qualitative social scientific approaches like surveys, experimentation, and observation, to address properly the given research questions, reinforced this decision. Therefore, in order to establish the proof to either validate or challenge the unqualified historical assumptions behind various hypotheses and theories about Chinese organized crime, I decided to implement a qualitative, document-based, case study approach.

In *Methods of Social Research*, Kenneth Bailey noted several advantages to document study. Documents, he stated, "allow research on subjects to [which] the researcher does not have physical access, and thus cannot study by any other method." Documents allow for nonreactivity on the part of the subject(s) being studied. That is, it seems highly unlikely that writers wrote these documents with the knowledge they would be studied by a criminal justice researcher 100 years after their publication and, hence, "felt unnatural, self-conscious, or bothered by the 'guinea pig' effect."[42]

The documents used in this study allow for a longitudinal analysis of the subject, provide for a large sample size, and are of relatively high quality. In this particular case, the study benefits from the standardized format associated with the newspaper articles. Such standardization, Bailey observed, "facilitates comparison across time for the same newspaper, and comparison across different newspapers at one point in the same time." The documents used here also allow for the capturing of spontaneous actions and feelings that may not occur at a time and place specified or expected by the researcher. Consequently, we can have much more faith in both the results of the study and the generalizations they spawn.[43]

Despite these advantages, document study does have its limitations. As Bailey explained, "many documents used in social research were not originally intended for research purposes," hence "the various goals and purposes for which [they] are written can bias them in various ways." Documents also survive selectively; they are written on paper that corrodes and they take up space in files that may need to be cleansed. A good example of this is the destruction of years worth of police documents by the New York Police Department during the 1970s, documents that included those compiled during the years covered in this study.⁴⁴ Fortunately many of the surviving documents tend to overlap with the information contained in destroyed police documents. For example, names, addresses, and affiliations that could have been found in police documents are also found in court papers and newspaper reports.

Documents also often provide incomplete accounts "to the researcher who has no prior experience with or knowledge of the events or behavior discussed." For instance, when tailored to a specific audience, or written without allowances for unknown future readers, these documents "assume specific knowledge that researchers unfamiliar with specific events [and personalities] will not posses."⁴⁵

Another disadvantage of document study cited by Bailey is the lack of information, possibly because it was either destroyed or never recorded. Yet another is sampling bias, which occurs when all of the potential respondents from which the sample could be drawn are not included. For example, this study does not take into account Chinese language documents because none of those available addressed the issues at hand. Finally, the data collected must be adjusted for comparability over time. In the course of this study, for example, it was noted that opium smuggling occurred for a different reason (tariff avoidance) in the past than it does today (it is an illegal narcotic).⁴⁶

The relative lack of Chinese-language sources did not preclude information provided by Chinese individuals, a point reflected in the sources used in John Kuo Wei Tchen's highly detailed treatment of New York City's Chinatown before 1882, *New York Before Chinatown*.⁴⁷ Indeed, the documents cited in this study and Tchen's cite many English-speaking Chinese, as well as those who spoke through translators. Missing from the data are the particular cultural nuances about and perspectives on our conflict that could only come from Chinese-language sources.

To compensate for this, I followed the advice of criminologist Ko-lin Chin. In *Chinatown Gangs*, Chin suggested that, "in order to understand Asian crime groups, the research and law enforcement communities need to broaden their perspectives."⁴⁸ I tried to broaden mine by becoming intimately familiar with the aforementioned literature on the Chinese-American experience, as well as that on Chinatown and its institutions. Though obviously not a replacement for having the language skill, the literature—much written by those who do understand Chinese—served as a frame of reference throughout this case study.

Also missing from some documents is information that was not recorded in the first place. On the one hand, it is reasonable to assume that some information would have been included, like the addresses of individuals captured in an opium raid or the background of a would-be assassin. On the other hand, the existence of documentary evidence pertaining to other types of information is highly unlikely. For instance, photographs and wiretaps of police officers, magistrates, and politicians receiving kickbacks from On Leong or Hip Sing do not exist, nor were the parties involved eager to write these actions down.

Finally, though the documents often reflect the biases of their writers and sources, these biases were identified and clarified in follow-up reports on the subjects in question or by comparing the respective coverage of the same incident in the large number of rival newspaper reports, court papers, and other available documents. Nevertheless, the data generated from the available sources are quite comprehensive, can be controlled reasonably for bias, and present very few outliers that would lead one to question the historical validity of the data. In the end, the logistical difficulties inherent in this study are similar to those one would encounter in researching other ethnic groups and criminal enterprises at the beginning of the twentieth century.[49]

Analyzing the Facts

By looking at the data in chronological order I was able to make improved descriptive inferences. Descriptive inference is "the process of understanding an unobserved phenomenon on the basis of a set of observations."[50] Chinese organized crime, this study's unobserved phenomenon, is best understood through contemporary observations of its activities. In this case, however, contemporary observers did not report on organized crime *per se*, but on the criminal activities and related events, groups, and individuals in Chinatown It is important to stress that the concept of organized crime as we understand the team today was not in place at the time the data were gathered. This designation comes only after the data are applied to today's organized crime theory.

Clearly, the descriptive inferences generated can only be as good as the observations made by the press, the predominant source of data for this study. At first glance, it would seem that the general quality of journalism during this era of muckraking and yellow journalism would undermine the value of its observations. C. N. Reynolds ran into this problem in 1935 when he consulted the blatantly racist, Sinophobic treatments found in California newspapers covering the tong wars. On a less insidious level, he also observed that "very little of this material ... is free from the deep coloring of an outside, Occidental mind that fails to sense the existence of basic cultural elements accounting for the appearance of the tongs and for the subsequent evolution of their activities."[51]

Fortunately, New York newspapers were far less Sinophobic in their treatment of the Chinese than newspapers from western states, though ethnocentrism was a common occurrence. For example, although a reporter might comically describes the decapitation of chickens as part of the oath-taking ceremony for Chinese testifying in the courts, the New York newspapers were not crying out for laws preventing Chinese from testifying in courts in the first place, as was the case on the West Coast.[52]

The fundamental problem that dogged reporters covering New York City's tong wars was the "cultural ignorance" of the "Occidental mind." As Dillon noted in his study, the press had difficulty in piecing together the existence and role of tongs in Chinatown. For example, the simple task of getting the names of organizations right—let alone understanding their role and function in the community—was made nearly impossible by "a host of variant spellings, mispronunciations and bad translations." Adding to the difficulty, the organized criminals obviously did not want the truth about their businesses made public to their non–Chinese neighbors. Dillon explained that each syndicate had a few English-speaking members "who scanned the newspapers to keep their societies posted, and dealt with American lawyers and other English-speaking people when necessary. But they passed no secrets to the 'foreign devils.'"[53] Indeed, these spokesmen served as spin doctors for their syndicate's interests.

For the purposes of this study, however, New York City press accounts prove quite reliable at providing the "who, what, when, where, why, and how" of the events in question. Altogether, they are quite thorough, particularly regarding events and personalities in Chinatown. This is because Chinatown was within fifteen minutes walking distance to New York's City Hall and police headquarters, busy police precincts, Tammany Hall, and even *The New York Times* itself. Also, it was located right at a major transportation junction, the Chatham Square elevated train station. Chinatown was at the center of three major ethnic enclaves—Italian, Irish, and Jewish—as well as the saloons and vice industries of the Bowery District. All of these enclaves made for promising stories, so it comes as no surprise that they were frequented by a number of reporters for either professional or personal reasons. Considering the widespread American fascination with all things Chinese at the time[54] and the geographical proximity of Chinatown to major institutions, events, and personalities, reports from Chinatown were a likely sell to one's editors.

The two most problematic areas in a reporter's coverage of a tong war story concerned the "whos" and "whys." The problem of identifying the actors and organizations in this drama came from the lack of standardization in reporting Chinese names. For the most part, until reporters saw the name of a Chinese person or organization on an official document (e.g., a coroner's report or grand jury indictment), chances are it was spelled phonetically. As a result, a name like Eng would become Ong, Hong, or On. Fortunately, as was the practice of the day, reporters almost always included the address of the subjects mentioned, making it easier to determine that two, three or four seemingly unrelated names might all refer to one individual or organization.[55]

Reporters sometimes attempted to explain why events in Chinatown occurred, but often these explanations seemed to facilitate the agenda of the parties involved; others were limited in scope. In short, they were only as reliable as their sources. Many times, however, the reporters often avoided the "why" question. Therefore, the "why" usually came out of the coverage of relevant criminal trials or in the statements of other observers. Also, the "why" became clearer when the organizations involved began to put their spin on events. Some reasons become evident when the individual reports are viewed in context and on a timeline. Certain patterns become apparent, providing the larger meaning behind the seemingly random gambling raids, acts of violence, and political alliances and infighting.

Creating a database of all individuals, organizations, and addresses mentioned in the source material reinforced the timeline. In order to analyze the structure of criminal interaction between the On Leong Tong, the Hip Sing Tong, and other actors, network charting was implemented in this study. This is a method used by both historically minded anthropologists and anthropologically minded historians. It is an anthropological technique that allows the researcher to construct relationships between individuals and organizations in the field. The network "maps" developed from this research are extremely important because they allow the researcher to focus his or her observations in time and space.[56]

The use of network charting to determine social networks that existed in the past presents an interesting challenge. Because this study is historical in nature, it cannot make use of interviews, surveys, and direct or participant observations as a means of expanding and elaborating on the networks. For these reasons, the network maps constructed for this study were relatively rudimentary, able only to present relationships found in, or inferred from, the historical record.

In spite of this handicap, there are enough data so that network maps created were quite strong, shedding more than adequate light on the political, economic, social, and criminal relationships[57] of On Leong and Hip Sing members within and outside of Chinatown. For example, the criminal affiliation of a raided gambling establishment could be determined by linking the name of one of those arrested to either the Hip Sing Tong or the On Leong Tong. Similarly, Hip Sing Tong and On Leong Tong connections to the upperworld could be established by researching the lawyers defending the accused in court. Likewise, a lawyer may have strong Tammany or reform connections. Therefore, by developing a timeline and maintaining a name, organization and address database to establish a series of relationships among professional criminals, upperworld clients, and politicians, Block's methodology in *East Side-West Side*, "grounding detail upon evidence and generalization upon detail," is emulated in this study.[58]

Chapter Notes

Preface

1. Recent work by two scholars have addressed this possibility with regard to African-American organized crime [Sean Patrick Griffin, *Organized Crime in Philadelphia, 1968–1984: On Exploitation and Urban Politics*, Ph.D. dissertation (University Park, PA: The Pennsylvania State University, 2000) and Robert M. Lombardo, "The Black Mafia: African-American Organized Crime in Chicago, 1890–1960," *Crime, Law & Social Change: An International Journal* 38:1 (July 2002): 33–65]. The only article on Chinese organized crime is the one on which this book is based, Jeffrey Scott McIllwain, "From Tong War to Organized Crime: Revising the Historical Perception of Violence in Chinatown," *Justice Quarterly* 14:1 (March 1997): 25–52.

2. Jay Albanese, *Organized Crime in America*, 3rd ed. (Cincinnati, OH: Anderson, 1996): 145.

Chapter 1

1. "Prepared Statement of Senator Nunn," as found in United States Senate, Permanent Subcommittee on Investigations of the Committee on Governmental Affairs, *Asian Organized Crime* (Washington, D.C.: U.S. Government Printing Office, 1992): 2.

2. "Opening Statement of Senator Roth," *Ibid.*: 4.

3. Ko-lin Chin, Robert J. Kelly, and Jeffrey Fagan, "Chinese Organized Crime in America," in *Handbook of Organized Crime in the United States*, Robert J. Kelly, Ko-lin Chin, and Rufus Schatzberg, eds. (Westport, CT: Greenwood, 1994): 236.

4. Ko-lin Chin, *Chinese Sub-culture and Criminality: Non-traditional Crime Groups in America* (New York: Greenwood Press, 1990): 146.

5. William Kleinknecht, *The New Ethnic Mobs: The Changing Face of Organized Crime in America* (New York: Free Press, 1996): 291–292.

6. Bill Kurtis (prod.), "The Dragons of Crime," *Arts & Entertainment's Investigative Reports* (Stornoway Productions, 1994).

7. "Testimony of William S. Sessions," in United States Senate Permanent Subcommittee on Investigations of the Committee on Governmental Affairs, *Asian Organized Crime*, Hearings held 3 October and 5–6 November 1991 (Washington, D.C.: GPO, 1992): 12–14.

8. United States Senate Permanent Subcommittee on Investigations of the Committee on Governmental Affairs, *Asian Organized Crime: The New International Criminal*, Hearings held 3 October, 18 June and 4 August 1992 (Washington, D.C.: GPO, 1992).

9. "White House Background Briefing on President Clinton's Initiative Against Trafficking," *Federal News Service* (June 18, 1993).

10. Pennsylvania Crime Commission, *1991 Report* (St. David's, PA: Pennsylvania Crime Commission, 1991): 27.

11. Works evaluated to establish these terms: Howard Abadinsky, *Organized Crime* (4th ed.) (Chicago: Nelson-Hall, 1994); Albanese, *Organized Crime in America*; David Black, *Triad Takeover: A Terrifying Account of the Spread of Triad Crime in the West* (London:

Sidgwick & Jackson, 1991); Martin Booth, *The Triads: The Growing Global Threat from the Chinese Criminal Societies* (New York: St. Martin's Press, 1990); Fenton Bresler, *The Chinese Mafia* (New York: Stein and Day, 1981); Ko-lin Chin, *Chinatown Gangs: Extortion, Enterprise, and Ethnicity* (New York: Oxford University Press, 1996):8. Chin, *Chinese Triad Societies*; Ko-lin Chin, *Smuggled Chinese: Clandestine Immigration to the United States* (Philadelphia: Temple University Press, 1999); Chin, Kelly, and Fagan, "Chinese Organized Crime in America"; Ko-lin Chin, Jeffrey Fagan, and Robert J. Kelly, "Patterns of Chinese Gang Extortion," *Justice Quarterly* 9:4 (December 1992): 625–646; James Durbo, *Dragons of Crime: Inside the Asian Underworld* (Ontario: Octopus, 1992); Dennis J. Kenney and James O. Finckenauer, *Organized Crime in America* (Belmont, CA: Wadsworth, 1995); Stephen Fox, *Blood and Power: Organized Crime in Twentieth-Century America* (New York: Penguin, 1989); Kleinknecht, *The New Ethnic Mobs*; Kurtis, "The Dragons of Crime"; Willard H. Meyers, III, "The Emerging Threat of Transnational Organized Crime in the East," *Crime, Law & Social Change: An International Journal* 24 (1996); Willard H. Meyers, III, "Orb Weavers—The Global Webs: The Structure and Activities of Transnational Ethnic Chinese Criminal Groups," *Transnational Organized Crime* 1:4 (1996): 1–36; Pennsylvania Crime Commission, *1991 Report*; Gerald L. Posner, *Warlords of Crime: Chinese Secret Societies—The New Mafia* (New York: Penguin, 1988); President's Commission on Organized Crime, *Organized Crime of Asian Origin* (Washington, D.C.: U.S. Government Printing Office, 1984); President's Commission on Organized Crime, *The Impact* (Washington, D.C.: U.S. Government Printing Office, 1984); Frank Robertson, *Triangle of Death: The Inside Story of the Triads—The Chinese Mafia* (London: Routledge and Kegan Paul, 1977); Jeffrey Robinson, *The Merger: The Conglomeration of International Organized Crime* (Woodstock, NY: Overlook Press, 2000); Paul Smith (ed.), *Human Smuggling: Chinese Migrant Trafficking and the Challenge to America's Immigration Tradition* (Washington, D.C.: The Center for Strategic and International Studies, 1997); Claire Sterling, *Thieves' World: The Threat of the New Global Network of Organized Crime* (New York: Simon & Schuster, 1994); Calvin Toy, "A Short History of Asian Gangs in San Francisco;" *Justice Quarterly* 9:4 (December 1992): 647–665; United States Senate, *Asian Organized Crime*; United States Senate, *Asian Organized Crime: The New International Criminal*;

12. Daniel Bell, "Crime as an American Way of Life: A Queer Ladder of Social Mobility," *The Antioch Review* 13 (June): 131–154.

13. Though the earlier documents are ripe with ethnocentrism or clearly dominated by racist perspectives and intents, the record of Chinese organized criminality and its intricate and substantial involvement with the social system of organized crime in the United States is quite public (easily accessible in any research library or appropriate on-line research databases) and impossible to dismiss. Setting aside literally thousands of primary source records held by archives, museums, and libraries across the nation for the time being, see, for example, United States Congress, Joint Special Committee to Investigate Chinese Immigrants, *Report* (Washington, D.C.: U.S. Government Print-ing Office, 1877); California Legislature, Senate Special Committee on Chinese Immigration, *Chinese Immigration, Its Social, Moral, and Political Effect* (San Francisco, CA: State Printing Office, 1878); Willard B. Farwell, *The Chinese at Home and Abroad: The Report of the Special Committee of the Board of Supervisors of San Francisco on the Condition of the Chinese Quarter of that City* (San Francisco, 1885); *Memorial—The Other Side of the Chinese Question: Testimony of California's Leading Citizens to the People of the United States and the Honorable Senate and House of Representatives* (San Francisco, February 1886); Alan A. Block, "History and the Study of Organized Crime," *Urban Life: A Journal of Ethnographic Research* 6 (January 1978): 455; United States Industrial Commission, *Report of the U.S. Industrial Commission on Highbinder Tongs* (Washington, D.C.: U.S. Government Printing Office, 1901); E. V. Robbens, "Chinese Slave Girls: A Bit of History," *Overland Monthly* LI (1909): 100–102; United States Bureau of Immigration, *Report* (Washington, D.C.: U.S. Government Printing Office, 1920); Ching Chao Wu, *Chinatowns: A Study of Symbiosis and Assimilation*, Ph.D. dissertation. (Chicago: University of Chicago, 1928); Eng Ying Gong and Bruce Grant, *Tong War!* (New York: Nicholas Brown, 1930).; C. N. Reynolds, "The Chinese Tongs," *American Journal of Sociology* XL (1935): 612–623; Yun, *Chinatown Inside Out*; Harry J. Anslinger and Will Oursler, *The Murderers: The Story of the Narcotics Gangs* (New York: Farrar, Straus and Cudahy, 1962); Richard H. Dillon, *The Hatchet Men: The Story of the Tong Wars in San Francisco's Chinatown* (New York: Coward-McCann, 1962); and George E. Paulsen, "The Yellow

Peril at Nogales: The Ordeal of Collector William M. Hoey," *Arizona and the West* 13 (1971): 113–128.

Why these and similar sources have never been mined by criminologists, particularly organized crime scholars, is unknown. Some radical criminologists, however, provide interesting perspectives that relate to this phenomenon. Perhaps the discipline of criminology is too defined by its ethnic and class homogeneity, thereby dominated by mainstream assumptions, perspectives, approaches, and concerns. Perhaps this lack of attention is a reflection of the general historical competency in the discipline. Perhaps traditional topics and approaches are considered safe, thereby providing criminologists easier roads to tenure, promotion, and publication. Perhaps criminology is simply too dominated by sociological approaches, thereby limiting other useful perspectives.

Whatever the reason, this general historical insensitivity is alarming. I do not mean to imply that all criminologists possess and manifest this attitude. Certainly, many do not. However, generally speaking, in terms of research and education, the discipline of criminology should place more emphasis on training criminologists to be historically aware and capable of historical research. After all, it is in the best interest of the discipline to get its historical facts straight, rather than basing theories on the shifting sands of historical naiveté.

14. Block, *East Side-West Side:* 10.
15. For more on the subject of mythology and organized crime, especially as it pertains to "traditional" organized crime, see Joseph L. Albini, *The American Mafia: Genesis of a Legend* (New York: Appleton, Century, Crofts, 1971); Joseph L. Albini, "The Mafia and the Devil: What They Have in Common," in Patrick J. Ryan and George E. Rush, *Understanding Organized Crime in Global Perspective: A Reader* (Thousand Oaks, CA: Sage Publications, 1997): 63–70; Joseph L. Albini and Bronislaw J. Bajon, "Witches, Mafia, Mental Illness and Social Reality: A Study in the Power of Mythical Belief," *International Journal of Criminology and Penology* 6 (1978): 285–294; Alan A. Block, *East Side-West Side;* Alan A. Block, "History and the Study of Organized Crime"; Gary W. Potter and Philip Jenkins, *The City and the Syndicate: Organizing Crime in Philadelphia* (Lexington, MA: Ginn, 1985); Philip Jenkins and Gary Potter, "The Politics and Mythology of Organized Crime: A Philadelphia Case-Study," *Journal of Criminal Justice* 15:6 (1987): 473–484; McIllwain, "From Tong War to Organized Crime."

Chapter 2

1. For example, see Donald Cressey, *Theft of a Nation: The Structure and Operations of Organized Crime* (New York: Harper & Row, 1969).
2. For example, see Francis Ianni, *Black Mafia: Ethnic Succession in Organized Crime* (New York: Simon & Schuster, 1974): 19; Francis A. J. Ianni and Elizabeth Reuss-Ianni, *A Family Business: Kinship and Social Control in Organized Crime* (New York: Russell Sage Foundation, 1972), and Francis Ianni and Elizabeth Reuss-Ianni (eds.), *The Crime Society: Organized Crime and Corruption in America* (New York: Times-Mirror, 1976).
3. For example, see Alan A. Block (ed.), *The Business of Crime: A Document Study of Organized Crime in the American Economy* (San Francisco: Westview Press, 1991) and Peter Reuter, *Disorganized Crime: Illegal Markets and the Mafia* (Cambridge: M.I.T. Press, 1986).
4. For example, J. A. Barnes, "Class and Committees in a Norwegian Island Parish," *Human Relations* 7 (1954): 39–58; E. Bott, *Family and Social Networks* (London: Tavistock, 1957); J. C. Mitchell (ed.), *Social Networks in Urban Settings* (Manchester, England: Manchester University Press, 1969); and Jeremy Boissevain, "The Place of Non-Groups in the Social Sciences," *Man* 3 (1968): 542–556.
5. Stanley Wasserman and Katherine Faust, *Social Network Analysis: Methods and Applications* (New York: Cambridge University Press, 1994): 12–13.
6. *Ibid.*: 9.
7. *Ibid.*: 4.
8. *Ibid.*: 17.
9. *Ibid.*: 18.
10. *Ibid.*: 18–19.
11. *Ibid.*: 19.
12. *Ibid.*: 20.
13. In addition to Jeffrey Scott McIllwain, "Organized Crime: A Social Network Approach," *Crime, Law and Social Change: An International Journal* 32 (1999): 301–323, the article that serves as the foundation for this chapter and the next, please consider other criminological applications of social network theory: Nigel Coles, "It's Not What You Know—It's Who You Know That Counts: Analysing Serious Crime Groups as Social Networks, *The British Journal of Criminology* 41:4 (2001): 580–594; Donald Liddick, "Political Fund-raising, Patron-Client

Relations, and Organized Criminality: Two Case Studies, *Journal of Contemporary Criminal Justice* 17:4 (2001): 346–357; Carlo Morselli, "Structuring Mr. Nice: Entrepreneurial Opportunities and Brokerage Positioning in the Cannabis Trade," *Crime, Law and Social Change: An International Journal* 35:3 (2001): 203–244; Gail Myers, Gene McGrady, Clementine Marrow, et. al., "Weapon Carrying Among Black Adolescents: A Social Network Perspective," *American Journal of Public Health* 87:6 (1997): 1038–1040; Gary Potter and Larry Gaines, "Organizing Crime in 'Copperhead County': An Ethnogrpahic Look at Rural Crime Networks," in Jay Albanese (ed.), *Contemporary Issues in Organized Crime* (Monsey, NY: Criminal Justice Press, 1995): 61–86; and Jerzy Samecki, *Delinquent Networks: Youth Co-offending in Stockholm* (Cambridge, UK: Cambridge University Press, 2001).

14. Henner Hess's seminal work on the same subject should not be overlooked [Henner Hess, *Mafia & Mafiosi: Origin, Power and Myth* (New York: New York University Press, 1998)]. For other examples of related social network research, see Jeremy Boissevain, "Patronage in Sicily," *Man* 1 (1966): 18–33; Jeremy Boissevain, "Poverty and Politics in a Sicilian Agro-Town," *International Archives of Ethnography* 50 (1960): 198–236; Jeremy Boissevain, *Friends of Friends: Networks, Manipulators and Coalitions* (Oxford: Basil Blackwell, 1973); Francis Ianni, *Black Mafia*; Jane Schneider, "Family Patrimonies and Economic Behavior in Western Sicily," *Anthropological Quarterly* 42 (1969): 109–129; Jane Schneider, "Of Vigilance and Virgins: Honor, Shame, and Access to Resources in Mediterranean Societies," *Ethnology* 10 (1971): 1–24; Peter Schneider, "Coalition Formation and Colonialism in Sicily," *Archives Europeennes de Sociologie (European Journal of Sociology)* 13 (1972): 255–267; Peter Schneider, Jane Schneider, and Edward C. Hansen, "Modernization and Development: The Role of Regional Elites and Non-corporate Groups in the European Mediterranean," *Comparative Studies in Society and History* 14 (1972): 328–350; Sydel F. Silverman, "Patronage and Community-Nation Relationships in Central Italy," *Ethnology* 4 (1965): 172–189; and Paul Friedrich, "A Mexican Cacicazgo," *Ethnology* 4 (1965): 190–209.

15. "Genuardo" is a pseudonym for a real town in Sicily.

16. Anton Blok, *The Mafia of a Sicilian Village, 1860–1960: A Study of Violent Peasant Entrepreneurs* (New York: Harper Torchbooks, 1974): xxvii.

17. This approach can be found in the influential work of Donald Cressey, *Theft of a Nation*.

18. Charles Tilly, "Foreword," in Blok, *The Mafia of a Sicilian Village: A Study of Violent Peasant Entrepreneurs* (New York: Harper Torchbooks, 1974): xiii.

19. Ibid.: xiii–xiv.
20. Ibid: xiv–xv.
21. Ibid.: xxviii.
22. Ibid.: xxix.

23. Norbert Elias and J. L. Scotson, *The Established and the Outsiders: A Sociological Enquiry into Community Problems* (London: Frank Cass & Co., 1965): 11–12, as quoted in Ibid.

24. Elias and Scotson, *The Established and the Outsiders*: 21–22, as quoted in Ibid.: xxx.

25. Ibid.: 9–10.
26. Ibid.: 12.

27. Alan A. Block. Interview with author. State College, PA (11 October 1996).

28. Block, "History and the Study of Organized Crime": 467.

29. Block, *East Side-West Side*: 3.
30. Ibid.: 10.

31. Kenney and Finckenauer, *Organized Crime in America*: 32.

32. Block, "History and the Study of Organized Crime": 470.

33. Alan Block, "Introduction: The Business of Organized Crime," in Block, *The Business of Crime*: 8.

34. Ibid.: 15.

35. Alan Block, "Organized Crime: History and Historiography," in *Time, Space & Organized Crime*, 2nd ed. (New Brunswick, N.J.: Transaction, 1994): 57.

36. Block, "Introduction: The Business of Organized Crime": 15.

37. Block, *East Side-West Side*: 10. This system is hinted at in the previously published works of Solomon Korbin and Richard Cloward and Lloyd Ohlin. Korbin studied delinquent subcultures in areas with high reports of delinquency. He posited that the "degree of integration" between underworld and upperworld actors in a community directly related to the form of delinquent subcultures in that community. Specifically, he maintained that if illegal activity was systematic and organized, and underworld leaders interacted on social, economic, and political levels with legitimate leaders of the community, commonality of purpose, goals, and security would develop between the two [Solomon Korbin, "The Conflict Values in Delinquency Areas," *American Socio-*

logical Review 16 (1951): 653–661]. Basing their work in part on Korbin's, Cloward and Ohlin developed "differential opportunity" theory. This generally addresses "illegitimate opportunity structures," a set of illegitimate means to achieve societal goals. As part of this theory, they contended that a "criminal subculture" developed in fully integrated communities. This criminal subculture allows juveniles to serve almost as an apprentice group for adult-run organized crime concerns [Richard Cloward and Lloyd Ohlin, *Delinquency and Opportunity: A Theory of Delinquent Gangs* (New York: Free Press, 1960)].

38. Block, *East Side-West Side.*: 10–11.
39. *Ibid*.: 58.
40. *Ibid*.: 11.
41. *Ibid*.: vii.
42. *Ibid*.: 11.
43. *Ibid*.
44. *Ibid*.: 183.
45. *Ibid*.
46. *Ibid*.: 129.
47. *Ibid*.: 159.
48. *Ibid*.: 159.
49. *Ibid*.: 160.
50. *Ibid*.: 246.
51. *Ibid*.: 245.
52. *Ibid*.: 246.
53. *Ibid*.: 222.
54. *Ibid*.: 239.
55. Charles A. Reich, "The New Property," *The Yale Law Journal* 73 (April 1964).
56. Block, *East Side-West Side*: 239.
57. For studies on the role of social networks in patron-client relationships in the American political sphere, see David Hammack, "Problems in the Historical Study of Power in the Cities and Towns of the United States, 1800–1960," *American Historical Review* 83 (April 1978): 323–349 and Alex Weingrod, "Patrons, Patronage, and Political Parties," *Comparative Studies in Society and History* X (June 1968): 377–400.
58. Block, *East Side-West Side*: 252. For more on the need for informal, adaptable networks, in this case in a rural context, see Robert S. Davis and Gary W. Potter, "Bootlegging and Rural Criminal Entrepreneurship," *Journal of Crime and Justice* 14:1 (1991): 145–159.
59. *Ibid.*
60. Timothy Gilfoyle, *City of Eros: New York City, Prostitution and the Commercialization of Sex* (New York: Norton, 1992).
61. David R. Johnson, "A Sinful Business: The Origins of Gambling Syndicates in the U.S., 1840–1887," in David Bayley (ed.), *Police and Society* (Newbury Park, CA: Sage, 1977): 29–55.
62. David R. Johnson, "The Origins and Structures of Intercity Criminal Activity, 1840–1920: An Interpretation," *Journal of Social History* 15 (Sumner 1982): 593–605.
63. Mark H. Haller, "Bootleggers as Businessmen: From City Slum to City Builders," in *Crime & Justice in American History 8: Prostitution, Drugs, Gambling and Organized Crime, Part 2*, Eric H. Monkkonen, ed. (New York: K.G. Saur, 1992): 294–312.
64. Mark H. Haller, "The Changing Structure of American Gambling in the Twentieth Century," *Journal of Social Issues* 35 (1979): 87–114; Haller's "social world" is used in a synonymous manner to Block's "social system."
65. Mark H. Haller, "Organized Crime in Urban Society: Chicago in the Twentieth Century," *Journal of Social History* 5 (Winter 1971–1972): 210–234.
66. Block, "Organized Crime": 53.

Chapter 3

1. Meyers, "The Emerging Threat of Transnational Organized Crime in the East": 183. The concept of *guanxi* in a criminal context is not the sole province of academics. M. Cordell Hart of the Financial Crimes Enforcement Network of the United States Department of the Treasury and others involved with the International Association of Asian Criminal Investigators have taken the lead in making *guanxi* a fundamental frame of reference for all criminal justice practitioners involved with Chinese criminality [e.g., M. Cordell Hart, "Money and 'Guanxi': Keys to Understanding Crime by Asians," A paper presented for a study on Global Organized Crime (Washington, D.C.: Center for Strategic and International Studies, 8 March 1996].
2. Sterling Seagrave, *Lords of the Rim: The Invisible Empire of the Overseas Chinese* (New York: G. P. Putnam's Sons, 1995).
3. Block, "Organized Crime": 41.
4. Adrian Praetzellis and Mary Praetzellis, *Archaeological and Historical Studies of the IJ56 Block, Sacramento, California: An Early Chinese Community* (Rohnert Park, CA: Anthropological Studies Center of Sonoma State University, 1982) and Adrian Praetzellis, Mary Praetzellis, and Marley Brown III, "Artifacts as Symbols of Identity: An Example from Sacramento's Gold Rush

Era Chinese Community," *Living in Cities: Current Research in Urban Archaeology* No. 5 (1987): 38–47. See also Roberta S. Greenwood, "The Overseas Chinese at Home," *Archaeology* 31:5 (1978): 42–49; R.L. Schuyler (ed.), *Archaeological Perspectives on Ethnicity in America: Afro-American and Asian-American Culture History* (Farmingdale, N.Y.: Baywood Publishing, 1980); Eugene M. Hattori, Mary K. Rusco, and Donald R. Touhy (eds.), "Archaeological and Historical Studies at Ninth and Amherst, Lovelock, Nevada," *Nevada State Museum Archaeological Services Reports*, (Carson City, NV, 1979); and David L. Felton, Frank Lortie, and Peter D. Schulz, *The Chinese Laundry on Second Street: Papers on Archaeological and Historical Data Recovered from Selected Sites*, (Nevada City, CA: Tahoe National Forest, 1984).

5. J. T. Omohundru, *Chinese Merchant Families in Iloilo* (Athens, Ohio: Ohio University Press, 1981) and J. T. Omohundru, "Trading Patterns of Philippine Chinese: Strategies of Sojourning Middlemen," in K. Hunter (ed.), "Economic Exchange and Social Interaction in Southeast Asia: Perspectives from Prehistory, History, and Ethnography," *Michigan Papers on South and Southeast Asia* 13 (Ann Arbor, MI, 1979): 113–136.

6. Omohundru, *Chinese Merchant Families in Iloilo*: 84, 114.

7. Meyers, "The Emerging Threat of Transnational Crime from the East": 183.

8. *Ibid.*: 184.

9. *Ibid.*: 185. For more on *guanxi* and Chinese criminal networks, see Meyers, "Orb Weavers—The Global Webs."

10. Meyers, "The Emerging Threat of Transnational Crime from the East": 185–186.

11. *Ibid.*: 186.
12. *Ibid.*: 186–187.
13. *Ibid.*: 187.
14. *Ibid.*: 188.
15. *Ibid.*
16. *Ibid.*
17. *Ibid.*: 188–189.

18. Thorsten Sellin, *Culture Conflict and Crime* (New York: Social Science Research Council, 1938). Sellin's theory was a major contributor to the development of a variety of subculture theories in criminology, among them Albert Cohen's subculture of delinquency theory [Albert Cohen, *Delinquent Boys The Culture of the Gang* (New York: The Free Press, 1955)]; Richard Cloward's and Lloyd Ohlin's differential opportunity theory [Cloward and Ohlin, *Delinquency and Opportunity*]; and Marvin Wolfgang's and Franco Ferracuti's subculture of violence theory [Marvin Wolfgang and Franco Ferracutti, *The Subculture of Violence: Towards an Integrated Theory in Criminology* [London: Tavistock, 1967)].

19. According to Dian Murray, "*hui*" has no precise English equivalent, therefore the terms "society" and "association" are used interchangeably in English. Dian H. Murray, in collaboration with Qin Baoqi, *The Origins of the Tiandihui: The Chinese Triads in Legend and History* (Stanford, CA: Stanford University Press, 1994): 1.

20. *Ibid.*: 1–2.

21. Eve Armentrout Ma, *Revolutionaries, Monarchists, and Chinatowns: Chinese Politics in the Americas and the 1911 Revolution* (Honolulu, HI: University of Hawaii Press, 1990): 14.

22. *Ibid.*: 15–16.

23. For example, see Bresler, *The Chinese Mafia*; Robertson, *Triangle of Death*; and Posner, *Warlords of Crime*.

24. This seemingly care-free and frequent application of the term Mafia (e.g. Russian Mafia, Black Mafia, Chinese Mafia, etc.) to describe any group of organized criminals by the media, academics, and the government is a ripe subject for research from a labeling or symbolic interactionist perspective [e.g., George Mead, *Mind, Self, and Society* (Charles W. Morris, ed. Chicago: University of Chicago Press, 1934) and Howard S. Becker, *Outsiders: Studies in the Sociology of Deviance* (New York: Free Press, 1963)]. For example, what "baggage" does the term Mafia imply when it is applied to non-Sicilian organized crime groups? How does the label Mafia affect investigations of, and societal reactions to, these organizations? How does the label Mafia affect the self-perception of these organized criminals? Is the label Mafia appropriate, or a misnomer? If so, what term or terms should be used in its place?

25. Chin, *Chinese Triad Societies*: 39.
26. *Ibid.*

27. Chin, *Chinesse Sub-culture and Criminality: Non-traditional Crime Groups in America* (New York: Greenwood Press, 1990); 28. This point is elaborated upon in Murray, *The Origins of the Tiandihui*.

28. The oaths and strategies of the societies are translated and listed in Chin, *Chinese Sub-culture and Criminality*: 155–161.

29. Chin, *Chinese Triad Societies*: 70.

30. Dillon, *The Hatchet Men*. It should be noted that other Chinese organizations, both restrictive and non-restrictive, undertook the same functions to varying degrees.

31. *Ibid.*
32. *Ibid.*
33. Stanford Morris Lyman, *The Asian in North America* (Santa Barbara, CA: ABC-Clio, 1977): 263–264.
34. Chin, *Chinese Triad Socities*: 39–65.
35. *Ibid.*: 72.
36. Chin, *Chinese Sub-culture and Criminality*: 53–54.
37. Chin, *Chinese Triad Societies*: 86–89.
38. *Ibid.*
39. Chin, *Chinese Sub-culture and Criminality*: 59.
40. *Ibid.*: 59–60.
41. *Ibid.*: 59. More on Triad oaths can be found in Dian Murray, *The Origins of the Tiandihui*: 239–246.
42. Chin, *Chinese Sub-culture and Criminality*: 142–143.
43. *Ibid.*
44. Chin, *Chinese Triad Societies*: 6.
45. Chin, *Smuggled Chinese.*
46. Chin, *Chinatown Gangs*: 21–34.
47. *Ibid.*: 5–6.
48. *Ibid.*: 5. Calvin Toy also disregarded the long history of Chinese street gangs in San Francisco, viewing the issue as beginning after the relaxation of immigration restrictions during the 1960s (Toy, "A Short History of Asian Gangs in San Francisco").
49. Chin, *Chinese Sub-culture and Criminality*: 60.
50. *Ibid.*: 146.
51. See Dillon, *The Hatchet Men* and Gong and Grant, *Tong War!*.
52. Chin, *Chinese Triad Societies*: 72–76.
53. *Ibid.*: 85–94.
54. For example, see the Asian organized crime sections in leading texts on organized crime: Howard Abadinsky, *Organized Crime* (4th ed.) (Chicago: Nelson-Hall, 1994); Albanese, *Organized Crime in America*: 151, 158–159; and Kenney and Finckenauer, *Organized Crime in America*: 256–260. It should be noted that scholars are not alone in this ahistorical approach. Consider the work of journalists Black, *Triad Takeover*: 141–143 and Posner, *Warlords of Crime*: 206–212; 239.
55. Stephan Thernstrom, "Notes on the Historical Study of Social Mobility," *Comparative Studies in Society and History* 10 (1968): 162.

Chapter 4

1. Marlon K. Hom, *Songs of Gold Mountain: Cantonese Rhymes from San Francisco Chinatown* (Berkeley, CA: University of California Press, 1987): 288. Hom appears to have placed two traditionally distinct vices, food and drink, and combined them, adding the fourth vice, opium. Since opium was a relatively new vice (1800s), this re-classification makes sense.
2. *Ibid.*
3. *Ibid.*: 289–300.
4. As found in and translated by Hom, *Ibid*: 294.
5. Paul C. P. Siu (John Kuo Wei Tchen, editor), *The Chinese Laundryman: A Study of Social Isolation* (New York: New York University Press, 1987): 250.
6. *Ibid.*: 253.
7. Hom, *Songs of Gold Mountain*: 289–300.
8. *Ibid.*: 301.
9. Ivan Light, "From Vice District to Tourist Attraction: The Moral Career of American Chinatowns, 1880–1940," *Pacific Historical Review* 43:3 (August 1974): 368–369. Light also stated that "in New York City's Chinatown, largest on the East Coast, Chinese-owned vice resorts proved so lucrative that Irish competitors invaded the district. By 1890, shady Irish were operating vice resorts in New York's Chinatown, but drawing their trade only from white men." This, however, appears to be an exaggeration of the situation, for it was the Chinese who "invaded" a bastion of Irish-run vice on the Bowery and turned the location into a Chinatown. For many years, Irish and Chinese vice establishments coexisted, but eventually the Irish gave way as the Chinese population increased substantially.
10. *Ibid.*: 372.
11. For samples of this history, see Timothy Brook and Bob Tadashi Wakabayashi (editors), *Opium Regimes: China, Britain and Japan, 1839–1952* (Berkeley: University of California Press, 2000); Gail Hershatter, *Dangerous Pleasures: Prostitution and Modernity in Twentieth-Century Shanghai* (Berkeley, CA: University of California Press, 1997); Hunt Janin, *The India-China Opium Trade in the Nineteenth Century* (Jefferson, NC: McFarland & Company, Inc., 1999); Brian G. Martin, *The Shanghai Green Gang: Politics and Organized Crime, 1919–1937* (Berkeley, CA: University of California Press, 1996); Kathryn Meyer and Terry M. Parssinen, *Webs of Smoke: Smugglers, Warlords, and the History of the International Drug Trade* (Lanham, MD: Rowman & Little-field, 2002); Dian H. Murray, "Migration, Protection, and Racketeering: The Spread of the Tiandihui within China," in David Ownby and Mary Som-

mers Heidhues (eds.), *"Secret Societies" Reconsidered: Perspectives on the Social History of Modern South China and Southeast Asia* (New York: M.E. Sharpe, 1993): 177–189; Murray, *The Origins of the Tiandihui*; Dian H. Murray, *Pirates of the South China Coast, 1790–1810* (Stanford, CA: Stanford University Press, 1987);

12. David T. Courtwright, *Violent Land: Single Men and Social Disorder from the Frontier to the Inner City* (Cambridge, MA: Harvard University Press, 1996): 160.

13. According to Dillon, coolie "gained wide acceptance as a synonym for Chinaman in the vocabulary of the Americans. It was an Anglo-Indian word, not a Chinese term at all, and came from the Bengali or Tamil word kuli which signified 'burden bearer' and which originally meant 'bitter work'" (Dillon, *The Hatchet Men*: 14–15).

14. *Ibid.*: 91. According to Ma, "the overwhelming majority of these immigrants were adult males. Most were Cantonese: people who came from the city of Canton or its Pearl River delta hinterland, in the southern coastal province of Kwangtung. About ninety percent of this group in North America were Punti Cantonese. The next largest group was the Hsiangshan, and the remainder were Hakka from Kwangtung" [Ma, *Revolutionaries, Monarchists, and Chinatowns*: 9].

15. According to the *United States Census of Population* (1940), there were 34,933 Chinese immigrants in the United States in 1860; 63,199 in 1870; 105,465 in 1880; and 107,488 in 1890. Beginning in the 1900 census, and bottoming-out in the 1920 census, the number of Chinese immigrants declined (89,863 in 1900; 71,531 in 1910; and 61,639 in 1920). This was due to the large number of Chinese men repatriating to China in the wake of the Boxer Rebellion, the Chinese Revolution, and the race-inspired difficulties faced by Chinese in the United States.

16. Ma, *Revolutionaries, Monarchists, and Chinatowns*.

17. Seagrave, *Lords of the Rim*.

18. Hom, *Songs of Gold Mountain*: 5.

19. Lisa See, *On Gold Mountain* (New York: St. Martin's Press, 1995): 6.

20. Courtwright, *Violent Land*: 153.

21. Calvin Lee, *Chinatown, U.S.A.* (Garden City, NY: Doubleday & Company, 1965): 12. If the immigrant was not under the credit-fare system, they sought their own employment.

22. Ma, *Revolutionaries, Monarchists, and Chinatowns*: 10–11.

23. *Ibid.*: 12.

24. Stewart Creighton Miller, *Unwelcome Immigrant: The American Image of Chinese, 1785–1882* (Berkeley, CA: The University of California Press, 1969): 15.

25. *Ibid.*: 201.

26. *The Missoula and Cedar Creek Pioneer* (22 June 1871).

27. Miller, *Unwelcome Immigrant*: 15.

28. Susan Craddock, *City of Plagues: Disease, Poverty and Deviance in San Francisco* (Minneapolis: University of Minnesota Press, 2000): Book jacket.

29. Miller, *Unwelcome Immigrant*: 193.

30. "Field, J., Dissenting," *Chew Hong v. United States*, 12 U.S. 536, 567 (1984).

31. Thomas G. Dyer, *Theodore Roosevelt and the Idea of Race* (Baton Rouge, LA: Louisiana State University Press, 1980): 139.

32. With regard to the fondness for the flesh of dogs, cats and rats, in 1883 leaders of New York City's Chinatown threatened slander lawsuits if such stories continued to appear in the press. Miller cites various stories re-electing these alleged culinary desires up to the year 1883 (Miller, *The Unwelcome Immigrant*: 186).

33. The Chinese and blacks were the targeted groups [David Musto, *The American Disease: Origins of Narcotic Control* (expanded edition) (New York: Oxford University Press, 1987): 5–6].

34. *Ibid.*: 244–245.

35. Sarah E. Henshaw, "California Housekeepers and Chinese Servants," *Scribner's Monthly*, XII (1876): 739.

36. *New York Daily Tribune* (2 October 1903).

37. Miller, *The Unwelcome Immigrant*: 186.

38. Mark Twain, *Roughing It* (New York: Harper & Brothers, 1924).

39. A fine source of primary documents relating to this experience can be found in Philip S. Foner and Daniel Rosenberg, editors, *Racism, Dissent, and Asian Americans from 1850 to the Present: A Documentary History* (Westport, CT: Greenwood Press, 1992).

40. Ruthanne Lum McCunn, *Chinese American Portraits: Personal Histories, 1828–1988* (San Francisco: Chronicle Books, 1988): 156.

41. As summarized in *Ibid.*: 156.

42. *Ibid.*: 156, 158.

43. *Ibid.*: 156, 159.

44. For examples of these fights, please see Andrew Gyory, *Closing the Gate:*

Race, Politics, and the Chinese Exclusion Act (Chapel Hill: University of North Carolina Press, 1998); Charles McClain, *In Search of Equality: The Chinese Struggle against Discrimination in Nineteenth-Century America* (Berkeley, CA: University of California Press, 1994), and Lucy Salyer, *Laws as Harsh as Tigers: Chinese Immigrants and the Shaping of Modern Immigration Law* (Chapel Hill: University of North Carolina Press, 1995),
    45. Courtwright, *Violent Land*: 167.

Chapter 5

1. Block, *East Side-West Side*: 159.
2. Myers, "The Emerging Threat of Transnational Organized Crime from the East": 185–186.
3. *Ibid.*
4. For example, see Lucie Cheng Hirata, "Free, Indentured, Enslaved: Chinese Prostitutes in Nineteenth-Century America," *Signs: Journal of Women and Culture in Society* 5 (1979) and Light, "From Vice District to Tourist Attraction."
5. For background on how prostitution was operated in China, see Hershatter, *Dangerous Pleasures*.
6. Note that the reduction in the gender ratio after 1900 was not due to an increase in the immigration of females. Rather it resulted from the repatriation of Chinese men that began in the 1890s as a result of the Scott Act, the weak American economy, and racial pogroms.
7. Hirata, "Free, Indentured, Enslaved."
8. Benson Tong, *Unsubmissive Women: Chinese Prostitutes in Nineteenth-Century San Francisco* (Norman, OK: University of Oklahoma Press, 1994): 193.
9. Lisa See, *On Gold Mountain* (New York: St. Martin's Press, 1995): 17.
10. As found in *Ibid.*: 15–16.
11. As found in Shih-Shan Henry Tsai, *The Chinese Experience in America* (Bloomington, IN: Indiana University Press, 1986): 40–41.
12. Tong, *Unsubmissive Women*: 126–158.
13. Hirata, "Free, Indentured, Enslaved": 7–8.
14. *Ibid.*: 8.
15. See, *On Gold Mountain*: 17. As was the case for immigrants' because of their proximity to trade routes, Canton and Hong Kong were the major sources of prostitutes going to the United States.
16. Hirata, "Free, Indentured, Enslaved": 8–9.
17. *Ibid.*: 10.
18. Hom, *Songs of Gold Mountain*: 19.
19. Hirata, "Free, Indentured, Enslaved": 10–11.
20. *Ibid.*: 11.
21. *Ibid.*: 12.
22. *Ibid*: 11.
23. Peter Reuter provides an excellent analysis of the concept of monopoly as applied to illegal markets for goods and services [Reuter, *Disorganized Crime*].
24. Hirata, "Free, Indentured, Enslaved": 12–13.
25. Dillon, *The Hatchet Men*: 223–227.
26. Hirata, "Free, Indentured, Enslaved": 12–13.
27. Marion Goldman, "Sexual Commerce on the Comstock Load," *Nevada Historical Society Quarterly* (1978): 98–129.
28. *Ibid.*
29. Dillon, *The Hatchet Men*.
30. Beck, *New York's Chinatown*: 108.
31. *Ibid.*: 17.
32. *Ibid.*: 17–19.
33. Light, "From Vice District to Tourist Attraction": 370–371.
34. For more on the process by which Chinese prostitutes left the trade, see Tong, *Unsubmissive Women*: 159–191. and Judy Yung, *Unbound Feet: A Social History of Chinese Women in San Francisco* (Berkeley: University of California Press, 1995).
35. Light, "From Vice District to Tourist Attraction": 370–371.
36. *Ibid.*
37. Robbens, "Chinese Slave Girls": 102.
38. Dillon, *The Hatchet Men*: 113.
39. *Ibid.*: 86.
40. *Ibid.*: 197.
41. Robbens, "Chinese Slave Girls": 102.
42. Hirata, "Free, Indentured, Enslaved" and Dillon, *The Hatchet Men*.
43. Gilfoyle, *City of Eros*.
44. Wu, *Chinatown*: 202.
45. *Ibid.*: 206.
46. Dillon, *The Hatchet Men*: 62.
47. Edward M. Brecher and others, *Licit & Illicit Drugs: The Consumers Union Report on Narcotics, Stimulants, Depressants, Inhalants, Hallucinogens, & Marijuana—Including Caffeine, Nicotine, and Alcohol* (Boston: Little, Brown, & Company, 1972): 42.
48. *Ibid.*: 42–44.
49. *Ibid.*: 44. For a complete listing of laws, regulations, and ordinances passed concerning opium on the federal, state, and

local levels during this era, see Charles E. Terry and Mildred Pellens, *The Opium Problem* (Montclair, NJ: Patterson Smith, 1928): 745.

50. For more information on Chinese immigrant smuggling, please see Hsu, Madeline. "Gold Mountain Dreams and Paper Son Schemes: Chinese Immigration Under Exclusion." *Chinese America: History and Perspectives* (1997): 46–60; Erika Lee, "Enforcing the Borders: Chinese Exclusion along the U.S. Borders with Canada and Mexico, 1882–1924," *The Journal of American History* 89:1 (June 2002); Jeffrey Scott McIllwain, "Corruption, Bureaucracy and Organized Crime: Federal Law Enforcement and Chinese Immigrant Smuggling Syndicates in and around San Diego, 1897–1901," a paper presented to the American Society of Criminology (November 1999) and Jeffrey Scott McIllwain, "Opportunity, Adaptation and Criminal Enterprise: Immigrant Smuggling during the Exclusion Era," a paper presented to the Academy of Criminal Justice Sciences (March 2000).

51. "Collector Saunders's Work," *The New York Times* (4 February 1895): 3.

52. Dillon, *The Hatchet Men*: 65–66. "A Heavy Opium Seizure," *The New York Times* (28 February 1897): 1.

53. "A Heavy Opium Seizure," *The New York Times*: 1; and "All San Francisco's Opium Seized," *The New York Times* (3 March 1897): 2.

54. "A Heavy Opium Seizure" refers to a statute of February 1887 that restricted the right to import opium to Caucasians. Furthermore, "a treaty between the United States and China binds [the United States] to forbid the importation of opium into American ports by Chinese agents."

55. "A Heavy Opium Seizure," *The New York Times*. Kwong Fong Tai & Co. is "Fong Tai & Co." in this article.

56. "All San Francisco's Opium Seized," *The New York Times*. Kwong Fong Tai & Co. is "Qwong Fong Tai & Co." in this article.

57. Tsai, *The Chinese Experience in America*: 39–40.

58. McIllwain, "From Tong War to Organized Crime."

59. For more on Chinese opium smuggling practices in the United States, see Jeffrey Scott McIllwain, "An Equal Opportunity Employer: Chinese Opium Smuggling Syndicates in and around San Diego during the 1910s," *Transnational Organized Crime* 4:2 (1999).

60. As quoted in Becher, *Licit & Illicit Drugs*: 44. The Secretary of the Treasury wrote the reference to the tongs.

61. Tsai, *The Chinese Experience in America*: 39–40

62. *Ibid.*

63. Becher, *Licit & Illicit Drugs*: 44–45.

64. Tsai, *The Chinese Experience in America*: 39–40.

65. Note that this is just reflective of legal importation of smoking opium. As the 19th century progressed, prohibitive duties were placed on the good, duties that encouraged smuggling so as to pocket the difference of created by non-payment of the duties (McIllwain, "An Equal Opportunity Employer").

66. David T. Courtwright, *Dark Paradise: Opium Addiction in America before 1940* (Cambridge, MA: Harvard University Press, 1982): 86.

67. *Ibid.*: 63–64.

68. *Ibid.*: 63–64. "'Lower class,'" added Courtwright, "in this context was almost certainly a euphemism for prostitutes."

69. *Ibid.*: 70.

70. *Ibid.*: 64.

71. *Ibid.*: 65.

72. *Ibid.*: 86.

73. *Ibid.*

74. For example, see Meyers and Parssinen, *Webs of Smoke*; Alfred McCoy, *The Politics of Heroin: CIA Complicity in the Global Drug Trade* (Brooklyn, NY: Lawrence Hill Books, 1991); David E. Kaplan, *Fires of the Dragon: Politics, Murder, and the Kuomintang* (New York: Antheum, 1992); and Anslinger and Ousler, *The Murderers*.

75. See McIllwain, "An Equal Opportunity Employer."

Chapter 6

1. Hom, *Songs of Gold Mountain*: 25.

2. Despite being considered one of the Four Vices, gambling has a long, ingrained history in Siu, *The Chinese Laundryman*: 228.

3. Culin also described various games of dice and dominoes in another essay, but did not relate them to organized criminal enterprise [Stewart Culin, "Chinese Games with Dice and Dominoes," *Report of the National Museum* (1893)].

4. Culin actually uses the spelling *fan t'an*, but the more common spelling is used here.

5. Stewart Culin, "The Gambling Games of the Chinese in America," *Series in Philology, Literature and Archaeology* 1:4

(Philadelphia: University of Pennsylvania Press, 1891): 1–2.
6. *Ibid.*
7. Siu, *The Chinese Laundryman*: 229.
8. Culin, "The Gambling Games of the Chinese in America": 6–7, 11.
9. *Ibid.*: 6–7.
10. *Ibid.*: 9–10.
11. *Ibid.*: 10–11.
12. *Ibid.*.
13. Siu, *The Chinese Laundryman*: 231.
14. As quoted in Dillon, *The Hatchet Men*: 217.
15. Gilfoyle, *City of Eros.*
16. As quoted in Tsai, *The Chinese Experience in America*: 39.
17. W. Maitland, "The Chinaman in California and South Africa," *Contemporary Review* 88 (1905): 821–822.
18. Johnson, "A Sinful Business": 29.
19. *Ibid.*
20. *Ibid.*: 35.
21. *Ibid.*
22. Light, "From Vice District to Tourist Attraction": 374.
23. Robert Wells Ritchie, "The Wars of the Tongs," *Harper's Weekly* 54 (27 August 1910): 8–9.
24. Siu, *The Chinese Laundryman*: 231.
25. Wu, *Chinatown*: 197.
26. *Ibid.*: 198.
27. This assumption is made after a reading of Dillon, *The Hatchet Men*, Eng Ying Gong and Bruce Grant, *Tong War!* (New York: N.L. Brown, 1930) and C.Y. Lee, *Days of the Tong Wars* (New York: Ballantine Books, 1974).
28. Dillon, *The Hatchet Men*: 172. Until approximately 1880, however, there was no particular term for Chinese criminals. Dillon cited police officer Delos Woodruff as coining the term "highbinders" during publicly-reported testimony made sometime during the 1870s. Appearing before the court, Woodruff answered a question from the bench by saying, "'A lot of highbinders came to the place (...).'" The judge then interrupted the officer, asking him what he meant by "highbinders." "Why," replied Woodruff, "a lot of Chinese hoodlums." According to Dillon, "from that point on, Chinese murderers, pimps, blackmailers, gunmen, professional gamblers, and toughs of all kinds in San Francisco began to be known as highbinders." At some unknown time, when some of these highbinders used a hatchet or cleaver in an act of violence, the term "hatchet man" was born (*Ibid.*: 52).
29. McIllwain, "From Tong War to Organized Crime."
30. Glick, *Shake Hands with the Dragon*: 261–265.
31. Wu, *Chinatown*: 223.
32. Dillon, *The Hatchet Men*: 184–185.
33. *Ibid.*; Gong and Grant, *Tong War!* and Stanford Morris Lyman, *Chinatown and Little Tokyo: Power, Conflict and Community among Chinese and Japanese Immigrants in America* (New York: Associated Faculty Press, 1986).
34. *Ibid.*: 225.
35. Lyman, *Chinatown and Little Tokyo*: 203.
36. *Ibid.*: 206.
37. *Ibid.*: 216.
38. Hirata, "Free, Indentured, Enslaved": 18.
39. *Ibid.*: 19.
40. *Ibid.*: 19–20.
41. As quoted in *Ibid.*: 259–260.
42. A point also illustrated in Clare V. McKanna, Jr., "Chinese Tongs, Homicide, and Justice in Nineteenth-Century California," *Western Legal History* (13:2 (Summer/Fall 2000): 205–238.

Chapter 7

1. David C. Hammack, *Power and Society: Greater New York at the Turn of the Century* (New York: Columbia University Press, 1982): 33.
2. *Ibid.*
3. *Ibid.*: 60–63.
4. For Lexow material consult New York State Senate, *Report and Proceedings of the Senate Committee Appointed to Investigate the Police Department of the City of New York* (Albany, 1895). For Mazet material consult New York State Assembly, *Final Report of the Special Committee of the Assembly Appointed to Investigate the Public Officers and Departments of the City of New York and the Counties Therein Included* (Albany, 1900).
5. Gilfoyle, *City of Eros*: 251–253.
6. *Ibid.*: 268. It should be noted that Gilfoyle never addressed Chinese prostitution in his research. This is despite the idea of Chinese "slave girls" and opium-induced "white slavery" being popular at the time. Given the thoroughness of his study, this leaves us with two possible conclusions: First, Chinese-operated prostitution did not exist for there is no record of its suppression, or, second, it did exist but was heavily protected via a system of police and political graft. Given that others provide evidence of its existence in New York City's Chinatown, as well as the patterns found in

other Chinatowns across the United States, it seems safe to rely on the second choice, especially when one notes the ward strength of Big Tim Sullivan's Tammany machine and the rampant police corruption in the area.

7. *Ibid.*: 268–269.

8. Miller, *The Unwelcome Immigrant*: 184. For more on this "trickle" and how it led to the forming of New York's Chinatown, please see Tchen, *New York before Chinatown*.

9. Beck, *New York's Chinatown*: 11.

10. "Quimbo Appo," was "a man of great intelligence, gifted with a mind whose keenness startled all white men who came in contact with him." Once a respectable tea merchant, Beck related that Quimbo Appo's fondness for drink—"at such times he transformed into a fiend, with an insatiable craving for blood"—led him to slash the throat of his wife, "a woman of the slums." Sentenced to prison, he was pardoned in 1863 through the influence of Christian friends. Once out, he killed a Pole in a street fight and was sent away to serve five more years. Released once again, he married an Irish woman named "Cork Mag," and their domestic violence led to another year in jail for Quimbo Appo. Before being sent to prison once again in 1875, this time for killing a neighbor, a Mrs. Fletcher, he and Cork Mag had a child who was named George Appo. After three years of his final sentence, Quimbo Appo's "mind gave way and the prison physicians declared him to be hopelessly insane." He was subsequently transferred to the State Hospital for the Criminal Insane at Matteawan where he spent his final years (Beck, *Chinatown*: 9–10). Tchen offers a more scholarly, balanced account of Appo that clearly illustrates that the treatment of Appo by the press was a microcosm of the manner in which the Chinese community as a whole was portrayed to the American people. John Kuo Wei Tchen, *New York Before Chinatown: Orientalism and the Shaping of American Culture, 1776–1882* (Baltimore, MD: The Johns Hopkins University Press, 1999). 90–93, 96, 159–163, 229, 284–291 and 294).

11. "Chinamen in New York," *New York Times* (26 December 1856). For more on Quimbo Appo, please see Tchen, *New York before Chinatown*: 90–93, 96, 159–163, 284–291 and 294.

12. Miller, *The Unwelcome Immigrant*: 184.

13. As quoted in Renqiu Yu, *To Save China, to Save Ourselves: The Chinese Hand Laundry Alliance of New York* (Philadelphia: Temple University Press, 1992): 13.

14. A full discussion of these changing attitudes towards Chinese in New York is the central theme of Tchen's excellent work, *New York before Chinatown*.

15. Victor Nee and Brett de Barry Nee, *Longtime Californ': A Documentary Study of an American Chinatown* (New York: Pantheon Books, 1972): 21–22.

16. Dillon, *The Hatchet Men*.

17. Gong and Grant, *Tong War!*: 148.

18. Beck, *New York's Chinatown*: 8, 12.

19. Wong Chin Foo, "The Chinese in New York," *The Cosmopolitan* 5 (March–October 1888): 297–311. Wong Ching Foo (Huang Qingfu) was a prominent Chinese "activist and gadfly" who came to "champion Chinese in the Americas." For more on this important figure in Chinese-American history, see Tchen, *New York Before Chinatown*: 233, 250, 251, 253–258, 268–269, 281, 283, 292 and 294.

20. Foo, "The Chinese in New York": 297.

21. "Chinese in New York," *New York Times* (26 December 1873).

22. Sante, *Low Life*: 144.

23. Jacob A. Riis, *How the Other Half Lives* (reprint edition): (New York: Bedford Books, 1996): 121.

24. *Ibid.*: 121–122.

25. Gong and Grant, *Tong War!*: 149.

26. Dunshee, *As You Pass By*: 153. Note that Doyers Street is spelled Doyer Street in some sources. I have standardized it throughout this study as the former.

27. Dunshee, *As You Pass By.*: 58.

28. Yu, *To Save China, to Save Ourselves*: 12.

29. Foo, "The Chinese in New York": 300.

30. Helen F. Clark, "The Chinese of New York Contrasted with Their Foreign Neighbors," *The Century* 53 (November 1896–April 1897): 106.

31. Beck, *New York's Chinatown*: 46.

32. "There are but a few Chinese prostitutes here, but their places are filled by white women of the most degraded class, hundreds of whom occupy apartments in Chinatown and minister exclusively to the passions of the Chinese" (Beck, *New York's Chinatown*: 29).

33. Obviously the number 9,156 does not equate the population estimates Beck provided earlier for both Chinatown proper or the Chinese community in the metropolitan area (*Ibid.*: 8 and 12). Since Beck does not provide his methods in any

of these cases, this contradiction cannot be explained.

34. Beck, *New York's Chinatown*: 91–94. Chinese theater is discussed generally in Lois Rodescape, "Celestial Drama in the Golden Hills: The Chinese Theater in California, 1849–1869," *California Historical Society Quarterly* 23:2 (June 1944): 97–116.

35. "Business in Chinatown Falls Off," *New York Times* (26 July 1900): 3. For a basic history of the Six Companies, see William Hoy, *The Chinese Six Companies* (San Francisco: Chinese Consolidated Benevolent Association, 1942).

36. "Six Companies Disbands," *New York Daily Tribune* (3 February 1897): 1 and "The Six Companies Retire," *New York Daily Tribune* (7 February 1897): III:5.

37. Note that the Six Companies was also known as the Chinese Consolidated Benevolent Association (Hoy, *The Chinese Six Companies*).

38. Leong Gor Yun, *Chinatown Inside Out* (New York: B. Mussey, 1936).

39. In his book, Beck called it the "Chong Wah Gong Shaw." However, the I have taken the liberty of replacing Beck's spelling with the one generated by contemporary Chinese scholars and will do so throughout the rest of this work.

40. Beck, *New York's Chinatown*: 13–14.
41. *Ibid.*: 19–20.
42. Yu, *To Save China, to Save Ourselves*: 17.
43. *Ibid.*
44. Yun, *Chinatown Inside Out*: 77.
45. Yu, *To Save China, to Save Ourselves*: 17.
46. Beck, *New York's Chinatown*: 17–19.
47. *Ibid.*: 18.
48. Yun, *Chinatown Inside Out*: 40–51.
49. The basic property right was different than the other procedures established by the CCBA to make sure debtors paid their creditors before selling their business and moving away. As discussed in the preliminary hearing of Lee Sing for the shooting of Mock Duck in 1904, a Chinese business "is never sold without its being posted in Chinatown in a public place." Half of the selling price "is paid on deposit and the other half in two or three weeks [after the notice is posted] in order that the creditors [of the business] may collect." [*The People, on Complaint of Mock Duck v. Lee Sing* (10 January 1905, etc.). City Magistrates' Court, First Division, First District. New York Public Library. Attached to *The People v. Mock Duck* (20 March 1902, etc.). Court of General Sessions. City and County of New York. Part II. New York Public Library.]

50. Yun, *Chinatown Inside Out*: 41–42.
51. *Ibid.*: 45.
52. *Ibid.*: 48–49.
53. *Ibid.*: 50.
54. *Ibid.* This is my paraphrased version of his question.
55. *Ibid.*: 52.
56. Beck, *New York's Chinatown*: 72.
57. *Ibid.*.
58. Also known as the Mei Chi Party.
59. Beck, *New York's Chinatown*: 21.
60. *Ibid.*: 16.
61. "Tongs Clash Again," *The New York Daily Tribune* (19 September 1904): 1.
62. Beck refers to the On Leong Tong as "The On Leon Society."
63. Beck, *New York's Chinatown*: 135.
64. Tchen listed Tom Lee's name as Wang A. Ling (a.k.a. Leeng); however, he does not state which name is his real name and which is a paper name (Tchen, *New York before Chinatown*: 242).
65. "Prosperous Chinese Arrested for Voting," *New York Times* (17 August 1904): 7.
66. "The On Leong Dinner," *The New York Daily Tribune* (13 February 1900): 6 and "Chinese New Year's Feast," *The New York Times* (13 February 1900): 18.
67. "Prosperous Chinese Arrested For Voting," *The New York Times*.
68. Beck, *New York's Chinatown*: 204–206.
69. *Ibid.*: 286.
70. Gong and Grant, *Tong War!*: 157.
71. Lee, *Chinatown, U.S.A.*: 35.
72. Gong and Grant, *Tong War!*: 152–157.
73. Tchen states that the Chinese Freemasons in New York City were the Sam Hop Hui (Sanhohui). The Sam Hop Hui "was an underground oppositional society reputedly founded by Buddhist monks in the early seventeenth century, during the early years of the Manchu (Qing) Dynasty, to work toward returning China to Chinese (Han) rule." Tchen added, "In order to adapt to American society, members of the brotherhood borrowed the name and some of the language of the Masons." Tom Lee (Wang A. Ling) was a founding member. Tchen states that the Chinese Freemasons were "egregiously misunderstood in the decades to come." Tchen argues that the New York Chinese Freemasons was not a criminal organization, as many non-Chinese viewed the organization (Tchen, *New York before Chinatown*: 241–242). Yet the Chih Kung Tong, also called the Chinese

Freemasons, clearly had chapters, including the one in New York, involved with criminal activity at various times. Whether the Chih Kung Tong and Sam Hop Hui were one in the same could not be determined.
 74. Gong and Grant, *Tong War!*: 152–157. I could not locate corroborating evidence for this alleged action by Mock Duck.
 75. Beck, *New York's Chinatown*: 133. Note that Beck equates highbinders with The Hip Sing Tong.
 76. *Ibid.*: 132–133.
 77. *Ibid.*: 120, 124.
 78. Yun, *Chinatown Inside Out*: 81–82.
 79. *Ibid.*
 80. *Ibid.*: 74.
 81. Sante, *Low Life*: 143–144.
 82. See Tchen, *New York before Chinatown*: 260–283.

Chapter 8

 1. For a short take on an entertainer's life of "passing that hat" at Bowery establishments, as well as short glimpses of various saloons and characters of the Bowery, see Lawrence Bergreen, *As Thousands Cheer: The Life of Irving Berlin* (New York: Viking Press, 1990): 14–31.
 2. Gong and Grant, *Tong War!*: 150–151; Harlow, *Old Bowery Days*.
 3. Cornelius Willemse, *Behind the Green Lights* (New York: Knopf, 1931).
 4. A. F. Harlow, *Old Bowery Days: The Chronicles of A Famous Street* (New York: D. Appleton & Company, 1931): 428–435, and Maxwell F. Marcuse, *This Was New York!: A Nostalgic Picture of Gotham in the Gaslight Era* (New York: LIM Press, 1969): 46.
 5. Harlow, *Old Bowery Days*: 428–435, and Marcuse, *This Was New York!*: 46. Considering the narcotic effect of opium, this was quite a comical, not to mention impossible, performance geared toward the naive.
 6. This is evident in his popular and widely read memoirs (co-authored by the proprietor of *The Police Gazette* publishing house, Richard K. Fox),: "But I guess blokes like Carnegie and Rockefeller hez got more dan a million—I t'ink dey must hev two millions ennyhow. But if I had dere cush I wouldn't be buildin' no readin' rooms, en libraries, en t'ings like dat. Nixey, dey ain't no good. A guy wot's hungry can't eat de cover off a book, kin he, an' if he's out uv work how is a brown-stone front goin' ter put him next?" [Chuck Connors, *Bowery Life* (New York: Richard K. Fox Publishing Company, 1904): 4].
 7. Harlow, *Old Bowery Days*: 428–435 and Marcuse, *This Was New York!*: 46. The 1903 banquet had the distinction of being disrupted by a cigar-snatching, bottle-and-glass-breaking, and hatchet-wielding Carrie Nation.
 8. However, "honest" graft, graft originating not from vice but from political patronage and power over the "new property" inherent in municipal government, was still allowed and expected.
 9. This explains why the Committee of Five never produced a written record of vice in Chinatown [Oliver E. Allen, *The Tiger: The Rise and Fall of Tammany Hall* (New York: Addison-Wesley, 1993): 203–204, 211–212 and 220]. The assumption that Sullivan was allowed to continue relationships with vice establishments comes from his involvement with the "Becker-Rosenthal Affair" in 1912 (as described on page 220 in the above), as well as his efforts leading to the removal of Police Commissioner Theodore Bingham in 1909 because of Bingham's attempts to clean up vice establishments surrounding Chatham Square (Luc Sante, *Low Life: Lures and Snares of Old New York* [New York: Vintage, 1991, 272]). For more on Tammany Hall, see *Ibid.*, Gustavus Meyers, *The History of Tammany Hall* (New York: Boni & Liveright, 1917); Elliot Rosenberg and Louis Eisenstein, *A Stripe of Tammany's Tiger* (New York: R. Speller, 1966); Morris Robert Werner, *Tammany Hall* (Garden City, New York: Doubleday, Duran & Company, 1928).
 10. Harlow, *Old Bowery Days*: 487–522.
 11. Sante, *Low Life*: 226. Sante's assertion makes sense. Whether or not Chinatown vice entrepreneurs paid for this "protection" is unknown. However, when one considers the close relationship between certain high-profile Chinese leaders (who also had vested interest in vice operations) and Tammany Hall, and the many political favors the latter did for the former, it is safe to infer that such a relationship existed. Yet there is no evidence to suggest Tammany-affiliated street gangs did any of the collecting from the Chinese. As a matter of fact, there is no evidence of any of these street gangs ever directly causing problems for the Chinese community, despite the fact Chinatown was the dividing line between Monk Eastman and Five Points territory. Therefore, it is logical to assume that Chinese organized criminals either paid Tammany agents directly, or else they had their attorneys or some other representative do the same.
 12. Otto L. Bettmann, *The Good Old*

Days—They Were Terrible! (New York: Random House, 1974): 96–97.

13. *Ibid.*

14. Gong and Grant, *Tong War!*: 151; "Gambling in Chinatown," *The New York Times* (9 September 1900): 26. The Chinese owners of the dens paid weekly tribute to those Chinese who controlled this vice in Chinatown. They extorted "a tax of 7 percent on all winnings at fan-tan and pigow, the tariff increasing to 14 percent on winnings over $25; late payments were assessed an additional fee of $10 (*Ibid.* and Sante, *Low Life*: 227).

15. Light, "From Vice District to Tourist Attraction": 382.

16. *Ibid.*: 369–370.

17. Frank Moss, *The American Metropolis: From Knickerbocker Days to the Present Time*, Vol. Two (New York: Peter Fenelon Collier, Publisher, 1897); 104

18. Yun, *Chinatown Inside Out*: 212–213.

19. Moss, *The American Metropolis*, Vol. 2: 427.

20. Titus would later come under public scrutiny for his leadership of the Police Headquarters Detective Bureau. The detectives in the Bureau were accused by District Attorney William Travers Jerome of running a fence operation for the thieves they were charged with arresting ["Police Fence?," *The Evening Sun* (5 April 1902) and "Nettled by Titus, Jerome Threatens," *New York Herald* (6 April 1902)].

21. I could not find any other mention of the Oriental Benevolent Society (4 Mott Street). However, the Ming Tuck Tong is mentioned in an 8 August 1899 article which describes the organization as "Chinatown's Parkhurst Society." The article reported the beating of one Ming Tuck Tong member named Chu Wong, an uptown laundryman and "fervid orator against the gamblers," by a dozen "gamblers" in front of 24 Pell Street. The article also reported, "So thoroughly Wong made himself disliked by the Chinese sports that a chuckle could be heard in twenty different places when watchful eyes saw him enter Pell Street yesterday morning alone." When police arrived on the seen, they arrested the badly beaten Chu Wong and one of his assailants and charged each with disorderly conduct. Since the raids stopped soon after, it appears the Ming Tuck got their message ["Chinatown Jumps on Reformer," *New York Press* (9 August 1899)].

In addition to this reference, Gong and Grant state that the "Ming Dock Tong" was comprised mostly of men from the Hock San District or from the Chin Family group. They assert that its leader, Chin Sam, sought to make it a "front rank" tong. If this is the case, then these raids probably just used the banner of reform to hide their true agenda: a poorly timed, ineffectual power play against those who controlled Chinatown's gambling (Gong and Grant, *Tong War!*: 152).

22. Who this referred to is unclear, but since Tom Lee lived in uptown and was known as the controller of Chinatown gambling, it is probably him.

23. "Men Baffled in Chinatown Raid," *The Morning Telegraph* (1 December 1898).

24. "Titus to Continue Raids on Chinese," *New York Herald* (2 December 1898).

25. "Seventeen Chinamen Held," *New York Times* (9 January 1899).

26. Beck, *New York's Chinatown*: 96.

27. *Ibid.*: 328.

28. *Ibid.*: 96.

29. Yun, *Chinatown Inside Out*: 212–213.

30. Beck, *New York's Chinatown*: 96.

31. *Ibid.*: 97.

32. Moss, *The American Metropolis*, Vol. 2: 406.

33. *Ibid.*

34. *Ibid.*: 427–428.

35. Tyler Anbinder, *Five Points: The 19-Century New York City Neighborhood that Invented Tap Dance, Stole Elections, and Became the World's Most Notorious Slum* (New York: The Free Press, 2001): 411–415.

36. *Ibid.*

37. *Ibid.*

38. *Ibid.*

39. Moss, *The American Metropolis*, Vol. 2: 414.

40. Beck, *New York's Chinatown*: 125.

41. Moss, *The American Metropolis*, Vol. 2: 406.

42. Beck, *New York's Chinatown*: 125.

43. Clark, "The Chinese of New York Contrasted with Their Foreign Neighbors": 110. She refers to the Hip Sing Tong as the "Hip Shing Tong."

44. Frank Moss had a different take on the Hip Sing, as well as some patronizing advice to Clark: Miss Clark, he said, "falls into an amusing error, when she speaks of the Hop Sing Tong as the New York Branch of the dread 'Highbinder' or 'Hatchet' Association; the truth being that the organization which she mentions is a benevolent corporation chartered under the laws of New York, approved by the Supreme Court, and expressly designed to aid the Chinese to learn American ways, and to advance them in religion and mutual helpfulness. In this case the oppo-

nents of the Chinese corporation got Miss Clark's ear and exercised their natural virtue of prevarication. They all do it. It is no wonder that occasionally we make mistakes in our judgment of these people, for they are our opposites in nearly every trait or custom." [Moss, *The American Metropolis*: 421–422]. By the end of the first Hip Sing/ On Leong Tong War, Moss would realize his own "mistakes in judgment" regarding the Hip (Hop) Sing.

45. Beck, *New York's Chinatown*: 126–127.
46. *Ibid.*: 103.
47. *Ibid.*: 103.
48. Moss, *The American Metropolis*, Vol. 2: 427–428.
49. Beck, *New York's Chinatown*: 76–78.
50. Stephen Crane, "Opium's Varied Dreams," in *Stephen Crane: Tales, Sketches, and Reports*, Fredson Bowers, ed. (Charlottesville, VA: University of Virginia Press, 1973): 365.
51. Sante, *Low Life*: 142.
52. Crane, "Opium's Varied Dreams": 365.
53. Riis, *How the Other Half Lives*: 123.
54. *Ibid.*: 123–124.
55. Augustine E. Costello, *Our Police Protectors: A History of the New York Police*, reprint ed. (Montclair, N.J.: Patterson Smith, 1972): 516–517. Costello, along with Max F. Schmittberger, were key witnesses against police corruption during the Lexow Committee Hearings [James F. Richardson, *The New York Police: Colonial Times to 1901* (New York: Oxford University Press, 1970): 206].
56. The law read: "Every person who opens or maintains, to be resorted to by other persons, any place where opium, or any of its preparations, is sold or given away, to be smoked at such place; and any person who at such place sells or gives away any opium, or its said preparations, to be there smoked or otherwise used, and any person who visits any such place for the purpose of smoking opium or its said preparations, shall be deemed guilty of a misdemeanor, and, upon conviction thereof, shall be punished by a fine not exceeding five hundred dollars, or by imprisonment in the penitentiary not exceeding three months, or by such fine and imprisonment." As found in Costello, *Our Police Protectors*: 517.
57. *Ibid.*: 523.
58. Edward Robb Ellis, *The Epic of New York* (New York: Coward-McCann, 1966): 421. Ellis notes that a "gambling den" operated along with the "opium dive."
59. Costello, *Our Police Protectors*: 523–524.
60. *Ibid.*
61. *Ibid.*: 524.
62. *Ibid.*
63. *Ibid.*
64. *Ibid.*
65. "6,000 Opium Users Here," *New York Times* (1 August 1908): 6.
66. Light, "From Vice District to Tourist Attraction": 371–372.
67. *Ibid.*: 371–372.
68. For more on opium smuggling networks, please see Jeffrey Scott McIllwain, "An Equal Opportunity Employer: 31–54.
69. This "raw opium" was most likely the medicinal variety. Chinese opium smugglers operating in the U.S. were known to convert imports of medicinal opium (on which there was not tax or a light tax) and process it into opium suitable for smoking.
70. Beck, *New York's Chinatown*: 144.
71. "Get Opium Worth $5,000," *New York Times* (5 October 1903): 3; "Opium Arrests Continue," *New York Times* (5 October 1903): 5; *United States of America against John M. Schneider* (U.S. Circuit Court, Southern District of New York, Criminal Case Files, Box 66: Cr.C.-2968, John M. Schneider), U.S. National Archives—New York Branch.
72. "One Chin Fooled 3 Sleuths," *The New York Sun* (23 February 1905).
73. Anbinder, *Five Points*: 413–415.
74. For more on the multiethnic nature of smuggling syndicates, see McIllwain, "An Equal Opportunity Employer." Jeffrey Scott McIllwain, "Bureaucratic Rivalry, Corruption and Organized Crime: Enforcing Exclusion in San Diego, 1897–1902," *Western Legal History* (forthcoming)
75. "Opium Smugglers Warned," *New York Times* (14 May 1895): 1.
76. "Took Bribe to Aid Raid," *New York Daily Tribune* (6 December 1903): 3.
77. Yun, *Chinatown Inside Out*: 218–219.
78. *Ibid.*
79. "Say Chinaman Was Murdered," *New York Daily Tribune* (26 October 1903): 12; "Highbinder Crime," *New York Commercial Advertiser* (26 October 1903).
80. 19 Pell Street is the reported residence of Hip Sing leader Mock Duck ["Drew Lots for Shooting," *New York Times* (4 November 1904): 7].
81. *The People v. Yee Wah and Louie Young* (New York District Attorney Closed Case Files, New York Municipal Archives).

82. "Police Raid Many Chinatown Dens," *The New York World* (21 February 1906).
83. All of these findings are replicated in McIllwain, "An Equal Opportunity Employer."
84. Shumsky, "Tacit Acceptance": 665.
85. Yun, *Chinatown Inside Out*: 370.
86. See Table Three.
87. Riis, *How the Other Half Lives*: 123.
88. Beck, *New York's Chinatown*: 29.
89. *Ibid*.: 108.
90. Yun, *Chinatown Inside Out*: 228.
91. Beck, *New York's Chinatown*: 108.
92. *Ibid*.: 29.
93. "Rescuing Angel of the Little Slaves of Chinatown," *New York Times* (30 April 1905): 4:4. Clark referred to the Hip Sing by their more popular name, the Highbinders.
94. Beck, *New York's Chinatown*: 118.
95. This is not to say that On Leong members, with their own powerful and influential *guanxi* networks, did not engage in the prostitution trade. I simply could not find direct or indirect evidence of their involvement in this enterprise.
96. This does not mean racism did not exist, a point aptly made by John Kuo Wei Tchen in *New York before Chinatown*. It just means that the gross level of anti-Chinese agitation, laws and ordinances, and violence that was commonplace in the West was relatively absent in New York (hence New York's migratory appeal to many Chinese living in the West during the 1880s and 1890s).

Chapter 9

1. Carl Glick, *Shake Hands with the Dragon* (New York: Whittlesy House, 1941): 127. The New York Daily News recently ran a three part series on Mock Sai Wing that provides a summary of his life [Jay Maeder, "Mock Duck: Red Flags," *New York Daily News* (20 June 1999); Jay Maeder, "Mock Duck: Blood of the Flower," *New York Daily News* (21 June 1999); Jay Maeder, "Mock Duck: Blood of the Rooster," *New York Daily News* (22 June 1999).]
2. *The People of the State of New York vs. Mock Duck* (6 June 1912, etc.), Trial Transcript Preservation Project, John Jay College of Criminal Justice, New York: 90.
3. Glick, *Shake Hands with the Dragon*: 259–261. Mock Wah's specific tong affiliation was not provided and I could not discover other sources to fill this gap.

4. Kwang Dock Tong: aka Kwong Duck Tong.
5. Lee, *Chinatown, U.S.A.*: 35.
6. Sante, *Low Life*: 227.
7. Herbert Asbury, *The Gangs of New York: An Informal History of the Underworld* (New York: Blue Ribbon Books, 1939): 303–304.
8. Glick, *Shake Hands with the Dragon*: 127.
9. Mock Duck also testified in this trial that he was acquitted of another unknown charge in 1897, but the Court would not allow Mock Duck to say any more because only convictions, not arrests and acquittals, could be admissible into the record. [*The People v. Mock Duck* (20 March 1902, etc.), Court of General Sessions, City and County of New York. Part II (document located in the New York Public Library): 521–522.]
10. One biographer stated that Mock Duck smoked opium, specifically chandu, not dross, opium. Chandu was a pure, clean smoking opium, while dross was made from the residue of chandu and any number of other possible adulterants. No other source mentioned or hinted that Mock Duck smoked opium. [McKelway, *True Tales from the Annals of Crime and Rascality*: 54.]
11. Chin Gin: aka Loo Shoo.
12. "Chinaman Found Stabbed Through the Heart," *New York Times* and "Mystery about Chinaman's Death," *New York Press*. As far as I could find, the press did not mention this suicide when it actually occurred.
13. Loo Choo: aka Loo Hee Bean, Loo Hee, and Choo Loo.
14. "Chinaman Found Stabbed Through the Heart," *New York Times*; "Mystery about Chinaman's Death," *New York Press*; and "Loo Hee Was Murdered," *New York Press* (31 August 1899).
15. *Ibid*.
16. *Ibid*.
17. "The On Leong Dinner," *New York Daily Tribune*. Beck stated that the restaurant was named Me Heong Lau and that it was a first-class establishment. Beck also noted that 14 Mott Street housed the Wing Yuen Tai lottery (Beck, *New York's Chinatown*: 49, 104).
18. "Chinaman Found Stabbed Through the Heart," *New York Times*.
19. It is not known if this is the Wo Kee (aka Wah Kee) who's mercantile served as the cornerstone for Chinatown.
20. "Loo Hee Was Murdered," *New York Press*.

21. Mock Duck's residence is established in "Drew Lots for Shooting," *New York Times*.
22. "Chinese Rioters in Court," *New York Herald* (5 September 1899).
23. "Chinatown Riot," *New York Journal* (4 September 1899).
24. *The New York Herald* stated that "Ching" Sam stabbed "Charles" Lee ("Chinese Rioters in Court," *New York Herald*). According to Gong and Grant, this was the first use of a handgun to resolve a conflict in New York City's Chinatown, thus "marking a new era of tong warfare" (Gong and Grant, *Tong War!*: 156). I could not corroborate this assertion
25. Ching On: aka Chin On. According to the *Herald*, two other men were arraigned for assaulting McClusky as well. Their names were reported as Wong Lum of 586 Morris Avenue, Manhattan, and Lee Sam of 973 Kent Avenue, Brooklyn (*Ibid.*).
26. "Chinatown Riot," *New York Journal*.
27. The four were the previously mentioned Wong Lum, Lee Sam, Ching Sam, and Chin On. The fifth was Lee Gum of 24 Pell Street. All were charged with felonious assault ("Chinese Rioters in Court," *New York Herald*). It should be noted that Gong and Grant provide a completely different interpretation of the same riot. According to them, Chin Sam (aka "Four Flusher Sam") was the head of the Ming Dock Tong, most of whom came from the Hock San District or Chin family group. Chin Sam tried to "place his tong in the front rank," but was unsuccessful. Gong and Grant stated that the riot mentioned above was actually a fight between the Ming Dock Tong and the Hock San District Guild. The subject of their quarrel was unclear. The Ming Dock Tong, however, reportedly disbanded after the shooting, a result of the Hock San District Guild's demand "that all members of theirs who belonged to the Ming Dock Tong—and there were quite a few, although they did not fight—should resign. This was carried out and left only members of the Chin family to defend Four Flusher Sam. But they rallied to his aid and he was acquitted" (Gong and Grant, *Tong War!*: 152–156).
  I discounted this interpretation after I placed the riot in the context of the three-year struggle within the Chinese hand laundry industry in New York. The Ming Dock Tong and Hock San District Association may have had a role in the quarrel, a point made possible by Gong and Grant's failure to mention a cause for their rift, but neither organization was mentioned in the extensive press accounts or in Beck's *New York's Chinatown*, which discussed the Chinese laundry industry in detail.
28. The Chinese Laundryman's Association: aka The Chinese Laundryman's Union. According to Beck, the Chinese Laundryman's Association had its headquarters in Chinatown's City Hall at 16 Mott Street, and it was represented by the CCBA [Beck, *New York's Chinatown*: 21].
29. Yu, *To Save China, to Save Ourselves*: 9.
30. *Ibid.*: 9–10.
31. Beck, *New York's Chinatown*: 58.
32. Yu, *To Save China, to Save Ourselves*: 11.
33. *Ibid.*: 12.
34. Beck, *New York's Chinatown*: 62.
35. "Tong" is "hong" in the original. According to Beck, "hong" means "guild." It stands to reason, then, that hong is most likely a phonetic translation of tong, which can also mean guild.
36. *Ibid.*: 58–61.
37. My research confirms Yu's assertion.
38. Yu, *To Save China, to Save Ourselves*: 31.
39. "Chinatown Riot," *New York Journal*.
40. Beck, *New York's Chinatown*: 58.
41. *Ibid.*: 60.
42. *Ibid.*: 59–60.
43. Jim Sang: aka Jim Seng, Ah Ting.
44. Lou Yen's laundry was located at 144 East 15th Street. Yee Sing's was located at 203 West 14th Street.
45. "Chinese Burglar Nabbed," *The Sun* (21 November 1898); "Chinese Burglar Caught," *New York Daily Tribune* (21 November 1898); "Chinese Burglar Arrested," *New York Times* (21 November 1898); and "Chinamen," *New York Journal* (22 November 1898). The owners of the other laundries were not named.
46. "Chinamen," *New York Journal*.
47. The complete differences in the two incidents reported this day prevent me from concluding that the "Ah Ting" mentioned in *Ibid.* is the same man as Ah Hop Sing mentioned in "His Enterprise Ruins Ah Hop Sing," *New York Herald* (22 November 1898).
48. *Ibid.*
49. Once again, outside of the application of the word highbinder to the parties involved with the struggle, there is no direct evidence to support the assertion the Hip Sing Tong sided with the dissidents. Rather, it is inferred from the facts presented in accounts of the laundry con-

flict. It is also inferred from the fact that open violence between the Hip Sing Tong and organizations associated with the men behind the Chinese Laundry Association began soon after.

50. Gong and Grant, *Tong War!*: 156.

51. Mock Duck's financial contribution to New York's Hip Sing is mentioned in *Ibid.*: 160.

52. Reported as both "Dop Sang Kong Saw" and "Chinese Laundryman's Association" in "Stiffen Prices for Stiffening Linen," *New York Daily Tribune* (14 March 1901): 9; and "Chinese Laundry Trust," *New York Daily Tribune* (27 September 1901): 6. Reported earlier as "Tap San Kan Shaw" or "Laundryman's Union" in "Chinamen," *New York Journal.*

53. I could not locate further information on these two organizations.

54. "Stiffen Prices for Stiffening Linen," *New York Daily Tribune.*

55. "A Chinese Laundry Trust," *New York Daily Tribune.*

56. "Chinese May Move to Williamsburg," *New York Times* (6 August 1906): 14.

57. For example, see *The New York Daily Tribune* (17 July 1900): 2; "Business in Chinatown Falls Off," *The New York Daily Tribune* (26 July 1900): 3; "Ruffians Attack Chinamen," *The New York Daily Tribune* (31 July 1900): 3; and "Mob Bombards a Chinaman," *The New York Daily Tribune* (19 August 1900): 7.

58. "Alarm Felt in Chinatown," *The New York Daily Tribune* (17 July 1900): 3.

59. "Driving Back the Allies," *The New York Daily Tribune* (14 July 1900): 3.

60. "Exodus from Chinatown," *The New York Daily Tribune* (24 July 1900): 3.

61. *Ibid.*

62. "What Can Chinatown Eat," *The New York Daily Tribune* (19 August 1900): Illustrated Supplement, I:5. If these goods were scarce, one can assume opium was scarce as well.

63. Lung Kin: aka Long Kin and Loang Kin. It could not be determined if Charlie Lee was or was not the same man shot by Chin Sam on 3 September 1899.

64. "Murder in Chinatown," *New York Daily Tribune* (13 August 1900); "Chinaman Killed in Faction Fight," *New York Herald* (13 August 1900); *New York Times* (13 August 1900); "Murder in Chinatown," *The Sun* (13 August 1900); and "Chinese Armed to Kill One Another," *New York Press* (13 August 1900).

65. *Ibid.*

66. *Ibid.* Nine days later, on Monday, August 20, a Brooklyn laundryman named Lin Neuy died of a gunshot wound to the abdomen that he received at 17 Mott Street, across the street from Chinatown's City Hall and the On Leong Headquarters. Based on the available evidence, it does not appear that this incident was related to the fight at 9 Pell Street. Police were quick to rule the incident a suicide after three Chinese men, professed friends of Lin Neuy, stated that he did so out of despair over the fact he was in love with a white girl who would have nothing to do with them. The white girl to whom they referred was most likely a prostitute, for Lin Neuy, having just sold his laundry for several hundred dollars that morning, went to a house in the rear of 17 Mott Street and visited a woman who lived in room No. 10. Some witnesses asserted that some white men who hung around the resort saw his roll of money and robbed him. When Lin Neuy resisted, he was shot. When a reporter asked one of these witnesses why the police would report a murder as a suicide, the man replied: "The police want to keep things quiet down here. They get big sums of money for keeping still about a lot of things. The people who live in that house (referring to the back part of No. 17 Mott-St.) pay for protection" ["Chinese Say Its Murder," *New York Daily Tribune* (22 August 1900): 6].

67. Ah Fe: aka Ah Fee.

68. "Chinese in Anger at Murder Trial," *New York Press* (14 April 1901).

69. Once again, Mock Duck resided at 19 Pell Street.

70. "Chinaman Shoots Wildly," *New York Times* (22 September 1900): 4 and "Chinaman Killed in Fight," *New York Daily Tribune* (22 September 1900): 6.

71. "Highbinders in Chinatown," *New York Daily Tribune* (14 April 1901): 6 and "Chinese in Anger at Murder Trial," *New York Press.* Garvan's quote referred to the "Ip Sing Tong." Though given as Garvin here, the A.D.A.'s name is Garvan in later reports. Hence the use of "Garvan" in the text.

72. "Highbinders in Chinatown," *New York Daily Tribune.* The identity of the Lung Gag Gong is unknown. This is most likely the result of an interpretation glitch on the part of the reporter. What is important is that it was clear that Tom Lee had strong ties to the Chinese Freemasons, otherwise known as the Chih Kung Tong.

73. "The 'Good Chinaman' in Danger," *New York Daily Tribune* (21 April 1901): 3.

74. "Boston Chinaman to Be Tried Here," *New York Daily Tribune* (11 July 1901): 5.

75. *Ibid.*
76. "Objections to Chinamen," *New York Times* (19 February 1902): 2.
77. *Ibid.*
78. Moss, *The American Metropolis*, Vol. 2: 421–422.
79. *Ibid.*: 414.
80. "Chinamen Much Excited," *New York Times* and "May Swear Chinamen by Chickens' Blood," *The World*.
81. Despite the sensationalism ascribed to it in the press, there seems to be validity behind such a practice. As Beck observed, "The Chinese ritual for swearing is very simple. When the witness is called a sharp knife is given him. He grasps it in his right hand and with his left he holds a live chicken. Then he cuts off the chicken's head. Next he takes the oath written on a paper in his own language, which he burns with incense, and then he is ready" (Beck, *New York's Chinatown*: 190). Posner explained that the use of a chicken during an oath is an important ritual in the Sun Yee On Triad in Canton: "Each recruit then knelt in front of the altar again and this time a cock was passed in front of him and then the incense master would chop its head off with one blow from a sword. He would tell the recruits that they would die like that if they ever betrayed the society, and the cut head was mixed in a bowl of wine together with the blood from the cock's body. That bowl was taken to each recruit, who would cut the middle finger of his left hand with a long needle and put some drops of blood into the bowl while saying that if he revealed the Triad secrets, then blood would be let out of the five holes of his body" (Posner, *Warlords of Crime*: 52).
82. *The People v. Mock Duck* (20 March 1902, etc.): 64–65.
83. The following details of the trial are drawn from *Ibid.*: *passim*.
84. *Ibid.*: 600–602.
85. *Ibid.*: 602–604.
86. "Mock Duck Jury Disagrees Again," *The Sun* (3 April 1902).
87. *The People v. Mock Duck* (20 March 1902, etc.): 755
88. Gong and Grant, *Tong War!*: 156–157.
89. Beck, *New York's Chinatown*: 135. and Moss, *The American Metropolis*, Vol. 2.
90. Beck, *New York's Chinatown*: 132–133 and Moss, *The American Metropolis*, Vol. 2.
91. A few years later, Dr. Sun Yat-sen relied on the protection of the Chih Kung Tong, especially its New York branch, during his exile in the United States [Glick, *Shake Hands with the Dragon*: 283–298].
92. Kleinknecht, *The New Ethnic Mobs*: 104.
93. Lee, *Chinatown, U.S.A.*:
94. Ma, *Revolutionaries, Monarchists, and Chinatowns*: 24–25.
95. Chin, *Chinese Sub-culture and Criminality*.
96. "Hip Sing on Top, On Leong on Run," *The Sun* (12 December 1904).
97. Gong and Grant, *Tong War!*: 157.
98. "Gambling in Chinatown," *New York Times*.
99. Gong and Grant, *Tong War!*: 156–157.
100. *The People v. Mock Duck* (20 March 1902, etc.): *passim*.
101. Beck, *New York's Chinatown*: 135.
102. "Hip Sing on Top, On Leong on Run," *The Sun* and "Chinese Prisoners Let Go," *The Sun* (14 February 1905).

Chapter 10

1. "Chinese Raid Fails," *The Evening Sun* (22 December 1902); "Chinamen Fool 'Em," *The Evening Sun* (22 January 1903); "Police Raid on Jerome Tip," *New York Times* (25 January 1903); and "Nabbed Chinamen," *The Evening Sun* (2 February 1903).
2. "Chinese Shot, Is Arrested," *New York Evening Journal* (2 December 1902); "Hop Sing Shoots Uncle, Hong Gee," *The World* (19 September 1903); "Highbinder Crime," *Commercial Advertiser*, and "Say Chinaman Was Murdered," *New York Daily Tribune*.
3. "Rival Bands Battle in Chinatown Streets," *New York Times* (30 September 1902): 3; "Battle in Poolroom," *New York Times* (5 October 1902): 3; "'Monk' Eastman Gang Let Go," *New York Times* (6 October 1902): 14; and "Leader Foley Settles Feud," *New York Times* (2 October 1902): 10.
4. Gong and Grant, *Tong War!*.
5. *Ibid.*: 164–165.
6. *Ibid.*: 158–160.
7. *Ibid.*: 162–164. When and why this fight was to occur is a mystery. It may be associated with another reported event, or it may not. I could not locate corroborating evidence for this claim, as well as the others Gong and Grant made about the Scientific Killer during this time frame.
8. *Ibid.*: 158–160. I could not find any corroborating evidence for this story.

9. *Ibid*: 164–165.
10. Moss, *The American Metropolis*, Vol. 2: 415–416.
11. Sante, *Low Life*: 127. The veracity of these specific quotes is highly questionable, however the sentiments they reveal are very telling.
12. "Reign of Terror in Chinatown Now," *New York Daily Tribune* (13 August 1905): IV/1.
13. Sante, *Low Life*: 127–128. Nowhere in the press accounts or in *Tong War!* is this incident, or anything resembling it, mentioned.
14. "Parkhurst Man Raids Chinese to Get Police," *New York Herald* (22 July 1904) and "Chinamen in Court," *The Evening Sun* (22 July 1904). Apparently, Titus was promoted since his last dealings with Chinatown.
15. "Prosperous Chinese Arrested For Voting," *The New York Times*.
16. His sentence is unknown. Only one indictment and plea could be found in the National Archive [*The United States of America v. Tong Kee Hang alias William Hang* (27 September 1904) U.S. Circuit Court, Southern District of New York, Criminal Case Files, Box 60, D-3414—William Hang], National Archives, New York City].
17. In addition to searching press accounts, I attempted to locate the files for Tom Lee and Charles Foon Foos in the National Archives, but to no avail.
18. "Tongs Clash Again," *The New York Daily Tribune*. Those arrested include Kip Loch Chong of 14 Mott Street, Lee Lay of 32 Mott Street, Jim Lang, Charley Lee and Sam Yuck of 18 Mott Street, and Lee Yup (no address given), all alleged members of the Hip Sing Tong.
19. "War of Tongs on Again," *The New York Daily Tribune* (18 October 1904): 2.
20. *Ibid*.
21. "War of Tongs Again in Court," *The World* (25 February 1905).
22. Gong and Grant, *Tong War!*: 166–169.
23. "War of Tongs on Again," *The New York Daily Tribune*.
24. Court testimony states that the shooting occurred at 13 Pell Street [*The People, on Complaint of Mock Duck v. Lee Sing*].
25. Lee Sing: aka Wing Sing and Low Roy.
26. "Shooting in Chinatown," *The New York Times*; "Drew Lots for Shooting," *The New York Times* (4 November 1904): 7; and "Chinese Assassins Work," *The Sun* (4 November 1904). The news reports mistakenly give Mock Duck's age as 27 (he was 25).
27. "Police in Pay of the On Leong Tong?," *The World* (8 November 1904). This quote refers to Lee Sing as Low Roy.
28. *The People, on Complaint of Mock Duck v. Lee Sing*: 81–86.
29. Gong and Grant, *Tong War!*: 166.
30. "Armor Clad Chinese Battle on the Bowery," *The New York Times* (26 November 1904): 2. This account mistakenly switched the affiliations of aggressors and victims. The *Times* corrected this mistake in follow-up reports.
31. The man Gong and Grant call Huey Gow is most likely the previously mentioned Huie Kin, however I could not determine this for sure. Indeed, perhaps the presidency of the Hip Sing Tong changed hands between members of this powerful family, or perhaps the actual identity of the president of the tong was not clear to either Gong and Grant or the press. Then again, maybe this is the same individual and this is a case of an individual being described by his paper name and given name. Either option is plausible. Regardless, what is clear in Gong and Grant's version is that the president of the Hip Sing was the primary target, not Mock Duck.
32. *The New York Times* reported that a Wong Lung was arrested (*Ibid.*). This may be Wong Lock in the Gong and Grant version.
33. Gong and Grant, *Tong War!*: 166–169.
34. "On Leong Have Stolen the Hip Sing's Crest," *The New York Times* (27 November 1904): 5.
35. "Tong Protected, Says Moss," *The Sun* (11 December 1904); "Says Murder Put on Chinaman Is Gamblers' Plot," *The World* (11 December 1904); and "Predicts Chinese Killings," *New York Times* (11 December 1904): 7.
36. "Predicts Chinese Killings," *The New York Times*.
37. "Chinamen Taken in Raid," *The New York Times* (12 December 1904): 7; "Bag of Chinese Gamblers," *The Sun* (12 December 1904); and "Raid on Pigtails," *The Evening Sun* (12 December 1904).
38. "Hip Sing on Top, On Leong on Run," *The Sun*.
39. E.F. Price may be Ed Price. If so, this brings up an interesting development in the rivalry between the two tongs. In 1897, Frank Moss identified Ed Price as "The legal champion of the powerful Lee family, storekeepers, gamblers and all...."

[Moss, *The American Metropolis*, Vol. 2: 44415–416]. If this is the same man, the Hip Sing scored a major victory by gaining the services of their adversary's former attorney. The On Leong and the Lee family would have surely lost *mianzi* as a result.

40. "16 Hip Sing Tongers Soaked," *The Sun* (27 December 1904) and "Raid Ends in Sub-Cellar," *The New York Times* (28 December 1904): 12.

41. "Graft from Chinese—Moss," *The Sun* (12 December 1904).

42. "Wing Futs and Chus Cite Police Pickets," *The New York Times* (16 April 1905): 14. I assume they are Hip Sings due to their street addresses. Daniel O'Reilly could be a former Democratic Congressman from Brooklyn (1879–1881). However, because this is a common name, there is no way to verify this possibility ["Members of the U.S. House of Representatives Elected from Districts All or Partly within the Current Boundaries of New York City," in Kenneth T. Jackson (ed.), *The Encyclopedia of New York City* (New Haven, CT: Yale University Press, 1995): 482.

43. Reportedly, the detectives had a "'line'" that a suspected robber would be coming to 17 Mott Street, so they were staking out the address when the following incident occurred ["Chinaman Is Slain in Feud by Assassins," *The World* (31 January 1905)]. Whether the detectives were there for that reason or not is unknown. It does, however, raise suspicion as to the true motivation for their presence. Perhaps it was at the request of one of the two tongs. It simply could not be determined with certainty.

44. "Huie Fong First Victim of On Leong's Vengeful Decree," *The Sun* (1 February 1905). See also "Chinatown Man Shot Dead," *The Sun* (31 January 1905) and "New Murder Marks Chinatown Feud," *The World* (1 February 1905).

45. "Armor Clad Chinese Battle on the Bowery," *The New York Times*. 10 1/2 Bowery was reported in this article as Hip Sing Headquarters.

46. "Chinamen Taken in Raid," *The New York Times*.

47. "Huie Fong First Victim of On Leong's Vengeful Decree," *The Sun*.

48. "War of Tongs Again in Court," *The World* (25 February 1905).

49. "Huie Fong First Victim of On Leong's Vengeful Decree," *The Sun*. If Huie Kin was Gong and Grant's Huey Gow, then Huie Kin had a solid basis for his testimony. If Gong and Grant's version of events surrounding the On Leong attack on 25 November 1904 are correct, Huie Kin had already been the target of at least one assassination attempt [Gong and Grant, *Tong War!*: 166–169]. This was in addition to the On Leong attempt to "wipe out" the Huie family at 12 Pell Street in early October 1904 ("War of Tongs Again," *The New York Daily Tribune*].

50. "War of Tongs Again," *The New York Daily Tribune*.

51. "Cops Swarmed About Tom Lee," *The Evening Sun* (4 February 1905).

52. This group included the On Leong Tong's Secretary and public relations specialist, Lee Moy (aka Lee Loy), who discussed the reward during his testimony on behalf of Yee Lee, whose preliminary hearing was being held in The Tombs Court that day. The three others had $1,000 each on their heads.

53. See "Price Put on Tom Lee's Head," *The World* (2 February 1905); "Tom Lee Marked," *The Evening Sun* (3 February 1905); "Chinatown's Mayor Marked for Murder," *The World* (3 February 1905); "Chinamen Rejoice with Hand on Gun," *The World* (4 February 1905); and "Cops Swarmed About Tom Lee," *The Evening Sun*.

54. "Held Chinese by the Queue," *The World* (13 February 1905); "Raid of Chinese Netted 75 Cents," *The Evening Sun* (13 February 1905); and "Chinese Prisoners Let Go," *The Sun*.

55. "Chinese Prisoners Let Go," *The Sun*.

56. Ong Fong: aka Ong Fang and Dong Fong.

57. "Old Chinaman Shot in Feud of the Tongs," *The New York Times* (25 February 1905): 2 and "Two Chinese Feudists Held," *The Evening Telegram* (25 February 1905).

58. Ibid.

59. Ong Fong was latter sentenced to Sing Sing prison for no less than fifteen months and no more than five years for the murder. ["Dong Fong Sent to Prison," *The New York Times* (16 May 1905): 4.]

60. Moss, *The American Metropolis*, Vol. 2: 414–415. Moss also received help from "the ingenious and persistent Wong Get" and the "jolly good-natured Huey Gow."

61. Ju Hong: aka J. Ging.

62. "Chinatown in Terror; Mock Duck Is Back," *The World* (18 March 1905).

63. "The Hip Sing Tong Marks Men to Die," *The World* (19 March 1905); "Nab Mock Duck, Chinese Terror," *The Evening Sun*; "Mock Duck's Wings Clipped," *The*

Sun (21 March 1905); and "Mock Duck Held for Old Murder," *The World* (21 March 1905).

64. "Frank Moss and Jerome in Tiff over Mock Duck," *The Evening Telegram* (22 March 1905) and "Hip Sing Saddest Day," *The Sun* (22 March 1905).

65. Goff was chief counsel to the Lexow Committee and later became a Recorder for the Court of General Sessions. As a Recorder, he was the municipal judge of "first instance" for some tong war related cases [e.g., "Bad Mock Duck Not So Very Bad," *The Evening Sun* (12 April 1906)].

66. Richardson, *The New York Police*: 237–238.

67. *Ibid.*: 206–207.

68. "Hits Jerome Again," *The Evening Sun* (10 February 1903) and "O'Reilly Seeks M'Adoo's Arrest," *The Evening Post* (25 May 1904).

69. "200 Cops Raid Chinatown," *The Sun* (24 April 1905); "McAdoo's Men Swoop Down on Chinatown," *The World* (24 April 1905); "On Leong Held on Hip Sing's Nod," *The Evening Sun* (24 April 1905); and "Chinese Puzzle Result of Wholesale Raids," *The New York Times* (25 April 1905): 8. The number of those arrested varies from each report.

70. O'Reilly was previously mentioned as a Hip Sing attorney ["Wing Futs and Chus Cite Police Pickets," *The New York Times*]. Because Elizabeth Street cops were used to make the raids, they arrested a large number of Hip Sing as well.

71. "200 Cops Raid Chinatown," *The Sun*; "McAdoo's Men Swoop Down on Chinatown," *The World*; "On Leong Held on Hip Sing's Nod," *The Evening Sun*; and "Chinese Puzzle Result of Wholesale Raids," *The New York Times*.

72. "Chinese Puzzle Results in Wholesale Raids," *New York Times*.

73. *Ibid.*

74. How this was done was not stated in the press.

75. "Hip Sing on Top of Tom Lee," *The Sun* (27 April 1905); "Tom Lee Arrested on Graft Charge," *The World* (27 April 1905); and "Chinatown's Mayor Now in Police Toils," *The New York Times* (27 April 1905): 7.

76. *Ibid.* "Jim Wing: aka Jim Wang."

77. "Chinatown's Mayor Now in Police Toils," *The New York Times*.

78. "No Autos in Chinatown," *The New York Times* (28 April 1905): 1.

79. "Police Descend on Hip Sings," *The New York Times* (31 May 1905): 9.

Chapter 11

1. Gong and Grant, *Tong War!*: 170–174; "Three Shot Dead in Chinese Theater," *The New York Times* (7 August 1905): 1; and "Hip Sings Held for Murders After Raid," *The World* (7 August 1905); and "Two Chinamen Killed," *The New York Daily Tribune* (7 August 1905): 1.

2. *Ibid.* Three killed may not seem like a big deal in today's society, but back then this sort of brazen attack was unheard of and carried a lot of emotional weight with a shocked public.

3. "Raid Chinese Laundry," *The New York Daily Tribune* (7 August 1905): 4.

4. "Mock Duck Held for Murder," *The Sun* (8 August 1905), and "Chinatown's Quiet, but Trouble's Afloat," *The New York Times* (8 August 1905): 12.

5. "Alibi of Mock Duck," *The New York Times* (8 August 1905): 6.

6. "Undesirable Chinamen," *The New York Times* (8 August 1905): 6.

7. This is a substantial component of the mythology of New York's Chinatown and tong wars and I believe this article is the "smoking gun" behind it. However, data derived from the primary source material does not even begin to validate such a number. Perhaps the sheer emotion of the Chinese Theater Massacre simply lent itself to this exaggeration.

8. Most likely, this was not the case, even though it was an easy inference to make. Other evidence more convincingly suggests that Mock Duck was a powerful and influential member of the New York branch of the Hip Sing Tong from its early stages and that it was Huey Gow who crafted the Parkhurst strategy, though Mock Duck assisted in its development and took the lead in implementing it.

9. "Reign of Terror in Chinatown Now," *The New York Daily Tribune*.

10. "Chinese War Again," *The New York Daily Tribune* (12 August 1905): 1; "Five on Leong Kill a Hep Sing Member," *The New York Times* (13 August 1905): 3; "Another Tong Victim," *The New York Daily Tribune* (13 August 1905): 4; "Revenge of the Ong Leong Tong," *The World* (13 August 1905); and "Tong Midnight Murder Squad," *The Sun* (13 August 1905).

11. "$3,000 on Tom Lee's Head," *The New York Times* (15 August 1905): 5; "Four After Tom Lee," *The New York Daily Tribune* (15 August 1905): 8; and "Try to Pick Off 'Mayor' Tom Lee," *The World* (15 August 1905).

12. "Tongs Fight Again; Four Shot This Time," *The New York Times* (21 August 1905): 1; "On Leong Tong's Inning," *The New York Daily Tribune* (21 August 1905): 1; "Accused of Pell Street Shooting," *The New York Daily Tribune* (22 August 1905): 3; "Four More Shot in Chinatown Feud," *The World* (21 August 1905); and "Four Shot in Chinatown," *The Sun* (21 August 1905).

13. "Chinese Leaders Angry," *The New York Daily Tribune* (22 August 1905): 3.

14. "To End War of Tongs," *The New York Daily Tribune* (30 August 1905): 1.

15. "Hip Sing Men Guilty," *The New York Daily Tribune* (30 August 1905): 1; "Damaging for Mock Duck," *The Evening Post* (29 August 1905); "Mock Duck Is Arrested for Tong Tragedy," *The Evening Journal* (29 August 1905); and "Mock Duck Held," *The Evening Sun* (29 August 1905).

16. "Fatal Shooting Followed By Fight," *The New York Times* (18 October 1905): 1; "Loie Sung's Murder Was All A Mistake," *The New York Daily Tribune* (19 August 1905): 18; and "Chinaman Shot in War of the Tongs," *The World* (18 October 1905). Moy Gung ran to 14 Mott Street (On Leong territory) where he was arrested. Apparently, the Wang Company had recently joined the tong war on the side of the On Leong Tong. If so, this would have been an interesting alliance, since Frank Moss noted in 1897, history that the aristocratic Lees ("Lis") "hated" the "plebian" Wangs; the former engaged in store-keeping and gambling, the latter in laundry work [Moss, *The American Metropolis*, Vol. 2: 405–406]. The reason for this possible alliance is unknown. It helps explain, however, how Moy Gong secured as his counsel Frank Lloyd, the longtime counsel of Tom Lee and the On Leong Tong.

17. *Ibid.*

18. "Raid Many Chinese," *The New York Daily Tribune* (15 January 1906): 12; "Police Raid Chinatown," *The New York Times* (15 January 1906): 14; and "Chinatown Raids," *The Evening Sun* (15 January 1906).

19. "Hip Sings Pay Debt," *The New York Daily Tribune* (25 January 1906): 2; "2 Killed From Ambush in Chinatown Battle," *The New York Times* (25 January 1906): 6; and "Two Killed in Chinatown Battle," *New York Herald* (25 January 1906).

20. *Ibid.*

21. "2 Killed From Ambush in Chinatown Battle," *The New York Times* and "Hip Sing Pay Debt," *New York Daily Tribune.*

22. "Chinese Killed Were to Testify at Murder Trial," *The World* (25 January 1906).

23. "Mr. Waldo Visits Tongs," *The New York Daily Tribune* (27 January 1906): 4 and *The New York Times* (27 January 1906): 16.

24. "Truce in Chinatown," *The New York Daily Tribune*; and "Against All Weapons," *The New York Daily Tribune* (31 January 1906): 14; and "Chinatown's Warriors Agree to Real Peace," *The New York Times* (31 January 1906): 8.

25. Wong Quon Sing: aka Chong Pon Sing. Wong Quon Sing was selected here because the Hip Sing President was referred to by this name numerous times in future news reports.

26. "Peace of Chinatown is Merely a Merger," *The New York Times* (1 April 1906): 5.

27. "Rival Tongs at Peace," *The New York Daily Tribune* (3 February 1906): 10 and "Tongs to Give Up Gambling and Shooting," *The New York Times* (3 February 1906): 16.

28. "Peace That Is Viewed Askance," *The New York Times* (8 February 1906): 8.

29. Wong Quon Sing: aka Chong Pon Sing

30. Yep Shung: aka Yip Shung.

31. "Fear Peace Dinner," *The New York Daily Tribune* (12 February 1906): 12; *The New York Times* (12 February 1906): 5. Rosenberg's name is spelled "Eli," not "Ely," in these articles as opposed to other sources. Ware and Rosenberg's relationship with the Hip Sing Tong is found in "Truce in Chinatown" and "Against All Weapons," *The New York Daily Tribune*; and "Chinatown's Warriors Agree to Real Peace," *The New York Times.*

32. "New Tong in Field," *The New York Daily Tribune* (13 February 1906) and "There's a New Tong in Chinatown Now," *New York Times* (13 February 1906): 12.

33. *Ibid.*

34. "Fear Peace Dinner," *The New York Daily Tribune* and *The New York Times* (12 February 1906).

35. Mock Duck's affiliation was addressed in *The People of the State of New York vs. Mock Duck.*

36. This reasoning assumes Mock Duck and Wong Get did not voluntarily accept their new designations as a way to further the interests of the Hip Sing Tong. This altruistic sacrifice for the betterment of the organization is common in tong-related criminal activity. Whether voluntary or not, however, the same goals stated above would have been achieved.

37. "Mock Duck Arrested," *New York*

Daily Tribune (21 February 1906): 10; "Police Raid Many Chinatown Dens," *The World*; and "Mock Duck in the Tombs," *The Globe* (21 February 1906).

38. "Mock Duck Held in $5,000 for Trial," *The World* (24 February 1906).

39. "Bad Mock Duck Not So Very Bad," *The Evening Sun*.

40. Perhaps a relative of former Democratic Congressman for Manhattan (1863–1865) Anson Herrick ["Members of the U.S. House of Representatives Elected from Districts All or Partly within the Current Boundaries of New York City," Jackson, *The Encyclopedia of New York City*: 481].

41. A longtime Democratic justice and judge in New York City, he was a Congressman from 1901 to 1915 and from 1919 to 1921. [Reynolds, Clifford, *Biographical Directory of the American Congress, 1774–1961* (Washington, D.C.: U.S. GPO, 1961): 953].

42. Due to the illegibility of the microfilmed newspaper article, the name could read Hoe Puch, not Hoe Poch.

43. "Tong Killings Pause and Chinatown Feasts," *The New York Times* (29 March 1906): 9. The CCBA was referred to as the "Chong Wah Kong Shore" in this article.

44. "Fear Peace Dinner," *The New York Daily Tribune*.

45. "Peace of Chinatown Is Merely a Merger," *The New York Times*.

46. "Steps to Abolish Chinatown," *The New York Daily Tribune* (6 March 1906): 2; "For Bronx Chinatown," *The New York Daily Tribune* (25 July 1906): 3; "Chinatown in Bronx," *The New York Times* (26 July 1906): 6; "Chinatown May Move to Williamsburg," *The New York Times*; (6 August 1906): 14; "For A New Chinatown," *The New York Times* (8 August 1906): 6; and "Chinatown Doomed to Make Room for Bowery Park," *The New York Times* (17 February 1907).

47. I conclude that they are one in the same because the article cited Chin Sam as being a leader of the powerful Chin family, a position made clear during his trial six years before. Refer to Chapter Seven for more information on Chin Sam. Why Chin Sam was connected to this particular allegation and to Tom Lee is not known, though one can speculate that his position in the Chinese community assured common interests with Lee, as well as opportunities to make money from gambling.

48. "A Ripple in Chinatown," *New York Times* (9 May 1906): 3.

49. The suggestion that the Consul reportedly made was that the two tongs, "in a petition to District Attorney Jerome and Police Commissioner Bingham," support the proposal that "gambling establishments be wiped out of Chinatown." In the light of the other evidence, it is my opinion that this suggestion was leaked to the reporter in attempt to mislead him and, hence, the public, of the true nature of the conflict (the On Leong attempt to freeze-out the Hip Sing Tong with the creation of the new Chinatown).

50. "Tongs with Knives Again," *New York Daily Tribune* (22 May 1906): 14.

51. See Eng and Grant, *Tong War* and the three Jay Maeder articles on "Mock Duck," *The New York Daily News*.

Chapter 12

1. This point is well documented in works like Sterling Seagrave's historical and sociopolitical analysis of overseas Chinese communities, Al McCoy's highly regarded examination of the Golden Triangle opium trade, Willard Meyer's analysis of the structure and activities of transnational ethnic Chinese criminal groups, George Paulsen's study on Chinese immigrant smuggling across the United States/Mexico border, Anthony Chan's study of the Western armament trade to China after World War I, Meyers and Parssinen's study of the Chinese opium trade, Hirata's description of the international and domestic traffic of Chinese prostitutes, and my previous study on the origins of opium smuggling on the California/Baja California border [Seagrave, *Lords of the Rim*; Alfred W. McCoy, *The Politics of Heroin*; Meyers, "The Emerging Threat of Transnational Organized Crime from the East;" Paulsen, "The Yellow Peril at Nogales;" Anthony Chan, *Arming the Chinese: The Western Armaments Trade in Warlord China, 1920–1928* (Vancouver, BC: University of British Colombia Press, 1982); Hirata, "Free, Indentured, Enslaved"; and McIllwain, "An Equal Opportunity Employer"].

2. Chin, *Chinese Sub-culture and Criminality*; Chin, *Chinese Triad Societies*; Lyman, *Chinatown and Little Tokyo*; Murray, *The Origins of the Tiandihui*; and Murray, *Pirates of the South China Coast*.

3. For example, see Yong Chen, *Chinese San Francisco, 1850–1943: A Trans-Pacific Community* (Palo Alto, CA: Stanford University Press, 2000); Gyory, *Closing the Gate*; McClain, *In Search of Equality*; Salyer, *Laws as Harsh as Tigers*; Seagrave, *Lords of the Rim*; Tchen, *New York before Chinatown*; Yung, *Unbound Feet*.

4. The author fully recognizes that

the "American" social system of organized crime was an amalgam of traditions of organized criminality from the host of nations represented in the United States, a product of cross-cultural exchange that includes Chinese traditions as well.

5. The potential for such an occurrence is very real, a point made in the recent revelation that the Democratic National Committee and the Clinton Administration knowingly or unknowingly received suspect donations from Chinese organized criminals and, perhaps, the communist government of the People's Republic of China. It has been reported that these donations were made to influence policy in a variety of areas. Though glaringly evident in a basic review of the evidence published to date, the roles of *guanxi* and the social system of organized crime in these events have not been discussed. This is because almost all of the American media and policymakers have no understanding of the utility of these academic concepts and their relevance to the scandal.

6. Abadinsky, *Organized Crime* (4th ed.); Albanese, *Organized Crime in America*; Fox, *Blood and Power*; and Kenney and Finckenauer, *Organized Crime in America*.

7. Block, "Aw! Your Mother's in th Mafia: Women Criminals in Progressive New York," *Contemporary Crises* 1 (1977): 5–22; Block, "History and the Study of Organized Crime;" Block, "The Snowman Cometh: Coke in Progressive New York," Criminology 17 (1979); Block, *East Side-West Side*; Gilfoyle, *City of Eros*; Haller, "The Changing Structures of American Gambling;" Hirata, "Free, Indentured, Enslaved;" Philip Jenkins and Gary Potter, "The Politics and Myth of Organized Crime: A Philadelphia Case Study," *Journal of Criminal Justice* 15 (1982): 593–605; Johnson, "The Origins and Structure of Intercity Criminal Activity, 1840–1920;" Light, "From Vice District to Tourist Attraction;" and Paulsen, "The Yellow Peril at Nogales."

8. Peter Novick, *That Noble Dream: The 'Objectivity Question' and the American Historical Profession* (New York: Cambridge University Press, 1988).

9. Block, *East Side-West Side*: 10.

10. Crime is not the only area where this "insularity" myth has been refuted. The well-researched and well-argued work of Charles McClain, Ralph James Mooney, John R. Wunder, Lucy E. Sayler, and Sterling Seagrave provide examples from the fields of law, the courts, economics, politics, and social life.

McClain attested to the fact that the Chinese community actively fought discriminatory laws passed against them. He argued that their prolific—and rather effective—use of the law and the courts to lessen or eradicate the effect of hostile and discriminatory local, state and federal legislation shows that the Chinese wanted to stay in the United States. Furthermore, their actions exemplified the fact that they did not want to be relegated to squalid, culturally-insular enclaves. Rather the Chinese wanted to remain active components of the social, political, and economic system of the United States [Charles McClain, *In Search of Equality*].

The work of Mooney [Ralph James Mooney, "Matthew Deady and the Federal Judicial Response to Racism in the Early West," *Oregon Law Review* 63 (1985): 561–644], Sayer [Sayer, *Laws as Harsh as Tigers*], and Wunder [John R. Wunder, "The Chinese and the Courts in the Pacific Northwest: Justice Denied?," *Pacific Historical Review* 52 (May 1993): 191–211] all provide similar evidence from the realm of the courts and the law. As for Seagrave, he provided an economic analysis of overseas Chinese to illustrate just how interconnected their communities were with the economic, political and social systems of their host nations [Seagrave, *Lords of the Rim*]. They also engaged in the same enterprises as Chinese settlers in other countries [Meyers, "The Emerging Threat of Transnational Organized Crime from the East" and Seagrave, *Lords of the Rim*].

Appendix

1. Michael S. Hindus, "The History of Crime: Not Robbed of Its Potential, But Still on Probation," in *Criminology Review Yearbook*, Egnon Bittner and Michael Messinger, eds.(Newbury Park: CA: Sage, 1979): 217–241.

2. Gilfoyle, *City of Eros*; Haller, "The Changing Structure of American Gambling in the Twentieth Century": 87–114; Block, *East Side-West Side*; Johnson, "The Origins and Structure of Intercity Criminal Activity": 593–605; Alan A. Block, "Aw! Your Mother's in the Mafia": 5–22; Alan A. Block, *East Side-West Side*.

3. Roger Lane, "Urban Police and Crime in Nineteenth-Century America," in *Crime and Justice in American History: Police and Crime Control, Part 2*, Eric Monkkonen, ed. (New York: K. G. Saur, 1992): 439.

4. *Ibid*.

5. Gary King, Robert O. Keohane, and Stanley Verba, *Designing Social Inquiry: Scientific Inference in Qualitative Research* (Princeton, NJ: Princeton University Press, 1994): 16.
6. *Ibid.*: 17.
7. *Ibid.*
8. *Ibid.*
9. Richard A. Myren and Carol Henderson Garcia, *Investigation for Determination of Fact: A Primer of Fact* (Pacific Grove, CA: Brooks/Cole Publishing Company, 1989): 18.
10. As found in *Ibid.*
11. *Ibid.*: 19.
12. Block, "History and the Study of Organized Crime,": 455.
13. For example, Ko-lin Chin, *Chinese Sub-culture and Criminality*; Chi-Ling Kuo, *Social and Political Change in New York's Chinatown: The Role of Voluntary Associations* (New York: Praeger, 1977); Gwen Kinkead, *Chinatown: A Portrait of a Closed Society* (New York: Harper Collins, 1992); Lyman, *Chinatown and Little Tokyo*; Bernard Wong, *Chinatown: Economic Adaptation and Ethnic Identity of the Chinese* (New York: Holt, Rinehart and Winston, 1982); and Bernard Wong, *Patronage, Brokerage, Entrepreneurship and the Chinese Community in New York* (New York: AMS Press, 1988).
14. Primary sources are defined by Kenneth Bailey as "eyewitness accounts written by people who experienced the particular event or behavior" [Kenneth Bailey, *Methods of Social Research* (New York: The Free Press, 1978): 266].
15. Beck, *New York's Chinatown*; Moss, *The American Metropolis*, Vol. 2; Glick, *Shake Hands with the Dragon*; Yun, *Chinatown Inside Out*.
16. Ching Chao Wu, *Chinatowns*.
17. John Stewart Burgess, *A Study of the Characteristics of the Cantonese Merchants in Chinatown, New York, as Shown by Their Use of Leisure Time* (M.A. Thesis, New York: Columbia University, 1909).
18. Beck, *New York's Chinatown*: 1.
19. Beck calls the On Leong Tong the On Leon Tong in his work. For the sake of consistency, I have changed future Beck references to the On Leon Tong to the On Leong Tong.
20. Beck, *New York's Chinatown*: 135.
21. *Ibid.*: 122–133; 283–286.
22. Betsy Huang, "The Redefinition of the 'Typical Chinese' in Gish Jen's Typical American," *Hitting Critical Mass: A Journal of Asian American Cultural Criticism* 4:2 (Summer 1997). She does qualify her criticism of Beck's prejudice by recognizing "the apparent 'inscrutable' qualities of his subjects."
23. Gong and Grant, *Tong War!*
24. For example, see Asbury, *The Gangs of New York*; Dillon, *The Hatchet Men*; Kenneth Holcomb Dunshee, *As You Pass By* (New York: Hastings House, 1952); Harlow, *Old Bowery Days*; Lee, *Days of the Tong Wars*; Marcuse, *This Was New York!* and Sante, *Low Life*. *Tong War!* also lends itself heavily to treatments of conflict in San Francisco's Chinatown.
25. For the details of the Valachi analogy, please see Block, "History and the Study of Organized Crime."
26. Dillon, *The Hatchet Men*.
27. Lee, *Days of the Tong Wars*.
28. For a historiography and examples of the yellow peril genre, see Don Hutchison, *It's Raining Corpses in Chinatown* (Mercer Island, WA: Starmount House, 1991).
29. Martín Booth, *The Triads: The Growing Global Threat from the Chinese Criminal Societies* (New York: St. Martin's Press, 1990).
30. Chin, *Chinese Sub-culture and Criminality*: 63.
31. Gong and Grant, *Tong War!*; Dillon, *The Hatchet Men*; Lee, *Days of the Tong Wars*.
32. Michael D. Maltz, "Crime Statistics: A Historical Perspective," *Crime and Delinquency* (January 1977): 32–40.
33. Eric Monkkonen, "Municipal Reports as an Indicator Source: The Nineteenth-Century Police," *Historical Methods* 12:2 (Spring 1979): 57–63.
34. "Loo Hee Was Murdered," *The Sun* (31 August 1899); "Mystery About Chinaman's Death," *The New York Press* (31 August 1899); and "Chinaman Found Stabbed Through the Heart," *The New York Times* (31 August 1899).
35. Haven Emerson and Harriet E. Hughes, *Population, Births, Notifiable Diseases, and Deaths Assembled for New York City, New York, 1866–1938: From Official Records* (New York: The DeLamar Institute of Public Health, College of Physicians and Surgeons, Columbia University, 1941): Nos. 163–171 inclusive. According to the authors, it was "assumed that since 1866 all deaths in New York City have been reported" (*Ibid.*: I).
36. Reynolds, "The Chinese Tongs": 612–623; Dillon, *The Hatchet Men*; and Ko-lin Chin, *Chinese Triad Societies, Tongs, Organized Crime, and Street Gangs in Asia and the United States*, Ph. D. dissertation (Philadelphia: Temple University, 1986).

37. The scrapbooks are located in the New York City Municipal Archives, New York, New York.

38. The author searched for stories about, but not limited to, the following subjects: Chinatown, Chinese, China, Hip Sing Tong, On Leong Tong, gambling, opium, prostitution, slavery, immigration, laundries, murders, obituaries, local and state politics, The New York City Police Department, the various courts within New York City, the New York County District Attorney's Office, reform, the Parkhurst Society, the Committee of Five, the Committee of Fifteen, and the Mazet Committee.

39. These newspapers include *The Brooklyn Daily Eagle, The New York Daily News, The Commercial Advertiser, The New York Daily Tribune, The Evening Post, The New York Evening Journal, The Evening Sun, The New York Herald, The Evening Telegram, The New York Journal, The Globe, The New York Press, Harper's Weekly, The New York Times, The Morning Telegraph, The Sun, The New York American, The World,* and *The New York American and Journal.*

40. The Society for the Prevention of Crime was more commonly known as the Parkhurst Society. The Reverend Charles Parkhurst was its head.

41. Monkkonen, "Systemic Criminal Justice History": 14.

42. Bailey, *Methods of Social Research*: 267–268.

43. *Ibid.*: 268.
44. *Ibid.*: 269.
45. *Ibid.*
46. *Ibid.*: 270–271.
47. Tchen, *New York Before Chinatown.*
48. Chin, *Chinatown Gangs.*

49. Consider the methodological issues addressed in C. N. Reynolds, "The Chinese Tongs": 612–613.

50. King, Keohane, and Verba, *Designing Social Inquiry*: 55.

51. Reynolds, "The Chinese Tongs": 612–613.

52. "Chinamen Much Excited," *New York Times* (20 February 1902) and "May Swear Chinamen by Chickens' Blood," *The World* (20 February 1902).

53. Dillon, *The Hatchet Men*: 178.

54. Jane Hunter, *The Gospel of Gentility: American Women Missionaries in Turn-of-the-Century China* (New Haven, CT: Yale University Press).

55. Similarly, the "name problem" would constitute a problem for the criminal justice system as well until the development and adoption of fingerprinting as a means of criminal identification.

56. This methodology was used in Ianni, *Black Mafia.*

57. The social system of organized crime.

58. Block, *East Side-West Side*: 11.

Bibliography

Articles

Albini, Joseph L., and Bronislaw J. Bajon. "Witches, Mafia, Mental Illness and Social Reality." *International Journal of Criminology and Penology* 6 (1978): 285–294.
Barnes, J. A. "Class and Committees in a Norwegian Island Parish." *Human Relations* 7 (1954): 39–58.
Bell, Daniel. "Crime as an American Way of Life: A Queer Ladder of Social Mobility." *The Antioch Review* 13 (June): 131–154.
Block, Alan A. "Aw! Your Mother's in the Mafia: Women Criminals in Progressive New York." *Contemporary Crises* 1 (1977): 5–22.
_____. "History and the Study of Organized Crime." *Urban Life: A Journal of Ethnographic Research* 6 (January 1978): 455–474.
_____. "Patronage in Sicily." *Man* 1 (1966): 18–33.
_____. "Poverty and Politics in a Sicilian Agro-Town." *International Archives of Ethnography* 50 (1960): 198–236.
_____. "The Snowman Cometh: Coke in Progressive New York." *Criminology* 17 (1979).
Boissevain, Jeremy. "The Place of Non-Groups in the Social Sciences." *Man* 3 (1968): 542–556.
Chin, Ko-lin, Jeffrey Fagan, and Robert J. Kelly. "Patterns of Chinese Gang Extortion." *Justice Quarterly* 9:4 (December 1992): 625–646.
Coles, Nigel. "It's Not What You Know—It's Who You Know that Counts: Analysing Serious Crime Groups as Social Networks." *The British Journal Of Criminology* 41:4 (2001): 580–594.
Davis, Robert S., and Gary W. Potter. "Bootlegging and Rural Criminal Entrepreneurship." *Journal of Crime and Justice* 14:1 (1991): 145–159.
Friedrich, Paul. "A Mexican Cacicazgo." *Ethnology* 4 (1965): 190–209.
Goldman, Marion. "Sexual Commerce on the Comstock Lode." *Nevada Historical Society Quarterly* (1978): 98–129.
Greenwood, Roberta S. "The Overseas Chinese at Home." *Archaeology* 31:5 (1978): 42–49.
Haller, Mark H. "The Changing Structure of American Gambling in the Twentieth Century." *Journal of Social Issues* 35 (1979): 87–114.
_____. "Organized Crime in Urban Society: Chicago in the Twentieth Century." *Journal of Social History* 5 (Winter 1971–1972): 210–234.
Hammack, David. "Problems in the Historical Study of Power in the Cities and Towns of the United States, 1800–1960." *American Historical Review* 83 (April 1978): 323–349.
Hirata, Lucie Cheng. "Free, Indentured, Enslaved: Chinese Prostitutes in Nineteenth-Century America." *Signs: Journal of Women in Culture and Society* 5 (1979): 3–29.
Hsu, Madeline. "Gold Mountain Dreams and Paper Son Schemes: Chinese Immigration Under Exclusion." *Chinese America: History and Perspectives* (1997): 46–60.

Huang, Betsy. "The Redefinition of the 'Typical Chinese' in Gish Jen's Typical American." *Hitting Critical Mass: A Journal of Asian American Cultural Criticism* 4:2 (Summer 1997).
Jenkins, Philip, and Gary Potter. "The Politics and Myth of Organized Crime: A Philadelphia Case Study." *Journal of Criminal Justice* 15 (1987): 473–484.
Johnson, David R. "The Origins and Structure of Intercity Criminal Activity, 1840–1920: An Interpretation." *Journal of Social History* 15 (Summer 1982): 593–605.
Kinder, Douglas Clark. "Bureaucratic Cold Warrior: Harry J. Anslinger and Illicit Narcotics Traffic." *Pacific Historical Review* L (1981): 169–191.
_____, and William O. Walker. "Stable Forces in a Storm: Harry J. Anslinger and United States Foreign Policy, 1930–1962." *Journal of American History* 72 (March 1986): 908–927.
Korbin, Solomon. "The Conflict Values in Delinquency Areas." *American Sociological Review* 16 (1951): 653–661.
Lee, Erika. "Enforcing the Borders: Chinese Exclusion along the U.S. Borders with Canada and Mexico, 1882–1924." *The Journal of American History* 89:1 (June 2002): 54–86.
Liddick, Donald. "Political Fund-raising, Patron-Client Relations, and Organized Criminality: Two Case Studies." *Journal of Contemporary Criminal Justice* 17:4 (2001): 346–357.
Light, Ivan. "From Vice District to Tourist Attraction: The Moral Career of American Chinatowns, 1880–1940." *Pacific Historical Review* 43:3 (August 1974): 367–394.
Lombardo, Robert M. "The Black Mafia: African-American Organized Crime in Chicago, 1890–1960." *Crime, Law & Social Change: An International Journal* 38:1 (July 2002): 33–65.
Maltz, Michael D. "Crime Statistics: A Historical Perspective." *Crime and Delinquency* (January 1977): 32–40.
McKanna, Clare V., Jr. "Chinese Tongs, Homicide, and Justice in Nineteenth-Century California." *Western Legal History* 13:2 (Summer/Fall 2000): 205–238.
McIllwain, Jeffrey Scott. "Bureaucratic Rivalry, Corruption and Organized Crime: Enforcing Exclusion in San Diego, 1897–1902." *Western Legal History* (forthcoming).
_____. "An Equal Opportunity Employer: Chinese Opium Smuggling Syndicates in and around San Diego during the 1910s." *Transnational Organized Crime* 4:2 (1999).
_____. "From Tong War to Organized Crime: Revising the Historical Perception of Violence in Chinatown." *Justice Quarterly* 14:1 (March 1997): 25–52.
_____. "Organized Crime: A Social Network Approach." *Crime, Law and Social Change: An International Journal* 32 (1999): 301–323.
Meyers, Willard H., III. "The Emerging Threat of Transnational Organized Crime in the East." *Crime, Law & Social Change: An International Journal* 24 (1996): 181–222.
_____. "Orb Weavers—The Global Webs: The Structure and Activities of Transnational Ethnic Chinese Criminal Groups." *Transnational Organized Crime* 1:4 (1996): 1–36.
Monkkonen, Eric. "Municipal Reports as an Indicator Source: The Nineteenth-Century Police." *Historical Methods* 12:2 (Spring 1979): 57–63.
_____. "Systemic Criminal Justice History: Some Suggestions." *The Journal of Interdisciplinary History* 9:3 (Winter 1979): 451–464.
Mooney, Ralph James. "Matthew Deady and the Federal Judicial Response to Racism in the Early West." *Oregon Law Review* 63 (1985): 561–644.
Morselli, Carlo. "Structuring Mr. Nice: Entrepreneurial Opportunities and Brokerage Positioning in the Cannabis Trade." *Crime, Law and Social Change: An International Journal* 35:3 (2001): 203–244.
Myers, Gail, Gene McGrady, Clementine Marrow, et. al. "Weapon Carrying Among Black Adolescents: A Social Network Perspective." *American Journal of Public Health* 87:6 (1997): 1038–1040.
Paulsen, George E. "The Yellow Peril at Nogales: The Ordeal of Collector William M. Hoey." *Arizona and the West* 13 (1971): 113–128.
Praetzellis, Adrian, Mary Praetzellis, and Marley Brown III. "Artifacts as Symbols of Identity: An Example from Sacramento's Gold Rush Era Chinese Community." *Living in Cities: Current Research in Urban Archaeology* 5 (1987): 38–47.
Reich, Charles A. "The New Property." *The Yale Law Journal* 73 (April 1964).
Reynolds, C. N. "The Chinese Tongs." *American Journal of Sociology* XL (1935): 612–623.
Rodescape, Lois. "Celestial Drama in the Golden Hills: The Chinese Theater in California, 1849–1869." *California Historical Society Quarterly* 23:2 (June 1944): 97–116.
Schneider, Jane. "Family Patrimonies and Economic Behavior in Western Sicily." *Anthropological Quarterly* 42 (1969): 109–129.

_____. "Of Vigilance and Virgins: Honor, Shame, and Access to Resources in Mediterranean Societies." *Ethnology* 10 (1971): 1–24.
Schneider, Peter. "Coalition Formation and Colonialism in Sicily." *Archives Europeennes de Sociologie (European Journal of Sociology)* 13 (1972): 255–267.
_____, Jane Schneider, and Edward C. Hansen. "Modernization and Development: The Role of Regional Elites and Non-corporate Groups in the European Mediterranean." *Comparative Studies in Society and History* 14 (1972): 328–350.
Shumsky, Neil Larry. "Tacit Acceptance: Respectable Americans and Segregated Prostitution, 1870–1910." *Journal of Social History* 19 (1986): 665–679.
Silverman, Sydel F. "Patronage and Community-Nation Relationships in Central Italy." *Ethnology* 4 (1965): 172–189.
Thernstrom, Stephan. "Notes on the Historical Study of Social Mobility." *Comparative Studies in Society and History* 10 (1968): 162–172.
Toy, Calvin. "A Short History of Asian Gangs in San Francisco." *Justice Quarterly* 9:4 (December 1992): 647–665.
Weingrod, Alex. "Patrons, Patronage, and Political Parties." *Comparative Studies in Society and History* X (June 1968): 377–400.
Wunder, John R. "The Chinese and the Courts in the Pacific Northwest: Justice Denied?" *Pacific Historical Review* 52 (May 1993): 191–211.

Books, Edited Volumes, Memorials, Monographs, and Papers

Abadinsky, Howard. *Organized Crime*. 4th ed. Chicago: Nelson-Hall, 1994.
Albanese, Jay. *Organized Crime in America*. 3rd ed. Cincinnati, OH: Anderson, 1996.
Albini, Joseph L. *The American Mafia: Genesis of a Legend*. New York: Appleton, Century, Crofts, 1971.
Allen, Oliver E. *The Tiger: The Rise and Fall of Tammany Hall*. New York: Addison-Wesley, 1993.
Anbinder, Tyler. *Five Points: The 19th-Century New York City Neighborhood that Invented Tap Dance, Stole Elections, and Became the World's Most Notorious Slum*. New York: The Free Press, 2001.
Anslinger, Harry J., and Will Oursler. *The Murderers: The Story of the Narcotics Gangs*. New York: Farrar, Straus and Cudahy, 1962.
Asbury, Herbert. *The Gangs of New York: An Informal History of the Underworld*. New York: Alfred A. Knopf, 1927; New York: Blue Ribbon Books, 1939.
Bailey, Kenneth. *Methods of Social Research*. New York: The Free Press, 1978.
Beck, Louis. *New York's Chinatown*. New York: Bohemia Publishing Company, 1898.
Becker, Howard S. *Outsiders: Studies in the Sociology of Deviance*. New York: Free Press, 1963.
Bergreen, Lawrence. *As Thousands Cheer: The Life of Irving Berlin*. New York: Viking Press, 1990.
Bettmann, Otto L. *The Good Old Days—They Were Terrible!* New York: Random House, 1974.
Black, David. *Triad Takeover: A Terrifying Account of the Spread of Triad Crime in the West*. London: Sidgwick & Jackson, 1991.
Block, Alan A. *East Side-West Side: Organizing Crime in New York, 1930–1950*. 2nd ed. New Brunswick, N.J.: Transaction, 1983.
_____ (ed.). *The Business of Crime: A Document Study of Organized Crime in the American Economy*. San Francisco: Westview Press, 1991.
Blok, Anton. *The Mafia of a Sicilian Village, 1860–1960: A Study of Violent Peasant Entrepreneurs*. New York: Harper Torchbooks, 1974.
Boissevain, Jeremy. *Friends of Friends: Networks, Manipulators and Coalitions*. Oxford: Basil Blackwell, 1973.
Booth, Martin. *The Triads: The Growing Global Threat from the Chinese Criminal Societies*. New York: St. Martin's Press, 1990.
Bott, E. *Family and Social Networks*. London: Tavistock, 1957.
Brecher, Edward M., et al. *Licit & Illicit Drugs: The Consumers Union Report on Narcotics, Stimulants, Depressants, Inhalants, Hallucinogens, & Marijuana—Including Caffeine, Nicotine, and Alcohol*. Boston: Little, Brown, & Company, 1972.
Bresler, Fenton. *The Chinese Mafia*. New York: Stein and Day, 1981.
Brook, Timothy, and Bob Tadashi Wakabayashi (eds.). *Opium Regimes: China, Britain and Japan, 1839–1952*. Berkeley: University of California Press, 2000.

Chan, Anthony. *Arming the Chinese: The Western Armaments Trade in Warlord China, 1920–1928.* Vancouver, BC: University of British Colombia Press, 1982.
Chauncey, George. *Gay New York: Gender, Urban Culture, and the Making of the Gay Male World, 1890–1940.* New York: Basic Books, 1994.
Chen, Yong. *Chinese San Francisco, 1850–1943: A Trans-Pacific Community.* Palo Alto, CA: Stanford University Press, 2000.
Chin, Ko-lin. *Chinatown Gangs: Extortion, Enterprise, and Ethnicity.* New York: Oxford University Press, 1996.
_____. *Chinese Sub-culture and Criminality: Non-traditional Crime Groups in America.* New York: Greenwood Press, 1990.
_____. *Smuggled Chinese: Clandestine Immigration to the United States.* Philadelphia: Temple University Press, 1999.
Cloward, Richard, and Lloyd Ohlin. *Delinquency and Opportunity: A Theory of Delinquent Gangs.* New York: The Free Press, 1960.
Cohen, Albert. *Delinquent Boys: The Culture of the Gang.* New York: The Free Press, 1955.
Connors, Chuck. *Bowery Life.* New York: Richard K. Fox Publishing Company, 1904.
Costello, Augustine E. *Our Police Protectors: A History of the New York Police.* Reprint edition. Montclair, N.J.: Patterson Smith, 1972.
Courtwright, David T. *Dark Paradise: Opium Addiction in America before 1940.* Cambridge, MA: Harvard University Press, 1982.
_____. *Violent Land: Single Men and Social Disorder from the Frontier to the Inner City.* Cambridge, MA: Harvard University Press, 1996.
Craddock, Susan. *City of Plagues: Disease, Poverty and Deviance in San Francisco.* Minneapolis: University of Minnesota Press, 2000.
Cressey, Donald. "Chinese Games with Dice and Dominoes." *Report of the National Museum.* 1893.
_____. *Theft of a Nation: The Structure and Operations of Organized Crime.* New York: Harper & Row, 1969.
Culin, Stewart. "The Gambling Games of the Chinese in America." *Series in Philology, Literature and Archaeology* 1:4. Philadelphia: University of Pennsylvania Press, 1891.
Dillon, Richard H. *The Hatchet Men: The Story of the Tong Wars in San Francisco's Chinatown.* New York: Coward-McCann, 1962.
Dower, John W. *War Without Mercy: Race & Power in the Pacific War.* New York: Pantheon Books, 1986.
Dunshee, Kenneth Holcomb. *As You Pass By.* New York: Hastings House, 1952.
Durbo, James. *Dragons of Crime: Inside the Asian Underworld.* Ontario: Octopus, 1992.
Dyer, Thomas G. *Theodore Roosevelt and the Idea of Race.* Baton Rouge, LA: Louisiana State University Press, 1980.
Elias, Nobert, and J. L. Scotson. *The Established and the Outsiders: A Sociological Enquiry into Community Problems.* London: Frank Cass & Co., 1965.
Ellis, Edward Robb. *The Epic of New York.* New York: Coward-McCann, 1966.
Felton, David L., Frank Lortie, and Peter D. Schulz. *The Chinese Laundry on Second Street: Papers on Archaeological and Historical Data Recovered from Selected Sites.* Nevada City, CA: Tahoe National Forest, 1984.
Foner, Philip S., and Daniel Rosenberg (eds.). *Racism, Dissent, and Asian Americans from 1850 to the Present: A Documentary History.* Westport, CT: Greenwood Press, 1992.
Fox, Stephen. *Blood and Power: Organized Crime in Twentieth-Century America.* New York: Penguin, 1989.
Gilfoyle, Timothy. *City of Eros: New York City, Prostitution and the Commercialization of Sex.* New York: Norton, 1992.
Glick, Carl. *Shake Hands with the Dragon.* New York: Whittlesy House, 1941.
Gong, Eng Ying, and Bruce Grant. *Tong War!* New York: N.L. Brown, 1930.
Gyory, Andrew. *Closing the Gate: Race, Politics, and the Chinese Exclusion Act.* Chapel Hill: University of North Carolina Press, 1998.
Hammack, David C. *Power and Society: Greater New York at the Turn of the Century.* New York: Columbia University Press, 1982.
Harlow, A. F. *Old Bowery Days: The Chronicles of a Famous Street.* New York: D. Appleton & Company, 1931.
Hart, M. Cordell. "Money and 'Guanxi': Keys to Understanding Crime by Asians." A paper for a study on Global Organized Crime. Washington, D.C.: Center for Strategic and International Studies (8 March 1996).

Hattori, Eugene M., Mary K. Rusco, and Donald R. Touhy (eds.). "Archaeological and Historical Studies at Ninth and Amherst, Lovelock, Nevada." *Nevada State Museum Archaeological Services Reports.* Carson City, NV, 1979.
Hershatter Gail. *Dangerous Pleasures: Prostitution and Modernity in Twentieth-Century Shanghai.* Berkeley, CA: University of California Press, 1997.
Hess, Henner. *Mafia & Mafiosi: Origin, Power and Myth.* New York: New York University Press, 1998.
Hom, Marlon K. *Songs of Gold Mountain: Cantonese Rhymes from San Francisco Chinatown.* Berkeley, CA: University of California Press, 1987.
Hoy, William. *The Chinese Six Companies.* San Francisco: Chinese Consolidated Benevolent Association, 1942.
Hunter, Jane. *The Gospel of Gentility: American Women Missionaries in Turn-of-the-Century China.* New Haven, CT: Yale University Press.
Hutchison, Don. *It's Raining Corpses in Chinatown.* Mercer Island, WA: Starmount House, 1991.
Ianni, Francis, *Black Mafia: Ethnic Succession in Organized Crime.* New York: Simon & Schuster, 1974.
____, and Elizabeth Reuss-Ianni (eds.). *The Crime Society: Organized Crime and Corruption in America.* New York: Times-Mirror, 1976.
Ianni, Francis A. J., and Elizabeth Reuss-Ianni. *A Family Business: Kinship and Social Control in Organized Crime.* New York: Russell Sage Foundation, 1972.
Janin, Hunt. *The India-China Opium Trade in the Nineteenth Century.* Jefferson, NC: McFarland & Company, Inc., 1999.
Kaplan, David E. *Fires of the Dragon: Politics, Murder, and the Kuomintang.* New York: Antheum, 1992.
Kenney, Dennis J., and James O. Finckenauer. *Organized Crime in America.* Belmont, CA: Wadsworth, 1995.
King, Gary, Robert O. Keohane, and Stanley Verba. *Designing Social Inquiry: Scientific Inference in Qualitative Research.* Princeton, NJ: Princeton University Press, 1994.
Kinkead, Gwen. *Chinatown: A Portrait of a Closed Society.* New York: HarperCollins, 1992.
Kleinknecht, William. *The New Ethnic Mobs: The Changing Face of Organized Crime in America.* New York: The Free Press, 1996.
Kolb, Lawrence, and A. G. Du Mez. *The Prevalence and Trend of Drug Addiction in the United States and Factors Influencing It.* Treasury Department. U.S. Public Health Service. Reprint No. 924. Washington, D.C.: U.S. Government Printing Office, 1924.
Kuo, Chi-Ling. *Social and Political Change in New York's Chinatown: The Role of Voluntary Associations.* New York: Praeger, 1977.
Laswell, Harold, and Jeremiah McKenna. *Organized Crime in an Inner City Community.* Springfield, VA: National Technical Information Service, 1972.
Lee, C. Y. *Days of the Tong Wars.* New York: Ballantine Books, 1974.
Lee, Calvin. *Chinatown, U.S.A.* Garden City, N.Y.: Doubleday & Company, 1965.
Lyman, Stanford Morris. *The Asian in North America.* Santa Barbara, CA: ABC-Clio, 1977.
____. *Chinatown and Little Tokyo: Power, Conflict and Community among Chinese and Japanese Immigrants in America.* New York: Associated Faculty Press, 1986.
Ma, Eve Armentrout. *Revolutionaries, Monarchists, and Chinatowns: Chinese Politics in the Americas and the 1911 Revolution.* Honolulu, HI: University of Hawaii Press, 1990.
Marcuse, Maxwell F. *This Was New York!: A Nostalgic Picture of Gotham in the Gaslight Era.* New York: LIM Press, 1969.
Martin, Brian G. *The Shanghai Green Gang: Politics and Organized Crime, 1919–1937.* Berkeley, CA: University of California Press, 1996.
McClain, Charles. *In Search of Equality: The Chinese Struggle against Discrimination in Nineteenth-Century America.* Berkeley, CA: University of California Press, 1994.
McCoy, Alfred. *The Politics of Heroin: CIA Complicity in the Global Drug Trade.* Brooklyn, NY: Lawrence Hill Books, 1991.
McCunn, Ruthanne Lum. *Chinese American Portraits: Personal Histories, 1828–1988.* San Francisco: Chronicle Books, 1988.
Mead, George. *Mind, Self, and Society.* Charles W. Morris (ed.). Chicago: University of Chicago Press, 1934.
Meyer, Kathryn, and Terry M. Parssinen. *Webs of Smoke: Smugglers, Warlords, and the History of the International Drug Trade* Lanham, MD: Rowman & Littlefield, 2002.
Meyers, Gustavus. *The History of Tammany Hall.* New York: Boni & Liveright, 1917.

Miller, Stewart Creighton. *Unwelcome Immigrant: The American Image of Chinese, 1785–1882.* Berkeley, CA: The University of California Press, 1969.
Mitchell, J. C. (ed.). *Social Networks in Urban Settings.* Manchester, England: Manchester University Press, 1969.
Moss, Frank. *The American Metropolis: From Knickerbocker Days to the Present Time,* Vols 1–3. New York: Peter Fenelon Collier, Publisher, 1897.
Murray, Dian H. *Pirates of the South China Coast, 1790–1810.* Stanford, CA: Stanford University Press, 1987.
_____, in collaboration with Qin Baoqi. *The Origins of the Tiandihui: The Chinese Triads in Legend and History.* Stanford, CA: Stanford University Press, 1994.
Musto, David. *The American Disease: Origins of Narcotic Control.* Expanded edition. New York: Oxford University Press, 1987.
Myren, Richard A., and Carol Henderson Garcia. *Investigation for Determination of Fact: A Primer of Fact.* Pacific Grove, CA: Brooks/Cole Publishing Company, 1989.
Nee, Victor, and Brett de Barry Nee. *Longtime Californ': A Documentary Study of an American Chinatown.* New York: Pantheon Books, 1972.
Novick, Peter. *That Noble Dream: The "Objectivity Question" and the American Historical Profession.* New York: Cambridge University Press, 1988.
Omohundru, J. T. *Chinese Merchant Families in Iloilo.* Athens, Ohio: Ohio University Press, 1981.
Posner, Gerald L. *Warlords of Crime: Chinese Secret Societies—The New Mafia.* New York: Penguin, 1988.
Potter, Gary W., and Philip Jenkins. *The City and the Syndicate: Organizing Crime in Philadelphia.* Lexington, MA: Ginn, 1985.
Praetzellis, Adrian, and Mary Praetzellis. *Archaeological and Historical Studies of the IJ56 Block, Sacramento, California: An Early Chinese Community.* Rohnert Park, CA: Anthropological Studies Center of Sonoma State University, 1982.
Reuter, Peter. *Disorganized Crime: Illegal Markets and the Mafia.* Cambridge: M.I.T. Press, 1986.
Richardson, James F. *The New York Police: Colonial Times to 1901.* New York: Oxford University Press, 1970.
Riis, Jacob A. *How the Other Half Lives.* Reprint edition. New York: Bedford Books, 1996.
Robertson, Frank. *Triangle of Death: The Inside Story of the Triads—The Chinese Mafia.* London: Routledge and Kegan Paul, 1977.
Robinson, Jeffrey. *The Merger: The Conglomeration of International Organized Crime.* Woodstock, NY: Overlook Press, 2000.
Rosenberg, Elliot, and Louis Eisenstein. *A Stripe of Tammany's Tiger.* New York: R. Speller, 1966.
Ruth, David E. *Inventing the Public Enemy: The Gangster in American Culture, 1918–1934.* Chicago: University of Chicago Press, 1996.
Salyer, Lucy E. *Laws as Harsh as Tigers: Chinese Immigrants and the Shaping of Modern Immigration Law.* Chapel Hill, N.C.: University of North Carolina Press, 1995.
Samecki, Jerzy. *Delinquent Networks: Youth Co-offending in Stockholm.* Cambridge, UK: Cambridge University Press, 2001.
Sante, Luc. *Low Life: Lures and Snares of Old New York.* New York: Vintage, 1991.
Schuyler, R. L. (ed.). *Archaeological Perspectives on Ethnicity in America: Afro-American and Asian-American Culture History.* Farmingdale, N.Y.: Baywood Publishing, 1980.
_____. *Lords of the Rim: The Invisible Empire of the Overseas Chinese.* New York: G. P. Putnam's Sons, 1995.
Seagrave, Sterling. *The Soong Dynasty.* New York: Harper & Row, 1985.
See, Lisa. *On Gold Mountain.* New York: St. Martin's Press, 1995.
Sellin, Thorsten. *Culture Conflict and Crime.* New York: Social Science Research Council, 1938.
Siu, Paul C. P. *The Chinese Laundryman: A Study of Social Isolation.* John Kuo Wei Tchen (ed.). New York: New York University Press, 1987.
Smith, Dwight. *The Mafia Mystique.* New York: Basic Books, 1975.
Smith, Paul (ed.). *Human Smuggling: Chinese Migrant Trafficking and the Challenge to America's Immigration Tradition.* Washington, D.C.: The Center for Strategic and International Studies, 1997.
Sterling, Claire. *Thieves' World: The Threat of the New Global Network of Organized Crime.* New York: Simon & Schuster, 1994.

Tchen, John Kuo Wei. *New York before Chinatown: Orientalism and the Shaping of American Culture, 1776–1882.* Baltimore, MD: The Johns Hopkins University Press, 1999.
Terry, Charles E., and Mildred Pellens. *The Opium Problem.* Montclair, NJ: Patterson Smith, 1928.
Tong, Benson. *Unsubmissive Women: Chinese Prostitutes in Nineteenth-Century San Francisco.* Norman, OK: University of Oklahoma Press, 1994.
Tsai, Shih-Shan Henry. *The Chinese Experience in America.* Bloomington, IN: Indiana University Press, 1986.
Twain, Mark. *Roughing It.* New York: Harper & Brothers, 1924.
Wasserman, Stanley, and Katherine Faust. *Social Network Analysis: Methods and Applications.* New York: Cambridge University Press, 1994.
Werner, Morris Robert. *Tammany Hall.* Garden City, New York: Doubleday, Duran & Company, 1928.
Willemse, Cornelius. *Behind the Green Lights.* New York: Knopf, 1931.
Wolfgang, Marvin, and Franco Ferracuti. *The Subculture of Violence: Towards an Integrated Theory in Criminology.* London: Tavistock, 1967.
Wong, Bernard. *Chinatown: Economic Adaptation and Ethnic Identity of the Chinese.* New York: Holt, Rinehart and Winston, 1982.
_____. *Patronage, Brokerage, Entrepreneurship and the Chinese Community in New York.* New York: AMS Press, 1988.
Yu, Renqiu. *To Save China, to Save Ourselves: The Chinese Hand Laundry Alliance of New York.* Philadelphia: Temple University Press, 1992.
Yun, Leong Gor. *Chinatown Inside Out.* New York: B. Mussey, 1936.
Yung, Judy. *Unbound Feet: A Social History of Chinese Women in San Francisco.* Berkeley: University of California Press, 1995.

Contributions to Edited Volumes, Conference Papers, Introductions and Prefaces

Albini, Joseph "The Mafia and the Devil: What They Have in Common." In Patrick J. Ryan and George E. Rush (eds). *Understanding Organized Crime in Global Perspective: A Reader.* Thousand Oaks, CA: Sage Publications, 1997: 63–70.
_____. "Syndicated Crime: Its Structure, Function, and Modus Operandi." Francis Ianni and Elizabeth Reuss-Ianni (eds.). In *The Crime Society: Organized Crime and Corruption in America.* New York: Times-Mirror, 1976: 24–41.
Albini, Joseph L., and Bronislaw Bajon. "Witches, Mafia, Mental Illness and Social Reality: A Study in the Power of Mythical Belief." (1978): 285–294.
Block, Alan A. "Introduction: The Business of Organized Crime." In Alan Block (ed.). *The Business of Crime: A Document Study of Organized Crime in the American Economy.* San Francisco: Westview Press, 1991.
_____. "Organized Crime: History and Historiography." In Alan A. Block. (ed.). *Time, Space & Organized Crime.* 2nd ed. New Brunswick, N.J.: Transaction, 1994: 21–68.
Chin, Ko-lin, Robert J. Kelly, and Jeffrey Fagan. "Chinese Organized Crime in America." In Robert J. Kelly, Ko-lin Chin, and Rufus Schatzberg (eds.). *Handbook of Organized Crime in the United States.* Westport, CT: Greenwood, 1994.
Crane, Stephen. "Opium's Varied Dreams." In Fredson Bowers (ed.). *Stephen Crane: Tales, Sketches, and Reports.* Charlottesville: University of Virginia Press, 1973.
Haller, Mark H. "Bootleggers as Businessmen: From City Slum to City Builders." In Eric H. Monkkonen (ed.). *Crime & Justice in American History 8: Prostitution, Drugs, Gambling and Organized Crime, Part 2.* New York: K.G. Saur, 1992: 294–312.
Hindus, Michael S. "The History of Crime: Not Robbed of Its Potential, But Still on Probation." In Egnon Bittner and Michael Messinger (eds.). *Criminology Review Yearbook.* Newbury Park: CA: Sage, 1979: 217–241.
Johnson, David R. "A Sinful Business: The Origins of Gambling Syndicates in the U.S., 1840–1887." In David Bayley (ed.). *Police and Society.* Newbury Park, CA: Sage, 1977: 29–55.
Lane, Roger. "Urban Police and Crime in Nineteenth-Century America." In Eric Monkkonen (ed.). *Crime and Justice in American History: Police and Crime Control, Part 2.* New York: K. G. Saur, 1992: 438–480.

McIllwain, Jeffrey Scott. "Corruption, Bureaucracy and Organized Crime: Federal Law Enforcement and Chinese Immigrant Smuggling Syndicates in and around San Diego, 1897–1901." A paper presented to the American Society of Criminology (November 1999).

———. "Opportunity, Adaptation and Criminal Enterprise: Immigrant Smuggling during the Exclusion Era." A paper presented to the Academy of Criminal Justice Sciences (March 2000).

"Members of the U.S. House of Representatives Elected from Districts All or Partly within the Current Boundaries of New York City." In Kenneth T. Jackson (ed.). *The Encyclopedia of New York City*. New Haven, CT: Yale University Press, 1995: 482.

Murray, Dian H. "Migration, Protection, and Racketeering: The Spread of the Tiandihui within China." In David Ownby and Mary Sommers Heidhues (eds.). *"Secret Societies" Reconsidered: Perspectives on the Social History of Modern South China and Southeast Asia*. New York: M.E. Sharpe, 1993.

Omohundru, J. T. "Trading Patterns of Philippine Chinese: Strategies of Sojourning Middlemen." In K. Hunter (ed.). "Economic Exchange and Social Interaction in Southeast Asia: Perspectives from Prehistory, History, and Ethnography." *Michigan Papers on South and Southeast Asia* 13. Ann Arbor, MI, 1978: 113–136.

Potter, Gary, and Larry Gaines. "Organizing Crime in 'Copperhead County': An Ethnographic Look at Rural Crime Networks." In Jay Albanese (ed.). *Contemporary Issues in Organized Crime*. Monsey, NY: Criminal Justice Press, 1995: 61–86.

Schatzberg, Rufus. "African American Organized Crime." In Robert Kelly, Ko-lin Chin, and Rufus Schatzberg (eds.). *Handbook of Organized Crime in the United States*. Westport, CT: Greenwood Press, 1994: 189–212.

Tilly, Charles. "Foreword." In Blok, Anton. *The Mafia of a Sicilian Village, 1860–1960: A Study of Violent Peasant Entrepreneurs*. New York: Harper Torchbooks, 1974.

Court Cases

Chew Hong v. United States, 12 U.S. 536, 567 (1984).

The People of the State of New York vs. Mock Duck (6 June 1912, etc.). Trial Transcript Preservation Project, John Jay College of Criminal Justice, New York, New York.

The People, on Complaint of Mock Duck v. Lee Sing (10 January 1905, etc.). City Magistrates' Court, First Division, First District. New York Public Library. Attached to *The People v. Mock Duck* (20 March 1902, etc.). Court of General Sessions. City and County of New York. Part II. New York Public Library.

The People v. Yee Wah and Louie Young (18 February 1906). New York District Attorney Closed Case Files. Series # 54451, Box 695, Shelf # 113356. New York Municipal Archives.

The People v. Mock Duck (20 March 1902, etc.). Court of General Sessions. City and County of New York. Part II. New York Public Library.

The United States of America v. John M. Schneider (12 January 1932). U.S. Circuit Court, Southern District of New York. Criminal Case Files, Box 66: Cr.C.-2968, John M. Schneider. U.S. National Archives—New York Branch.

The United States of America v. Tong Kee Hang alias William Hang (27 September 1904), U.S. Circuit Court, Southern District of New York, Criminal Case Files, Box 60, D-3414—William Hang, National Archives, New York Branch.

Dissertations and Theses

Burgess, John Stewart. *A Study of the Characteristics of the Cantonese Merchants in Chinatown, New York, as Shown by Their Use of Leisure Time*. M.A. Thesis. New York: Columbia University, 1909.

Chin, Ko-lin. *Chinese Triad Societies, Tongs, Organized Crime, and Street Gangs in Asia and the United States*. Ph.D. dissertation. Philadelphia: Temple University, 1986.

Griffin, Sean Patrick. *Organized Crime in Philadelphia, 1968–1984: On Exploitation and Urban Politics*. Ph.D. dissertation. University Park, PA: The Pennsylvania State University, 2000.

Wu, Cheng Tsu. *Chinese People and Chinatown in New York City*. Ph.D. dissertation. Worcester, MA: Clark University, 1958.

Wu, Ching Chao. *Chinatowns: A Study of Symbiosis and Assimilation.* Ph.D. dissertation. Chicago: University of Chicago, 1928.

Documentaries

Kurtis, Bill (prod.). "The Dragons of Crime." *Arts & Entertainment's Investigative Reports.* Stornoway Productions, 1994.

Government Documents

California Legislature. Senate Special Committee on Chinese Immigration. *Chinese Immigration, Its Social, Moral, and Political Effect.* San Francisco, CA: State Printing Office, 1878.

Emerson, Haven, and Harriet E. Hughes. *Population, Births, Notifiable Diseases, and Deaths Assembled for New York City, New York, 1866–1938: From Official Records.* New York: The DeLamar Institute of Public Health, College of Physicians and Surgeons, Columbia University, 1941.

Farwell, Willard B. *The Chinese at Home and Abroad: The Report of the Special Committee of the Board of Supervisors of San Francisco on the Condition of the Chinese Quarter of That City.* San Francisco, 1885.

Memorial—The Other Side of the Chinese Question: Testimony of California's Leading Citizens to the People of the United States and the Honorable Senate and House of Representatives. San Francisco, February 1886.

New York State Assembly. *Final Report of the Special Committee of the Assembly Appointed to Investigate the Public Officers and Departments of the City of New York and the Counties Therein Included.* Albany, 1900.

New York State Senate. *Report and Proceedings of the Senate Committee Appointed to Investigate the Police Department of the City of New York.* Albany, 1895.

Pennsylvania Crime Commission. *1991 Report.* St. David's, PA: Pennsylvania Crime Commission, 1991.

President's Commission on Organized Crime. *The Impact.* Washington, D.C.: U.S. Government Printing Office, 1984.

President's Commission on Organized Crime. *Organized Crime of Asian Origin.* Washington, D.C.: U.S. Government Printing Office, 1984.

Reynolds, Clifford. *Biographical Directory of the American Congress, 1774–1961.* Washington, D.C.: U.S. GPO, 1961.

Seabury, Samuel. *Final Report of Samuel Seabury, Referee.* Presented to the New York Supreme Court, Appellate Division, First Judicial Department, 1931.

United States Census of Population, 1940.
United States Census of Population, 1960.
United States Census of Population, 1970.

United States Bureau of Immigration. *Report.* Washington, D.C.: U.S. Government Printing Office, 1920.

United States Bureau of Immigration. *Report of the U.S. Industrial Commission on Highbinder Tongs.* Washington, D.C.: U.S. Government Printing Office, 1901.

United States Congress. Joint Special Committee to Investigate Chinese Immigrants. *Report.* Washington, D.C.: U.S. Government Printing Office, 1877.

United States Senate. Permanent Subcommittee on Investigations of the Committee on Governmental Affairs. *Asian Organized Crime.* Washington, D.C.: U.S. Government Printing Office, 1992.

United States Senate. Permanent Subcommittee on Investigations of the Committee on Governmental Affairs. *Asian Organized Crime: The New International Criminal.* Washington, D.C.: U.S. Government Printing Office, 1992.

Interviews

Morris, Richard. Interview with the author. New York, NY (21 May 1996).
Block, Alan A. Interview with the author. State College, PA (11 October 1996).

Newspapers and Magazines

The Century:
    Clark, Helen F. "The Chinese of New York Contrasted with Their Foreign Neighbors." 53 (November 1896–April 1897): 104–113.

Contemporary Review:
    Maitland, W. "The Chinaman in California and South Africa." 88 (1905): 821–822.

The Cosmopolitan:
    Foo, Wong Chin. "The Chinese in New York." 5 (March–October 1888): 297–311.

Federal News Service:
    "White House Background Briefing on President Clinton's Initiative Against Trafficking." 18 June 1993.

Harper's Weekly:
    Alexander, J. W. "American Opium Smokers: Interior of a New York City Opium Den." 8 October 1891: 684.
    Barnard, Frederick. "The Sketch." In "Reminiscences of a Ramble Through the Chinese Quarter of New York." 25 August 1888: 629.
    Bode, W. W. "Searching Chinese Immigrants for Opium at San Francisco." 7 January 1882: 5.
    Frenzeny and Tavernier. "Sketches in 'China-town,' San Francisco." 22 May 1875: 421.
    Ritchie, Robert Wells. "The Wars of the Tongs." 54 (27 August 1910): 8–9.

The Missoula and Cedar Creek Pioneer:
    [Title not available.] 22 June 1871.

The New York Commercial Advertiser:
    "Figures in the Police Changes" *Saturday Pictorial Review* (5 January 1901): 1.
    "Highbinder Crime." 26 October 1903.

The New York Daily News:
    Maeder, Jay. "Mock Duck: Blood of the Flower." 21 June 1999.
    _____. "Mock Duck: Blood of the Rooster." 22 June 1999.
    _____. "Mock Duck: Red Flags." 20 June 1999.

The New York Daily Tribune:
    "Accused of Pell Street Shooting." 22 August 1905: 3.
    "Against All Weapons." 31 January 1906: 14.
    "Alarm Felt in Chinatown." 17 July 1900: 3.
    "Another Tong Victim." 13 August 1905: 4.
    "Boston Chinaman to Be Tried Here." 11 July 1901: 5.
    "Business in Chinatown Falls Off." 26 July 1900: 3.
    "Chinaman Killed in Fight." 22 September 1900: 6.
    "Chinese Burglar Caught." 21 November 1898.
    "Chinese Laundry Trust." 27 September 1901: 6.
    "Chinese Leaders Angry." 22 August 1905: 3.
    "Chinese Say Its Murder." 22 August 1900: 6.
    "Chinese War Again." 12 August 1905: 1.
    "Driving Back the Allies." 14 July 1900: 3.
    "Exodus from Chinatown." 24 July 1900: 3.
    "Fear Peace Dinner." 12 February 1906: 12.
    "For Bronx Chinatown." 25 July 1906: 3.
    "Four After Tom Lee." 15 August 1905: 8.
    "The 'Good Chinaman' in Danger." 21 April 1901: 3.
    "Highbinders in Chinatown." 14 April 1901: 6.
    "Hip Sing Men Guilty." 30 August 1905: 1.
    "Hip Sings Pay Debt." 25 January 1906: 2.
    "Loie Sing's Murder Was All a Mistake." 19 August 1905: 18.
    "Mr. Waldo Visits Tongs." 27 January 1906: 4.
    "Mob Bombards a Chinaman." 19 August 1900: 7.
    "Mock Duck Arrested." 21 February 1906: 10.
    "Murder in Chinatown," 13 August 1900.
    "New Tong in Field." 13 February 1906.
    "The On Leong Dinner." 13 February 1900: 6.
    "On Leong Tong's Inning." 21 August 1905: 1.
    "Raid Chinese Laundry." 7 August 1905: 4.

"Raid Many Chinese." 15 January 1906: 12.
"Reign of Terror in Chinatown Now." 13 August 1905: IV:1.
"Rival Tongs at Peace." 3 February 1906: 10.
"Ruffians Attack Chinamen." 31 July 1900: 3.
"Say Chinaman Was Murdered." 26 October 1903: 12.
"Six Companies Disbands." 3 February 1897: 1.
"The Six Companies Retire." 7 February 1897: III:5.
"Steps to Abolish Chinatown." 6 March 1906: 2.
"Stiffen Prices for Stiffening Linen." 14 March 1901: 9.
"To End War of Tongs." 30 August 1905: 1.
"Tongs Clash Again." 19 September 1904: 1.
"Tongs with Knives Again." 22 May 1906: 14.
"Took Bribe to Aid Raid." 6 December 1903: 3.
"Truce in Chinatown." 31 January 1906: 14.
"Two Chinamen Killed." 7 August 1905: 1.
"War of Tongs on Again." 18 October 1904: 2.
"What Can Chinatown Eat." 19 August 1900: Illustrated Supplement, I:5.
[Title not available] 17 July 1900: 2.
[Title not available] 2 October 1903.

The New York Evening Journal:
"Chinese Shot, Is Arrested." 2 December 1902.
"Mock Duck Is Arrested for Tong Tragedy." 29 August 1905.

The New York Evening Post:
"Damaging for Mock Duck." 29 August 1905.
"O'Reilly Seeks M'Adoo's Arrest." 25 May 1904.

The New York Evening Sun:
"Bad Mock Duck Not So Very Bad." 12 April 1906.
"Chinamen in Court." 22 July 1904.
"Chinamen Foil 'Em." 22 January 1903.
"Chinatown Raids." 15 January 1906.
"Chinese Raid Fails." 22 December 1902.
"Cops Swarmed About Tom Lee." 4 February 1905.
"Hits Jerome Again." 10 February 1903.
"Mock Duck Held." 29 August 1905.
"Nab Mock Duck, Chinese Terror." 20 March 1905.
"Nabbed Chinamen." 2 February 1903.
"On Leong Held on Hip Sing's Nod." 24 April 1905.
"Police Fence?" 5 April 1902.
"Raid of Chinese Netted 75 Cents." 13 February 1905.
"Raid on Pigtails." 12 December 1904.
"Tom Lee Marked." 3 February 1905.

The New York Evening Telegram:
"Frank Moss and Jerome in Tiff over Mock Duck." 22 March 1905.
"Two Chinese Feudists Held." 25 February 1905.

The New York Globe:
"Mock Duck in the Tombs." 21 February 1906.

The New York Herald:
"Chinaman Killed in Faction Fight." 13 August 1900.
"Chinese Rioters in Court." 5 September 1899.
"His Enterprise Ruins Ah Hop Sing." 22 November 1898.
"Nettled by Titus, Jerome Threatens." 6 April 1902.
"Parkhurst Man Raids Chinese to Get Police." 22 July 1904.
"Titus to Continue Raids on Chinese." 2 December 1898.
"Two Killed in Chinatown Battle." 25 January 1906.

The New York Journal:
"Chinatown Riot." 4 September 1899.
"Chinamen." 22 November 1898.

The New York Morning Telegraph:
"Men Baffled in Chinatown Raid." 1 December 1898.

The New York Press:
"Chinatown Jumps on Reformer." 9 August 1899.

"Chinese Armed to Kill One Another." 13 August 1900.
"Chinese in Anger at Murder Trial." 14 April 1901.
"Loo Hee Was Murdered." 31 August 1899.
"Mystery About Chinaman's Death." 31 August 1899.

The New York Sun:
"Bag of Chinese Gamblers." 12 December 1904.
"Chinatown Man Shot Dead." 31 January 1905.
"Chinese Assassins Work." 4 November 1904.
"Chinese Burglar Nabbed." 21 November 1898.
"Chinese Prisoners Let Go." 14 February 1905.
"Four Shot in Chinatown." 21 August 1905.
"Graft from Chinese—Moss." 12 December 1904.
"Hip Sing on Top of Tom Lee." 27 April 1905.
"Hip Sing on Top, On Leong on Run." 12 December 1904.
"Hip Sing Saddest Day." 22 March 1905.
"Huie Fong First Victim of On Leong's Vengeful Decree." 1 February 1905.
"Loo Hee Was Murdered." 31 August 1899.
"Mock Duck Held for Murder." 8 August 1905.
"Mock Duck Jury Disagrees Again." 3 April 1902.
"Mock Duck Wings Clipped." 21 March 1905.
"Murder in Chinatown." 13 August 1900.
"One Chin Fooled 3 Sleuths." 23 February 1905.
"16 Hip Sing Tongers Soaked." 27 December 1904.
"Tong Midnight Murder Squad." 13 August 1905.
"Tong Protected, Says Moss." 11 December 1904.
"200 Cops Raid Chinatown." 24 April 1905.

The New York Times:
"Alibi of Mock Duck." 8 August 1905: 6.
"All San Francisco's Opium Seized." 3 March 1897: 2.
"Armor Clad Chinese Battle on the Bowery." 26 November 1904: 2.
"Battle in Poolroom." 5 October 1902: 3.
"Business in Chinatown Falls Off." 26 July 1900: 3.
"Chinaman Found Stabbed Through the Heart." 31 August 1899.
"Chinaman Shoots Wildly." 22 September 1900: 4.
"Chinamen in New York." 26 December 1856.
"Chinamen Much Excited." 20 February 1902.
"Chinamen Taken in Raid." 12 December 1904: 7.
"Chinatown Doomed to Make Room for Bowery Park." 17 February 1907.
"Chinatown in Bronx." 26 July 1906: 6.
"Chinatown May Move to Williamsburg." 6 August 1906: 14.
"Chinatown's Mayor Now in Police Toils." 27 April 1905: 7.
"Chinatown's Quiet, but Troubles Afloat." 8 August 1905: 12.
"Chinatown's Warriors Agree to Real Peace." 31 January 1906: 8.
"Chinese Burglar Arrested." 21 November 1898.
"Chinese in New York." 26 December 1873.
"Chinese New Year's Feast." 13 February 1900: 18.
"Chinese Puzzle Result of Wholesale Raids." 25 April 1905: 8.
"Collector Saunders's Work." 4 February 1895: 3.
"Dong Fong Sent to Prison." 16 May 1905: 4.
"Drew Lots for Shooting." 4 November 1904: 7.
"Fatal Shooting Followed by Fight." 18 October 1905: 1.
"Five On Leong Kill a Hep Sing Member." 13 August 1905: 3.
"For a New Chinatown." 8 August 1906: 6.
"Gambling in Chinatown." 9 September 1900: 26.
"Get Opium Worth $5,000." 5 October 1903: 3.
"A Heavy Opium Seizure." 28 February 1897: 1.
"Leader Foley Settles Feud." 2 October 1902: 10.
"Loo Hee Was Murdered." 31 August 1899.
"'Monk' Eastman Gang Let Go." 6 October 1902: 14
"No Autos in Chinatown." 28 April 1905: 1.

"Objections to Chinamen." 19 February 1902: 2.
"Old Chinaman Shot in Feud of Tongs." 25 February 1905: 2.
"On Leong Have Stolen the Hep Sing's Crest." 27 November 1904: 5.
"Opium Arrests Continue." 5 October 1903: 5.
"Opium Smugglers Warned." 14 May 1895: 1.
"Peace of Chinatown Is Merely a Merger." 1 April 1906: 5.
"Peace that Is Viewed Askance." 8 February 1906: 8.
"Police Descend on Hip Sings." 31 May 1905: 9.
"Police Raid Chinatown." 15 January 1906: 14.
"Police Raid on Jerome Tip." 25 January 1903.
"Prosperous Chinese Arrested for Voting." 17 August 1904: 7.
"Predicts Chinese Killings." 11 December 1904: 7.
"Raid Ends in Sub-Cellar." 28 December 1904: 12.
"Rescuing Angel of the Little Slaves of Chinatown." 30 April 1905: 4:4.
"A Ripple in Chinatown." 9 May 1906: 3.
"Rival Bands Battle in Chinatown Streets." 30 September 1902): 3.
"Seventeen Chinamen Held." 9 January 1899.
"Shooting in Chinatown." 3 November 1904: 1.
"6,000 Opium Users Here." 1 August 1908: 6.
"Three Shot Dead in Chinese Theater." 7 August 1905: 1.
$3,000 on Tom Lee's Head." 15 August 1905: 5.
[Title not available] 13 January 1985: A1.
[Title not available] 13 August 1900.
[Title not available] 27 January 1906: 16.
[Title not available] 12 February 1906: 5.
"2 Killed from Ambush in Chinatown Battle." 25 January 1906: 6.
"There's a New Tong in Chinatown Now." 13 February 1906: 12.
"Tong Killings Pause and Chinatown Feasts." 29 March 1906: 9.
"Tongs Fight Again; Four Shot This Time." 21 August 1905: 1.
"Tongs to Give Up Gambling and Shooting." 3 February 1906: 16.
"Undesirable Chinamen." 8 August 1905: 6.
"Wing Futs and Chus Cite Police Pickets." 16 April 1905: 14.

The New York World:
"Chinaman Is Slain in Feud by Assassins." 31 January 1905.
"Chinaman Shot in War of Tongs." 18 October 1905.
"Chinamen Rejoice with Hand on Gun." 4 February 1905.
"Chinatown in Terror; Mock Duck Is Back." 18 March 1905.
"Chinatown's Mayor Marked for Murder." 3 February 1905.
"Chinese Killed Were to Testify at Murder Trial." 25 January 1906.
"Four More Shot in Chinatown Feud." 21 August 1905.
"Held Chinese by the Queue." 13 February 1905.
"The Hip Sing Tong Marks Men to Die." 19 March 1905.
"Hip Sings Held for Murder after Raid." 7 August 1905.
"Hop Sing Shoots Uncle, Hong Gee." 19 September 1903.
"May Swear Chinamen by Chickens' Blood." 20 February 1902.
"McAdoo's Men Swoop Down on Chinatown." 24 April 1905.
"Mock Duck Held for Old Murder." 21 March 1905.
"Mock Duck Held in $5,000 for Trial." 24 February 1906.
"New Murder Marks Chinatown Feud." 1 February 1905.
"Police in Pay of the On Leong Tong?" 8 November 1904.
"Police Raid Many Chinatown Dens." 21 February 1906.
"Price Put on Tom Lee's Head." 2 February 1905.
"Revenge of the On Leong Tong." 13 August 1905.
"Says Murder Put On Chinaman is Gambler's Plot." 11 December 1904.
"Tom Lee Arrested on Graft Charge." 27 April 1905.
"Try to Pick Off 'Mayor' Tom Lee." 15 August 1905.
"War of Tongs Again in Court." 25 February 1905.

Overland Monthly:
Robbens, E. V. "Chinese Slave Girls: A Bit of History." LI (1909): 100–102.

Scribner's Monthly:
Henshaw, Sarah E. "California Housekeepers and Chinese Servants." XII (1876):   739.

The Washington Times:
  28 January 1986: 1A.

Non-cited Primary Sources

Butler Library, Columbia University, New York, New York
  Collection of Tammaniana The Edwin Patrick Kilroe Collection. Rare Book and Manuscript Collection.
  The Society for the Prevention of Crime Collection. Rare Book and Manuscript Collection.
The Lloyd Sealy Library, John Jay College, New York, New York:
  Trial Transcript Preservation Project.
New York Municipal Archives, New York, New York:
  New York County District Attorney's Records.
  Police Court/Magistrate Court Records.
  Supreme Court Records.
United States National Archives, New York Branch, New York, New York:
  Chinese Exclusion Act Files.
  Federal Court Records.

Index

Ah Chung 112
Ah Fe 136, 140–141, 148, 161, 176
Ah Fee *see* Ah Fe
Ah Hop Sing 132–133
Ah Lip 119
Ahearn, Manhattan Borough President 177
Albanese, Jay 2
Albany, New York 120
Albini, Joseph 1, 37
alien conspiracy 184
Andbinder, Tyler 111
Appo, Quimbo 86
arrest, substitution for 110
arrests, gambling 109, 150, 156–157, 159, 160, 165, 166, 171, 175
arrests, opium 117, 118–121, 171
arson 141, 150
associations: district 30, 32, 45, 74, 75, 93, 192; family/clan 30, 32, 74, 75, 93, 102, 127, 192; general 86–87, 126, 136; guilds (labor/craftsmen/trade/business) 30, 75, 78, 192; political 30, 74, 92–99; religious 30; voluntary 30, 99–104, 127, 143–144; *see also* tongs; Triads

Bachelor Society 42, 51, 103, 107, 125
Bailey, Kenneth 198–199
Bank of British Colombia 61
bao (obligation to repay) 26–27, 50
Barlow, Magistrate 176
Barry, John 112
Beck, Louis 85, 88, 91, 94, 96, 99, 100–101, 102, 109–110–111, 113–114, 123–124, 131–132, 143, 191–193
Bell, Daniel 1, 8
Belleville, New Jersey 131
Berlin, Irving 105
Bing Ching Union 108
Bingham, Theodore 84
blackmail *see* extortion
Blanchard, Justice 158
Block, Alan 8, 15–23, 25, 37, 186, 189, 202
Blok, Anton 13–15, 16, 18
Bloody Angle 169
Boissevain, Jeremy 15
boo how doy (also highbinder and hatchetmen) 35, 50, 53, 55, 57, 67, 72, 73, 74–79, 102, 112, 113, 126, 128–129, 132, 133, 146, 148, 152–154, 159, 161
Booth, Martin 194
Boston, Massachusetts 137, 153, 159
bounty 137, 159, 161
The Bowery 105–107, 125–126, 135
Boxer Rebellion 135, 136
Brague, Stephen 138, 140

Breen, Magistrate 166
British Columbia, Canada 118–119
The Bronx, New York 131, 177
Brooklyn, New York 88, 130, 132, 148, 177
Brooks, Nicholas 109, 136, 155
Buffalo, New York 120–121, 137
Burgess, John Stewart 191
Burlingame Treaty 48
Burlington, Vermont 119

Canada 118, 125
Cantor, Eddie 105
Chatham Club 105
Chauncey, George 189
Cheng Hun Sing 176
Chentung Liang Chiang 170
cheui 41; *see also* opium
Chih Kung Tong 32, 33, 36, 75, 102, 136–137, 140–146, 172
Chin, "Four Flusher" Sam 178
Chin, Ko-lin 6, 31, 32–34, 35–37, 144, 184, 194, 195, 199
Chin Fin 177
Chin Gin 129
Chin Sam 130
Chin Ying 172
China, Diplomatic Missions in United States 90, 93–94, 170, 173, 176

245

China Lobby 186
Chinatown: Boston 85,
  101, 124; Philadelphia
  85, 121–122; New York
  City 35–36, 55, 85–92,
  105–126, 185, 191–193,
  194; Sacramento 25;
  San Francisco 52, 71,
  78, 87, 95, 124, 168, 186;
  Vancouver 124
Chinatown Bill 120
Chinese-Americans: burial traditions 96, 98;
  Christianity and 86,
  139–140, 151; conflict
  between 76–77, 103;
  criminalization of 47–
  49, 102, 116–117; legislation against 42, 48–49,
  51, 59–60, 65–66, 124–
  125; migration 87, 131,
  134, 135; racism against
  45–47, 58–59, 65, 87,
  88–90, 125–126, 135–
  136, 138–139, 141–142,
  166–169; stereotypes of
  45–46, 47–48, 88–90,
  104, 105–106, 116–117,
  166–169, 192–193
Chinese Chamber of
  Commerce, New York
  95
Chinese Consolidated
  Benevolent Association
  (CCBA) 32, 78, 90,
  94–99, 103, 108, 109,
  111, 126, 130, 132–134,
  145, 176, 192
Chinese Exclusion Act see
  Exclusion, Chinese
Chinese Laundryman's
  Association 99, 130–
  134
Chinese Laundryman's
  Union 132
Chinese Freemasons 32;
  see also Chih Kung Tong
Chinese Reform Association 173
Chinese Six Companies
  30, 31, 57–58, 87, 93–
  94, 99, 127
Chinese Theater, New
  York City 92, 166, 169,
  170, 173, 175
Ching Lung Lin 120
Ching On 130
Chong Bock 158

Chong Pon Sing see Wong
  Quon Sing
Chong Wah Gong Shaw
  see Chinese Consolidated Benevolent
  Association
Chop Sing Tong 131, 132
Chow Young 163
Chu Chung Society 130,
  132
Chu Family Association
  see Clan of Chu
Chu Fong 101
Chu Gow's Port Arthur
  Chart House 176
Chu Wing Kin 158
Chuck Connors Association 100, 106
Cincinnati, Ohio 84
Clan of Chu 158
Clark, Helen 90, 113, 124
Clemens, Samuel 47
Clinton, William Jefferson
  7
"code of silence" 163
Colan, City Court Judge
  176
Committee of Five 106,
  176
Connors, Chuck 105, 168,
  176
contracts 44–45, 51–52
Corr, Detective 152
Corrigan, Assistant District Attorney 163
corruption 6, 36, 49, 54,
  57, 70–72, 78, 84–85,
  103, 106–107–114, 117,
  120, 122, 125–126, 138,
  146, 147, 149, 155–157,
  160–163, 175, 177–178,
  185, 186
Corsiglia, Giovanni 122
Costello, Augustine 116–
  118
courts, testimony of Chinese in 31, 49, 138–140,
  200
Courtwright, David 64–
  66
Cowing, Rufus 140
Craddock, Susan 46
Crane, Stephen 115–116
Credit-fare system 44, 60–
  61, 133
Cressey, Donald 1
Croker, Richard 106
Cuba 121

Culin, Stewart L. 67–70
Cullin, Leslie 61
cultural integration see
  social integration
culture conflict 29, 139
Cunniff, Detective 171

Davidson, H.R. 61
Devery, Bill 106–109, 162
Dillon, Richard 31–32,
  55, 57, 58, 59, 61, 74,
  193, 195, 200–201
Dinnean, Thomas 173
disease see public health
Don Kim 170–171
Dong Fong 161; see also
  Ong Fong
Dong Sue 137
Dong Wah 171
dou 41; see also gambling
Drescher, Policeman 169
Duck, Mock see Mock
  Duck
Duffy, Detective 171
Dutch East Indies 121
Dyer, Thomas 47

Eastman, Monk 169
Eggers, Acting Captain
  151, 164–165, 168
Elias, Nobert 14–15
Empire Reform Association 176
England 121
enterprise syndicate 19,
  43, 49, 50, 77, 79, 84–
  85, 104, 125–126, 158,
  184, 185
ethnic identity 26
ethnic succession 8
ethnicity trap 2, 37, 186
excise law 165
Exclusion, Chinese 35,
  44, 48, 54, 55, 120
extortion (also blackmail)
  19, 50, 73, 78, 95, 101,
  103, 107–08, 112, 120,
  126, 144, 160, 164–165

face see mianzi
factionalism 33, 34, 108
Fagan, Jeffrey 6
fan tan 67, 68, 70, 89,
  103, 107, 109
Fan Tan Syndicate 99,
  109–121, 144, 145
Farwell, Willard 70
Faust, Katherine 11–13

Index

Federal Bureau of Investigation 5
Field, Stephen 46
Five Points 111
Five Points Gang 106, 147, 169, 186
Flammer, Charles 152
Flood, Captain 122, 156
Foley, Tom 147, 176
Foo, Wong Ching 88, 90
Fook Yuen *see* opium, brands
Foos, Charles Foon 150
Foreign Miners Tax 49
Foster, Warren W. 172–176
Four Brothers Association 102
Four Vices 41–43, 92, 185
Fulton Market 140
Fung Y. Mow 176

Galby, Customs Inspector 119
Gambler's Union 108
gambling 41–43, 67–73, 84, 89, 101, 102, 103, 106, 107–114, 122, 125–126, 127–128, 143, 144, 158, 163–165, 166, 177, 179, 185
gangs, Chinese 35; *see also* boo how doy
Garcia, Carol Henderson 190
Gardner, Charles 162
Garvan, Assistant District Attorney 137, 156, 176
Geary Act 48
Gibson, Otis 52
Gilfoyle, Timothy 22, 58, 70, 84, 186, 189
Gin Gum 153, 159, 166, 168, 169, 172, 173, 175
Ging, J. *see* Ju Hong
Glaze, George 138, 140
Glick, Carl 74, 128, 191
Goff, John 162, 176
Gold Mountain 43
Golden Star Massacre 36
Golden Venture 7
Goldfogle, Henry 176
Gong, Eng Ying "Eddie" 90, 101, 134, 142, 144, 147, 153, 155, 166, 193–194
Gong Yeong 171
Goo Wing Ching 136

Grand Trunk Railroad 121
Grant, Bruce 90, 101, 134, 142, 144, 147, 153, 155, 166, 193–194
Grant, Ulysses S. 57
Great Britain 59
Green Gang 31
guanxi 25–29, 30–34, 50, 58, 60–61, 76, 93, 98, 100, 101, 122, 125–126, 134, 146, 176, 184, 185
Guy Maine 173

Haller, Mark 23, 37, 186, 189
Hamilton, Agent 174
Hammack, David 83
Hang, William A. 150
Harvey, James B. 131
hatchetmen *see* boo how doy
Herlihy, Thomas 136
Herrick, D. Caddy 176
Hess, Henner 15
Hickey, Detective
highbinders *see* boo how doy
Hip Sing Tong 32, 36, 74, 95, 101–104, 110–114, 122, 124, 125–126, 127–129, 133–138, 142–146, 147–165, 166–179, 186, 192, 193, 201, 202
Hip Yee Tong 53
Hirata, Lucie Cheng 51–58, 77, 186
Hoboken, New Jersey 132
Hoe Poch 176
Hogan, Inspector 171
Hom, Marlon 41, 53–54, 67
Homer, Winslow 86
homicide 121–122, 129, 136–137, 151, 155, 158–159, 160, 166, 169, 170, 171–172
Hong Kong 31, 44, 53, 118
Houghton, Assistant U.S. Attorney 150
Hoyt, Charles M. 107
Huang, Betsy 192
Huang Pang 32
Huang Qingfu *see* Wong Ching Foo
Huey Gow 148, 149, 152, 155, 159, 173, 176

hui 30–34; *see also* associations
Huie Fong 151, 158–159
Huie John Wok 170
Huie Kin 151–152, 155, 159
Huie See 170
Huie Yee 170
Hung Mun Triad Society 143
Hup Lee 169, 172

Ianni, Francis 1
immigrant smuggling, Chinese 35, 48, 60–61, 66, 197
immigration, Chinese 43–46, 197
India 118, 121
industrial racketeering 78
International Opium Commission 118

Jack the Ripper 169
Japan 121
Jenkins, Philip 186
Jerome, William Travers 147, 161–163, 167, 168, 175, 176, 197
Jersey City, New Jersey 88, 131
Jiang Hu 34, 184
Jim Sang 132
Johnson, David 22–23, 37, 71–72, 186, 189
Jolson, Al 105
Jolson, Harry 105
Jong, Charlie 169
Ju Hong 161
Jue Chu 176

Kear, Captain 158, 161
Kelley, Robert 6
Kenny, John 105
Keohane, Robert 190
Kernochan, Deputy Assistant District Attorney 163, 169, 171
kidnapping 44, 47, 51, 53, 54, 55, 77
King, Gary 190
Kit Fu Shah 173
Kleinknecht, William 6
Koumintang, Eastern United States Branch 95
Kurtis, Bill 6

Kwang Duck Tong 101, 127
Kwong Fong Tai Company 61

labor brokering 44–45
labor racketeering 78, 104, 130–135, 144
La Cosa Nostra 1, 5, 15, 16
Laing Yue 101–102
Landes, David 17
Lane, Roger 189
Lang, Policeman 160
laundries 88, 90, 130–135, 144
Laundryman's Protective Association 134
Lavelle, Scotty 176
Lee, Calvin 101, 143
Lee, Charlie 130, 178
Lee, Charlie 136
Lee, C.Y. 193
Lee, Tom 100, 105, 111–113, 120, 126, 134–135, 137–138, 140, 143–146, 149–151, 153, 159–161, 164–165, 168, 169, 171–173, 177–178, 185
Lee, Tuck C. 122
Lee Chung 171
Lee Company see Fan Tan Syndicate) 144, 145, 157
Lee Dock 170–171
Lee Doong 177
Lee Family Association 101
Lee Foy Man 177
Lee Fung 120
Lee Fung Chang 120
Lee Gong Yee 176
Lee King 121
Lee Loy see Lee Moy
Lee Moy 159
Lee Shew 101
Lee Sing 152–153
Lee Soon 172
Lee Toy 171, 172
Lee Wah Lung Company 114
Lee Yu 160
Levy, Abraham 138, 175–176
Lexow Committee 84, 107, 138, 149, 161–163
Li Gin 171
Li Ho 171
Li Hung Chang 90, 105

Li Yook 171
Li Yuen see opium, brands
Lian Cheng (Lun Sing) Gong Suo Association 94–95
Light, Ivan 42–43, 72, 107, 118, 186
Lloyd, D. Frank 152
Lo Ping 114
Loang Kin see Lung Kin
loansharking 114
Lock Wing 170
Loie Sung 171
Long Kin see Lung Kin
Loo Choo 129
Loo Lin 130
Loo Tom 130
Lord, Assistant District Attorney 163
Los Angeles, California 121
lottery, Chinese 68–70, 103, 112, 114, 122, 175
Lottery Agent's Union 114
Lou Yen 132
Louie Foung 159
Louie Yong Hock 101, 142
Louis Quong 173
Louis Young 122
low gui gow (messengers) 124
Low Roy see Lee Sing
Loy Fook 170–171
Luie Fong 151
Lung Gag Gong see Chih Kung Tong
Lung Kin 136–137
Lyman, Stanford Morris 31–32, 76–77, 184

Ma, Eve Armentrout 30, 44, 143
Macao 121
mafia 13–15
The Mafia 1, 6, 15, 37, 102, 103, 113
Mafia Mystique 186
mafiosi 13–15
Maitland, W. 71
Maltz, Michael 195
Marcus, Samuel 153
Marx, Assistant U.S. Attorney 150
Mazet Committee 84, 138
Mazzaki, Mary 136
McAdoo, Police Commissioner 164–165, 168

McAvoy, Magistrate 175
McCarthy, City Court Judge 176
McClelan, George B. 177
McClintock, Thomas 150, 152, 155, 157, 160, 164, 175
McClusky, Detective 130
McCormick, Superintendent 163
McCullagh, Captain 117
McDonald, Detective 172
McLaughlin, A.F. 122
McLellan, Robert S. 164
McLelland, Agent 174
Mee Shing Gong Shaw see Mei Chi Party
Mei Chi Party 95, 99
Meriwether, Lee 78
methods: clarifying names 201; data analysis 200–202; document study 198–202; network analysis 201–202; use of historical data 190–198
Mexico 118
Meyer, Maurice 158
Meyers, Willard 25–29, 37, 184
mianizi (face) 27, 41, 50, 102, 139, 145, 151, 153, 174, 175
Miller, Detective 171
Miller, Stewart Creighton 45, 47
Ming Duck Tong 108
missionaries 45, 52, 57, 58
Mock Duck 102, 122, 126, 127–129, 134, 137–138, 140–142, 144–146, 147–150, 152–165, 166–177, 185, 196
Mock Sai Wing see Mock Duck
Mock Wah 127
Mock Wing 127, 134
Mock Wing Ching 136
moneylending see loansharking
Monk Eastman Gang 106, 147, 186
Monkkonen, Eric 195, 198
Montreal, Canada 119
Moss, Frank 111, 113, 138, 139, 140–142, 143, 149,

153, 156, 158, 161–163, 172, 176, 191, 197
Moy Dong Yue 101, 142
Moy Gung 171
Moy Tow 173
Mullins, Paddy 105
Murphy, Charles Francis 106
Murray, Dian 30
Myren, Richard 90

New Jersey 148
New Orleans, Louisiana 84, 121
new property 21
New York City, history 83–85
New York Police Department (NYPD) 84, 100, 111, 164, 198–199
New York Union *see* Chop Sing Tong
Newman, Jacob 174
Ning Yang Hui Guan Association 94–95
Nixon, Lewis 176
Norfolk, Virginia 121
norms *see* Triad norms and values
Nott, C.J. 170
Nunn, Sam 5

O'Connor, Captain 177–178
O'Hare, Stephen J. 163
O'Leary, "Jerry" 121
O'Reilly, Daniel 158, 163
Ommen, Magistrate 156
Omohundru, J.T. 26
On Leong Tong 32, 36, 95, 99–101, 111–114, 120, 129–130, 134–138, 140–146, 147–165, 166–179, 186, 192, 201, 202
Ong Fang *see* Ong Fong
Ong Fong 160–161
opium 41–43, 58–66, 84, 88, 89–90, 102, 103, 105, 106, 107, 112, 113, 114–118, 125–126, 185; brands 119; smuggling 60–64, 114–118
opportunity, criminal 8, 16, 22, 25, 34, 43, 49, 54, 66, 73, 77, 87, 98, 102, 118, 125–126, 127, 134, 158, 184
organized crime: definition 10–11, 24; history and the study of 1–2, 8–9, 15–17, 34–37, 189–202; multiethnic nature of 36, 42–43, 55, 59, 64–65, 72, 107, 114–126; power and 19–21, 43, 52, 100, 103, 114, 134, 145, 184, 185; racism and 125–126, 184–185, 187; relations with attorneys and 54, 57; theories 8, 10
organized criminals: Italian 1–2, 15, 106, 113, 193; Jewish 1–2, 15, 106; Sicilian 13–15, 193
Oriental Benevolent Association *see* Chinese Consolidated Benevolent Association

Page Law 48, 54
Paginelli, Mary 136
pai gow 107, 120, 160; *see also* gambling
pak kop piu *see* lottery, Chinese
Parker, Andrew D. 108
Parkhurst, Charles 84, 138, 149, 162, 197
Parkhurst Society *see* Society for the Prevention of Crime
Passaic, New Jersey 150
Passaic Steam Laundry 131
patronage 21–22, 26
Paulsen, George E. 186
peace agreement 171, 172–179
Peddler's Union 99
The Pelham 105
Pennsylvania Crime Commission 7
Philadelphia, Pennsylvania 121
Philbin, District Attorney 137
The Philippines 121
Phillips, John 136
piu 41; *see also* prostitution
policy 175; *see also* lottery, Chinese
Poolon Kun Cee Club 86–87
Portland, Oregon 101

Potter, Gary 186
power syndicate 19, 43, 49, 50, 57, 73–79, 98, 103, 104, 112, 126, 129, 144–145, 158, 184, 185
Powers, Detective 152
Pratt, Harvey J. 137
Price, Edmond E. 111, 152, 157
price fixing 130–135
Prohibition 186
property rights 78, 96, 98, 103, 112, 125–126, 179, 185
prostitution 41–43, 51–58, 64, 66, 70, 77–78, 84–85, 101, 102, 103, 107, 113, 114, 122–126, 127, 185
protection 43, 53, 58, 78, 79, 85, 95, 98, 101, 102, 103, 105, 107–111–114, 117, 124, 126, 132, 133, 136, 144, 146, 150, 157
public health 46, 65, 118

Quan Kai 119; *see also* opium, brands
Quinqing (mutual reciprocity) 27
Quong Jon 122
Quong Lo 130
Quong Ying Lung Company 99

Reich, Charles 21
reform 72, 108, 115, 138, 140, 149, 153, 155, 162–163, 179
renqing (right to request favors) 26–27, 50
Reynolds, C.N. 195, 200
Richmond, Indiana 150
Riis, Jacob 88, 116, 123
Ritchie, Robert Wells 72–73
Robbens, E. V. 57, 58
Roosevelt, Theodore 47, 84
Rosano and Company 61
Rosenberg, Ely 173
Roth, William 5

Sacramento, California 70
St. Louis, Missouri 84, 150
Sam Jin 121

250　Index

Sam Kee 122
Sam Sing 171
San Francisco, California 44, 49, 57, 59, 70, 84, 121, 127, 128, 131, 134, 143, 148, 153, 161, 168
Sang Chung 101
Sante, Luc 106–107, 128, 150
Schmittberger, Max 163
Schneider, Jane 15
Schneider, John 120
Schneider, Peter 15
Scholer, Coroner 166, 170
Scotson, J.L. 14–15
Scott Act 48, 64
Seattle, Washington 121
See, Lisa 44–45, 51, 53
Sellin, Thorsten 29
Sessions, William 6
Sexton, John 100
Shafer, Robert Jones 190
Shah, F.F. 170
Shan Lock Wing 176
Shields, Commissioner 150
Shumsky, Neil 122
Sidewalk Ordinance 49
Sin Que 136, 141
Sing Dock ("The Scientific Killer") 148, 155, 166
Sing Me Tong 131, 132
Sing Moh 157
Sing Sing Prison 137
Singleton, Joseph H. 176
Siu, Paul C.P. 67, 70
Six Companies *see* Chinese Six Companies
Slater, Mike 105
Smith, Charley "The Hog" 169
Smith, Dwight 37
smoking opium *see* opium
Smoking Opium Exclusion Act 65

social change 14–15, 22, 24, 186
social Darwinism 47
social function 27–29, 30, 77, 79, 84, 98, 103, 104, 113
social integration 29, 32–33
social mobility 8, 26–29, 37, 185
social networks 9, 11–13, 22–24, 37, 84–85, 124, 125–126, 184; Chinese *see* guanxi; Sicilian 13–15
social structure 16–17, 27–29
social system of organized crime 17–18, 24, 36, 49, 50, 125–126, 134, 184, 185, 190; New York City 15–17, 36, 179
social world of organized crime 18, 134, 162, 179
Society for the Prevention of Crime (Parkhurst Society) 85, 92, 138, 147, 149–150, 152–158, 160–165, 166, 168, 173–176, 197
Society for the Prevention of Cruelty to Children 85
Society for the Suppression of Vice 85
Standish, Detective 164
Star Rescue Mission 176
Steam Laundryman's Association 134
Steen, Magistrate 176
Steinert, Magistrate 176
Strong, William L. 101
Sue Sing 136, 140–141
suicide 121–122, 129
Sullivan, "Big" Tim 106
Sun Chung Lung 101
Sun Tzu 187
Sung, Joe "The Plug" 114

Taishan 94
Tam Wah Toy 151, 159
Tammany Hall 84, 90, 100, 105–106, 111, 130, 135, 138, 149, 197
Tap San Kan Shaw Tong *see* Chinese Laundryman's Association
Taylor, R.H. 120
Tchen, John Kuo Wei 199
The Tenderloin 115–116
testimony *see* courts, testimony of Chinese in
Thernstrom, Stephan 37
Ti Sin *see* opium, brands
Ti Yuen *see* opium, brands
Tilly, Charles 13
Titus, Captain 108–110, 130, 135, 150
Tom Lee *see* Lee, Tom
Tom Sue 170
Ton Bok Woo 148, 173
Tong, Benson 51, 52
Tong, F. Froman 173, 176
tong(s) 30, 31–34, 73, 74, 77–78, 95, 98, 106
tong war(s) 32, 76–77, 87, 102, 104, 146, 147–165, 166–179, 185, 193–195, 166–179
tourism 90, 165
Tracy, Captain 169, 171, 172
Train, Arthur 140
Transfiguration Church 112
Triad(s) 30–31, 143–144, 194; initia-tion 31; norms and values 31, 33–34, 144
tribute *see* protection
truce *see* peace agreement
Tsai, Shih-Shan 52

Ung Quong 170–171
Ung Taing 171
Unger, Henry 138